M000222136

BUREAUCRACY IN AMERICA

The Administrative State's Challenge to
Constitutional Government

BUREAUCRACY IN AMERICA

The Administrative State's Challenge to Constitutional Government

Joseph Postell

UNIVERSITY OF MISSOURI PRESS
COLUMBIA

Publication of this volume has been supported with a gift from the Kinder Institute on Constitutional Democracy.

ISBN: 978-0-8262-2123-0
Library of Congress Control Number: 2017932480

∞™ This paper meets the requirements of the
American National Standard for Permanence of Paper
for Printed Library Materials, Z39.48, 1984.

Typeface: Caslon and Trajan

Studies in Constitutional Democracy

Justin B. Dyer and Jeffrey L. Pasley, Series Editors

The Studies in Constitutional Democracy Series explores the origins and development of American constitutional and democratic traditions, as well as their applications and interpretations throughout the world. The often subtle interaction between constitutionalism's commitment to the rule of law and democracy's emphasis on the rule of the many lies at the heart of this enterprise. Bringing together insights from history and political theory, the series showcases interdisciplinary scholarship that traces constitutional and democratic themes in American politics, law, society, and culture, with an eye to both the practical and theoretical implications.

Previous Titles in Studies in Constitutional Democracy

Lloyd Gaines and the Fight to End Segregation
James W. Endersby and William T. Horner

John Henry Wigmore and the Rules of Evidence:
The Hidden Origins of Modern Law
Andrew Porwancher

To My Parents, John and Laura Postell

CONTENTS

ACKNOWLEDGMENTS

Tʜɪs ʙᴏᴏᴋ ᴡᴏᴜʟᴅ not have been completed without the help and encouragement of many. I am extremely grateful for Ashland University and the Ashbrook Center for Public Affairs, which first introduced me to the study of political thought and American constitutionalism. This book was ultimately inspired by wise counsel from my dissertation advisor, Ronald J. Pestritto. He first taught me and others about the importance of administrative law, and then advised me that a dissertation on the administrative state would be a worthwhile and engaging project. I am most indebted to him for not only the inspiration for this book but also the patient and thoughtful advice he has offered on too many occasions to count.

I am especially grateful to those who provided helpful comments and suggestions on various drafts of the manuscript. Tiffany Miller and Johnathan O'Neill read early drafts and helped me to express more clearly the import of various parts of the argument. Gary Lawson offered his legal expertise to this non-lawyer and enabled me to clarify aspects of the book. Paul Moreno and Aditya Bamzai read the manuscript carefully and provided me with excellent comments and suggestions for improvement. Several of my students and interns over the years assisted me with research on this project, especially Garrett Coon, Neville Haynes, Johnathan Knight, and Mark Palmisano.

Others have read portions of the argument and offered helpful feedback and encouragement. Philip Hamburger not only supported this project but also pointed me towards sources and arguments with which I was unfamiliar. David Alvis, David Azerrad, Eric Claeys, Steve Ealy, Michael Greve, Shep Melnick, Sidney Milkis, Peter Myers, Anthony Peacock, Jeremy Rabkin, Richard Reinsch, James Stoner, and Adam White commented on various aspects of the arguments in this book and encouraged me to write about administrative law in various outlets. Matthew Spalding especially encouraged me to make public arguments on the relationship of American constitutionalism and the regulatory state, and frequently provided me with a platform to test these arguments. Without his advice and counsel this book would never have come to fruition.

I completed this book while beginning a teaching career at the University of Colorado-Colorado Springs. My colleagues and the University have supported me beyond my hopes. In particular, Joshua Dunn and James Null patiently supported my research goals through academic advice and practical assistance. Raphael Sassower offered helpful advice for sharpening my proposal and the thesis of the book as a whole. I could not ask for a more supportive environment at UCCS and thank my colleagues for their help.

My deepest gratitude is to my wife, Allison Postell, who has sacrificed in countless ways to make this book possible. Her patience and fortitude are a source of constant admiration. Our son, Luke, has given me both joy and purpose in seeing this project to completion. This book is dedicated to my parents, John and Laura Postell. Their support and pride in their son's path inspired me to press on in the face of difficult challenges, and I will always be indebted to them for their selfless encouragement of my career, even when it cost them greatly.

BUREAUCRACY IN AMERICA

The Administrative State's Challenge to
Constitutional Government

INTRODUCTION

THE RISE OF the modern administrative state is the most important political development in America over the past century. Today, most policies are enacted not by Congress and the president but by administrative agencies. Their personnel are not elected by the people, but they make, enforce, and adjudicate rules all at once, based on their expertise in the specific policy areas entrusted to their care. As Chief Justice John Roberts argued in the 2013 case *City of Arlington v. FCC*, "Although modern administrative agencies fit most comfortably within the Executive Branch, as a practical matter they exercise legislative power, by promulgating regulations with the force of law; executive power, by policing compliance with those regulations; and judicial power, by adjudicating enforcement actions and imposing sanctions on those found to have violated their rules. The accumulation of these powers in the same hands is not an occasional or isolated exception to the constitutional plan; it is a central feature of modern American government."[1]

The overwhelming influence of what has been called the "fourth branch" over politics compels us to seek to understand the historical, theoretical, and political foundations of administration in its present form. This book contributes to our understanding of the administrative state by describing how principles of American constitutionalism, such as representation, the rule of law, and the separation of powers, have influenced the development of the administrative state through administrative law, broadly understood. Arguments about these principles have affected the structure, powers, procedures, and judicial review of administrative agencies from the Founding to today.

By examining legislative debates over setting up agencies, judicial review of agency decisions, and presidential actions seeking to claim authority over the use of administrative power, this book aims to show that there has always been a tension between administrative power and American constitutionalism. Principles of American constitutionalism have been used to temper and to reduce administrative discretion in important ways, seeking to reconcile these competing aims of establishing the rule of law and strengthening administrative power. As the historian Arthur Bestor explained in a classic article, American constitutionalism exercises a "configurative" influence on political development.[2] The administrative state's development has been shaped profoundly by the fundamental principles of American constitutionalism. Yet while this struggle in administrative law has profoundly affected the way in which the administrative state functions, it has failed to reconcile adequately the ideas and principles that guide both administrative power and constitutionalism, leaving both progressives and conservatives dissatisfied.

This dissatisfaction has reached a fever pitch over the past two years, and both on the Supreme Court and in the popular media the administrative state has become a lightning rod for criticism. Charles J. Cooper has recently observed that in the 2014–2015 Supreme Court term Justice Clarence Thomas authored "four opinions . . . that call into question the constitutionality of the massive and largely unaccountable bureaucracy that we commonly refer to as the administrative state."[3] Chief Justice Roberts's opinion in *City of Arlington*, quoted earlier, suggests that other justices share Thomas's reservations about the constitutional legitimacy of our bureaucracy. Outside the Court, prominent newspapers are publishing articles that issue scathing attacks on the administrative state and the "fourth branch of government."[4]

One might think that this is a new development, and that the administrative state is now only beginning to experience a crisis of legitimacy. This thesis dovetails nicely with the idea that a more radical and conservative element has arisen in American politics, with unprecedented attacks on the legitimacy of modern government. But it is inaccurate. Administrative power and the administrative state has *always* suffered a crisis of legitimacy, because of the tension between administrative power and American constitutionalism. In fact, thirty-five years ago James Freedman published a book titled *Crisis and Legitimacy: The Administrative Process and American Government*, describing the historical tension that has persisted between the ideals of constitutional government and administrative law.[5] Freedman traced the crisis of legitimacy back to the very origins of the modern administrative state, and connected them to the challenge that the administrative state posed to critical features of American constitutionalism, including the separation of powers, and the departure from the idea of an independent judiciary. While Freedman was not a critic of the administrative state he acknowledged the challenge that it posed to earlier conceptions of constitutionalism, and took those objections very seriously.

Recently scholars sympathetic to the modern administrative state have begun to accept implicitly the notion that the administrative state posed a constitutional challenge to the American political system, but have argued that this problem was cured by incorporating elements of American constitutionalism into the alien administrative process that was created in the twentieth century. Daniel Ernst's *Tocqueville's Nightmare*, Joanna Grisinger's *The Unwieldy American State*, and Anne Kornhauser's *Debating the American State* all recognize the challenge of administrative power and argue that American government has successfully coped with this challenge by softening it through administrative law.[6] As this book argues, administrative law has indeed been *justified* on the grounds that it would alleviate the problems of modern administrative government, but it has generally failed to achieve this objective.

These defenses of the modern administrative state build upon earlier attempts to shore up the foundations of the administrative state, especially John Rohr's *To Run a Constitution* and Jerry Mashaw's *Creating the Administrative Constitution*.[7] The former argued for the compatibility of the administrative state and core principles of American constitutionalism, while the latter used early American history to demonstrate that administrative power was pervasive and administrative discretion common in America prior to the Civil War. Both of these earlier attempts are engaged at length and ultimately disputed in this book, particularly in chapters one through four. In spite of the best efforts of the defenders of the administrative state, its problems are still evident to constitutional lawyers as well as the general public. The crisis of legitimacy has not subsided.

Nevertheless, we still await a full explanation and analysis of the ground of this crisis of legitimacy. Two of the most prominent criticisms of the administrative state, while important, fail to capture the full scope of the theoretical and historical tension between administrative government and the American constitution. Theodore Lowi's *The End of Liberalism* offered a powerful criticism of the problem that delegation of power to agencies posed to good government, and especially the problem of interest group liberalism that the administrative state facilitates.[8] Lowi's contribution focused more directly on the practical political difficulties created under the institutional dynamics of the administrative state, as opposed to the broader historical and theoretical problem of administration in a constitutional system. More recently, Philip Hamburger's *Is Administrative Law Unlawful?* connects the rise of administrative government with the return to prerogative power, a shift fundamentally

antithetical to the rule of law.[9] While an impressive and powerful effort con-
necting the modern administrative state to earlier rejections of the rule of
law, particularly the sixteenth- and seventeenth-century English monarchy,
Hamburger leaves out much of American history in his analysis. Therefore
there remains a need to fill in these details to connect the problem of the administrative state to specifically American principles and American historical
developments. That is the objective of this book.

An Overview of Administrative Law

This book examines the historical evolution and development of administrative power in the United States, from midway through the colonial period
to the present. It focuses specifically on the constitutional and legal status of
administrative power: its relationship to the other powers specifically mentioned in the U.S. Constitution, how it is to be structured based on constitutional principles such as representation and the separation of powers, and the
role of judicial review in ensuring administrative power is exercised in accordance with law. Therefore it focuses heavily on what is called administrative
law in many political science departments and in the American law school
curriculum, even though it is not strictly speaking a book about administrative
law. Rather, it is a book about the historical relationship of political thought,
American constitutionalism, and the exercise of administrative power.

Given the panoramic scope of this study, it is of course inevitable that many
subjects cannot be treated with the degree of depth that they merit. This is a
challenge endemic to any project that attempts to connect legal and historical
developments across multiple eras and subject matters. Nevertheless, important benefits are derived from charting the trends and developments that have
occurred throughout American legal history. Narrowly focusing on each legal
issue as a distinct subject threatens to miss the ways in which fundamental
ideas of constitutionalism explain, underlie, and connect important legal doctrines that affect the way public policy is made today. To compensate where I
have been forced to sacrifice depth for brevity, I have attempted to point the
reader to secondary research that elaborates on specific topics through the
endnotes.

The integrative approach of this book distinguishes it from much of the
existing scholarship on the administrative state. By examining the relationship
between these aspects of American government, this book presents a broader
and more historically and philosophically informed picture of the growth of
administrative power and its tension with important principles of American
constitutionalism than what is found in strictly legal examinations focusing

on specific legal questions using a case law approach. Nevertheless, the reader who is interested in the relationship between the administrative state and American constitutionalism may profit from a brief summary overview of major questions in administrative law that will be discussed throughout the chapters of this book and which serve to organize much of the analysis of the book.

A first and fundamental set of issues in administrative law has to do with the nondelegation doctrine: the principle that the legislature may not delegate legislative power to administrative agencies. The first sentence of Article I of the U.S. Constitution declares that "all legislative powers herein granted shall be vested in a Congress of the United States." On this textual basis, and on the broader principle that legislative power cannot be further delegated out of the hands in which the people themselves have delegated it, there has been a consistent argument in American politics that administrative agencies are constitutionally forbidden from exercising legislative power.[10] A related issue in administrative law is whether and to what extent the legislature may delegate the power of adjudication over to administrative actors rather than courts vested with the protections granted by Article III of the Constitution. Since Article III of the Constitution grants the judicial power to the federal courts of law, which are empowered to decide cases and controversies "arising under . . . the laws of the United States," it seems that administrative agencies cannot be given the power to decide particular cases involving the laws passed by Congress. Yet as Chief Justice Roberts suggested in his dissent in *City of Arlington*, agencies today routinely exercise this power of adjudication. As we will see, these issues of delegation—of both legislative and judicial power—have arisen repeatedly throughout American history, framing the way in which administrative power is to be established.

A second set of issues concerns the status of independent administrative power within the American constitutional framework. In particular, an ongoing debate centers on whether discretionary power can be delegated by Congress to administrative actors, given that the Constitution seems to vest all executive power in the hands of the president, the only elected official in the executive branch. Since the president is given the entire executive power by Article II of the Constitution, constitutional questions are raised when Congress tries to grant discretion to officers below the president, not subject to the president's supervision. A related aspect of this issue concerns the president's power over the appointment and removal of personnel within the executive branch. Just as the president would gain control over, and therefore responsibility for, administrative decisions that are subject to his personal oversight, so he would also gain control and responsibility by having the power to hire or fire any administrative official in the bureaucracy. As with issues of delegation, these issues have been contested many times throughout the history of our republic.

Third, administrative law also governs the procedural adequacy of agency actions being challenged. Agencies are required by both the Constitution and organic statutes to follow certain procedures before taking action. These procedural requirements are deemed necessary to protect parties who are affected by agency action, and also to ensure that the agency is exercising reasoned judgment when it makes a final decision. From the very beginning of American history the question of administrative procedure has been an arena in which the constitutionality of administrative power has been disputed.

A fourth set of issues focuses on the nature and scope of judicial review of administrative decisions. Within this area there are several analytically distinct questions, all of which reduce to the question of the relationship between judicial and administrative power. The first question is the extent to which courts should defer to administrative agencies' findings of fact. For instance, if the Environmental Protection Agency finds that a certain level of smog is a threat to health, this finding of fact may be challenged in court. Judges may defer to the expertise of the agency on this question, or substitute their own judgment for that of the EPA. The former approach is characteristic of deference, while the latter is characteristic of de novo review, in which the court finds the facts anew. A second question arising under the scope of judicial review is the extent to which reviewing courts substitute their own judgment for that of the agency on questions of legal interpretation. Because they are charged with carrying out statutory provisions and implementing laws which grant them authority over regulatory programs, administrative agencies often interpret statutes as they make decisions. The EPA's determination of what constitutes a pollutant is a necessary step in implementing the Clean Air Act, but it also raises questions of statutory interpretation. Agencies also interpret other sources of law such as the Constitution and their own rules and regulations. When they do this, courts charged with reviewing an agency's action must determine the appropriate scope of review of the legal interpretation. Should courts, as experts in legal interpretation, decide the question themselves, or defer to the superior expertise of the agency? A third aspect of scope of review issues involves judicial review of the reasonableness of an administrative decision that does not fit neatly into a finding of law or fact. These decisions may be considered policy choices made by the agency in carrying out the functions delegated to it by Congress, where the choice does not hinge upon some finding of fact or interpretation of law. In this case, the court is reviewing an exercise of agency policymaking, and questions arise over the appropriate level of scrutiny that should be extended over the decision. Thus with regard to judicial review of the substance of an agency decision, courts may set up different levels of deference depending on whether the question is one of fact, of law, or of policy.

The fifth and final set of issues in administrative law has to do with access to judicial review in the first place. In order to engage in litigation over administrative policies one must have standing to sue an agency, and the timing of the suit must be appropriate. If an agency has not engaged in a final action, a court may not yet be authorized to intervene. If the court does not limit which parties may challenge administrative decisions in court, citizens may use litigation to single-handedly hamstring administrative decisions that need to be implemented. This would transform the legal process into a political process in which those who disagree with an agency's policy would use litigation to win a battle lost in the halls of the agency. Consequently courts, interpreting the Constitution and the statutes which address these questions, are required to define which parties can bring legal challenges to agencies and when they can do so. The answer to these questions—which has varied significantly throughout American history—is an important factor in determining the role of the judiciary in checking administrative power.

All of these questions have been hotly disputed on the basis of competing constitutional principles and visions from the Founding to today. This contest over the legal and constitutional legitimacy of administrative government has profoundly influenced the manner in which the administrative state functions, and therefore the way in which public policy is made by our national government.

The Development of Administrative Power

Unlike most books on the administrative state this book begins in the colonial era, as the American colonists grappled with administrative bodies constructed by the Crown to manage their internal affairs. Through that experience, and especially through the experience of setting up inadequate administrative institutions during the Revolutionary War, the Framers of the Constitution learned important lessons about the constitutional principles that should inform the structure of administration. These lessons were evident at the Constitutional Convention and during the debates over the ratification of the Constitution. By the time the Constitution was ratified, the principles of constitutional administrative power were largely, though not entirely, established: lawmaking by elected representatives, unity and responsibility in the executive, the separation of powers, and judicial review of administrative action.

These principles were reinforced as the new government took shape and encountered practical difficulties that were not (and could not have been) anticipated by those who framed and ratified the Constitution. The structure and powers of the federal departments and the scope of judicial review of administrative decisions were issues unaddressed during the Founding, but the principles of American constitutionalism were applied to these questions to produce a unique brand of administrative law. The president's responsibility for administration was preserved through ensuring his ability to intervene personally to direct administrative decisions, Congress kept administrative discretion to a minimum, and the courts embraced the use of common law actions to ensure judicial review of administrative action. Some controversies over the president's ability to appoint administrators and the scope of judicial review marked the Jacksonian period, but this traditional constitutional approach to administrative law largely prevailed from the beginning of American history to the Civil War.

Even after the Civil War, as Chapter Four argues, the traditional approach persisted, in the face of new issues such as the abuse of patronage and railroad regulation. While the conventional view of administrative law maintains that these issues sparked a revolution in administrative practice, and the birth of the modern administrative state, a careful examination of the record shows that reformers sought to eliminate the abuses of economic regulation without devising radically new regulatory institutions. Rather, these reforms of the 1880s followed earlier patterns featuring clear statutory rules, judicial enforcement, presidential control, and avenues for judicial review. It was not until the twentieth century, Chapter Five argues, that a new theory of administration's place in the constitutional system was advanced. Progressive reformers devised a new theory of administration that rejected the separation of powers and representation, and worked to enact practical reforms that gave greater authority to regulatory agencies and greater judicial deference to their decisions.

These trends continued during the New Deal, but the Administrative Procedure Act was intended to introduce greater legal checks and balances, including greater accountability for rulemaking, separation of functions within agencies, and more judicial oversight of the administrative process. The objective was not to return to the traditional model of administration and the constitutional principles undergirding that model, but to reintroduce these principles in new forms, accommodating the administrative state and seeking to ameliorate the threat it posed to the Constitution. Modern administrative law was born with the passage of the APA in 1946, but as Chapters Seven and Eight explain, it has not suppressed the conflict over the legitimacy of the administrative state. In many respects the post-APA objections over the administrative state have been voiced by progressives and liberals who, contrary to their progressive predecessors, pressed for greater judicial oversight of the administrative state and less discretion for bureaucracy. Paradoxically, the conservative response to the changes they made to administrative law doctrines was to call for greater presidential control of administration and more judicial deference to administrative decisions.

The administrative state's troubled history, the failure of administrative law to vindicate the legitimacy of the administrative state, and the ongoing debate over the status of bureaucracy in America demand historical exploration and an appreciation for the ongoing relevance of basic principles of American constitutionalism to how government works today. This book attempts to illuminate the history of the constitutional and legal dimensions of administrative power in our unique form of government. This history reveals that the controversy over bureaucracy in America will never be fully settled, but that it would be helpfully informed by taking a broader view of the challenge it poses to constitutional government.

CHAPTER ONE

An Improved Science of Administration

Administration and the American Founding

By the time the Framers reached the Philadelphia Convention in 1787 and established the U.S. Constitution, they had acquired extensive experience to guide them in establishing administrative structures. Their experience with administrative power in the colonial period, at the state level during the Revolutionary War, and at the national level during the same period, guided them in establishing administrative power in the new government. Though they did not specify in great detail the kind of administrative regime they sought to construct in the Constitution itself, they had reached clarity on certain fundamental constitutional principles. These principles were repeatedly articulated in the debates at the Convention and in the ratifying debates, as illustrated in the state ratifying conventions and in writings such as *The Federalist*. This chapter begins with an examination of the lessons of experience that informed the debates and decisions made at the Constitutional Convention in 1787, before proceeding to examine the debates at the Convention and during the ratification of the Constitution.

Colonial Experience
The American Colonies were established with a variety of institutional arrangements, but the essential institutional dynamic in each colony was the same. As Judith Best has explained, "Although there were three kinds of colonies in America—royal, proprietary, and corporate—the general experience in the American colonies was one of continuous struggle between colonial governors and colonial assemblies."[1] Royal colonies were those in which the governor was royally appointed; proprietary colonies allowed the proprietor to choose the governor with the approval of the crown. Only in the corporate

colonies (Connecticut and Rhode Island) were the governors popularly elected. By 1760 most of the colonies were royal colonies.[2]

The colonies possessed essentially the same forms of government regardless of type, with a governor, a bicameral legislature (in most cases), and a "Governor's Council," composed from the upper house of the legislature, which advised the governor on executive decisions, served as the highest appeals court in the colony, and acted as one half of the legislative branch—combining legislative, executive, and judicial functions.[3] The members of the council were selected by the crown or proprietor, but typically the governor's preferences were followed.[4] The lower houses were elected and were referred to variously as the House of Burgesses, the General Court, or the Assembly. Justices of the peace, county courts, and circuit courts constituted the judicial structure beneath the Governor's Council. The governor served (sometimes alone, sometimes with the Council) as the chancellor with jurisdiction in equity cases.[5] Appeals from the colonial courts were heard by the crown's Privy Council.[6]

Colonial governors were vested with important powers and were supervised by royal authorities such as the English Board of Trade, a committee of the English Privy Council. These authorities could recall governors who violated their orders. In addition to a standard set of executive powers, the governor could summon, prorogue, and dissolve the legislature—powers, which were controversial and which were frequently used throughout the eighteenth century.

The colonial assemblies retained the power to initiate legislation and control taxing and spending. Legislation could be vetoed by governors or the Privy Council but the assemblies possessed autonomy on fiscal matters. The colonists quickly learned that a legislature could use its fiscal powers to wrest control over executive and administrative personnel, and the colonial legislatures gradually became ascendant over the governors as a result of the shrewd employment of their financial powers.[7] In New York, New Hampshire, and North Carolina, governors went without pay for several years in the 1720s and 1730s as assemblies stopped appropriating funds for their offices.[8] While this tactic was helpful in checking overzealous executives, it would eventually become a lamentable tactic that enervated the basic functions of government during the Revolution.

In sum, colonial government featured representative lower houses of the legislature, combined with governors and upper houses, which were unrepresentative and tended to advance royal interests. This set up a dynamic between legislative and executive power in which the latter was viewed with great suspicion. For the most part, however, administration was situated not in the executive but in the judicial branch, which (in contradistinction to today) was the real engine of colonial regulation and administration.

Judicial Administration: A State of Courts

The most extensive powers in the colonies fell under the judicial heading. As William Nelson has explained, "Colonial government, unlike our own, did not consist of a vast bureaucracy with clear chains of command reaching upward to central political authorities. Instead there were a number of courts, whose judges and subordinate officers were appointed and in part enforced law enacted by political authorities but met in various localities under scrutiny of the community as a whole."[9] The courts, in short, were in most cases the administrators.

The structure of the judicial power in colonial Massachusetts illustrates the general principles followed in the colonies, which were based on the English system.[10] Power was organized into three tiers. The first tier consisted of individual courts of the justices of the peace, which were appointed by the governor and council of the colony (though colonial assemblies often checked or assumed this authority).[11] These justices had both civil and criminal jurisdiction within the county in which they served and could impose limited fines and criminal punishments such as imprisonment for twenty-four hours or whipping. Justices of the peace were highly accountable to the local communities they served.[12] They were essentially agents of local communities for carrying out the regulation of their own affairs.

Appeals from the decisions of the justices of the peace were to county-based courts. In Massachusetts appeals went to the Court of General Sessions of the Peace ("Sessions") in criminal matters, and to the Inferior Court of Common Pleas in civil matters. These courts were composed of all of the justices of the peace in each county sitting together. They met routinely (Sessions met quarterly in Massachusetts) and heard appeals in criminal matters, with trial by jury.[13] In addition, these courts served as "the chief administrative agenc[ies] of the county, having supervision, among other things, of county property, roads, and the poor."[14] In Massachusetts Sessions courts "served their counties as regulatory agencies." They "supervised colony finances; regulated highways; controlled the establishment of inns and liquor retailers; . . . exercised a kind of pure-food jurisdiction," and so forth.[15] It was the county courts, then, that performed most of the regulatory and administrative duties in the colonies.[16] The regulatory bodies, then, were composed of local justices of the peace, keeping the community in charge of regulation and administration.

Above the county courts and at the next rung of the judicial ladder typically sat the general circuit courts, often composed of the governor and the council, but sometimes (as in Massachusetts) consisting of full-time judges appointed by the governor and council. Some colonial charters also allowed for appeal

to the Privy Council in England once colonial appeals had been exhausted. In
Massachusetts, for example, the Privy Council could hear appeals from cases
where the amount in controversy surpassed three hundred pounds.[17]

Guarding the Guardians

If officers frequently held "coercive power of a criminal, administrative, and
civil nature," how did the colonists prevent such power from being exercised
arbitrarily?[18] The answer to this question reveals much of the "administrative
law" of the colonial period—the methods by which administrative power
would be limited by law.

The colonial approach contrasts dramatically with that of the present day.
Since courts were the only agencies "that had jurisdiction to fine or otherwise
punish and hence ultimately coerce people who broke the law," they were the
administrative agencies of the colonies.[19] Administrative law did not start with
judicial review of administrative activity; the courts were the administrators
themselves.[20] In the rare cases where administrative officers such as assessors,
sheriffs, and selectmen had the power to coerce citizens, courts had supervision over the legality of their actions—what we normally associate with administrative law today, namely, the judicial review of administrative action.
Courts commonly overturned administrative action, for instance granting tax
abatements by overturning assessors' decisions on grounds of reasonableness.[21]

In addition, administrative officials themselves "were subject to common
law actions for damages whenever in the exercise of their duties they committed a wrong."[22] Sheriffs were liable not only for their own misconduct but
also for that of their deputies. Constables and jailers who lost prisoners could
be sued. Improper arrests and invasions of property were proper subjects of
lawsuits. Illegal searches of property could be remedied by damage actions
against the offending officers. And as Paul Moreno explains, "If a tax collector
took too much of one's property, one had to sue him to recover the excess."[23]

To protect themselves from such actions, administrators in many juris-
dictions sought general warrants and writs of assistance. Established by the
Navigation Act of 1696, writs of assistance were general warrants, signed by
judges, which gave customs officers open-ended authority to invoke probable
cause and search warehouses and other private property for illegal or untaxed
goods. These writs were valid for the entire life of the official rather than for
single searches.[24] Suits for trespass were inapplicable because the writ shielded
the official from liability.[25] Yet as Philip Hamburger explains, in 1761 when
Parliament reauthorized the writs (following the death of King George II),

"a rejection of administrative warrants became one of the foundations of the American Revolution."[26] Among others, James Otis opposed the issuance of these writs and appealed to the Massachusetts Superior Court "to demolish this monster of oppression, and tear into rags this remnant of Star Chamber tyranny."[27] It was "the worst instrument of arbitrary power" through which "Custom house officers may enter our houses when they please . . . and whether they break through malice or revenge, no man, no court can inquire."[28] Otis therefore emphasized not just the power of invasion that the writs granted, but also the inability to challenge the searches in a court of law after the fact.

Though Otis lost in 1761, he inspired further resistance to such writs, and laid the groundwork for their abolition. (John Adams went so far as to declare that Otis "hurried away all before him. American Independence was then and there born.")[29] When the 1767 Townshend Revenue Act reinstated writs of assistance and authorized colonial courts to issue them, courts refused to do so.[30] Complaints about the writs abounded in Revolutionary era pamphlets, including Samuel Adams's "Rights of the Colonists," which appeared in 1772:

"Each of these petty officers so made is intrusted with power more absolute and arbitrary than ought to be lodged in the hands of any man or body of men whatsoever . . . full power and authority from time to time, at their and any of their wills and pleasures . . . to enter and go on board any Ship, Boat, or other Vessel . . . and also in the day time to go into any house, shop, cellar, or any other place." "Thus our houses and even our bed chambers, are exposed to be ransacked. . . . By this we are cut off from that domestic security which renders the lives of the most unhappy in some measure agreeable. Those officers may under color of law and the cloak of a general warrant, break through the sacred rights of the *domicile*."[31]

Thus, the American Revolution established as a basic principle of American constitutionalism that executive officers could not be placed above liability for following the law. Most of the state constitutions established after independence was declared contained bills of rights that expressly forbade general warrants.[32]

Finally, when a law imposed statutory penalties, these could be collected by private enforcers bringing actions against the lawbreakers. This arrangement gave ordinary citizens a pecuniary interest and incentive in enforcing the laws privately through lawsuits. These "qui tam" actions were extensively relied upon for enforcement rather than the employment of a full-time administrative officer, thus limiting the need for full-time bureaucratic enforcement. Administrative action could be shielded from arbitrariness by using private citizens, rather than the agencies themselves, as the prosecutorial mechanism.

"There was, in short, little that one acting on behalf of government could do without rendering himself liable to legal action in the event that he wronged another," Nelson concludes.[33] Courts acted not only as the first administrators and enforcers of laws, but also as the arena for review of administrative power when it was exercised by other officers. Through overturning official action, entertaining private suits enforcing statutory penalties, and holding administrative officers liable for damages, courts were an active part of the administrative process in colonial America. They were the colonial alternative to a vast administrative apparatus.

"I Will Breake Theare Heads":
Timid Officers and Assertive Citizens

The active role played by courts in colonial administration raises the question of how to restrain the courts themselves. The colonial response to this problem was to reduce judicial discretion as much as possible through making judges accountable to the community. Just as administrators such as justices of the peace were kept accountable through frequent elections, courts would be kept accountable through the common law and through juries.

The right to trial by jury was critically important to the American colonists because it provided a check against arbitrary power exercised by royally appointed judges. For this reason, as William Nelson explains, "[J]uries in prerevolutionary Massachusetts could ignore judges' instructions on the law and decide the law by themselves in both civil and criminal cases."[34] This ensured that the administration of the law, both in its development and in its application, would be accountable and therefore not arbitrary: "the law applied in the towns of Massachusetts on a day-to-day basis was not the product of the will of some distant sovereign" but rather the manners and customs of the people themselves.[35] The jury's power over both the interpretation and the application of law helped to keep judicial arbitrariness at bay.

The result of this structure of administrative power in the colonies was twofold. First, the absence of a powerful executive and administrative branch weakened the ability of the government to enforce law against the wishes of the community. Second, this phenomenon ensured that law was in accordance with custom, a principle central to the idea of common law. As Nelson explains, these features of administrative law "rendered formal institutions relatively weak."[36] "[S]ubordinate officials like sheriffs, deputy sheriffs, and constables," he continues, could enforce their judgments "only when local communities were willing to permit judgments to be enforced."[37]

This phenomenon is aptly illustrated by an episode Nelson relates. In this case a parson who led a dissenting religious sect was "threatened with coercion by a committee of the General Court." The citizen responded to the officers: "Let them come into my field, I will breake theare Heads. . . . I do not fear it, I can have anofe to assist me in that afare; Let them Come in to my field if they Dare, I will split theaire braines out."[38] This episode demonstrates that administrative officers, in practice, were relatively weak and lacked the authority to enforce their will on communities disposed to resist them.

Local Government Power:
From Consolidation to Separation

Colonial administration, therefore, rested upon courts as opposed to bureaucracies and used common-law actions to keep both judges and county officers accountable. The advantages of this approach were replicated by the structure of local government, especially in the townships in New England.

Towns were legal corporations that were represented in the legislature and were recognized as basic political units. In Massachusetts they were established by the General Court, which in the early colonial period appointed town officials and managed the towns' affairs. Eventually, the towns began meeting several times annually to exercise the taxing power, to elect town selectmen (the chief local officers), and to enact bylaws.[39] In New York, as opposed to Massachusetts, the township selected "overseers" rather than "selectmen." In Pennsylvania commissioners, elected by the people, eventually assumed powers to care for highways, assess property, and other local matters.[40] Thus in the New England colonies the towns were of greater significance than the counties, which were the most powerful political units in the middle and the southern colonies. In these colonies the chief local officers were sheriffs. Nevertheless, the judicial and administrative powers in these colonies were also largely in the hands of the county courts, whose members were appointed by the governor and council.

Even in the New England colonies, however, the town meeting did not dominate proceedings until relatively late in the colonial era. During the first few decades of the colonial period the town selectmen, and not the town meetings, exercised most coercive power. These bodies of selectmen were established because the town meetings, where everyone debated measures in person, were inefficient. In Dedham, a committee of seven selectmen was created because, in the town's words, "it hath been found by long experience that the general meeting of so many men" in person "have wasted much time to no small damage and business is thereby nothing furthered."[41] In Watertown a committee of three selectmen was established in 1634. In both cases the selectmen were annually elected, a fact that promoted accountability. As town officers, selectmen exercised many of the same functions that justices of the peace performed. They "enforced decisions of the town meetings, issued licenses, admitted new inhabitants, served as judges in certain disputes, supervised building of roads and fences, and looked after education and the poor."[42] From 1640 to 1680 in Massachusetts these officers combined legislative, executive, and judicial powers. They initiated bylaws—sometimes even without the consent of the town meeting itself—assessed taxes, appointed officials such as tithingmen, spent money, laid out highways, granted franchises to operate mills, supervised education, and judged cases involving property disputes and liability for livestock. They were the exemplars of lawmaker, prosecutor, judge, jury, and executioner. These selectmen could initiate and conclude action without the prior action of the town meetings. The meetings held a veto power over the selectmen but it was rarely used.[43]

Gradually, however, these powers were either reclaimed by the people of the town themselves or separated and transferred to other political actors. After 1680, the tide of power shifted to the town meetings. Beyond this date the legislative activities of the town selectmen ceased completely, and they were also stripped of their appointment powers. As a result, the selectmen became merely assessors and adjudicators, applying rather than making law. Thus at the local level administrative power was weakened as the colonists gained familiarity with the problems it posed to the rule of law. In short, administrative power moved from consolidation to separation in the Massachusetts towns. This tendency indicates that colonial Americans refused to subject themselves to potentially arbitrary authorities that could make, execute, and adjudicate law against individual citizens.

Furthermore, in both towns and counties, local officials were elected by local inhabitants, ensuring that administrative power would be exercised in an accountable manner. Administrative power was held highly accountable through annual elections and a highly engaged citizenry. As Morton Keller explains, "American politics [during the Colonial period] was not just a carbon copy of English ways. Local officials (though usually from leading families) were more frequently elected than appointed in America. . . . Instruments of self-governance abounded. Virginia's county courts and local justices of the peace, New England towns and their magistrates and selectmen, and colonial assemblies everywhere were virtually autonomous governing bodies."[44]

The American colonists' experience over an entire century preceding the Revolutionary War yielded important lessons for establishing and constraining administrative power. Administrative power was to be accountable through frequent elections. Town selectmen in Massachusetts were annually elected. Justices of the peace were kept accountable to colonial legislatures. Even *ad hoc* administrative committees were to report to the town meetings for confirmation of their decisions. In addition, a nascent practice of separation of functions is discernible in the gradual reduction of selectmen's consolidated functions. As the example of Massachusetts illustrated, the colonists were uncomfortable with vesting such wide-ranging power in the hands of a single body and gradually separated these powers by placing them in the hands of other officials or assuming them directly. Finally, the legal community developed basic protections for individual liberty in the face of administrative power, including rights to be free from unreasonable searches, the right to trial by jury, and the right to due process as opposed to summary administrative authority. These lessons would be reinforced through the lessons of experience, at both the state and national levels, during the Revolutionary War.

The Revolutionary War Experience

As scholars have documented, the state governments performed disastrously during the Revolutionary War. Because the first state constitutions were designed to curtail executive power and ensure legislative dominance, they produced inadequate administration. As Jefferson famously wrote, "Before the Revolution we were all good English Whigs, cordial in their free principles, and in their jealousies of their executive magistrates. These jealousies are all very apparent in all our state constitutions."[45] After learning the hard way through his own service in the Continental Congress, James Madison conceded in *Federalist no. 48*:

> The founders of our republics . . . seem never for a moment to have turned their eyes from the danger to liberty from the overgrown and all-grasping power of an hereditary magistrate. . . . They seem never to have recollected the danger from legislative usurpations; which by assembling all power in the same hands, must lead to the same tyranny as is threatened by executive usurpations.[46]

Like Madison, James Wilson understood that the framers of most of these initial state constitutions failed to consider the possibility of legislative tyranny. He observed that after the Revolutionary War "the executive and judicial as well as the legislative authority was now the child of the people," unlike the Colonial era, "but, to the two former, the people behaved like stepmothers. The legislature was still discriminated by excessive partiality; and into its lap, every good and precious gift was profusely thrown."[47] But the Framers learned from this experience that executive power cannot be neglected or made subservient in a well-functioning political system.

Committees of Public Safety: Veiling the Impetuous Vortex

The first mistake the states made during the Revolutionary War was apparent in the structure of the "Committees of Public Safety" established in response to military necessities. These temporary committees were relatively large bodies tasked with meeting basic and immediate exigencies such as military preparations. Virginia organized an eleven-member Committee of Public Safety; the Carolinas' numbered thirteen, while Maryland's committee was composed of sixteen members.[48] These committees were given considerable latitude over a wide range of military affairs (including financial and executive powers), subject to the ultimate authority of the legislative assemblies, which formally "retained the power of legislation."[49]

Though these committees of safety served a useful purpose in the midst of grave necessity, political leaders quickly learned about the importance of separating legislative and executive power adequately and supplying an independent and unitary executive. Many of the new states simply eliminated the temporary councils of safety as soon as they could. South Carolina moved to create a more regular plan of government by February 1776, and Georgia followed a few months later.[50]

New York's Committee of Safety, however, proved more resilient and was subjected to repeated attacks from those who favored a more regular organization of legislative and executive power. The state's Council of Revision, led by Governor George Clinton, used its veto to assert basic principles of administrative law and structure violated by the state's Committee of Safety. In February 1778 it vetoed "An act to prevent the exportation of flour, meal, and grain" as "inconsistent with the spirit of the Constitution" of New York.[51] The veto objected that the statute called the Council of Safety "a Legislative body, when in fact all legislative power is to be exercised by the immediate representatives of the people, in Senate and Assembly, in the mode prescribed by the Constitution." Citing the New York Constitution's provision that "no authority shall . . . be exercised over the people or members of this state, but such as shall be derived from and granted by them," the Council concluded that the measure was an invalid delegation of legislative power to an illegitimate body. This veto message in 1778 served as an early assertion of the nondelegation doctrine, which prohibited delegating legislative power to bodies not composed of immediate representatives and whose powers are not derived from the people.[52] These two principles—immediate legislative representation and the social compact—would reappear during the ratification of the Constitution during the 1780s.

The same veto asserted that "the court instituted by [the law] for the trial of intentional exports without license" violated protections of due process, for "the person who makes the seizure is . . . to determine the propriety of evidence and challenges, and yet in certain cases must be the prosecutor." The party whose property is seized, in addition, is "condemned to forfeit his property without a hearing." Furthermore, "by the bill mere suspicion alone, without any proof or evidence of intention to export without license, is sufficient to justify any committeeman, justice, sheriff, or other peace officer to seize and detain flour, &c."[53] Thus the Council of Revision objected to the exportation bill not only on delegation but also on rule of law grounds. An official who can seize property without a hearing, and who is allowed to devise his own procedures when challenged, is not a legitimate court, according to the Council's message.

The Council's veto was overturned by the state legislature. Still, the message demonstrates that by 1788 the executive and judicial branches had already developed constitutional arguments against the vesting of legislative power in bodies that were not granted authority directly by the people. Prominent figures such as George Clinton, John Jay, Robert Livingston, and Robert Yates were making these arguments as members of the state's Council of Revision. And these arguments gradually won out. Later in 1778 the Council successfully vetoed a measure to raise revenue through a tax on all personal property within the State of New York. The act provided for assessors not only to "ascertain the profits by such persons" to be taxed, but also to assess "at such rates . . . over and above the assessment hereby required on their real and personal estates . . . as they, the assessors, shall in their judgment think proper."[54] The assessors, in other words, were not merely charged with the ministerial task of determining the value of the property; they were empowered to adjust the rate at which the property would be taxed. The Council argued that "the Legislature are not authorized by the Constitution to delegate the right of determining, at discretion, how much shall be levied on all or part of the people to any body of men whatever, much less to the assessors." The job of the legislature, the Council maintained, was "to ascertain and declare the rate at which the people shall be taxed, and of the assessors to determine only the value or amount of the property of each individual."[55] In this case the Council successfully insisted upon the nondelegation of legislative power to the assessors and the separation of political functions.

Clinton's Council of Revision won other, similar victories by asserting the principles of nondelegation and separation of powers. The Council vetoed a 1780 measure providing for a Council of Safety during the recess of the legislature, on the grounds that the bill required "the person administering the Government . . . with the Council therein provided" to "exercise the powers of legislation; which by the Constitution, is vested in the Senate and Assembly, and cannot by them be delegated to others." By delegating the power to legislate to the Council of Safety the legislature had violated the nondelegation doctrine. In addition, the Council objected that "the person administering the government is by the bill subjected, in the execution of his office, to the control of a Council, when by the Constitution" it is vested in a Governor exclusively. The measure had not only violated the nondelegation doctrine; it had also undermined the unity and independence of the executive by subjecting him to the control of the Council of Safety during a recess of the legislature. Pernicious effects would follow these constitutional injuries, the Council concluded: it would "tend to embarrass government, and destroy its present energy."[56] Once again, Clinton's veto was successful and the bill was defeated.

Other states began to insist upon separation of powers principles in the face of the Councils of Safety. In 1781, for instance, the state of New Hampshire called a second Constitutional Convention to form a state Constitution. The Convention itself sent out an address accompanying its plan, which addressed the role of executive power in a separation-of-powers system. The Convention admitted that because of the perilous situation of the colonies in 1776, the state gave insufficient consideration to the structure of government in crafting its constitution: "That form which was the simplest . . . they adopted without that thorough discussion and calm deliberation which so important an object required." Given these difficulties, it conceded, "the legislative and executive powers of government were vested in one body, to wit, in a General Court, consisting of two branches, a House of Representatives and a Council." During the recess of the legislature, a "Committee of Safety" was empowered to exercise the executive power.[57]

The problem with this arrangement was immediately apparent: "many of the individuals who compose the aforementioned body, assist in enacting laws, in explaining and applying them, and in carrying them into execution."

The combination of these three powers produced numerous difficulties. Consequently, the 1781 Convention affirmed that "The three powers of government . . . we have thought proper to keep as separate and distinct as possible," for "If they should be all united, the government, would then be a complete system of tyranny. The same party would be legislator, accuser, judge, and executioner."[58] New Hampshire's call for a constitutional convention resulted from the clear problems that the committees of safety posed to individual liberty, due to their violations of the separation of powers principle.

While New York benefited from Clinton's leadership in asserting the principles of nondelegation and the separation of powers, in the other states the lessons in favor of executive unity and independence were hard learned. Almost all of the states elected their governors by the legislative branch, for short terms and with restrictions on re-eligibility. They also divided executive power through the use of an executive council with which the governor was required to share powers. Most minor administrative officials were chosen by the legislature (except in Maryland and Georgia, where many were elected by the people).[59] Most states also denied the veto power to their governors.

These institutional arrangements illustrated the extent to which the legislatures sought to swallow up all executive power and interfere with administration. Eventually, however, leaders of states beyond New York began objecting to such a system of legislative domination. In May of 1780 the Pennsylvania Council protested against "the interference of your Hon'ble House in matters merely of an executive nature."[60] In this case the legislature sought to overturn an adjudication already concluded by the executive, a practice that the Council deemed at odds with the need for an independent executive power.

Other states refused to adopt a unitary executive at the state level, choosing instead to divide up executive power into multi-member committees. In 1776 Massachusetts organized its government into a twenty-eight member council, which combined legislative, executive, and judicial powers (its Committee of Safety consisted of fewer members and was in place through July of 1775). Though this "seemed the wisest move at a time when acts were largely dependent upon expediency," the first few years of the Revolutionary War decisively debunked the experiment: "it was not long before the disadvantages arising from substituting an executive body of twenty-eight for a single executive became apparent."[61] When smallpox broke out in Boston in 1778 the General Court bypassed the council, declaring that any seven members could conduct business on behalf of the whole.[62] The inefficiency of this arrangement prompted Samuel Otis to write to Elbridge Gerry in November 1777, "There is great expectation of a new form of government in our state. I hope it will be a good one, and an executive power will be lodged somewhere; at present, if there is any, you will be puzzled to find it: hence the chariot wheels drag so slowly."[63] Still, the issue of executive power was particularly contentious in the framing of the Massachusetts Constitution of 1780. The town of Ashfield declared "it is our Opinniiun that we do not want any Goviner but the Goviner of the universe."[64] Eventually the advocates for a stronger executive power achieved victory in Massachusetts, but not until the effects of a weakened, divided, and dependent executive power became starkly apparent.

Through experience leaders of the new states learned important lessons. In Virginia, for instance, Jefferson famously described the phenomenon of legislative usurpation in his *Notes on the State of Virginia* thusly: "All the powers of government, legislative executive and judiciary, result to the legislative body." Although the powers were separate on paper, "no barrier was provided between these several powers . . . and the direction of the executive, during the whole time of [the state legislature's] session, is becoming habitual and familiar."[65] The nominal separation of powers in Virginia had become, in practice, the direction of all powers by the legislature. The lessons learned from state experience were reinforced by the inadequate structure for administration erected under the Articles of Confederation.

National Experience under the Articles of Confederation

The Framers' immense frustration at the inadequacy of administration under the Articles of Confederation provided the greatest inspiration to set administrative power on a firm footing under the Constitution. A careful examination of the problems they experienced under the Articles, therefore, is essential to understanding the role of administrative power within the constitutional system they established. The Articles of Confederation failed to set up a proper executive or judicial power. The only institution established under the Articles was the Continental Congress. The task of providing for administration would be accomplished through positive enactments of the Congress.

For six years, from 1775 to 1781, this approach failed dramatically. During this time the Continental Congress adopted a two-pronged approach to administration. First, it established *ad hoc* committees to take care of particular functions. Jerry Mashaw explains: "By one count the Continental Congress created 3249 different committees between 1774 and 1788. It created 498 in its 1783 session alone, giving the average representative something like twenty committee assignments."[66] Moreover, Congress retained control over these committees, which were composed of members of the legislature and which "operated under the direct supervision and control of the whole Congress."[67]

Therefore members were both legislators and administrators, with disastrous results. In the spring of 1775, the members of the Continental Congress rushed quickly to establish executive committees for carrying out basic functions. It created committees to secure ammunition, manufacture saltpeter, govern the army, supply and raise troops, raise revenue, and initiate relations with other powers. Each committee contained from three to thirteen members, "the latter number being usually selected for the more important ones, so that each colony might be represented."[68] The result was administrative sprawl, with "a legion of small boards, who neither took pains to render mutual assistance to each other, nor to preserve peace within their own ranks."[69] The inconveniences of this administrative method became apparent almost immediately. The military objectives Congress intended to pursue were consistently enervated by the dispersion of authority into so many boards and commissions, without a supervising body except that of the entire Congress itself.

The second approach involved the creation of relatively permanent administrative agencies to handle war, naval affairs, foreign relations, finance, and so on. Here, the Congress attempted to set up administrative departments but failed to construct them properly. Thus the result was the same under both approaches: the execution of Congress's policies was inefficient, and members of Congress continually tinkered with both the powers and the structure of these bodies. For example, the Board of War, composed of five members of the Congress, chaired by John Adams, was inundated with responsibilities related to raising and supplying troops and reporting to Congress. By the following March it was clear that the members of the Continental Congress could not manage the war effort and perform their legislative functions simultaneously. Structural reforms would be necessary to produce the necessary efficiency and responsibility they were seeking. Executive power would have to be separated out from and made independent of the Congress, so that independent executives could devote their full energies to the effort.

Congress took this step in October 1777, creating a new Board of War composed of members outside the Congress, but its multi-headed organization rendered it irresponsible and inefficient. Members of Congress could not hold the Board responsible because there was no single head in charge of the Board. Thus the Framers learned that such administrative bodies needed not only to be independent but also single-headed in order to ensure both efficiency and responsibility. The concentration of accountability in a single person, who was not a member of the legislature, and the continuity provided by a single figure's leadership ensured greater energy, efficiency, and responsibility to the ends set forth by the authorizing legislature.

The Shift to Single-Headed
Departments and the "Revolution of 1781"

These lessons were learned simultaneously through the experience of working with other departments, in which Congress followed largely the same process as that of the Board of War. From 1775 to 1781, in summary, the Continental Congress adopted a characteristic approach to administration, one that produced a perilously inefficient government. Congress normally dealt with administrative business through *ad hoc* administrative units rather than permanent departments with settled authority. Congress refused to delegate executive business to these units but consistently meddled in the business of administration. The use of multi-member boards, comprised of both legislators and members outside Congress, rather than single-headed departments was prevalent, and by 1781 members of the Congress understood this to be particularly problematic. One scholar states: "It is positively pathetic to follow Congress through its aimless wanderings in search of a system for satisfactory management of its executive departments. At no period between 1774 and 1781 can we find it pursuing any consistent line of action with reference to them. A humble committee served as the common origin of all. . . . There was, in short, no element of permanency to be found anywhere in the entire system."[70]

Congress's poor decision making hindered the war effort significantly. The dire situation faced by George Washington and his men at Valley Forge in 1777 and 1778 can be traced to Congress's meddling with the Commissary Department, which was charged with supplying the troops. The first Commissary General of the Continental Army, Joseph Trumbull, was frustrated in his efforts because Congress deprived him of control of the subordinates in the department. He ultimately resigned because of this feature. John Marshall ascribed his resignation to the "creation, in some of the subordinate offices, of an independence on the head of the department, and an immediate and direct dependence on Congress."[71] Congress established four deputies within the department who were to be appointed by the Congress, not by Trumbull. In addition, those deputies were not removable by Trumbull, but only by the legislature. Trumbull's frustration with this arrangement was evident in his letter of resignation to the Continental Congress, which asserted that "the head of every department ought to have control of it. In this establishment, an imperium in imperio is created."[72] After Trumbull's resignation Congress reorganized the department, affirming that the new Commissary General would have full power to appoint and remove subordinates at will, but it had to learn these lessons the hard way.

Ultimately, the problems of 1775–1781 stemmed from the inability of the Congress to see that a popular republican government was compatible with, and even required, the existence of a responsible and independent executive power. This inability was so great that John Adams and others favored "upon the genuine principles of a republic . . . a new election of general officers annually" rather than letting Washington make the appointments on the basis of his experience.[73] This inability to separate legislative and executive functions nearly scuttled the entire American Revolution.

Gradually, these lessons became so compelling that the Framers modified their preconceived notions against executive power. They came to see that boards and committees lacked efficiency and accountability, and that departments with single heads alleviated these problems. Alexander Hamilton was largely responsible for the "vigorous crusade against the boards" undertaken by the Congress.[74] As he wrote to Robert Morris in 1780: "We want a Minister of War, a Minister of Foreign Affairs, a Minister of Finance, and a Minister of Marine. There is always more decision, more dispatch, more secrecy, more responsibility, where single men, than where bodies are concerned."[75] Though these lessons had been learned the hard way, Hamilton was prepared by 1780 to ensure Congress would not repeat its previous errors.

The decisive shift finally arrived in February of 1781. In that month single-member secretaries of War and of Marine, and a Superintendent of Finance were established (a single Secretary of Foreign Affairs had been established the month prior). Illustrating the entrenched nature of opposition to energetic and independent executive institutions is the fact that Congress failed to select the first Secretary of War, Benjamin Lincoln, until October 1781. This was eight months after the office was created, and days after the British surrender at Yorktown.[76]

Bloodied but Not Beaten:
The Framers Craft an Administrative Constitution

The problems that the Continental Congress encountered eventually persuaded them of the need to revise their administrative arrangements. At the same time states were coming to see the need for independent executive power. Slowly but surely, critical principles of administrative constitutionalism were emerging as a result of eighteenth-century experience. Reliance on the judiciary as the agents of regulation and administration, accountability of administrators to the people, the availability of judicial review and legal checks to guard against administrative arbitrariness, separation of administrative power from legislative interference, and unitary executive structures were all becoming part of the new administrative constitutionalism.

By the time the delegates to the Constitutional Convention began deliberations in the summer of 1787, then, a relatively sophisticated set of principles governing the structure of administration had begun to emerge. Though the arguments for these principles were still nascent, many of the debates at the Convention and during the ratification of the Constitution followed the principles set forth in these early American discussions on how to reconcile administration with American constitutionalism. Although they had not resolved all questions regarding administration, nor reached complete unanimity even on certain fundamental principles, the process of framing and ratifying the Constitution enabled them to reach consensus on administration's place in the Constitution. Contrary to what Jerry Mashaw has recently asserted, there is no "hole" in the Constitution "where administration might have been."[77] The principles of administrative law that emerged from the debates surrounding administration during the framing and ratification of the Constitution can be discerned, though they are not well understood today.

"A Considerable Silence Ensued": A Unitary or a Plural Executive?

Debates on the executive power and the structure of administration were extensive at the Constitutional Convention. Of course, the question of representation was the most vexing of all questions encountered by the delegates, but that question was largely political. The problems representation presented concerned how to compromise on questions where interests were deeply entrenched. With executive and administrative power, however, the questions were more difficult on the theoretical level.

Three fundamental questions surrounding administrative power emerged at the Convention: first, should the executive branch be single- or multi-headed; second, should this executive power be made independent of the legislature; and third, should the concurrence of a council be required for the exercise of certain executive powers? These questions interacted with each other, so that the answer to one would affect the answer to another—a feature that only further complicated an already difficult matter.

The presentation of the Virginia Plan on May 29 introduced these questions to the Convention for the first time. Resolution Seven of the Plan was ambiguous on critical elements of executive power, merely suggesting that "a National Executive be instituted; to be chosen by the National Legislature for the term of _____ years." It would have provided this executive with "a general authority to execute the National laws" as well as "the Executive rights vested in Congress by the Confederation." Finally, it would be combined with "a convenient number of the National Judiciary" to form "a council of revision with authority to examine every act of the National Legislature" and exercise veto authority over laws passed by the legislature.[78] The plan was therefore silent on the question of how many executives would be at the head of the executive branch, and proposed to make the executive dependent on the legislature and combine it with a council drawn from the judiciary for the exercise of the veto.

Resolution Seven was taken up on June 1. After the resolution was read, James Wilson immediately moved to amend the resolution to read "that a national Executive to consist of a single person be instituted."[79] Wilson's call for a single-headed executive conformed to the lessons learned by the Continental Congress under the Articles of Confederation, where experience taught the delegates to abandon multi-headed agencies for single-headed departments. These points were repeated by several of the delegates, such as John Rutledge who argued that "A single man would feel the greatest responsibility and administer the public affairs best."[80] Wilson similarly "preferred a single magistrate, as giving most energy, dispatch, and responsibility to the office."[81]

Still, fear of executive power made them hesitate. Upon Wilson's motion, Madison reported in his notes, "A considerable pause ensuing and the Chairman asking if he should put the question, Dr. Franklin observed that it was a point of great importance and wished that the gentlemen would deliver their sentiments upon it."[82] Wilson's motion had induced a normally loquacious convention to silence—a silence so lengthy that the Chair nearly moved to vote on the motion without debate, at which point the distinguished Franklin had to exhort his colleagues to speak.

Franklin opened Pandora's Box with his request, and the delegates quickly jumped in on both sides of the question. Randolph—who had introduced the Virginia Plan—"strenuously opposed a unity in the Executive magistracy" as "the foetus of monarchy. . . . He could not see why the great requisites for the Executive department, vigor, dispatch & responsibility could not be found in three men, as well as in one man." While he granted that "The Executive ought to be independent" he argued that this would only be attainable if there were many at the head.[83] Elbridge Gerry preferred "annexing a Council (to the Executive) in order to give weight & inspire confidence," showing the link between the questions of unity and of a council.[84] Roger Sherman advocated letting the legislature vary the number of executives from time to time as it saw fit.

After Wilson once again defended the safety of a single-headed executive branch as "the best safeguard against tyranny" Madison moved to table the issue, arguing that the question would be easier to address after defining the extent of executive power. Moving on to this issue brought the Convention to its first confrontation with the nondelegation principle. Madison moved to define the executive power as the "power to carry into effect the national laws, to appoint such offices in cases not otherwise provided for, and to execute such other powers as may from time to time be delegated by the national legislature."[85] Was Madison suggesting that the legislature could delegate its powers to the executive?

The ambiguity in his motion was quickly challenged by Charles Pinckney, who suggested that the last clause—to execute such powers as may be delegated—was unnecessary since it was already included in the first clause, namely, the power to carry into effect the national laws. Regardless, he recommended amending the clause to read "to execute such other powers *not Legislative or Judiciary* in their nature as may from time to time be delegated.[86] Two propositions were therefore presented to Madison and the Convention: first, does the power to execute the national laws already include the power to execute powers that are periodically delegated by the legislature, and second, does the term "execute" by definition exclude the powers to legislate and adjudicate, or must that exclusion be positively specified?

Madison responded that he "did not know that the words" in the last clause "were absolutely necessary." He even argued that the power to appoint offices might be "included in the first number of the proposition" as naturally part of the executive power. He merely recommended retaining the last two clauses—with Pinckney's proposed alteration prohibiting the executive from exercising legislative or judicial power—because "cases might happen in which they might serve to prevent doubts and misconstructions."[87] Madison's response suggests that he believed the power to execute the national laws *already* entailed, by definition, the power to appoint offices and the power to execute such powers that might be delegated by the legislature. It also suggests that he did *not* think the power to execute such powers that might be delegated included legislative or judicial powers. In other words, Madison's response clearly indicates that he believed that not all powers delegated by the legislature were legislative or judicial. Some of them were strictly executive. And only those powers that were strictly executive could be legitimately delegated. All of this, his response suggests, is entailed in the very definition of executive power, such that Pinckney's restriction did not have to be positively specified, and that it was only necessary "to prevent doubts and misconstructions."

Madison's response shows a clear and conclusive commitment to the principle of nondelegation: that the legislature may not transfer legislative or judicial power over to the executive. But it also acknowledges that some powers can be delegated that are strictly executive in nature. However, the delegates were so committed to the nondelegation principle themselves that they struck the last clause of Madison's motion entirely, leaving out any suggestion that the executive may execute powers of any kind that might be delegated by the legislature.

Having accepted Madison's specification of the executive's powers, without the ability to execute such powers as might be delegated by the legislature, the Convention proceeded to discuss the method of selecting the chief executive. On this question the critical consideration was preserving the independence of the executive from the legislature. James Wilson was the first delegate to advance the idea of a popular election of the chief executive, though he admitted that "he was almost unwilling to declare the mode he wished to take place, being apprehensive that it might appear chimerical." Still, he declared that he advocated popular election in both the legislature and the executive "in order to make them as independent as possible of each other."[88] This consideration also prevailed in the discussion of removing the chief executive from office. George Mason, hardly an advocate of a powerful executive, still "opposed decidedly the making the Executive the mere creature of the Legislature as a violation of the fundamental principle of good Government."[89] Therefore he rejected Roger Sherman's proposal "that the National Legislature should have power to remove the Executive at pleasure."[90] A motion by John Dickinson to have the chief executive removable by the legislature, upon the application of a majority of the state legislatures, was also defeated. On these questions, with the exception of only a few delegates such as Sherman, there was widespread agreement that the mode of removal of the executive had to preserve the independence of the executive from the legislature. The Convention wrestled with the proper mode of electing the executive for months, however, due to practical problems with both legislative and popular selection. Eventually they would settle on the Electoral College as a method of keeping the executive independent from the legislature. A key failure of the Articles would not be replicated in this Constitution.

Having settled these matters, the Convention returned to the silence-inducing question of a single versus a plural chief executive. Pinckney moved again to establish a single chief executive, "suppos[ing] the reasons to be so obvious & conclusive in favor of one that no member would oppose the motion."[91] He was too optimistic. Randolph immediately "opposed it with great earnestness. . . . He felt an opposition to it which he believed he should continue to feel as long as he lived."[92] However, Randolph was opposed by most of the delegates who echoed arguments made earlier by Wilson and Morris, and which would be repeated by Hamilton in *The Federalist*. Pierce Butler "contended strongly for a single magistrate. . . . If one man should be appointed he would be responsible to the whole, and would be impartial to its interests. If three or more should be taken from as many districts, there would be a constant struggle for local advantages."[93] The Convention adjourned on June 2nd without deciding the question.

When debate resumed, Wilson added an additional reason in favor of unity in the executive: "The *tranquility* not less than the vigor of the Govt. he thought would be favored by it." A division in the executive would occasion "nothing but uncontrouled, continued, & violent animosities; which would not only interrupt the public administration; but diffuse their poison through" the entire government.[94] Finally the question was put to a vote, and the Convention decided on a single executive by a vote of seven states to three.

At this point in the Convention's deliberations several principles relevant to administrative law had emerged and it may be helpful to summarize them briefly. First, the Convention emphatically endorsed the principle of nondelegation. In fact, they went so far in defense of this principle as to eliminate all room for misconstruction by defeating Madison's motion even with Pinckney's revision that the executive could not execute powers "Legislative or Judiciary in their nature." The Convention had also endorsed the principle of unity and independence in the executive, though on this point there was less unanimity, particularly with regard to making the executive independent of the legislature.[95] The Convention had also offered many of the reasons in defense of this arrangement: greater energy and efficiency, greater safety due to accountability, and a greater tranquility as a result of eliminating internal rivalries in the administration of the laws.

Secondary questions of administrative structure, however, were left unanswered. Would there be a cabinet or a council to assist the chief executive? The greatest opponent of unity in the executive, Roger Sherman, asserted that all of the states attached "a Council of advice, without which the first magistrate could not act," suggesting the Convention follow this practice.[96] In addition, should departments be specified and established in the Constitution itself? If so, what would be their relationship to the chief executive? These questions would be addressed by the Convention later in the summer.

Structuring the Administrative Power:
Proposals for Councils and Departments

The idea of a council that would exercise power concurrently with the chief executive was one of the most persistently advanced ideas at the Convention. Even James Wilson and James Madison, among the most committed defenders of a unitary executive, favored joining the judiciary with the executive in a council of revision for the exercise of the veto power. Madison proposed the council of revision multiple times, failing repeatedly. Oliver Ellsworth pressed a similar idea in which certain ministers would be specified and joined to the president, along with the president of the Senate and the Chief Justice of the Supreme Court (thus joining all three branches of government). The notion of a council to be attached to the executive was so persistent that it was advanced at several of the ratifying conventions.

All of these proposals were rejected decisively and for similar reasons—reasons that are highly relevant to contemporary administrative law. Just as significant as the vigorous attachment of some delegates to a council is the fact that the proposals were consistently rejected. Ultimately, in spite of the persistence of this idea, the Framers concluded that the costs were too great to justify patterning executive power after the British model in this respect. The debates concerning the existence and role of a council attached to the president help to illustrate the prevailing views on the relationship between the chief executive and subordinate executive officers, an important and persistent question in administrative law.

The most intriguing proposal for an executive council at the Constitutional Convention was advanced by Gouverneur Morris and Charles Pinckney near the end of August. The Morris-Pinckney council clarified that this council would "advise [the president] in matters respecting the execution of his Office. . . . But their advice shall not conclude him, nor affect his responsibility for the measures which he shall adopt." The proposal would have established a much more detailed structure for the federal administration than the Constitution and thus deserves careful attention. Titled a "Council of State," the proposed council consisted of the Chief Justice, secretaries of Domestic Affairs, Commerce and Finance, Foreign Affairs, War, Marine, and State. Each secretary would be "appointed by the President and hold his office during pleasure," giving the president both appointment and sole removal power over his council. Each secretary was also given specific responsibilities in the Morris plan, similar to a statutory assignment of responsibility. The Secretary of Domestic Affairs, for instance, was required to "attend to matters of general police, the State of Agriculture and manufactures, the opening of roads and navigations, and the facilitation communications through the United States," and was tasked with recommending measures "as may tend to promote those objects."[97] Thus the proposal seemed to anticipate ministers within the executive department, accountable to the president, yet tasked with recommending legislation to Congress regarding the specific areas entrusted to them. This structure would resemble the British parliamentary system, but with important alterations: an independently selected president with exclusive control over subordinates within the administration. While this proposal would have fostered some interaction between the heads of departments and the legislature, it would not replicate some of the problematic features of the Articles of Confederation, such as legislative control over department heads and subordinate officers within the departments. The consistent arguments for unity and responsibility were influencing even those who advocated for some kind of council of state.

As a council, the Council of State could be convened by the president, who could submit matters for its consideration. The proposal explicitly stated that the president "may require the written opinions of any one or more of the members: But he shall in all cases exercise his own judgment . . . and every officer abovementioned shall be responsible for his opinion on the affairs relating to his particular Department."[98] The proposal was referred to the Committee of Detail, which reported it out to the full Convention two days later. The Committee of Detail called this "a Privy-Council" whose duty would be "to advise him in matters respecting the execution of his Office, which he shall think proper to lay before them; But their advice shall not conclude him, nor affect his responsibility for the measures which he shall adopt."[99]

The Committee's revised council proposal was not taken up by the Convention, and was eventually referred to the Committee on Postponed Matters, composed of eleven members, on August 31. Several days later the committee reported out several clauses but there was no mention of the proposal. One of the clauses reported, however, seemed to be based upon the proposal: the Written Opinions Clause, which declares that the president "may require the Opinion, in writing, of the principal Officer in each of the executive Departments." Saikrishna Prakash writes that "Evidently, the eleven-member committee reviewed the Morris-Pinckney plan, rejected it, and instead submitted the Written Opinions Clause. . . . The resemblance . . . to the language in the Morris-Pinckney plan is unmistakable."[100] Why did the Convention eliminate the council and retain the power to require written opinions from principal officers? George Mason, who offered one last proposal for a council based on geographical membership, suggested that the Committee on Postponed Matters eliminated the council provision because "it was judged that the President by persuading his Council, to concur in wrong measures, would acquire their protection for them."[101] When Mason's proposal was defeated, it appears that the Convention passed the Written Opinions Clause as a substitute.

One argument in favor of the Written Opinions Clause, versus the council proposal, was clearly the issue of administrative accountability and responsibility. As James Iredell would later explain at the North Carolina ratifying convention, Hamilton would argue in *The Federalist*, many members argued at the Constitutional Convention, executive responsibility demanded that the ultimate accountability for decisions lie in a single actor who maintained control over administrative decisions.[102] When the textual support for the unitary executive that does exist is understood in light of the debates that gave rise to it, it becomes clear that the Framers ardently wished to secure administrative responsibility and that presidential control over decisions was the chief way to achieve that objective.

Appointments and Inferior Officers

The Written Opinions Clause indicates that while the delegates at the Convention were not prepared to lay out in detail the structure of the executive branch beneath the president, they were willing to provide some guidance in the Constitution on the relationship between the president and subordinate administrative officers. The deliberations on the Inferior Officers Clause also offers some guidance as to this relationship between the chief executive and subordinates. When the provision for nominating officers was raised for consideration on September 7, James Wilson objected to the Senate's involvement in appointments "as blending a branch of the Legislature with the Executive. . . . Responsibility is in a manner destroyed by such an agency of the Senate."[103] Wilson was again raising his favorite argument about responsibility in attacking any role at all for the Senate in appointments. When Morris responded that "as the President was to nominate, there would be responsibility, and as the Senate was to concur, there would be security," Gerry presented the obvious objection: "The idea of responsibility in the nomination to offices is chimerical—the President can not know all characters, and can therefore always plead ignorance."[104] Gerry's objection to the executive's exclusive control over appointments was also based on the principle of responsibility. The difficulty was that the principle of responsibility does not apply in the case of many inferior officers, who are not traceable to the president due to the impossibility of knowing every appointee intimately.

Gerry's argument sheds light on the reasons for the inclusion of the Inferior Officers Clause: that "Congress may by law vest the appointment of such Inferior Officers as they think proper, in the President alone, in the Courts of Law, or in the heads of Departments." This clause was introduced by Gouverneur Morris—a strong proponent of executive power—on the penultimate day of the Convention.[105] In the brief debate over the clause, Madison asserted that "It does not go far enough if it be necessary at all—Superior Officers *below* Heads of Departments ought in some cases to have the appointment of the lesser offices."[106] Madison therefore envisioned a hierarchy of appointments in which the chief executive appointed the heads of the various departments, but where the lower offices within departments were selected by officers within the department—even, in some cases, those who were not themselves the heads of the department.

At the Convention, several important principles were articulated that demonstrated a connection between American constitutionalism and administrative law. A key principle, in keeping with the lessons learned during the Revolutionary period, was that administration should be made both independent and responsible through the mode of selecting administrative officers. There should be a single executive whose mode of election rendered him independent of the legislature. Inferior administrative officers need not be appointed by the president, but the delegates were suspicious of administrative arrangements that might vest independent powers in officers within the executive branch. The Morris-Pinckney proposal specified that the heads of departments could advise but not "conclude" the president's action. Even then it was rejected because it might serve as a pretense for undermining administrative accountability.[107] A further principle was that the executive branch should not receive powers legislative or judiciary in nature. The legislative and executive powers should be kept separate, and the administrative power could not legitimately extend to legislative activity. These principles would be articulated in terms of republicanism and the separation of powers during the ratification debates—most prominently in *The Federalist*.

Administration in the Ratification Debates: Republicanism, Responsible Administration, and the Separation of Powers

The Anti-Federalists were highly critical of the executive power as set up in the Constitution in general. The debates over the structure of the executive branch during the ratification process prompted some important comments from both sides on the constitutional principles that should guide the structure of administration.

The most sustained objection the Anti-Federalists leveled against the structure of the administration was the president's unified control over it. Though, as Herbert Storing has written, "Many Anti-Federalists thought that a unitary executive was necessary, for the sake of both efficiency and responsibility," they were not willing to extend the lessons of experience under the Articles as far as their Federalist counterparts.[108] Many of them continued to argue in favor of an executive council, particularly to check the president's power to appoint administrative officers.[109]

Federal Farmer, for example, acknowledged that every state "has uniformly shewn its preference for a single executive," but was quick to note that they also "directed the first executive magistrate to act in certain cases by the advice of an executive council." Unity in the executive would provide "discernment and decision" as well as "promptitude and uniformity," while retaining "a visible point serving as a common centre in the government, towards which" the people could "draw their eyes and attachments."[110] To this point he was largely in agreement with his Federalist counterparts on the virtues of a unitary executive. Yet in the case of appointments he suggested that the "power to appoint all other necessary officers" aside from inferior officers be lodged in "the first executive magistrate, advised and directed by an executive council of seven or nine members" not of his own choosing.[111] Cato agreed, saying that it was "obvious to the least intelligent mind . . . why, great power in the hands of a magistrate . . . may be dangerous to the liberties of a republic—the deposit of vast trusts in the hands of a single magistrate, enables him in their exercise, to create a numerous train of dependants [sic]." Given the vast nomination and appointment powers of the president, joined with other powers, Cato argued that "if the president is possessed of ambition, he has power and time sufficient to ruin his country." As a result of the lack of a constitutional council, he argued, the president would "generally be directed by minions and favorites, or a council of state will grow out of the principal officers of the great departments, the most dangerous council in a free country."[112]

The Anti-Federalists' arguments for an executive council were repeated in several of the state ratifying conventions. Melancton Smith proposed at the New York ratifying convention to amend the Constitution to provide "a council to advise the President in the appointment of officers." This council would be appointed by the Congress and its individual members would "always be responsible for their advice, and impeachable for malconduct in office."[113] In Virginia Mason repeated his proposal for a constitutional council to "aid the President in the discharge of his office."[114] In North Carolina the leading Anti-Federalist, Samuel Spencer, raised a proposal to provide the president with a "standing council, composed of one member from each of the states," in order to eliminate the dependence of the president upon the Senate and to diminish the Senate's powers.[115] The executive council idea was ably rebutted by the leading Federalist at the North Carolina convention, James Iredell.

Iredell, who would eventually serve on the U.S. Supreme Court, recurred to the principle of responsibility in arguing against a council of appointments. He first pointed to the Written Opinions clause that was, "in some degree, substituted for a council. . . . By this means [the president] will be aided by [the principal officers'] intelligence; and the necessity of their opinions being in writing, will render them more cautious in giving them, and make them responsible should they give advice manifestly improper. This does not diminish the responsibility of the President himself."[116] If, Iredell continued, the president had "a council by whose advice he was bound to act, his responsibility, in all such cases, must be destroyed. . . . It would be difficult often to know whether the President or counsellors were most to blame. A thousand plausible excuses might be made, which would escape detection." Under the Constitution, by contrast, "the President will personally have the credit of good, or the censure of bad measures; since, though he may ask advice, he is to use his own judgment in following or rejecting it."[117]

The debates surrounding executive councils at the ratification debates afforded another opportunity for defenders of the Constitution to outline the link between a unitary executive and the necessary degree of administrative responsibility. The idea of an executive council was so persistent that its ultimate rejection must be seen as significant, and the reasons for its rejection be understood as central to the administrative structure that the Framers were establishing.

Administration and Republican Government

One of the central questions during the ratification debates was whether the Constitution satisfied republican principles. Though these debates centered on the makeup of the legislative branch, particularly the term lengths, term limits, and number of representatives in that branch, in the course of defending the republican nature of the Constitution the Federalists were compelled to outline the basic principles of republican government. These principles bear significantly on significant questions of administrative structure.

Madison argued that the Constitution indeed creates a republican form of government. But before determining whether the Constitution creates a republican form of government, Madison first had to define the fundamental characteristics of republican government, a task that is more difficult than first appears. According to Madison, "Were an answer to this question to be sought, not by recurring to principles, but in the application of the term by political writers, to the constitutions of different states, no satisfactory one would ever be found."[118] The various definitions offered throughout history vary too greatly to offer much guidance. Thus, Madison was compelled to offer his own definition. He had already begun this task months earlier in his famous *Federalist 10*, in which he called "A Republic . . . a Government in which the scheme of representation takes place." But this provisional definition required defining the nature of representation, although even in *Federalist 10* Madison was clear that representation meant "the delegation of the Government . . . to a small number of citizens *elected by the rest*."[119] (One essay earlier, Hamilton identified "the representation of the people in the legislature by deputies of their own election" as one of the great modern improvements in political science).[120] The principle of election was central to Madison's understanding of republicanism even before he sought to define it in *Federalist 39*. As he would restate several weeks after writing *Federalist 39*, "The *elective* mode of obtaining rulers is the characteristic policy of republican government."[121] The notion of "virtual" representation offered by the British to the colonists was rejected by Madison as irreconcilable with republicanism.

Of course, the Founders did not create a Constitution where all of the representatives are elected directly by the people. If the principle of republican government is a scheme of representation where the powers of government are delegated to officials elected by the people, does this mean that the Senate, president, and federal courts are not republican institutions? Madison addressed this issue in his rather convoluted definition of republicanism in *Federalist 39*. There, he wrote:

We may define a republic to be, or at least may bestow that name on, a government which derives all its powers directly or indirectly from the great body of the people; and is administered by persons holding their offices during pleasure, for a limited period, or during good behavior. It is *essential* to such a government that it be derived from the great body of the society, not from an inconsiderable proportion, or a favored class of it. . . . It is *sufficient* for such a government that the persons administering it be appointed, either directly or indirectly, by the people; and that they hold their appointments [during pleasure, for a limited period, or during good behavior].[122]

A government must incorporate several elements to satisfy Madison's definition of republicanism: its powers must be "derive[d] directly or indirectly from the great body of the people," its officials must be "appointed, either directly or indirectly, by the people," the great body of the society (rather than a narrow class) must be eligible to serve in it, and those in office must be removable either by a superior authority, the end of their term, or impeachment due to bad behavior. What one first notices is the great latitude this three-part definition gives to the conception of republican government. If republicanism merely requires "that the persons administering [the government] be appointed, either directly or indirectly, by the people,"[123] then all of the national institutions are consonant with republican principles. The House "is elected immediately by the great body of the people." The president "is indirectly derived from the choice of the people." "Even the judges," Madison explains, are "the choice, though a remote choice, of the people themselves."[124] Some electoral connection, therefore, is a central component of Madison's notion of republicanism. Moreover, there is a clear distinction, repeated throughout *Federalist 39*, between "immediate" election and "indirect" choice of the people. But both methods are compatible with his standard of republicanism. This explains why the Convention was so deeply attached to the nondelegation principle. For a government to be republican, the legislators had to be those who were deputized by the people to represent them in the legislature. If the legislature were to transfer its powers to another department, it would no longer be satisfying the principle of representation and would be undermining republicanism.

In comparing Madison's definition of republicanism to contemporary administrative power, two questions emerge. The first question is what kind of connection must be present between citizens and officials in order to legitimize the exercise of coercive power. Madison's admission that officials in a republican form of government may be appointed "either directly or indirectly" might be interpreted to permit policymaking by officials who are only indirectly chosen by the people such as administrators are today. Second, since Madison's definition of representation demands that officials resist popular opinion if necessary, administrators who are far removed from practical politics might be seen as a reflection, rather than a contradiction, of Madison's understanding of republicanism. These two questions, raised recently by scholars, merit further attention.

The first question asserts that Madison's conception of republicanism can accommodate policymaking by unelected officials. After all, if republicanism merely requires *some* connection, however indirect or remote, between the people and federal officeholders, federal administrators today would satisfy the requirements of republican government. The manner of their selection, it may be urged, is no more remote than that of a U.S. senator (prior to the 17th Amendment) or a federal judge. The filling of an office by a civil service examination certainly does not provide an "immediate" connection, but it might be said to be an "indirect" appointment by the people. And presidential appointments (or appointments by heads of departments) are certainly "indirectly" based on popular elections.

In response to this argument, we must note that one of the critical elements of Madison's conception of republicanism is its practical ability to control the exercise of government power. Madison argued that representation must be structured in a way that controls and guides the use of delegated power in the interest of the people. This aspect of Madison's definition of republicanism *precludes* lawmaking by unelected—or even indirectly elected—officials.[125]

As just noted, Madison's definition of republicanism in *Federalist 39* repeatedly draws a distinction between direct (sometimes referred to as "immediate") and indirect elections. This is a phrase that both Madison and Hamilton used carefully and systematically throughout *The Federalist*. For instance, Hamilton in *Federalist 84* proclaims that the U.S. Constitution is "professedly founded upon the power of the people, and executed by their *immediate representatives and servants.*"[126] Hamilton made the same argument almost verbatim more than sixty essays earlier: "The fabric of American Empire ought to rest on the solid basis of THE CONSENT OF THE PEOPLE. The streams of national power ought to flow *immediately* from that pure original fountain of all legitimate authority."[127] While the choice of whether to follow the immediate influence of the people belongs to the representative, the relationship between the government and the people must be immediate.

Combining these statements with the principles of republican government set forth by Madison in *Federalist 39*, we may conclude that officials may be *appointed* either directly or indirectly by the people, but this does not mean that the connection between the people and their representatives can be anything less than "immediate." The manner in which officials are *chosen* is understood differently than the relationship between officials and the people once those officials are in office. For the theory of representation to be effectual in practice the connection between the people and their representatives must always be immediate, in the basic sense that the public, the sovereign authority, must be able to remove delinquent public officials from office. This means that the principle of election is a necessary condition for the preservation of representative government. Election can be applied indirectly, meaning that an elected official could fill another office through appointment; this would still satisfy the republican principle. What is impermissible, however, is to fill offices without the direct or indirect appointment of the people, such as by lottery or heredity. The manner of choosing an official can be indirect or remote but still representative. The crucial cord that cannot be severed is the principle of election.

This interpretation of Madison's definition of republicanism is at odds with John Rohr's *To Run a Constitution*, a book that attempts to reconcile the modern administrative state with the Constitution. One of Rohr's central claims is that the Founders' theory of representation is unconcerned with the relationship between the people and their representatives. In his view, the existence of elections does not make an office republican in character. Because the office of representative is derived from the Constitution, he explains, and not from the method of appointment, the officers of government "are all *equally* the object of a constitutional choice." Even though "they are most emphatically unequal in the scope and nature of their constitutional duties[,] . . . [t]heir offices . . . *ultimately* depend upon the same authoritative source."[128]

In this view, none of the branches of government has a special relationship or connection to the people. All of the branches of government have an equal connection to the people, namely, the constitutional connection. According to Rohr, this entails "the *irrelevance of election* to ground a superior claim to speak for the people."[129] The implications are clear. If government personnel are representatives of the people regardless of whether they are elected by the people, appointed by an elected official, or selected based on a civil service examination, then the electoral connection is not fundamental to republicanism. As Rohr concludes: "The fact that some offices are filled by election and others by appointment *says nothing about the connection between the people and the occupant of a particular office.*"[130]

This argument is at odds with Madison's understanding of the relationship between the people and officeholders. For Madison the manner in which the office is filled is critical to understanding the connection between the people and the occupant of the office. In *Federalist 52*, for instance, Madison stated clearly and emphatically: "As it is essential to liberty that the government in general, should have a common interest with the people; so it is particularly essential that the branch of it under consideration, should have an immediate dependence on, & an intimate sympathy with the people. Frequent elections are *unquestionably the only policy* by which this dependence and sympathy can be effectually secured."[131] In *Federalist 52*, the "branch . . . under consideration" is the Congress, and Madison used the phrase "immediate dependence" to describe the relationship that must exist between it and the people. The "only policy" that will "effectually" secure both dependence and sympathy between the legislature and the people is the institution of frequent elections, Madison asserted. This is why Madison concluded five essays later that "[The] aim of every political Constitution is or ought to be first to obtain for rulers, men who possess most wisdom to discern, and most virtue to pursue the common good of the society; and in the next place, to take the most effectual precautions for keeping them virtuous, whilst they continue to hold their public trust. The elective mode of obtaining rulers is the characteristic policy of republican government."[132] With regard to the legislative branch especially, Madison maintained that there must be an immediate dependence of the government on the people, through frequent elections. Hardly considering it irrelevant to the relationship between the government and the people, Madison staked the very existence of republicanism on the electoral connection between lawmakers and citizens.

In this view, representation must preserve the immediate connection between the people and their representatives in the legislature, thereby ensuring that the interest of representatives coincides with their duty to serve the people.[133] It demands that the representatives of the people are so situated that their interest will lie in discerning and pursuing the best interests of the people. The most obvious way to situate the representatives of the people to secure this end is to render their reelection contingent upon winning the favor of the people. Ensuring that the power of government is in the hands of the people's representatives ensures the security of the people because they are able to exercise control over their representatives. They are able to exercise control over their representatives because they are in charge of perpetuating their representatives' tenure in office. This explains why the Framers refused to grant legitimacy to the idea that the elected representatives in the legislature could delegate the lawmaking power to indirectly chosen officers in the executive branch.

In summary, the Federalists argued that representation was fundamental to republicanism. In their view political officials must be incentivized to exercise their powers in a manner conducive to the public good. Representation secures this practical end by making the representative's interest—reelection—one and the same with the representative's duty, namely, pursuing the public good.

In order to achieve this practical end, an immediate connection between the people and their representatives is required. Publius uses various phrases: "due dependence," "a proper responsibility," and "dependence on the suffrages of the people for his continuance in office," to express the necessity of an immediate connection through the principle of elections. All power must be derived from the people, who must have an immediate connection to their rulers. In some cases, indirect elections—appointment by an elected official, or by an official whose appointment can ultimately be traced to some immediate election—is legitimate. However, with regard to the making of binding laws, immediate election is the only method that promotes a common interest and sympathy between rulers and the people.

The second question asserts not that election is irrelevant to legitimizing administrative power but that it is actually detrimental to good policymaking, and that Madison would draw the same conclusion. This argument fixes on the nature of representation as articulated by Madison and Hamilton in *The Federalist*. According to this argument, Madison and Hamilton emphasized the need for representatives to resist popular opinion in certain situations, for the good of the country, and federal administrators have the same ability, thus vindicating some of the original purposes of representation.[134] This argument suggests that administrative policymaking is actually more consistent with the idea of republican government than any other potential alternative.

Thus in this view the modern administrative state "is entirely consistent with [the Founders'] concept of democratic theory."[135] Its central proposition is that "The Founders sought to create a system in which government could produce decisions that were imperfectly responsive to majority opinion by design."[136] The Senate, in particular, suggests that the Framers intended to design a system where policy would be made by elites insulated from the people. The implicit premise is that the "countermajoritarian" aspect of the administrative state is not distinguishable in principle from the original "countermajoritarian" yet popular institutions of the Founders' original design.

This argument is the inverse of Rohr's. Whereas Rohr claims that one is a "representative" of the people regardless of how one is elected, and therefore the electoral connection to the people is *irrelevant*, this argument claims that the connection of a representative to the people is *the same as* that of a bureaucrat to the people. In this view it is just as democratic to be governed by unelected bureaucrats as it is to be governed by senators who are elected in such a way that they can resist the immediate impulse of public opinion. Even if the Senate was designed to be removed from immediate public opinion through

its term lengths and mode of election, however, this would not vindicate policymaking by unelected administrators, for the simple reason that the Senate
is not authorized to make law without the concurrence of other institutions.

A closer examination of the way in which representation refines public
opinion suggests that there are critical differences between the way representation filters public opinion and the way in which the administrative process
does this. In *Federalist 63*, Madison defends the ability of the Senate to check
and resist public opinion in a famous passage:

> As the cool and deliberate sense of the community ought in all governments,
> and actually will in all free governments prevail over the views of its rulers; so
> there are particular moments in public affairs, when the people stimulated by
> some irregular passion, or some illicit advantage, or misled by the artful misrep-
> resentations of interested men, may call for measures which they themselves will
> afterwards be most ready to lament and condemn. In these critical moments,
> how salutary will be the interference of some temperate and respectable body of
> citizens, in order to check the misguided career, and to suspend the blow medi-
> ated by the people against themselves, until reason, justice, and truth, can regain
> their authority over the public mind?[137]

This passage reveals important differences between the Senate's insulation
from public will and that of modern administrators. First, it is critical to note
how the Senate is designed to correct the errors of the public in these "critical
moments." The purpose of the Senate is not to *thwart* the will of the public, but to *enlighten* it. Madison maintains that "in all free governments" the
"cool and deliberate sense of the community" will "prevail over the views of
its rulers."[138] The purpose of the Senate is simply to provide the cooling effect
necessary to allow reason to regain its control over the public mind, not to
operate independently of the people. The connection between the Senate and
the people is not severed in this process.

Second, Madison's explanation of the means by which the Senate accom-
plishes this cooling effect illustrates another difference between the Senate
and an independent bureaucracy. Superficial analysis of this passage leads one
to the conclusion that the Senate cools the public will simply by resisting
it. On the contrary, Madison says that the Senate must be a "temperate and
respectable body of citizens" in order to check the public passions. But the
Senate can only be respectable because of its connection to the people. As
Madison remarks elsewhere, representatives will "have been distinguished by

the preference of their fellow citizens." Therefore, "we are to presume, that in general, they will be somewhat distinguished also, by those qualities which entitle them to it."[139] Representatives may need to resist public opinion, but in Madison's view they can only do so if they are connected to the people through election.

Therefore, the purpose of the Senate is not simply to ignore the public will when it is in error; Madison maintains consistently that the public will is to prevail in republican governments. The purpose of the Senate is to enlighten or cool the public will so that it can rule according to reason rather than passion. In order for a governmental institution to do this, it has to be "respectable." As Madison remarks elsewhere, a "numerous legislature" is "best adapted to deliberation and wisdom, and best calculated to conciliate the confidence of the people and to secure their privileges and interests."[140] The legislature in general, and the Senate in particular, will be respectable and possess "the confidence of the people" by virtue of their connection to the people. The Senate fulfills this requirement in a way that an administrator cannot, because of the core differences in the design of the two institutions.

A second aspect of the Senate that allowed it to resist public opinion, at the time of the Founding, was the method of electing Senators. Under the original Constitution senators were to be elected indirectly by the state legislatures. This would seem to suggest that senators and bureaucrats are both equally legitimate lawmakers from a constitutional perspective. After all, if a legislative body can be severed from direct connection to the people, why is it illegitimate for administrative agencies, with a similarly indirect connection to the people, to make law?

Madison would have rejected this claim for several reasons, some of which have already been indicated. First, many administrative officers are not even indirectly selected by the people. They are chosen impersonally by a civil service examination. Second, as earlier mentioned, Madison explicitly granted that frequent elections for legislators are critical to ensuring that the government have a common interest and immediate sympathy with the people. Most decisively, however, is the fact that Senators alone do not make policy. Bureaucrats do. Senators are *part* of the policymaking process, but it is impossible for senators to make policy on their own according to the Constitution. The only way for senators to take part in a policymaking process is in concert with other, directly elected officials. Because of bicameralism and the requirement to present legislation to the president for signing, no indirectly elected member of the U.S. government may make law without the concurrence of a directly elected official.

This point was decisive at the Constitutional Convention. In one of Madison's famous speeches at the convention, on 31 May, he remarked that he "considered the popular election of one branch of the National Legislature as *essential* to every plan of free Government."[141] Free republican government, Madison argued, requires popular election of at least part of the legislative branch. Madison admitted that he "was an advocate for the policy of refining the popular appointments by successive filtrations." Yet he also remarked that he "thought it might be pushed too far," and "the people would be lost sight of altogether; and the necessary sympathy between them and their rulers and officers, too little felt." "[T]he great fabric to be raised would be more stable and durable," he continued, "if it should rest on the solid foundation of the people themselves."[142] Madison argued at the Convention that the legislative branch of government must be *at least in part* popularly elected.[143] A law-making process that takes place entirely in a body that is unelected would be inconsistent with republican principles. Given the fact that the Founders viewed it as "essential" that the legislative branch rest on the firm foundation of the people, we must conclude that there is a decisive difference between a legislative process that involves the Senate *and* the House of Representatives, involving at least one house that is popularly elected, and a process that takes place *entirely* within the confines of an unelected administrative agency.

Madison, admittedly, advocated that the immediate representatives of the people *not* follow the public will when the public is misled about its true interest. Therefore he defended certain institutional mechanisms that will allow for the representatives of the people to resist the public will when necessary. However, while Madison recommended that the representatives use their own, often superior judgment regarding whether to *follow* the will of the people, he did not recommend eliminating the immediate *connection* between the people and their representatives.

Administration and Unity in the Executive

Because of the centrality of representation by elected officials to the Framers' understanding of republicanism, they sought to extend popular control over administration to the greatest extent possible, consistent with the need for efficiency and energy in administration. Hamilton's analysis of administration and executive power in *The Federalist* is the classic illustration of the Constitution's use of a unitary executive to ensure both energy and accountability in the administration of the laws.

In *Federalist 37* Madison outlined the many challenges facing the Constitutional Convention, and one of the most daunting was the difficulty "in

combining the requisite stability and energy in Government, with the inviola-
ble attention due to liberty, and to the Republican form."[144] The Constitution
had to produce a republican government dedicated to liberty, but also a government that promoted stability and energy. Some of these objectives were in
tension, particularly the need for energy and the requirements of republicanism. Securing an energetic government required the institution of a powerful
executive, a notion that seemed to many at the Convention to be incompatible
with republicanism.

The tension between energy in the executive and republicanism was raised
again by Hamilton in *Federalist 70*. Hamilton opened his discussion of energy
in the executive by acknowledging the tension between these two principles.
"There is an idea, which is not without its advocates," he admitted, "that a
vigorous Executive is inconsistent with the genius of republican government."
However, he continued, those who favor republican government "must at least
hope that the supposition is destitute of foundation; since they can never admit its truth, without at the same time admitting the condemnation of their
own principles."[145] Strikingly, Hamilton argued that if there *were* a tension
between vigorous execution of the law and republican government, this would
require the Framers to abandon republicanism, not a strong executive.

Therefore, in Hamilton's view, the real question was not *whether* to have a
vigorous executive, but *how* to achieve this goal in the right way. "Taking it
for granted . . . that all men of sense will agree in the necessity of an energetic
executive," he wrote, "it will only remain to inquire . . . how far" energy can
"be combined with those other ingredients which constitute safety in the republican sense."[146] The solution to this problem, Hamilton maintained, was to
establish a unitary executive that would guarantee both energy in the administration of the laws and safety to the people.

Energy would obviously be promoted by a unitary executive, since "Decision, activity, secrecy, and dispatch will generally characterize the proceedings
of one man in a much more eminent degree than the proceedings of any greater number."[147] But how would unity in the executive promote safety? Granting
too much power to a single person seemed to them the very opposite of safety. Hamilton's response to this question rested on the two "circumstances" or
ingredients he identified that "constitute safety in the republican sense." The
first of these ingredients is "a due dependence on the people," the second, "a
due responsibility."[148] In a republican government, every official, including the
executive, must be responsible to, and dependent upon, the people. Unity in
the executive would promote both dependence and responsibility by enabling

greater public oversight and control over administration. When a good or bad policy can be clearly traced to a single official, and that official is dependent upon the people through election, these checks ensure that greater power can be entrusted to that official. As Hamilton explained, "one of the weightiest objections to a plurality in the executive . . . is that it tends to conceal faults, and destroy responsibility."[149] This is because "the plurality of the executive tends to deprive the people of the two greatest securities they can have for the faithful exercise of any delegated power; first, the restraints of public opinion, which lose their efficacy" because "of the division of the censure attendant upon bad measures among a number" and because "of the uncertainty on whom it ought to fall; and, second, the opportunity of discovering with facility and clearness the misconduct of the persons they trust."[150] In other words, plurality in the executive undermines both dependence and responsibility. It undermines dependence by hindering the ability of the people to remove officials for bad decisions. They are unable to discover "with facility and clearness the misconduct" to be punished. It undermines responsibility by allowing officials to elude accountability and misdirect public anger at other officials who can plausibly be blamed. This pretext for eluding accountability does not exist when one person alone has the final decision-making authority.

Having drawn the connection between unity in the executive and safety through dependence and accountability, Hamilton proceeded to discuss how unity in the executive might be undermined. This could happen "either by vesting the power in two or more magistrates of equal dignity and authority; or by vesting it ostensibly in one man, subject in whole or in part to the controul and co-operation of others, in the capacity of counsellors to him."[151] There are, in other words, two methods for undermining unity in the executive. The first is obvious and straightforward: vest power in "two or more magistrates of equal dignity and authority." Proposals for multi-member executives like those that existed under the early years of the Articles of Confederation undermined unity in the straightforward sense. But there is a second, subtler method for undermining unity: vest power "ostensibly in one man," but make that person's decision "subject in whole or in part to the control and co-operation of others." Proposals that would divide executive power between the president and other actors in the government would accomplish the same effect. In appointments, the requirement of cooperation from the Senate undermines accountability. Attempts to vest administrative power in the hands of officials who exercise independent authority that the president cannot control also undermines the safety that unity in the executive provides.

Hamilton's solution was to "politicize" administration by ensuring a clear line of accountability from administrative officers to an elected official under the control of the people. It is only through the restraints of public opinion, Hamilton suggested, that administration could be made safe in the republican sense. As he explained elsewhere in *The Federalist*: "The natural cure for an ill administration, in a popular or representative government, is a change of men."[152] This is accomplished not through insulating the administration from public opinion and the control of elected representatives, but the opposite: political control must be extended over the administration to ensure that administrative power is exercised safely. The people must be able to hold an elected official—the president—accountable for the goodness or badness of the national administration.

Administration and the Separation of Powers

In addition to the debate over the extent to which the Constitution satisfied the requirements of republicanism, the ratification debates also occasioned a debate on the nature of separation of powers. This debate also bears extensively on the question of how administrative power is to be situated in the constitutional system. As a preliminary matter it is important to note that the discussion on the separation of powers centered on both the theory of separation of powers as well as the practical implementation of that theory in the Constitution. There are, of course, many ways in which the separation of powers can be implemented in practice, and the Constitution did not reflect the only permissible method. Moreover, because the Constitution was given the sanction of the people at the end of the ratification process, it mandates the division of powers set forth in the document, without regard to whether it conforms to the pure theory of the separation of powers.

The separation of the legislative, executive, and judicial powers and offices of government into distinct departments was a political maxim as sacred as republican self-government. As Madison wrote in *Federalist 47*: "The accumulation of all powers legislative, executive, and judiciary in the same hands, whether of one, a few or many, and whether hereditary, self appointed, or elective, may justly be pronounced the very definition of tyranny."[153] But the principle of separation of powers is not self-executing, as the Revolutionary War era taught Madison and the other Framers. In 1787 there was no clear and established blueprint for how the powers were to be separated in the first place. Madison noted that a simple declaration against combining powers will not ensure the separation of powers in practice.[154] What is needed is an institutional arrangement that will make the principle effective in practice. Madison dedicated several essays in *The Federalist* to explaining the intricate arrangements needed to protect the separation of powers.

While the Constitution's opponents submitted that it violated "the political maxim, that the legislative, executive and judiciary departments ought to be separate and distinct,"[155] Madison attempted to show that some blending of powers is necessary to preserve the separation in practice. Prudence, he argued, dictates that "deviations . . . from the principle must be admitted" for the sake of securing the principle.[156] Deviating from the strict principle is acceptable but only for the sake of adhering to the principle in practice more effectively. All deviations from a strict separation of powers arrangement must be justified as helping to maintain the separation in practice. Deviations that reinforce the separation of powers cannot therefore be invoked as justification for deviations that undermine the separation of powers.

After reviewing and rejecting other proposals for maintaining the separation in practice, Madison explained in *Federalist 51* that the only way to maintain the separation of powers is to ensure that each branch has "a will of its own." This is accomplished by "giving to those who administer each department, the necessary constitutional means, and personal motives, to resist encroachments of the others."[157] Thus in Madison's argument the separation of powers cannot be accomplished unless both means and motives are present. As George Carey has written, "we cannot view the constitutional provisions apart from the 'personal motives' to which Publius refers because the latter supply the force that will render constitutional provisions effective."[158]

Madison presented an intricate design to ensure the existence of both constitutional means and personal motives. He argued that the "remedy" for legislative usurpation of power "is to divide the legislature into different branches; and to render them by different modes of election, and different principles of action, as little connected with each other" as possible.[159] The constitutional means specifically aim at dividing the legislative branch to prevent that branch from encroaching on the others. Furthermore, "[a]s the weight of the legislative authority requires that it should be thus divided, the weakness of the executive branch may require, on the other hand, that it should be fortified."[160] The veto power granted to the president was intended to empower the president to resist the potential encroachments of the legislature, which was already to be divided and constituted in such a way to prevent it from being unified itself. In short, the constitutional means supporting the separation of powers are designed not only to foster legislative-executive conflict, but even to foster intra-legislative conflict, in order that the separation of powers be maintained in practice. An integral part of the Founders' separation of powers, in short, is the separation or *division* of legislative power itself. The Constitution's separation of powers ensures that no single institutional actor can make law by itself.

Recent defenders of the modern administrative state have picked up on the Anti-Federalists' claim that the Constitution blended powers. They use this claim to argue that the Constitution's blending of powers justifies the combination of powers in the hands of modern agencies. John Rohr, for instance, has argued that the Constitution supports a combination of functions because it creates "the Senate as a body that exercises powers that are (1) legislative . . . (2) executive (when it 'advises and consents' . . .); and (3) judicial (when it sits as a court to try impeachments)." He concludes that these facts provide "*textual* evidence that the Framers were quite willing to place all three powers of government in one institution when circumstances so required."[161] If the Senate can exercise all three powers of government, why not let the Environmental Protection Agency do so as well?

In addition, Rohr argues that in *The Federalist* Madison "subscribes to a remarkably relaxed view of the separation of powers,"[162] finding the principle to be violated only "where the *whole* power of one department is exercised by the same hands which possess the *whole* power of another department."[163] The administrative state does not violate the separation of powers because "[t]his has never happened with an administrative agency. The powers of administrative agencies, unlike those of Congress, the president, and the courts, are always 'partial,' never '*whole*.' They are partial because they are exercised over a narrowly defined scope of governmental activity."[164] After all, modern agencies do not have comprehensive legislative powers but only have the power to make, execute, and adjudicate in limited policy areas such as broadcasting, workplace safety, environmental protection, and so forth.

Even at first glance, however, there are important differences between the combination of functions in the Senate and the combination of functions in administrative agencies. One important difference is that the combination of functions in the Senate is mandated by the text of the *Constitution*, which in Rohr's words is symbolic of "a solemn and authoritative act" of the people, as opposed to an act passed by the people "when they are under the influence of a momentary inclination."[165] A *statute* that combines legislative, executive, and judicial functions is characteristic of the latter as opposed to the former. In other words, a specifically constitutionally mandated combination of powers cannot be used to justify a combination of powers not specifically mandated by the Constitution. As mentioned earlier, even if there is blending of powers in the Constitution, that cannot be said to justify additional extra-constitutional blending of powers, for the simple reason that the Constitution mandated the former but not the latter.

A second and more important difference is that the combination of functions in the Senate is *for the sake of preserving* the separation of powers in practice. For the Founders, the combination of functions is not a deviation from the principle of separation of powers but, rather, the only way that the principle can be secured. In other words, the only justification for combining—or in Madison's words, "blending"—the powers of government in a department is for the sake of separating them in practice.

Third, Madison explains that both constitutional means and personal motives must be present to ensure the separation of powers is maintained in practice. An administrative agency constituted for a single, common objective would not have the motives to resist itself internally in the way that separation of powers requires. The different departments or functions within agencies develop the same interest, namely, the achievement of the objective set forth in the organic statute. In short, the motives necessary to ensure that each department has its own will are not secured by the administrative state.

To equate the combination of powers in the Senate to the combination of powers in a modern agency misunderstands the separation of powers in a fourth way, namely, a failure to consider the *causes* that make the separation of powers necessary in the first place. This cause is the inherent tendency of human beings to be biased in cases where their interest is personally involved. Montesquieu justified the separation of powers on the basis of human nature: the difficulty remedied by the separation of powers is the dangerous possibility that "the same monarch or senate that makes tyrannical laws will execute them tyrannically."[166] Madison himself points to *"The reasons on which Montesquieu grounds his maxim"* as "a further demonstration of his meaning."[167] He quotes two separate passages from Montesquieu, both of which point to the same cause for the necessity of the maxim, namely, the impulse in human beings to tyrannical behavior when acting as legislator, executioner, and judge in the same case.[168]

If the powers of government are separated, a defense against this problem is provided, for the self-interested official will be checked by members of the other departments who do not have the same interest in writing, applying, and judging a biased law in a biased manner. Viewed in light of the reasons upon which the separation of powers is grounded, it is clear that the combination of functions in an agency does not guard against the problem that necessitates the separation of powers in the first place. Even if an agency possesses all the power of legislating, executing, and judging the law "over a narrowly defined scope of government activity," such as securities fraud, there is no defense against the problem that the separation of powers seeks to remedy. The agency could write a law injurious to the rights of a particular industry, or a particular corporation. It could then enforce its law on a specific party and judge the party to be guilty of that law. There would be no check at any point in this process, for the same agency is at work throughout. Put differently, contrary to Rohr, the Environmental Protection Agency *does* have the "whole power" of legislating, as far as the need for separation of powers is concerned. This is because it can use that exclusive and complete power to make, execute, and adjudicate law on particular parties.

A Constitutional Administration

If one simply reads the text of the Constitution and calls it a day, it is easy to conclude that the Constitution offers little guidance on questions of administrative power and structure. To understand the relationship between the Constitution and administration requires an understanding of the historical context that led to the Constitutional Convention and careful analysis of the constitutional principles that were advanced during the Convention and in the ratification debates. The history and arguments provide sufficient context to deduce several important principles that bear directly on administrative law.

The first of these principles is based on the definition of republicanism— that all powers are derived directly or indirectly from the great body of the people, and that all political officials are elected either directly or indirectly by the people. At several points in *The Federalist* Madison placed election of representatives as the critical criterion that defines a republican form of government. This principle requires that all officials, including administrators, derive their authority from election or appointment by someone who is ultimately traceable to an elected official. It undergirds the requirement that legislative power remain in the hands of directly elected officials, as well as the principle of unity in the executive. Furthermore, the principle of separation of powers— on which all parties agreed—prohibited the consolidation of powers for any other reason than the preserving of the separation of powers in practice. It also led to the internal division of legislative power—the requirement that no single institutional actor can enact binding legislation. Some of the objections to the idea of an executive council were clearly based on separation of powers grounds. These and other institutional principles emerged out of the healthy debate that transpired during and after the Constitutional Convention.

Of course, not everyone agreed with the Framers and the Federalists about the principles that should guide administrative structure. Many Anti-Federalists and members of the Convention wanted a council annexed to the president for the exercise of certain functions. Many of them fought (successfully) for indirect election of one house of the legislature. Some of them even advocated a plural executive. Unanimity on the constitutional principles undergirding administration was not achieved, but a broad consensus did eventually emerge. This consensus obviously did not answer every question that would ultimately be raised about how to establish administration within constitutional boundaries, but it established the framework within which later efforts would operate.

CHAPTER TWO

Well-Regulated and Free

Administration and Constitutionalism in the Early Republic[1]

THE TOWN WAS Pittsburgh, Pennsylvania, and the year was 1816.[1] A visitor to the town wrote that "Dark dense smoke was rising from many parts," which "rendered it singularly gloomy." A few decades later the local newspaper suggested that the "vapors of our own smoky city, prevented the inhabitants of Pittsburgh from getting a good view" of the aurora borealis.[2] While most residents of Pittsburgh misunderstood the health consequences of their smoky environment,[3] they were not unaware of the effects that a well-developed, highly-integrated economy could produce, and the need for a reasonable system of regulation to account for these effects.

Politicians and statesmen in America prior to the Civil War did not live in an era far removed from present circumstances and concerns. Nor did they establish a laissez-faire economic system. They were well acquainted with many of the problems that we seek to address today through regulation, and their own circumstances required that they think carefully about the problems of regulation, administration, and constitutional government in a practical manner. As their experience was not too far removed from our own, so scholars can benefit from a close inspection of the decisions they made in setting up regulatory programs and administrative systems.

This chapter examines state and local regulatory and administrative arrangements prior to the Civil War before moving to an examination of national administration from 1789 to 1828 (generally understood to be the beginning of the Jacksonian period in American history). It examines state and local arrangements first because that is where much of the practical decisions were made. Nevertheless, important constitutional principles for administrative power were forged in a series of very important decisions at the national level during the early republic as well.

Local and State Administration

State and local governments during the early republic exercised broad regulatory powers that spanned all areas of economic life, from common carriers to banks and labor. Seen as a whole, the activities of states and localities during the antebellum period demonstrate the Founding generation's commitment to regulation.

Some of the activities of state and local governments are best understood as service-oriented rather than regulatory. Instead of governing and controlling the otherwise private interactions and market transactions between individuals or corporations, these service activities used government to provide tangible benefits to a class of citizens or to the public at large. Provision for the poor, the building of roads and highways, promotion of education, and subsidizing of private enterprise could all be categorized as service activity. State and local governments were extensively involved in these areas. By the 1750s Massachusetts required a poorhouse to be located in every county.[4] New York's welfare law in 1788 required that "Every city and town shall support and maintain their own poor."[5] New York State also spent millions in aid of agriculture and manufacturing between 1785 and 1825.[6] Pennsylvania issued loans "to industrial entrepreneurs who could not raise sufficient capital."[7] Other states such as Missouri also granted special loans and subsidies to promote agriculture.[8] These activities—providing education and poor relief, subsidizing certain economic activities, building roads—required administration to be carried out efficiently.

In addition to service activities, which did not impose coercion to control behavior, state and local governments imposed regulations that did involve coercion. Many of these regulations restricted the use of property so that others were capable of enjoying their property without injury or interference. For example, in the half century after the Revolution "plaintiffs could recover damages for a nuisance" for a variety of injuries, from factories emitting foul smells to draining a pond that causes another's well to dry up.[9] Regulations were often codified rather than left to the common law. In the 1830s, the state of Michigan authorized local officials to assign specific places for the practicing of trades that were offensive to other citizens or dangerous to the public health.[10] Activities such as the burying of the dead and the storage of gunpowder were extensively regulated in such statutes.[11] Augusta, Georgia, granted a charter of incorporation by the state government to enact its own bylaws, established an ordinance around 1807 "To Regulate the internal police and economy of the City of Augusta." This ordinance regulated nuisances "such as slaughter pens and privies, as well as the hours of business in the city market."[12] At the same time Pittsburgh enacted an ordinance fining anyone "who shall cast or deposit any dead carcase, garbage, noxious liquor, or other offensive matter on any street, square, lane or alley, or on the beach of any of the rivers within the bounds of the Borough, or shall keep the same within any inclosure, to the annoyance of the neighbourhood."[13] The city also established an ordinance in 1816 fining anyone who allowed his horses, hogs, or other livestock to run wild in the city.[14]

These kinds of regulations were designed to prevent liberty and property from being used in a manner that would become injurious to others. Thus this category of regulation also included ordinances forbidding certain activities on the grounds that they would be injurious to public morals. The State of South Carolina outlawed "billiard tables and bawdy houses within five miles of Columbia" to prevent the corruption of students at South Carolina College.[15] These kinds of prohibitions of billiard halls, gaming, and other diversions were widespread during the antebellum period. In New York State puppet shows, rope or wire dancing, and "other idle shows" could not be performed for profit.[16]

Another area of state and local regulation involved inspections and licensing. States established these programs widely during the Founding period. In Massachusetts and Pennsylvania, for example, inspections were required for a variety of commodities before they could be sold, including lumber, beef, tobacco, butter, bar iron, and salt.[17] These inspection laws were implemented in states as diverse as Connecticut, New York, Georgia, and Michigan.[18] The inspections covered packing and dimensions of containers, markings and stampings, and of course the quality of goods. States and localities also used licensing to regulate entry into various occupations, including lawyers, doctors, innkeepers, tavern owners, and auctioneers.[19] The licensing of liquor merchants enabled temperance advocates to stamp out perceived moral illnesses in society. In many states licensing programs were used essentially to forbid liquor sales altogether.[20]

Finally, state and local regulation governed common carriers and charters of incorporation to economic entities. In early America states granted specific charters of incorporation to specific entities by special incorporation. Since the states crafted special incorporation laws to apply to specific entities, they could use the chartering process to impose regulatory duties. Banks were often partially owned by the states that incorporated them, and some states set the maximum interest rates that banks could charge for loans in their charters. Vermont, for instance, included in one bank's charter a maximum rate of 6 percent on loans it issued.[21] Transportation companies were also regulated through special incorporation. Illinois required every chartered ferry keeper receiving a charter to display the "rates of ferriage . . . by law allowed."[22] The doctrine of "duty to serve" was concomitant with a special charter of incorporation; the law assumed that if the government granted permission to set up and operate a common carrier, the owners could be required "to grant equality of access to members of the community seeking to use them" and to comply with regulatory requirements.[23]

This brief overview, while by no means exhaustive, illustrates the extent of regulation that the Founding generation accepted as legitimate. Hardly dedicated to the idea of laissez-faire, the Founding generation saw no philosophical objection to these kinds of regulations. Most (but not all) regulation and administration in antebellum America was situated at the state and local levels. This overview provokes the question: how did communities in antebellum America carry out these responsibilities? What kinds of administrative officials and arrangements did they use to implement these regulations?

At the state and local levels the principles of administration differed to an extent from those which emerged at the national level. Generally, administrative power was checked by popular accountability through elections and a wide scope of judicial oversight. At the same time, the principle of separation of powers was applied rather loosely, creating arrangements that would have provoked strong objections had they been applied to national administration. These developments largely followed what had transpired during the colonial era. After the American Revolution "there came some significant changes in American local institutions, but there was no radical revolution, and the main features of the old systems continued," according to one scholarly account.[24] While there was great variation in state and local practices in early America, several principles of administrative law can be deduced from the administrative arrangements at the state and local levels during this period.

Local Administration: Decentralization and Accountability
The selection of administrative officers at the local level became significantly more democratic in the 1780s and 1790s. One scholar summarizes, "there was a distinct tendency in most states towards decentralization or an increase of local influence in choosing county officials, but this was to be exercised mainly through the members of the legislature, and direct election of the old appointive officials was established in only a few cases."[25] Administrative officials at the county level were typically appointed by the state legislatures rather than the governors, while some local offices were directly elected. In New Jersey, South Carolina, and Georgia justices of the peace were chosen by the

legislature, while in Delaware and North Carolina they were appointed but on the recommendation of the legislature. In Pennsylvania (and in Georgia, within a few decades of the Revolution) justices of the peace, sheriffs, commissioners, and assessors were popularly elected. New Jersey mandated in its state constitution that town constables be elected at annual town meetings. New York established a council of appointment to select all county officers, while continuing direct popular election of supervisors in the towns. A few states such as Massachusetts and New Hampshire provided for appointment of justices of the peace by the governor and the council, retaining the colonial method. Selectmen continued to be annually elected. Virginia provided for the commissioning of county officers by the governor, though nomination was made by the county justices of the peace.

In short, county administrative officers were more likely to be directly elected or appointed by the legislature (rather than the executive) after the American Revolution, and direct election of town officers was retained. Administration became more democratic and election of administrative officers was more common. As new states joined the union the democratization of administration continued. Kentucky at first provided for election of sheriffs and constables, then moved to the Virginia model of gubernatorial appointment based on nomination by the county courts. In the Northwest Territory townships were created on a geographical basis. The constables and overseers of the poor in the townships were appointed by the county courts, which played a role similar to that of the court of general sessions in many colonies. By 1800 town meetings were empowered to elect trustees, constables, road supervisors, and overseers of the poor, providing for a highly democratic administrative system in the Territory. In the states that emerged out of the Northwest Territory, such as Ohio, Indiana, and Illinois, the powers of the sessions courts were transferred to boards of elected county commissioners, while sheriffs and justices of the peace were made directly elective—a different arrangement from that which prevailed in some of the older states. Indiana's first state constitution in 1816 mandated the election of sheriffs and justices of the peace. Some states in the South, such as Mississippi and Alabama, allowed for appointment of justices of the peace but retained direct elections for sheriffs.

From the variety of administrative arrangements that emerged in the early republic, we can discern some general tendencies with regard to the accountability of local administrators. Local elections, especially for sheriffs and (in some cases) justices of the peace, were much more prevalent than in the colonial period. In the South, justices of the peace continued to function as both judicial and administrative officers, a holdover of the colonial era. In the

Midwestern states such as Pennsylvania, Ohio, Indiana, and Illinois, elected county boards of commissioners exercised the administrative functions, leaving the justices of the peace to play only a judicial role.

There was, in summary, a significant shift to direct electoral accountability with regard to local administrative officers in the early republic. This shift eventually worked its way back to the original colonies. New York's 1821 constitution abolished the council of appointment and provided for election of sheriffs and justices of the peace. Massachusetts transferred administrative powers to directly elected county commissioners in the 1820s, removing administrative powers from the courts of sessions. Nearly every other state followed suit in the 1820s and 1830s.[26] Thus one can observe not only a tendency towards direct election of administrators in the early republic but also the beginnings of a separation of functions, where judicial powers and administrative powers were increasingly separated. The inexorable and widespread tendency was to democratize administration and separate administrative and judicial power.

These democratically elected administrators exercised significant powers either as county officers or as powers delegated to local communities by the state government. In most states in early America, the state governments transferred authority to local governments to deal with local issues. The theoretical foundations of this local power were not clearly defined or agreed upon by politicians in the early republic. Nevertheless, state legislatures granted them generously throughout the early republic. The duties, powers, and mode of selecting local officials was often indicated in the statutes that established a municipal corporation. The Georgia state legislature incorporated Savannah in 1787 and Sunbury in 1791.[27] The Sunbury charter authorized property owners in the town to elect five commissioners who could adopt bylaws that were "not repugnant to the laws and constitution of the State."[28] Property owners in Savannah were required to meet annually to elect wardens, who would then choose a president from among the wardens. These offices were renamed to aldermen and mayor in 1791.[29] The wardens were authorized to make bylaws "conductive to the good order and government" of Savannah.[30] Macon was governed by a board of five commissioners, elected to annual terms. These commissioners "passed city ordinances, imposed fines, and levied taxes." They also appointed officials such as surveyors and bridge keepers, and generally kept the peace.[31] Columbia, South Carolina was organized similarly, with six wardens and an intendant composing a town council with authority to enact ordinances, set fines and penalties, care for the poor, and appoint minor officials.[32] The state legislature often created bylaws that the local officials were charged with implementing. In New York State until 1838 the state legislature "consumed countless hours and days overseeing the day-to-day affairs of counties, cities, and towns," until it finally passed a set of laws delegating responsibility to the local governments. County boards of supervisors were given powers to erect courthouses and jails, construct highways, and regulate the killing of game and the destruction of wild animals.[33]

Like county-level justices of the peace, the local officials such as wardens and commissioners also had the power to enforce the penalties of the local bylaws they created, as long as the penalties were sufficiently minor. More substantial penalties or civil disputes, as in the county system, could only be tried by the county courts. Though the commissioners and wardens had these powers, "to what extent this authority was exercised is far from clear" as a matter of actual practice.[34] Typically criminal punishments in the towns were only handed out by the council composed of the wardens (or commissioners, or aldermen, as they were variously named) sitting together.[35]

The city council acted as a kind of local legislature, composed of the elected officers variously named wardens, commissioners, or aldermen. While they enacted their own ordinances imposing fines for nuisances, crimes against the peace of the community, and the like, from time to time these local legislatures created boards and committees to investigate and report on various problems that needed to be addressed. In 1811 the city council of Augusta, Georgia, established a Committee of Health to investigate health concerns in the city and report issues to the local marshal. The marshal was "required to notify the owner and oversee the correcting of any dangerous conditions."[36] Macon, Georgia, created a board of health in 1834 and tasked it with removing minor health hazards such as dead animals and garbage. Any larger concerns were brought to the board of aldermen. As a result, the board was confined to encouraging healthful practices such as putting lime in cellars and privies.[37] Columbia, South Carolina, also created a board of health charged with regulating sanitation problems. The board inspected yards and cellars throughout the summer to prevent threats to public health.[38] Pittsburgh established a Sanitary Board composed of ten members in 1832 in response to an outbreak of Asiatic cholera. The board was authorized "to adopt and direct all such measures as they think necessary for averting the introduction of the frightful epidemic disease," including the authority to clean up refuse and other threats to public health in the town and appoint inspectors of cellars, privies, and other nuisances.[39] Money was appropriated by the local government to the board for general sanitary purposes.

Pittsburgh's health and sanitary committee seems, like those in Georgia and South Carolina, to have largely been confined to removal of nuisances that threatened public health and inspection of likely sources of such nuisances. It is unclear whether these boards possessed any larger powers than these to plan and regulate broad aspects of community life. Furthermore, many of these boards were composed of the local legislators themselves: Pittsburgh's board contained the mayor and three aldermen, along with a few other local officials already in existence.[40]

Local regulation and administration was a relatively messy affair, but the broad contours of power are evident. State legislatures created and authorized county and town officials to make bylaws, and to enforce them, but the lawmaking powers were defined in law. State legislatures often prescribed the laws to be made, and the enforcement of these laws required the local officials to sit as a council. Still, powers were extensively blended at the local level, and it was difficult to discern where lawmaking, enforcement, and judicial powers began and ended. Philip Hamburger suggests that "To the extent local determinations crossed into legislation, they are historical anomalies—inherited local exceptions from American constitutional principles rather than evidence of such principles. And because they occurred at the local level, they never posed the threat of centralized extralegal power that has come with [modern] federal administrative law."[41]

Rather than inherited local exceptions from American constitutional principles, I would suggest that these examples are so prevalent that they must be understood in light of American constitutional principles. First, because local officers such as justices of the peace, selectmen, commissioners, overseers, aldermen, and the like were highly accountable to the people through elections, these deviations from the principles of separation of powers were accepted. Second, as these local communities grew and their government structures became more sophisticated, they began to separate the powers of making bylaws, enforcing them, and judging them. Finally, while the creation of boards of health and sanitation and similar entities might appear to serve as a precedent for establishing an independent administrative body with lawmaking power, when one closely examines the activities of these boards in cities such as Columbia and Pittsburgh, it becomes clear that they carried out less significant powers.

Local administrative power, at times, sacrificed a strict version of the separation of powers for a strict version of electoral accountability. The people regulated their own affairs in these communities and the administrative officers served as instruments of the sense of the community. This approach to regulation and administration differed significantly from that which predominated at the state and national levels. There, questions of an independent executive, control over subordinate administrative officers, and the relationship between legislative and administrative power were debated more systematically.

State Legislatures Reluctant to Delegate

While power was blended and placed in the hands of locally elected officials who made bylaws and were involved in their enforcement at the local level, at the state level a different kind of administrative structure was prevalent. State administrative powers were controlled extensively by courts and by legislatures. As Tocqueville observed in *Democracy in America*, "In the New England states, the legislative power extends to more objects, than among us [in France]. The legislator penetrates in a way into the very heart of administration; the law descends into minute details . . . it thus encloses secondary bodies and their administrators in a multitude of strict and rigorously defined obligations."[42] This fear of entrusting too much power to administrative officials was a product of suspicion of government power. As Leonard White noted in his famous study of administration at the national level during the Federalist period, "Among a people as devoted to liberty as were eighteenth-century Americans, we would expect official discretion to be looked upon with concern and to be strictly limited."[43] White's assessment was true not only of national administration; it was an even truer expression when applied to state and local regulation. State legislatures were extremely reluctant to delegate responsibility over to administrative officials, even arguably encroaching on the legitimate and necessary responsibilities to be entrusted to administrative actors.

Numerous examples illustrate Tocqueville and White's description of early American administration. Pennsylvania's most prominent administrative agency, the state Canal Board, was weakened by the state legislature's unwillingness to delegate power to it. The Board was established in 1824 and its members selected by the Governor, but in 1829 the legislature changed the law to appoint members itself. Eventually the state substituted direct popular election of the Board members for both options.[44] It was authorized to set tolls and appoint collectors and lockkeepers but lost the power to set toll rates "by a statute binding the commissioners to a fixed scale of tolls throughout each year."[45] Long before the ratemaking power of the Interstate Commerce Commission would become a contentious political issue, the Pennsylvania legislature was stripping its Canal Board of the same power applied to waterways. Other regulations regarding how canals were to be built and repaired were enacted not by the Board itself but by the legislature. Even the Board's secretary argued that regulations regarding the public works "ought to be passed upon directly by the immediate representatives of the people," echoing

James Madison's use of the terms "direct" and "immediate" in the context of representation in *Federalist 39*.[46]

The legislature interfered not only with the Canal Board's power to enact regulations but also with its power to adjudicate claims of property owners injured by the construction of public works. A Board of Appraisers was established to settle these claims, with original jurisdiction over construction damages and appellate jurisdiction (from the decisions of the canal commissioners) over fire damages caused by railroad locomotives.[47] Yet the state legislature refused to grant judicial authority—such as the power to compel witnesses or to subvert trial by jury in damages cases—to the Board, and its individual determinations were often reversed by the state legislature, which would often grant larger damage awards than the Board.[48]

The developments in New York State were similar. Most of the legislature's activity in the first several decades of the nineteenth century "were judicial or administrative in character."[49] It entered into the details of administration incessantly, specifying the construction of jails and poorhouses, granting incorporation charters, and deciding specific relief cases and claims against the state. The state legislature retained authority over the appointment of most administrative officers, preventing the development of a unitary executive responsible for coordinating all of the decisions of the various agencies.[50] This practice continued until the 1840s when, as indicated earlier, the legislature delegated many of these responsibilities to the county supervisors and local authorities.[51]

In practice, therefore, prior to 1840 the New York state legislature was "the principal regulatory agency in state government. . . . Even when making policy of a general nature, such as establishing a prison or constructing a canal, the legislature frequently assumed direct administrative control."[52] The state's canal administration was divided between the Canal Fund Commission, composed of the elective state officers, and the Canal Commission. The former was responsible for financial matters related to the canal while the latter assumed control over the day-to-day administration of the canal. Together the two commissions formed the Canal Board. The Canal Commission was responsible for determining the routes of canals—significant authority when a canal is the primary method for moving goods to new markets.[53] The Canal Fund Commission wielded immense financial power given its significant financial holdings. Both of these delegations of power to an administrative agency, however, prompted stern objections on nondelegation grounds. One New Yorker objected that the Canal Board was "both dangerous in nature, and without . . . precedent in practice in any other free government." In 1838

Whigs succeeded in preventing further delegation of financial powers to the Canal Fund Commission by relying on the nondelegation doctrine.[54]

Cass Sunstein has written that the nondelegation doctrine "has had one good year, and 211 bad ones (and counting)."[55] The reason for this claim, Sunstein suggests, is that the nondelegation doctrine has only been enforced by the U.S. Supreme Court in one calendar year—during the New Deal in the critical year of 1935. The problem with this claim is that it only examines opinions by the U.S. Supreme Court where a statute was struck down as unconstitutional. This misses a very wide field of political practice, at the state level and in representative bodies, where the principle of nondelegation was applied. These cases remained out of the courts—and therefore out of Sunstein's limited view—because of the strength of legislators' conviction in the nondelegation principle. In many states in antebellum America the legislatures refused to delegate broad powers to administrative bodies, entered into the details of administration, constrained administrative actors, and appealed to the nondelegation doctrine to attack those who attempted to grant more discretion to administrators. If anything, the state legislatures were too meddlesome during the early republic, rather than eager to delegate authority to administrators.

The Judicial Role

The methods of administration that prevailed at the state level in antebellum America necessitated an active judiciary. This was required for two reasons. First, many regulations themselves required judicial decision for enforcement. Determinations about the application of law to particular circumstances were often left to the courts, rather than to administrative actors. This is because, as Paul Moreno writes, in early America "courts *were* the administrative branch. Nineteenth-century Americans administered their affairs through contract law" and other well-established common-law principles.[56] Because the common law covered many of the regulatory requirements local and state governments sought to enact into law, the judiciary decided cases applying the rules in practice.

A second reason that an active judiciary was a necessary component of antebellum administration was related to state legislatures' inclination to descend into the details of administration. Because statutes often specified the responsibilities of legislators in great detail, and they also provided legal recourse to those who were injured by an abuse of official discretion, courts were able to apply those statutes to determine the legal liability of officers when they stepped outside of the law. As Tocqueville explained, "society finds at its disposition only two means to oblige officials to obey the laws. It can confide a discretionary power in one of them to direct all the others and to discharge them in case of disobedience. Or instead it can charge the courts to inflict judicial penalties on offenders." American administrative law adopted the latter approach during this period. Because officials were elected, there was no supervising power within the executive branch to dismiss administrators who broke the law. Thus early Americans relied upon "judicial punishments as a means of administration."[57] "If a public official in New England commits a crime in the exercise of his duty," Tocqueville explained, "the ordinary tribunals are always called in to do justice upon him."[58]

As Tocqueville suggested, courts routinely became involved in administrative questions. Many laws provided for private enforcement of the law. "Informers," as they were often called, could bring suit against those who violated a law and collect some of the fine that the court would levy against the offender. Prohibition regulations, inspection laws, and other regulations were typically enforced in this manner.[59] In other contexts states allowed for appeals to courts for judicial review of administrative decisions—a phenomenon that much more closely resembles modern administrative law. Legislation passed in 1786, 1794, and 1812 in Massachusetts allowed those denied licenses by the town selectmen to appeal to courts to have the determinations overturned. In 1786 Massachusetts authorized courts "to overrule the town on the question of the necessity of a road and . . . to build and to collect costs from the recalcitrant corporations."[60] The courts could appoint assessors to calculate damages and costs in order to facilitate their adjudications in nuisance cases involving sewers, common fields, and the like.[61] Most of these decisions today would not be handled by the courts but by administrators.

Finally, courts sometimes reviewed the legality of administrative action on substantive grounds. This was a different kind of review; rather than taking action itself, adjudicating a suit against an administrative official, or reviewing an initial determination, in these cases the courts decided larger questions of legitimacy. In these kinds of cases the courts exercised a sort of review that we would equate to substantive review of administrative regulation today. In 1834, for example, the Massachusetts Supreme Judicial Court decided *Austin v. Murray*, in which the undertaker of the Catholic Church in Boston was charged with violating burial regulations promulgated by town selectmen in nearby Charlestown. The state passed a law granting the selectmen the power to establish regulations and penalties for violating their regulations. The selectmen established two regulations pursuant to this authority: that no person could bring a dead body into the town without the written permission of a majority of the selectmen, and a prohibition on burial in the town without a license granted by the selectmen.

Thomas Murray, the undertaker of the Catholic Church, challenged the town bylaws when he was charged for bringing dead bodies into the city without permission for internment in the Church's local cemetery. The court invalidated the bylaws as "an unreasonable infringement on private rights."[62] Interestingly, the parties conceded that the bylaw establishing a permission requirement was an unconstitutional delegation of power. But the selectmen argued that the licensing bylaw was valid and that Murray had violated it. In rejecting their argument, Justice Samuel Wilde opined that "A by-law to be valid, must be reasonable." It was not reasonable, he claimed, because it was not made in good faith. "[I]f this regulation or prohibition had been limited to the populous part of the town, and were made in good faith for the purpose of preserving the health of the inhabitants . . . it would have been a very reasonable regulation." But this regulation extended several miles into the country, "to the utmost limits of the town. Now such unnecessary restraint upon the right of interring the dead, we think essentially unreasonable."[63] In other words, the Massachusetts Supreme Judicial Court did not simply defer to the reasonableness of the licensing provision, on the grounds that it was delegated to the town selectmen. While the selectmen had legitimately been delegated this power (as opposed to the other bylaw, which was an unconstitutional delegation), they still had to exercise it reasonably, and the Court did not hesitate to evaluate the reasonableness of the regulation in this case. *Austin v. Murray* was cited for decades in defense of the proposition that courts may declare unreasonable bylaws void, even if the power to promulgate them is granted to administrative officers.[64]

As W. F. Willoughby of the Brookings Institution would remark nearly a century later about the extensive reliance on courts for administration in the early republic:

> The extent to which our courts in the past have been burdened with the task of acting as auxiliary agencies for securing the administration of public law is not generally appreciated. This has arisen from the emphasis that the English speaking people have placed upon rights and the deep-rooted belief that adequate protection of such rights can be secured only through the judicial branch of the government. As a necessary consequence of this position, the American people, in common with other English speaking people, have been loath to grant to administrative officers other than the most limited powers to enforce, through their own action, compliance with provisions of law.[65]

An Inefficient and Failed Administration?

These features of administrative law and power in antebellum America are often regarded by more modern scholars with derision. They argue that it is precisely these features of administration in early America—its accountability to the public, to the courts, and to elected officials—that condemned it to failure. In his study of antebellum Pennsylvania, for instance, Louis Hartz concludes that "However excellent the principles of rotation or election may have been as applied to legislative, gubernatorial, or even judicial offices, they clearly had serious shortcomings in the administrative field. . . . It was in the realm of administration, more clearly than anywhere else, that the age was misled by the glamour of its democratic dreams."[66] Pennsylvania's faith in democratic accountability "rationalized the reluctance of the legislature to delegate technical responsibilities, the enforcement of political rotation in administrative services, and the extension of the elective process" into the administrative system.[67] In his examination of New York, L. Ray Gunn similarly concludes that "the attributes of a political system which make it representative are not necessarily those most conducive to effective government." The "very representativeness" of New York "produced a bargaining style of politics and political outcomes" that prevented "the rational consideration of policy alternatives."[68] He concludes that "For all the accumulation of power by state officers" during this period, "administration, as Tocqueville correctly observed, was hardly imposing . . . the specific structures created exhibited characteristics directly contrary to modern nations of effective administration."[69]

While it is true that administration was weaker during the early republic than it is today, and their notions of effective administration are at odds with today's approach to administrative power, these scholars miss the virtues of the antebellum approach to administration. It avoided the creation of an elite bureaucracy, removed from public opinion and oversight, and unaccountable to judges and juries that would enforce the rule of law. As Ellis Hawley has explained, "in the nineteenth century we developed our own peculiar form of the modern state. It lodged power not in a bureaucratic elite, but in patronage-based political parties, local governmental units, and a strong judicial system."[70] The lack of a bureaucratic elite did not mean the absence of regulation but, rather, the existence of a constrained administrative apparatus that was tightly bound to public opinion and promoted self-government at the local level.

The development of administrative power at the state and local levels in antebellum America featured three interrelated principles. The first is the principle of election and accountability—that discretionary policy choices should be made by officials directly elected by the people. This meant that either directly elected administrators or directly elected legislators should be responsible for administrative decisions. The second is the principle of judicial accountability—that judges and juries are critical administrative actors who can make regulatory determinations and punish administrative officials by applying clear laws to specific cases. The rule of law was understood during this period to require clear rules and laws that could be enforced by judges and juries, eliminating the need for a vast administrative apparatus.

Third, and consequently, the administrative system of antebellum America relied on the connection, rather than the separation, of politics and administration. The theory of a scientific administration that should be removed from politics and vested in expert officers simply applying scientific expertise was, in the view of antebellum Americans, at odds with republican forms of government and the principle that all policy—even administrative policy—was to be determined by the people, deliberating on questions of the common good that could not be resolved by apolitical expertise. As a result of this view, the administrative structure that they created was heavily influenced and directed by a party system that used politics to direct administration.

Tocqueville offered a prescient analysis of early American administrative law. American administrative law adopted the second and safer of two methods of diminishing political authority. The first, he explained is simply to deprive government of the power to act by restricting its powers over particular objects. The second approach is the one that prevailed in antebellum America. It diminishes power "by dividing the use of [society's] forces among several hands. . . . In partitioning authority in this way one renders its action less irresistible and less dangerous, but one does not destroy it." This, Tocqueville explained, was their method to ensure that "authority is great and the official small, so that society would continue to be well regulated and remain free."[71] Early American policy was not driven by laissez-faire, but by the attempt to establish a society could be "well regulated and remain free."

The Foundations of National Administration

The structural principles on which administration was built at the national level differed in some important respects from local and state administration. While nondelegation was consistently practiced at all levels in the early republic, including the U.S. Congress, a stricter separation of powers resulting in a more independent and unitary executive power was followed. The power of judicial review was prevalent in the early republic, just as it was at the state and local levels in antebellum America.

Nondelegation

Scholars have offered very different assessments of whether Congress delegated legislative powers in its first several years of existence. On one side, legal
scholars Kenneth Culp Davis and Jerry Mashaw have insisted that Congress
did not follow a strong version of the nondelegation principle. Mashaw argues
that "From the earliest days of the republic, Congress delegated broad authority
to administrators, armed them with extrajudicial coercive powers, created systems of administrative adjudication, and specifically authorized administrative
rulemaking."[72] "[G]eneral claims that early congressional practice establishes
a narrow view of what could constitutionally be delegated to administrative
officials," he concludes, "are not convincing."[73] Davis pointed to several early
statutes enacted by the First Congress that vested discretionary powers in administrative actors—sometimes including the power to make regulations—as
evidence that early legislators did not take the doctrine seriously.[74] Statutes authorized federal courts "to make and establish all necessary rules for the orderly
conducting of business," gave courts the power to impose penalties in mari-
time cases, continued Revolutionary War pensions for one year "under such
regulations as the President of the United States may direct," and authorized
trade with Indian tribes by those persons licensed through the executive and
"governed . . . by such rules and regulations as the President shall prescribe."[75]

In response, several scholars have sought to distinguish the cases on which
Davis and Mashaw rely from actual delegations of legislative power. In this
view, advanced most effectively by Gary Lawson and Philip Hamburger, not
all delegations to make rules and regulations are delegations of legislative
power. Hamburger argues that "the natural dividing line between legislative
and nonlegislative power was between rules that bound subjects and those that
did not."[76] The executive rules delegated to administrative actors in the early
republic, he claims, "affected the public, but did not purport to bind them,"
and therefore cannot serve as precedents for delegation of legislative power to
administrative officials.[77] None of the statutes cited by Davis actually sought
to establish binding rules against subjects, Hamburger argues. To put it differently, Lawson concedes that "these statutes vest a good deal of discretion in
executive and judicial actors. But the nondelegation doctrine does not forbid
all executive and judicial discretion. It only forbids Congress from vesting the
kind of discretion in executive and judicial actors that falls outside of those
actors' constitutionally enumerated powers."[78] Statutes that delegate discretion, even the discretion to enact regulations, are not delegations of lawmaking
power if Lawson and Hamburger are correct. Only those regulations that are
legislative in nature—creating and establishing binding rules of conduct—are

examples of delegations of legislative power. Some of these powers to enact regulations, Lawson suggests, are merely designed to execute the laws rather than make them. For instance, with regard to the president's power to enact regulations continuing Revolutionary War pensions, Lawson suggests, the power "obviously concerns such matters as forms of application, procedures for determining eligibility, proof of claims, etc."[79] While these powers might be substantial, and create a great deal of discretion, they may not cross the line into legislative power.

Examining congressional activity in the early republic supports Lawson and Hamburger's interpretation that Congress adhered to a nondelegation principle and avoided delegating its legislative powers to the executive. Although early congresses struggled to delineate clearly the distinction between legislative and executive power, Leonard White concludes that "The priority of the legislative power was nevertheless acknowledged on all sides, and the jealousy with which Congress guarded its position was amply illustrated during the Federalist era."[80]

With regard to tariff laws and post roads, Congress was vigilant in retaining the power to make the law. Louis Jaffe notes that "Congress for many years wrote every detail of the tariff laws." In the tariff acts from 1789 to 1816, for example, Congress not only specified which products would be taxed, but also the rate at which they would be taxed.[81] Moreover, as Gary Lawson has pointed out, during the Second Congress a debate emerged over the detail Congress is required to include in statutes mapping out the route of post offices and post roads. Theodore Sedgwick, a prominent Massachusetts Federalist, believed that a general act giving the executive the authority to designate the specific route of post roads was not a delegation of legislative power. He admitted that "it was impossible precisely to define a boundary line between the business of Legislative and Executive," but "he was induced to believe, that as a general rule, the establishment of principles was the peculiar province of the former, and the execution of them, that of the latter."[82] Madison echoed this distinction in a later debate, where he distinguished "between the deliberative functions of the House and the ministerial functions of the Executive powers. . . . The fundamental principles of any measure, he was of opinion, should be decided in the House, perhaps even before a reference to a select committee."[83] Madison admitted that he "saw some difficulty in drawing the exact line between subjects of legislative and ministerial deliberations, *but still such a line most certainly existed.*"[84]

In these statements we find an affirmation of the nondelegation principle by both Federalists and Republicans. During the early republic the debate was often not over the legitimacy of the doctrine but over its application to specific cases. The legitimacy of the doctrine was unquestioned. Sedgwick and Madison both believed that a meaningful distinction could be drawn between the "deliberative" function of the "establishment of principles" and the "ministerial" function of the "execution" of principles.

In the period from 1790 to 1792, the question of the specificity of the law creating post roads was the subject of intense debate. However, as Leonard White explains, "With great persistence the Federalists tried on five successive occasions to vest the power in the executive but without success."[85] The statute that resulted is a perhaps comical illustration of the seriousness of the Framing generation with regard to the nondelegation doctrine. The law specified in detail the route of the post road:

> From Wisscassett in the district of Maine, to Savannah in Georgia, by the following route, to wit: Portland, Portsmouth, Newburyport, Ipswich, Salem, Boston, Worcester, Springfield, Hartford, Middletown, New Haven, Stratford, Fairfield, Norwalk, Stamford, New York, Newark, Elizabethtown, Woodbridge, Brunswick, Princeton, Trenton, Bristol, Philadelphia, Chester, Wilmington, Elkton, Charlestown, Havre de Grace, Hartford, Baltimore, Bladensburg, Georgetown, Alexandria, Colchester, Dumfries, Fredericksburg, Bowling Green, Hanover Court House, Richmond, Petersburg, Halifax, Tarborough, Smithfield, Fayetteville, Newbridge over Drowning creek, Cheraw Court House, Camden, Statesburg, Columbia, Cambridge and Augusta; and from thence to Savannah.[86]

Furthermore, Leonard White writes, referring matters to the various heads of departments for a report was "one of the central threads of early legislative-executive relations."[87] In particular, references to Alexander Hamilton, the Secretary of the Treasury, were challenged by early Republicans on the grounds that the legislature, not the executive, is given the power to make laws by the Constitution. In response to a proposal to refer a petition asking for the repeal of duties on distilled spirits to the Secretary of the Treasury, Representative William Branch Giles of Virginia protested that the matter was "cognizable by the House only."[88] Giles's view seems to have prevailed, as the proposal was defeated.

As the practice of referring proposals to executive agents became more widespread, the clamor against the practice increased. Early in 1792, Representative John F. Mercer of Maryland rose and proclaimed, "I have long remarked in this House that the executive, or rather the Treasury Department, was really *the efficient Legislature of the country*."[89] Later that year, Representative

Abraham Baldwin of Georgia argued that "The laws should be framed by the Legislature." The Treasury Act, he asserted, was "couched in such general language as to afford a latitude for the introduction of new systems, such as were never expected by the Legislature."[90] Mercer further remarked that "the power of the House to originate plans of finance" was "incommunicable."[91] In March of 1792, James Madison weighed in, submitting that "a reference to the Secretary of the Treasury on subjects of loans, taxes, and provision for loans, &c., was, in fact, a delegation of the authority of the Legislature, although it would admit of much sophistical argument to the contrary."[92] Just a few years into the new government, the nondelegation doctrine was proving to be a central principle in many legislative debates.

Importantly, the Federalists defending these practices did not reject the principle of nondelegation. Rather, they affirmed the propriety of relying on information received from department heads as long as Congress had the last word in passing legislation in response to the information. Representative William Smith responded to the delegation charge by reminding the House that "The ultimate decision . . . in no one point, is relinquished by such a reference. If such a reference was unconstitutional, he observed, much business had been conducted by the House in an unconstitutional manner, by repeated references to the Heads of Departments."[93] In other words, the Republicans and the Federalists agreed on the legitimacy of the nondelegation doctrine, but disagreed about whether it was violated by the practice of referring petitions and legislative matters to department heads for their advice and opinion. This illustrates the consensus and relevance of the nondelegation principle during the first few years of the republic.

The widespread affirmation of the nondelegation principle during the early republic was rooted in several of the most important statements from *The Federalist* about the division of powers in the national government. Although Madison admitted in *Federalist 37* that "no skill in the science of government has yet been able to discriminate, and define, with sufficient clarity, its three great provinces the legislative, executive, and judiciary" (just as he admitted in the debate in Congress), he and Hamilton had offered some guidance as to the difference between legislation and execution of law. In *Federalist 75* Hamilton addressed whether the power to make treaties was legislative or executive in nature, and concluded that it was part of both powers. Yet he also wrote that "it will be found to partake more of the legislative than of the executive character. . . . The essence of the legislative authority is to enact laws, or, in other words, to prescribe rules for the regulation of society." Madison echoed this definition of lawmaking in *Federalist 62* when he argued that "Law is defined to be a rule of action; but how can that be a rule, which is little known, and less fixed?" Both of these definitions affirmed that lawmaking power was the power to make rules that govern action, to promote the proper regulation of society.

If anything, as in the case of state legislatures, it could be argued that Congress entered too much into the details of administration. Rather than delegating its legislative powers routinely, it routinely settled matters of detail that could legitimately have been transferred to administrative officials. As Leonard White notes, "Congress itself decided upon the ports of entry and delivery rather than delegating this duty to the President or the Treasury," though "it allowed the President to establish excise districts." Congress also "specified what lighthouses were to be built."[94] Mashaw himself concedes that Congress "micromanaged administration, particularly Treasury administration, through specific instructions. Many statutes laid out in excruciating detail the duties of officers and of private parties subject to the legislation." The statute establishing a tax on Whiskey in 1791 "specifie[d] everything from the brand of hydrometer to be used in testing proof to the exact lettering to be used on casks that have been inspected and the wording of signs to be used to identify revenue officers."[95] Discretion to establish regulations governing these nonlegislative matters could arguably have been delegated to the Treasury department without violating the nondelegation doctrine, but legislators erred on the side of caution. They ensured that the "duties [of customs officers, collectors, and surveyors] were specified in considerable detail" to avoid unconstitutionally delegating such powers to unelected bureaucrats.[96]

From 1789 to 1828, Congress largely refrained from delegating its legislative powers to administrative officers, and did so because of its commitment to the constitutional principle of nondelegation. There were some temporary deviations in which Congress granted lawmaking power to administrators, most notably the infamous Embargo of 1807–1809. Jerry Mashaw writes that the embargo statutes "featured stunning delegations of discretionary authority both to the President and lower-level officials," and therefore it "has much to teach us about early understandings about the nondelegation doctrine."[97] In reality, the embargo was a temporary deviation from the typical policy decisions of the early republic, one that was nearly universally acknowledged as a colossal failure, and thus is of very limited value as an indication of what early American politicians regarded as legitimate.[98] Paul Moreno notes that the juries in common-law courts refused to enforce it in many causes, and "Republicans were compelled to shift enforcement . . . to the juryless admiralty courts," a decision that only exacerbated resistance.[99] Much more indicative of common practice was the more prevalent approach of limited and narrow delegations of discretion to administrative actors, not to make law but to enforce laws that were contained in the statutes passed by Congress.

Administrator-in-Chief? Presidential Control of Administration
In preparing to assume office as the first president of the United States, George Washington wrote to the Count de Moustier that the "impossibility that one man should be able to perform all the great business of the state" was "the reason for instituting the great departments, and appointing officers therein, to assist the supreme magistrate in discharging the duties of his trust."[100] Washington's statement would be repeated several times as the First Congress debated the structure of the executive departments. But this sentiment raised a question: if it is impossible for one person to assume such great responsibility, why does the Constitution seem to require it of the Chief Executive? Are the provisions for principal and inferior officers in the administration, contained in the Constitution, intended to indicate that discretionary administrative decisions should be spread throughout the administration, in order to take advantage of many hands and encourage specialization?

The early congresses generally rejected this position, opting instead to clarify repeatedly that administrators were under the control and supervision of the president, and served merely as his agents. As Leonard White summarized, "So far as subordinate officials were concerned, there is much evidence to show that they were intended to possess not more than a minimum [of official discretion]."[101]

When this minimal discretion was exercised in a manner that conflicted with the underlying laws that administrators were charged with implementing, Congress would often cry foul. One prominent example occurred in 1793 with Hamilton, the Secretary of the Treasury. Hamilton had allegedly used funds that were designated to pay foreign creditors for the repayment of the domestic debt. On the floor of the House, Madison responded with a scathing condemnation of Hamilton's conduct, quoting letters where Hamilton, "[t]he subordinate officer appeared in direct opposition to the Chief Magistrate. The agent was seen overruling, by his own orders, the orders of his principal."[102] Washington, following the law appropriating the money, had ordered that the money would be applied to the debt and Hamilton had acted contrary to the order. While Madison "did not deny that there might be emergencies . . . of so extraordinary a nature, as to absolve the Executive from an inflexible conformity to the injunctions of the law," in this case "no necessity appeared for the liberties which had been taken."[103] The only power which Congress had granted the Secretary of the Treasury, Madison maintained, was "the case of superintending the regular and ordinary collection of the revenue, and granting warrants for moneys issued from the Treasury, in pursuance of appropriations by law."[104] Loans were only to be "provided for by particular laws for the purpose," and the authority to direct these loans "was accordingly committed to the President, in order to secure for so special a trust, the highest responsibility to be found in the Government."[105] Madison summarized: "as the law authorizing loans exacts, for special reasons, the authority of the Secretary, in executing the loans, and the appropriation of them, must be derived from the President; and, consequently, where that authority fails, there can be no resort to the law establishing the Department, much less to any general discretion incident to his official character."[106] Although Washington had "employ[ed] the agency of the Secretary of the Treasury" to carry out the power Congress granted him, he could have used another officer. Regardless of "whatever agency he might prefer, his own instructions would always regulate the extent and exercise of the power conferred."[107] While Hamilton successfully defended himself in Washington's eyes, the episode illustrated the importance that many members of the early Congress placed on the responsibility of administrative subordinates to the chief executive. Even Hamilton conceded that point by arguing for his fidelity to the president's intentions.

Thus, while Congress might have hedged on a few occasions in setting up the administration on the question of unitary presidential control of administration, on the whole it established an administrative structure that confirmed the president's ability to direct and control the decisions of subordinate administrative officers. Presidents themselves operated even more decisively in favor of presidential control over administration. Washington proceeded under the theory of a unitary administration fully controlled by the president.[108] "No department head, not even Hamilton, settled any matter of importance without consulting the President and securing his approval," explains Leonard White.[109] He exchanged letters with his department heads, after which he would clearly convey his approval or disapproval of a proposed action, issued directives to his department heads, and objected when subordinate officers acted on substantive matters without his advance approval. Even before Congress created the new Cabinet Departments Washington issued a set of letters to his acting secretaries that clearly demonstrated he believed in the president's role as manager of national administration.[110] When a private citizen attended a council of Native Americans without Washington's approval, for instance, he sternly rebuked his Secretary of War that "Subordinate interferences must be absolutely interdicted, or counteraction of the measures of Governmt, perplexity and confusion will inevitably ensue."[111] Finally, although, as indicated earlier, the president's control over federal district attorneys was not explicitly established by the Congress, he directed U.S. attorneys in prosecutorial matters, specifically instructing them to refrain from prosecuting certain individuals.[112]

This control over subordinates who possessed only minimal discretionary powers trickled down into the various administrative departments. Hamilton limited the discretion possessed by subordinate officers on questions of revenue to prevent division and irresponsibility in the administration of the laws.[113] Washington refrained from interfering in the internal business of the various departments, but this did not entail the assignment of unsupervised, discretionary responsibilities in the hands of subordinates. As White explains, "Washington did not reach down into departmental operations, although much departmental business rose from subordinate levels to his desk."[114] Authority traveled only one way.

Adams followed the precedent set by Washington, though he retained department heads who were selected by his predecessor and who were more loyal to Hamilton than to him. Still, he took the same position on his constitutional right to trump the decisions of his department heads. As he wrote to Timothy Pickering—his own Secretary of State—in 1797, "The worst evil that can happen in any government is a divided executive; and, as a plural executive must, from the nature of men, be forever divided, this is a demonstration that a plural executive is a great evil, and incompatible with liberty. . . . This is my philosophy of government."[115] When Congress granted considerable power to the Treasury Secretary in an act establishing a Stamp Tax, Adams objected that "the office of the secretary of the treasury is, in that bill, premeditatedly set up as a rival to that of the President." This policy would continue, he predicted, "if we are not on our guard, till we have a quintuple or a centuple executive directory, with all the Babylonish dialect which modern pedants most affect."[116]

Thus the idea of a unitary executive under presidential control of administration was firmly set in the early years of the new republic by both the legislature and the executive. As White has written, "[D]uring the crucial years of 1790 and 1791. . . . No member, no committee of Congress, no party sought to lay hands on the independence of the executive branch. . . . In these early years Congress took care to maintain the unity of the executive branch by vesting the great bulk of administrative authority in the President and by placing him in a position to direct the affairs of every subordinate officer."[117] The arguments for unity in order to promote energy and responsibility, which had been consistently raised at the Convention and in the ratification debates, were still firmly in the minds of the early Congress. The statutes they enacted put the president clearly at the helm of the entire federal administration. "Embedded in these provisions was a congressional acceptance of the superior position of the President in relation to department heads."[118]

When Thomas Jefferson assumed office he sent a circular letter to his own department heads, explaining that his predecessors had "preserved an unity of object and action among [the departments]; exercised that participation in the suggestion of affairs which his office made incumbent upon him; and met himself the due responsibility for whatever was done."[119] He also indicated that he intended to adopt the same principles in his own management of the administration. Following Washington's example, Jefferson exercised control over prosecutions and directed district attorneys to cease prosecutions under the Alien and Sedition Acts.[120] Jefferson even resisted a circuit court decision that seemed to undermine his control over subordinate officers administering the Embargo Act. In *Ex Parte Gilchrist* a collector maintained that he had not believed a vessel was suspicious but that he was compelled to detain it because the president had instructed him to do so.[121] The circuit court maintained that the collector was required by law to exercise his own judgment in determining the intentions of a vessel; the president could not direct that determination. This seemed to maintain that the president did *not* have the authority to intervene personally to direct subordinates' decisions when Congress granted discretion to other administrative actors. The decision was relentlessly praised by Federalist newspapers and attacked by Republican papers. Jefferson himself was appalled and his Attorney General issued an opinion "that controverted [Justice] Johnson's statement of the law." Jefferson sent his Attorney General's opinion to collectors and told them "to ignore Johnson's opinion and follow the President's instructions."[122] Jefferson therefore asserted the president's constitutional power to control the actions of subordinate officers, even when a statute was silent on the question.

Subsequent presidents such as James Madison and James Monroe followed the precedents set by Washington, Adams, and Jefferson. Steven Calabresi and Christopher Yoo survey the decisions of Madison and conclude that he was "at all times during his long and remarkable career a defender of the unitary executive."[123] Monroe presents a more complicated example. As Secretary of State he asserted in a letter that the heads of departments "should be responsible to the Chief Executive Magistrate of the Nation. The establishment of inferior independent departments, the heads of which are not, and ought not to be members of the Administration, appears to me to be liable to many serious objections."[124] Monroe largely adhered to this principle as president, though his Attorney General William Wirt equivocated on the question of the president's power to direct the exercise of administrative powers. In 1823 Wirt suggested that it was not "the intention of the constitution, in assigning this general power to the President to take care that the laws be executed, that he should in person execute the laws himself." This was in direct opposition to how Washington and several members of the First Congress described the structure of administration. Nevertheless, Wirt concluded that the Take Care Clause only gave the president a "general superintendence" over subordinates rather than a "power to interfere" in their discretionary decisions. Consequently any law that assigns "a particular officer by name to perform a duty, not only is that officer bound to perform it, but no other officer," including the president, "can perform it without a violation of the law."[125]

According to Wirt's interpretation the president could not legally direct subordinate officers to take specific actions or make specific decisions if Congress vests that discretionary power in that officer by law. Wirt's position, however, wavered on this question, and it is not clear that Monroe ever shared the view of his Attorney General. Wirt maintained in other opinions that the president could exercise a "revising power" over the decisions of accounting officers and that the president had the constitutional power to order federal district attorneys to discontinue suits that they commenced.[126] Although Wirt's opinions revealed some minor opposition to direct presidential intervention in particular administrative decisions, it amounts to a small deviation from the general practice during the early republic. The first seven presidents and most early congresses clearly acknowledged the president's control over the exercise of discretionary administrative power by subordinates.

In this sense, despite the major differences between the two camps on significant public policy issues, the Federalists and the Jeffersonian Republicans largely agreed on the structural principles of administrative power. As Leonard White summarizes, "The Jeffersonian era in the field of administration was in many respects a projection of Federalist ideals and practice. The political differences between Jefferson and Hamilton turned out to be much more profound and significant than their differences in the manner and spirit of conducting the public business."[127] As Jefferson wrote to a Greek colleague in 1823:

We have, I think, fallen on the happiest of all modes of constituting the executive, that of easing and aiding our President, by permitting him to choose Secretaries of State, of finance, of war, and of the navy, with whom he may advise, either separately or all together, and remedy their divisions by adopting or controling [sic] their opinions at his discretion; this saves the nation from the evils of a divided will, and secures to it a steady march in the systematic course which the president may have adopted for that of his administration.[128]

Jefferson's view that the president could control the actions of subordinate administrative officials was shared by all of the early presidents, regardless of party persuasion. Steven Calabresi and Christopher Yoo argue that "by 1837, both the friends and enemies of presidential power over law execution agreed that the matter had been conclusively settled in the President's favor."[129] Although their view was sometimes challenged by Congress (and sometimes supported by it as well), presidents consistently believed that they could exercise control over administration as a result of their constitutional powers, and that practice had supported this interpretation of their constitutional powers.

What did this mean, however, for the president's power over administrative offices? After all, the Constitution had not granted total control of appointments to the president, and said nothing at all about how officers were to be removed. Still, regardless of how the questions of appointment and removal would be resolved, the early Congress clearly put the president at the head of administrative decisions.

Avoiding the "Monster of a Peculiar Enormity": The Removal Power
The issue of removing administrative officers posed greater difficulties. The Constitution's silence on the issue of removal led to a lengthy and robust debate in the First Congress about whether the Constitution required presidential removal of officers or whether the Congress could vest removal powers elsewhere. Though this debate eventually produced the famous "Decision of 1789," the outcome was not nearly as decisive as later actors would claim. The process by which the removal issue was settled produced only a murky, very tenuous precedent in favor of the president's constitutional removal power.

Ultimately, the First Congress explored four possibilities regarding the power to remove administrators: (1) either the president had the power to do so under the Constitution, (2) he could only do so with the advice and consent of the Senate (as with appointments), (3) administrators could not be removed except for "good behavior" (much like the tenure of federal judges), (4) or Congress could decide on the mode of removal as it saw fit. The complexity of the debate was increased by the ambiguity of the proposed provision for removal of the Department of Foreign Affairs, which presented the issue for the first time to the House of Representatives. Madison's motion provided for a secretary "removable by the president." Did this imply option 1 or 4? Was

Congress merely recognizing a constitutional power, or merely allowing the president to remove the secretary at pleasure?

Madison's proposal immediately provoked strong objections similar to those leveled against a strong executive at the Constitutional Convention. Giving the president sole authority over officers, many argued, would create a monarchical power that would corrupt the administration through the use of offices as bribes. Theoderick Bland proposed an amendment to Madison's motion that would require the Senate's advice and consent before the secretary could be removed, in order to avoid turning the president into a "monarch" possessing "absolute power over all the great departments of Government."

Madison forcefully responded by asserting the same arguments based on responsibility that carried the issue at the Convention. On the constitutional point, Madison pointed out that the executive power was vested in the president by Article II of the Constitution. If the power to remove is an executive function, which it must be, then only those specific exceptions from executive power listed in the Constitution (as with appointments) should be taken out of the president's hands. The Constitution's silence on removal, he concluded, meant that the president must have the constitutional power as a result of the general grant of executive power in the opening to Article II. Moreover, Madison continued, this is as it should be. Without department heads that are personally responsible to the president alone, he reasoned, the president could not be "responsible to the country" for the administration of the laws.

Fisher Ames argued, "The constitution places all executive power in the hands of the President, and could he personally execute all laws, there would be no occasion for establishing auxiliaries." But because of "the circumscribed powers of human nature in one man" the president "must therefore have assistants. But in order that he may be responsible to his country, he must have a choice in selecting his assistants, a control over them, with power to remove them."[130] Appealing to the grant of executive power to the president in Article II of the Constitution, Ames concluded that the president must have control over subordinates, and that the various department officials are merely auxiliaries to the president, who could personally make all administrative decisions if not for the limitations inherent in human nature. Theodore Sedgwick advanced the same argument, that if human nature made it possible, the Constitution would empower the president personally to make every single administrative decision:

> It will be agreed on all hands, that [the Secretary of Foreign Affairs] is merely to supply a natural incompetency in man. In other words, if we could find a

President capable of executing this and all other business assigned to him, it would be unnecessary to introduce any other officer to aid him. It is, then, merely from necessity that we institute such an office; because all the duties detailed in the bill are, by the constitution, pertaining to the department of the Executive Magistrate. . . . If, then, the Secretary of Foreign Affairs is the mere instrument of the President, one would suppose, on the principle of expediency, this officer should be dependent upon him.[131]

Concurring with Ames, Madison noted that if one viewed the Appointments Clause in isolation, it would make sense to divide the president's power to remove administrative officials with the Senate. However, he explained, "there is another part of the constitution . . . that part which declares that the executive power shall be vested in a President of the United States." Moreover, he continued, "there is another part of the constitution . . . the President is required to take care that the laws be faithfully executed." If he has the executive power, including the power to take care that the laws are executed faithfully, "he should have that species of power which is necessary to accomplish that end." There is a "species of control" in the hands of the president, therefore, "which seems to be required by the constitution," Madison concluded.[132] Both the clause vesting executive power in the president's hands and the power to take care that the laws be faithfully executed, Madison reasoned, required granting the president control over administrative decisions.

Representative John Vining of Delaware concurred with Ames and Madison. He argued that insulating administrators from the president's power to fire them would create a monster with multiple, independent heads: "What kind of a monster this will be, I do not pretend to say; whether it will have two heads, three heads, or four heads . . . but I will be bold to say it is a monster of a peculiar enormity; for gentlemen are putting the heads where the tails should be, or rather making it without any head at all."[133] For Vining, as for Madison and Ames, the president's removal power was connected to his general power to control every administrative decision: "I think where the responsibility is, and where the power of overseeing and controlling resides, that there also must be the power of removal."[134] Like Madison, who argued that the Constitution requires a "species of control" over administration to be granted to the president, Vining appealed to the president's "power of overseeing and controlling" administration. The removal power debate, in their view, was simply an extension of the president's general superintending power over administration—the power to remove was simply a tool by which the president could wield his constitutional power to control particular decisions.

In response to several arguments in the House rejecting the president's power to remove administrative officials, the proponents of the president's constitutional power to remove officials relied upon the basic theory of a unitary executive contained in several constitutional principles. As Elias Boudinot argued, the president's constitutional removal power "consists with the general principles of the constitution; because the executive power is given to the President, and it is by reason of his incapacity that we are called upon to appoint assistants. . . . If we establish an office avowedly to aid the President, we leave the conduct of it to his discretion. Hence the whole executive is to be left with him."[135]

The debate dragged on over several days. Finally, Egbert Benson introduced an amendment that clarified Madison's original motion. His amendment provided for a chief clerk who would assume the head of the Department of Foreign Affairs if the secretary "shall be removed from office by the President of the United States, or in any other case of vacancy." This amendment made it clear that the representatives were voting to acknowledge the president's constitutional removal power, not granting that power at its discretion. This amendment passed based on a coalition of those in favor of two options: the president's constitutional removal power and Congress's discretion to specify the mode of removal.

Once the amendment passed, Benson moved to strike Madison's original language regarding the removal of the secretary, since it would be redundant if the president possessed the constitutional power to remove him. This motion divided those who favored the first Benson amendment, but united the defenders of the president's constitutional removal power with those who opposed giving the president any power to remove the secretary. In other words, the "Decision of 1789" was reached by the House only after Madison's forceful reasoning, *combined* with clever political maneuvering to produce shifting coalitions in the House. At no point did a clear majority in the House support the position that the Decision was ultimately understood to take: that the president had the constitutional power to remove administrators. The Decision is more important for the powerful reasoning Madison employed than the fact that the House went along with him.

Once the debate reached the Senate, things looked even more dicey for the proponents of the president's removal power. William Maclay immediately moved to strike the critical portion of the Benson amendment affirming the president's removal power. Of course, the Senate deliberations were complicated by the fact that the Senate had an institutional interest in one of the options under consideration: to require the advice and consent of the Senate in removals. For a time it looked like Maclay's motion had the support of the Senate, but John Adams lobbied vigorously and produced a tie. Under the Constitution, Adams could break the tie as vice president. Adams voted to keep the language of the Benson amendment, and the Decision of 1789 was reached.

Although events in 1789 did not present a decisive consensus in response to the removal power question, the outcome convinced prominent politicians and jurists in the early republic that the issue was settled. William Smith, who was so prominent in opposing the president's constitutional removal power, wrote to James McHenry in 1797 that "If you look into the Debates of Congress you will find this subject fully handled; I was on that occasion on the wrong & Madison on the right side."[136] Even he had been converted by the "Decision of 1789." Prominent jurists such as James Kent and Joseph Story later declared the issue to be settled by the First Congress. Kent wrote that its decision "amounted to a legislative construction of the constitution, and it has ever since been acquiesced in and acted upon, as of decisive authority in the case."[137] Story proclaimed that the decision "has not been questioned on many other occasions."[138] Late in life, as the Whigs increasingly sought to insulate administrative officers from the president's removal power, Madison wrote in a letter that "The claim, on constitutional ground, to a share in the removal as well as the appointment of officers, is in direct opposition to the uniform practice of the Government from its commencement." To follow that policy now, he maintained, would "vary, essentially, the existing balance of power" and "expose the Executive, occasionally, to a total inaction . . . fatal to the due execution of the laws."[139]

In practice, early presidents operated as if they possessed the unconstrained discretion to remove subordinate officers at will. Although they did not engage in large-scale partisan removals to remake the administration in their party's image, the constitutional power to do so was never questioned by any president. Adams dismissed only a handful of officials during his administration. Jefferson was more forceful in ensuring that a suitable proportion of Jeffersonian Republicans occupied the executive branch, but he tried to use attrition rather than removal to achieve this objective. Madison only removed twenty-seven officials during his two terms in office, and Monroe and John Quincy Adams were just as restrained. These practices established a relatively clear precedent: the president had the constitutional power to remove officials at will, but this power should be used hesitatingly and sparingly. As a matter of policy, officers should be retained in office unless they behave in gross misconduct.

Congress, by contrast, did attempt to regulate the president's removal power indirectly, in a manner that did not question the president's constitutional removal power. The Tenure of Office Act of 1820 limited revenue collectors to a four-year term in office. If the president wished to retain the collector, the Senate would have to provide consent for another term. This seemed to promote the Senate's power, but it actually facilitated removals, since the president could simply do nothing to achieve the removal of a collector. Jefferson and Madison exchanged correspondence denouncing the Act. Jefferson warned that "it saps the constitutional and salutary functions of the President. . . . It is more baneful than the attempt which failed in the beginning of the government to make all officers irremovable, but with the consent of the Senate."[140] Madison agreed, declaring that it "is pregnant with mischiefs."[141] The Act had little value as precedent and little practical impact. It was passed without debate and President Monroe signed it without deliberating. He eventually came to see the problems with the bill and blunted its effect by simply renominating every collector when their terms expired.

To summarize, the practice of removals largely followed the Decision of 1789 during the first several decades of American history. The consensus was not universal and there were dissenters from the practices of the early presidents, and their arguments were beginning to mount. These dissenters would grow in number and influence after the inauguration of Andrew Jackson, and a major debate over the removal power would erupt during the Jacksonian administration, as the following chapter will discuss. For the first several decades of American history, however, there was general acceptance of the binding precedent established in the Decision of 1789.

Responsibility to Courts

If the Congress largely refrained from delegating legislative powers to administrative actors and acknowledged the president's control over nonlegislative discretionary powers exercised by subordinate officers, where did that leave the courts? Were they simply to stay out of administration and defer to the decisions made by the unitary executive branch? Some scholars suggest that this was the state of judicial review of administrative action during the early republic. Jerry Mashaw argues that "Unlike today's ubiquitous statutory provisions for judicial review of administrative action, there were very few such provisions in the early Republic. Direct review through mandamus, injunction, or appeal was extremely limited. Judicial review proceeded largely in collateral forms, forms described by one leading commentator as 'relatively unimportant common law remedies.'"[142]

Other examples suggest a more complicated story, one in which the courts were far more assertive in reviewing administrative action than Mashaw suggests.[143] Even if some statutes granted discretion to administrators, many others did not, and it was the courts' responsibility to enforce the law when it clearly forbade the actions taken by an officer. Officers were held personally liable for violations of law, and private rights of action ensured that citizens had access to the courts. When administrators violated the law they could be sued in state court through common law actions such as trespass.[144] Statutes subjected officials such as internal revenue officers to penalties for neglect or refusal to perform duty. Congress specified that inspections officers could be sued for damages if they neglected to perform their duty.[145] Sometimes Congress imposed stiff and severe penalties against officials for neglecting their duties. Death was the penalty to postal agents who embezzled or destroyed a letter containing money. More typical was the requirement that agents post bond to provide assurance that any fines or forfeitures they imposed illegally could be collected.[146]

Citizens could serve as private enforcers of law, acting as informers bringing violations of law to the attention of courts. Leonard White notes "over twenty instances" in which "Congress made provision for rewards to informers" in the early republic.[147] Courts could compel legal action from field agents when the law clearly mandated it. In *Ex Parte Gilchrist*, as indicated earlier, the owner of a vessel brought a mandamus action to get a clearance alleging that a collector had detained it in a manner inconsistent with the law. Administrative supervisors could bring suits to compel performance or recover money from subordinate officials who failed to carry out their responsibilities. By bringing suits on the bonds collectors were required to post supervisors could wield an important tool for ensuring compliance with their orders.[148] According to Leonard White the most critical elements of administrative art in the Federalist period included "Proper legal authority in official hands and responsibility to courts for its use."[149]

Often the courts were *themselves* the administrators, just as they were in the colonial period and at the state and local levels during the early republic. In many cases administrative enforcement was simply not authorized by Congress, leaving the enforcement of the law to the courts. The Sedition Act "authorized no administrative enforcement procedures whatever," instead relying on juries to make determinations of law and fact. This illustrated, White argues, "the settled determination of federal lawmakers to leave to courts the enforcement of penalties against the person of citizens." "Sanctions were principally judicial, not administrative in character."[150] Regulations of the merchant service, provisions governing employment in the cod fisheries, protection of patents and copyrights, were all enforced by courts rather than administrative agencies.[151] Collectors of revenue had to sue for recovery of penalties in a court of law, and "the penalties and forfeitures were imposed by the judge. The proceeding gave the court opportunity to decide upon the legality and correctness of the official decision."[152]

In other words, allowing courts to serve as the enforcement mechanisms ensured that the determinations of administrators would be scrutinized, both by judges and juries, depending on the nature of the decision being settled in court. "Judicial review was therefore an ultimate protection against error, bad judgment, partiality, or venality of the customs officers," writes White.[153] District judges sometimes held summary hearings to hear appeals in customs cases involving fines and forfeitures, and the Secretary of the Treasury would make a determination about mitigating or remitting the fine. The same procedure was followed for carriage owners who sought a revision of their classification for purposes of the carriage tax. However, no administrative determination was final, and fines were only collectible after a court judgment, ensuring that an independent judge could review these determinations.

The licensing scheme for vessels engaged in foreign commerce also relied principally on the courts. Though no sanctions were attached to engaging in trade in an unlicensed vessel, substantial benefits attended registration and licensing. The licensing scheme, however, included regulatory requirements such as compliance with inspection by revenue officers. Those who violated the terms of the license were subjected to fine and forfeiture "after judicial action, not revocation [of the license] by the collector."[154]

In cases where enforcement was administrative rather than judicial, Congress was sure to provide abundant legal protections to citizens who might be aggrieved by illegal administrative action. At every turn administrative officials understood that they were accountable to the courts in the exercise of their powers. U.S. Marshals, who were established in each federal district, could appoint deputies who were removable by the judiciary and who were required to enforce the decisions of the courts. They "were subject to the immediate direction and orders of the court, and reported their actions to the judge from day to day."[155]

On questions of substantive review of administrative action, the federal judiciary produced mixed results during the early republic. In several cases the courts protected administrative officers from extensive scrutiny and litigation, but there were prominent dissenters. In *Otis v. Watkins*, a collector enforcing the Embargo Act was challenged with respect to his assessment of a ship's

intention to violate the embargo. Collectors could detain a vessel if they believed it was intending to violate the Act, and a plaintiff challenged that a
collector must exercise reasonable care in coming to such a conclusion.[156] The
Supreme Court rejected this position, asserting that the law did not explicitly
require a standard of reasonable care and if a jury refused to find fault with
the collector the officer could not be held liable. Chief Justice John Marshall
dissented in the case. "It follows necessarily from the duties of forming an
opinion," he maintained, "that reasonable care ought to be used in collecting
the facts to be stated to the President."[157] Marshall stood for some standard
of reasonableness to which an administrator had to adhere in carrying out his
functions. As in *Austin v. Murray*, a reviewing court would be able to apply
this standard of reasonableness to ensure that discretionary actions were not
undertaken arbitrarily.[158] In this case, however, the collector was exempted
from such a standard by a majority of the Court.

Sometimes, therefore, Justice Marshall found himself dissenting in cases where the courts exempted administrators from judicial scrutiny. On the
whole, however, as Ann Woolhandler has argued, it was "the de novo model in
its various manifestations, which left the final say to the judiciary rather than
the executive," that "was the predominant form of judicial review of executive
action in the early Republic."[159] The approach of *Little v. Barreme* was typical.
In that case, the Court invalidated an order issued by President John Adams
to seize vessels sailing to and from French ports during the Quasi-War on the
grounds that it was inconsistent with the statute passed by Congress. In that
case John Marshall ruled that Captain George Little could be sued for damages for failing to comply with the law, and that the Court would be willing
to uphold the statute against an executive interpretation that was inconsistent
with it.[160] In short, the picture of an inactive and deferential judiciary, meekly
acquiescing in the decisions of federal administrators, simply does not depict
accurately the nature of judicial involvement in administration in this period.

Conclusion: Regulation and Administration under the Rule of Law

This chapter has demonstrated that early American history offers many examples and therefore much instruction on the role of administration in the
system of representation, the separation of powers, and the rule of law. The
critical features of the early approach to administration are evident, though
they differed at the state and local versus the national levels. At the state and
local levels, accountability was the critical principle. Officials like justices of
the peace sometimes blurred the lines between legislative, executive, and judicial power, but they were closely accountable to the citizens they governed.

At the national level, where accountability was more difficult to secure, arrangements were slightly different. Congress refused to delegate its legislative power to administrators, and it ensured that administrative responsibility through the president was preserved. Presidents were given broad powers to direct and control administrative subordinates.

Regardless of whether the administrator served at a local, state, or national level, the power of the judiciary to vindicate the rights of citizens and uphold the legal requirements on administrators was preserved. When an administrator's power was discretionary in nature, courts would not issue mandamus writs to control administrative action, but as *Austin v. Murray* and other cases make clear, courts still scrutinized administrative regulation to ensure reasonableness. Officers were personally liable for legal injuries done in the course of carrying out their duties. This ensured that a balance remained between administrators and the citizens they were supposed to serve. As Tocqueville so wisely explained, early administrative law ensured that society would be "well regulated and remain free."

CHAPTER THREE

Executive-Centered Administration

Administrative Law and Constitutionalism
During the Jacksonian Era

DURING THE JACKSONIAN era (1828–1860) the national government maintained a variety of sophisticated programs and worked out a body of administrative law that regulated the extent to which Congress could delegate powers
to administrative agencies, the appointment and removal of administrative
officers at multiple levels, the president's authority over administrative action,
and the scope of judicial review of administrative decisions. This chapter describes these developments and discusses their foundations in the principles of
American constitutionalism outlined in the previous chapters.

A brief summary of the national government's activities during this period
reveals that they were vast and significant, and that they also raised sophisticated and difficult questions of administrative law. Although the Jacksonian Democrats, who typically held power during this period, are frequently
portrayed as proponents of laissez-faire policies who kept the government's
activities to a minimum, government was actually a pervasive presence in citizens' daily lives.[1] The most well-known activities of the national government
involved the collection of revenue and the carrying of mail. In addition, the
federal government's accumulation of land during this period necessitated the
establishment of a land office and procedures for disbursing that land to citizens. One scholar claims that this "was the area of federal administration consistently most important to citizens during the first century of the Republic."[2]
Pensions for war veterans also had to be distributed by administrative officials
following administrative and statutory rules and procedures.

Less well-known are the federal government's activities relating to public health and the advancement of science and navigation. The national government established lifesaving stations to aid shipwrecked sailors along the

coasts leading into New York.[3] In response to an epidemic of steamboat boiler explosions, Congress passed legislation creating the U.S. Steamboat Inspection Service. Congress established a system for inspecting imported drugs in 1848. It also established various agencies for advancing scientific knowledge: the Coast Survey, Naval Observatory, and the Smithsonian (though the latter was funded by a private endowment).[4] Finally, the federal government also used the postal service to distribute smallpox vaccines, authorized by statute in 1813. (The experiment was short-lived; the government actually distributed the wrong vaccine and *caused* an outbreak of smallpox in Tarboro, North Carolina, and Congress repealed the statute in 1822).[5]

In short, while "[t]he federal government did very little in 1860 that it had not undertaken before 1830," it is also true that the federal government did a great deal throughout the Jacksonian era.[6] Consequently, this period reveals much about the way in which antebellum thinkers and political figures thought about the relationship of administrative power to core principles of American constitutionalism. The various questions they confronted are the subjects of the following sections.

Administrative Discretion and the Delegation of Legislative Power

As noted in Chapter One, many prominent members of the Constitutional Convention were forced to confront the question of how much discretion could be vested in the hands of administrative officers. The Constitution clearly mandated that all legislative powers be exercised by the people's representatives in Congress, under the theory (expressed in the *Federalist*) that only elected representatives could be trusted with the duty of legislation. But what this mandate meant in practice was unclear. Could legislation delegate discretionary powers to administrative officers? If so, how could these powers be distinguished from the legislative power members of Congress were required to exercise themselves?

Ships Passing in the Night: The Curious Case of the Steamships

Several episodes during the Jacksonian period addressed these issues, but the example typically cited as evidence in favor of broad legislative power vested in an administrative commission was the Steamboat Safety Act of 1852 (formally titled "An Act to Provide for the Better Security of the Lives of Passengers on Board of Vessels Propelled in Whole or in Part by Steam"), which amended an earlier measure passed in 1838. Explosions and fires on steamboats had become a national emergency by the 1830s and Congress repeatedly attempted to deal with the problem through legislation. A steamboat explosion killed sitting senator Josiah Johnson from Louisiana in 1833, and several members of the House of Representatives also perished in steamboat accidents. Johnson's death prompted Andrew Jackson himself to recommend "precautionary and penal legislation" by Congress on the issue.[7]

As the death toll rose, so also rose the pressure on Congress to act. In 1838 Congress undertook a first attempt at regulation, largely relying on existing inspection requirements and common law judicial remedies.[8] Inspections of boilers and hulls was established in the 1838 Act, but the district judges appointed the inspectors, and the law was not specific with regard to the safety standards that the inspectors should employ when examining vessels. Failure to comply with the Act's requirements to employ experienced engineers made ship owners and masters liable for damages caused by explosion.

The reason Congress did not establish more specific penalties and remedies in 1838 was not simply due to prevailing laissez-faire political ideas. Members of Congress did not understand the specific causes of these accidents and therefore were unable to proscribe specific practices in law. Some argued that "racing"—when engineers would tamper with the safety valves to allow more pressure to build in the boiler—was the primary problem. Others pointed to inferior building materials as the cause. Still others argued that the dearth of firefighting equipment, lifeboats, and other safety instruments on ships exacerbated problems that could be easily mitigated. Because in 1838 there was little agreement on the specific problem that caused loss of life on steamships, Congress could not identify specific solutions, and thus relied on negligence law as a second-best solution.

Deaths on steamships continued to mount, and Senator John Davis of Massachusetts consulted extensively with steamship experts and pushed a more comprehensive bill through Congress in 1852. This bill relied on local inspectors, supervised by nine supervising inspectors appointed by the president with the advice and consent of the Senate. In each district two inspectors were appointed, one to inspect hulls and the other to inspect boilers, by the collector of customs in that district, the district judge, and the supervising inspector. Detailed provisions in the law specified the dimensions of pumps, number of lifeboats, buckets, and axes on board, the level of water in boilers, and other requirements to guide inspectors in examining steamships.[9] In addition, the supervising inspectors were given power to make rules to govern their own conduct and the passing of ships in tight spaces.[10]

This bill is cited by several scholars, including Leonard White and Jerry Mashaw, as an example of independent regulatory commissions similar to those that became prevalent after 1900 in America. White argues that in this law

"Laissez faire thus gave way to public control in the interest of safety of persons and property."[11] Mashaw is even more forceful. He claims that "it combined something of the 'New Deal' independent regulatory commission with 'Great Society' health and safety regulation by delegating administrative authority to a multimember board that combined licensing, rulemaking, and adjudicatory functions."[12] He notes that the "Supervising Inspectors acting as a body were also given rulemaking authority," and that the supervising inspectors constituted "a semi-autonomous bureaucratic enterprise." The Board of Supervising Inspectors "combined the multimember structure, single-industry focus, and licensing/adjudication features of Progressive and New Deal regulatory commissions with the rulemaking capacities of later health and safety regulators like OSHA, NHTSA, and EPA," Mashaw writes.[13] This 1852 Act therefore, in this view, sets a precedent for later regulatory agencies established during the Progressive, New Deal, and Great Society eras in the twentieth century. The implications of this argument are clear. If it was constitutional in the minds of antebellum legislators, then surely the tension between modern regulatory agencies and the Constitution must be an invention of modern scholarship.

A close look at the congressional debates surrounding the 1852 Act, and the statute itself, however, reveals important differences between the inspection system established by the law and the modern regulatory agencies that are prevalent today. The rulemaking powers possessed by the supervising inspectors were far different from those exercised by agencies such as OSHA, EPA, and NHTSA. The supervising inspectors were given rulemaking power in two provisions of the law. The first, section 18, declared that the supervising inspectors "shall assemble together . . . once in each year at least, for joint consultation and the establishment of rules and regulations for their own conduct and that of the several boards of inspectors within the districts."[14] The language of this section clearly states that the supervising inspectors' rulemaking power is for governing "their own conduct" rather than binding those subject to their jurisdiction.

This section was probably designed to cover routine rules directing local inspectors' daily activities, such as how frequently to attend certain locations to carry out inspections. An exchange during the congressional debates supports this interpretation. Solon Borland, Senator from Arkansas, inquired about the possibility of adding an inspector for Arkansas in the statute. He argued that given the rise of steamboat traffic in Arkansas "My only object is to secure for our steamboat interest . . . facilities for inspection." Davis replied that by the provisions of the statute a supervising inspector will attend to inspections in places where there are no local inspectors. Borland asked "if a supervising inspector will be there sufficiently often to make the inspection?" To which Davis replied that "It lies in the discretion of the men to arrange their duties."[15] In other words, there were matters of internal administration left to the executive to determine by internal rulemaking. This power was not a general regulatory power but a power to establish internal procedures that were not binding on the public. Such rulemaking powers were common well before 1852, especially in the administration of customs under the Secretary of the Treasury. This provision of the statute, in other words, was likely intended to affirm this power of internal governance, and place it in the hands of the supervising inspectors to ensure the local inspectors' accountability to their superiors. (In support of this interpretation, it is worth noting that section 21 of the statute states that the supervising inspectors shall "as far as practicable by their established rules, harmonize differences of opinion when they exist in different boards.")

The second rulemaking power appeared in Section 29, and at first appears more supportive of Mashaw's claim that the supervising inspectors had broad rulemaking powers. This provision declared that "it shall be the duty of the supervising inspectors to establish such rules and regulations to be observed by all vessels in passing each other, as they shall from time to time deem necessary," and printed copies of these rules must be displayed on steamships.[16] Unlike the provision in section 18, this section granted the supervising inspectors the power to make binding rules governing steamship traffic. The provision's legislative history, however, suggests that the rulemaking power granted in this provision was minimal and provides little precedential value.

The original provision that Section 29 replaced (reproduced in Appendix A to this chapter) was extraordinarily detailed and elicited much debate. In introducing the legislation on July 7, 1852, John Davis explained that in order to address "disasters arising from collisions, snagging, and sinking . . . we have established safe rules for meeting and passing in narrow and unsafe channels, which, if observed, will prevent collisions. This provision embodies the usages of navigators on rivers."[17] The original, absurdly detailed provision was designed not to grant discretion to the supervising inspectors but simply to copy the existing rules navigators already used to avoid collisions in specific contexts. It prescribed actions such as on which side to pass, which boat should first ring its bell and how many times, and which boat should yield in a narrow channel, in minute and unnecessary detail. The fact that such minute traffic regulations were spelled out in the statute at first is an indication of how seriously the statute sought to *limit* administrative discretion.

Furthermore, when this provision became the subject of debate two days later it became clear that nobody understood what was required by the detailed rules spelled out specifically in the statute. There was confusion about which boat should be considered to be "ascending" and "descending" in tidewaters. When an amendment was proposed to specify in the statute that boats moving with the tide would be considered descending, Davis responded that it "may lead to confusion" in "navigating rivers that have tides in them" such as the Mississippi.[18] This is because in the Mississippi River the tide and the current run in opposite directions. As Senator Bayard explained, "the boat does not move with the tide. When we speak of a boat ascending a river, in the ordinary meaning of the terms, we mean that it is going from the mouth to its source. That is not the meaning in the tide-waters. In the Mississippi, I take it for granted that, though the tide may check the current, a boat never moves with the tide."[19] After much exasperation, Senator Rusk noted that "These regulations are intended for the rivers where there is a current, which makes it difficult for the boats to change their course. . . . What would be the result [of the amendment]? You would have to change the rules every time the tide ran up and back again; and there would be considerable danger of collision."[20] After the debate, the amendment to specify which boat was ascending and which was descending was defeated, and the Senate moved on to other alterations to the statute.

The detailed provision regarding ships passing in the night was not altered until August 25, when the House of Representatives sent over 150 amendments to the bill for adoption by the Senate. This provision contained in Section 29 was agreed to without debate in the House.[21] When the amendments reached the Senate, there was discussion about whether each amendment should be read aloud before the Senate voted on them. Senator Stockton argued that the Senate should read the amendments before voting on them, and he insisted in having each amendment read and voted on separately: "The bill is a most important one; and if it is passed at all, it should be done properly."[22] After four amendments were addressed in this manner, many senators called for the process to stop, given the confusion that resulted from having the Secretary of the Senate read the amendments aloud. Finally, Senator Atchison declared that "We have to take these things on trust, and I am prepared to swallow this steamboat bill on trust, just as we have done many others."[23] Seeing that defeat was imminent, Senator Stockton relented and the amendments were passed without being read by most of the senators.

In short, the provision granting the supervising inspectors rulemaking power over the passing of ships was a very specific power to dictate such minor regulations such as which ship must pass on which side in a narrow channel, how the ships are to signal each other, and the like. The final provision, less detailed than the original, allowed for the traffic regulations to be tailored to the specifics of each body of water, but was not even read aloud by the senators who passed the amendment. This was hardly a grant of general rulemaking power to an expert board. It was a specific power to make regulations about ships passing in the night, passed without debate and without scrutiny. Such a provision bears little resemblance to the expansive rulemaking powers of the modern administrative state.

In addition to the fact that the rulemaking powers of the supervisory inspectors were minor and narrow, the discretion of the inspectors was dramatically curtailed. The inspectors were granted licensing power in the Act, but the law mandated that "no license, registration, or enrolment, under the provisions of this or the act to which this is an amendment, shall be granted, or other papers issued by any collector . . . unless he shall have satisfactory evidence that all the provisions of this act shall have been fully complied with."[24] The inspectors' licensing discretion was constrained by detailed statutory provisions that outlined the equipment requirements for steamships. Section 2 required that all "combustible material" had to be at least eighteen inches away from sources of heat. Section 3 mandated that each ship of certain size have three double-acting pumps, with chambers at least four inches in diameter. Section 4 specified the size and material of lifeboats on steamships. Section 5 carefully detailed the required lifesaving and firefighting equipment, including the number of buckets and axes, that had to be on each steamship. Certain combustible materials could only be carried on board with a license, and had to be packed in a certain manner specified by the statute in Sections 7 and 8. The method for testing the hydrostatic pressure of boiler pumps was mandated in Section 9 of the Act, which specified the appropriate levels of pressure at which the boilers could operate. Section 12 mandated that water could not fall below three inches above the flue of a boiler. Finally, the statute mandated that boilers be constructed of quality iron and of plates at least one-quarter-inch thick. The boilers were required to be stamped "in such manner as the Secretary of the Treasury shall prescribe" with the name of the manufacturer, the place where they were made, and the quality of the iron with which they were made. Therefore, the inspectors were not free to exercise uncontrolled discretion regarding which steamships to license. They conducted essentially ministerial activities, checking the ships to ensure that they complied with very detailed statutory requirements. There was not a delegation of power to the inspectors to make legislative-style determinations regarding the specifications of steamships. These decisions were made by the statute, and the inspectors were charged simply with carrying out those requirements.[25]

Finally, the power of adjudication was more minimal than Mashaw suggests. Section 41 of the act declared that "all penalties imposed by this act may be recovered in an action of debt by any person who will sue therefor in any court of the United States." This provision was proposed as an amendment to the original act by Senator Hale of New Hampshire, who argued that "There are several penalties proposed in a great many sections [of the Act], while in others there is none." The purpose of his adding this provision to the Act was to "give a general jurisdiction in enforcing all penalties" to the courts.[26] Hale's amendment ensured that the actual enforcement of penalties specified in the Act would run through the judiciary. In addition, many penalties for violating the law simply imposed liability for damages rather than fine and imprisonment. Provisions such as these ensured that the adjudicatory functions of the inspectors would be minimal, and that the primary means of enforcement would be judicial.[27]

Administrative discretion surely existed during the Jacksonian period, but administrators were typically limited by specific statutory provisions and legislative power was not transferred to administrative bodies. When the supervising inspectors wished to require steamships to equip lights to prevent collisions, they petitioned Congress to change the law, rather than assuming a general rulemaking power to require their installation.[28] Legislators agreed that agencies' input should be sought to ensure that new laws are guided by their experience, but they retained the responsibility for actually writing the laws themselves. Senator Jefferson Davis, for example, insisted that it would be unwise "to legislate upon the minute details of patents and the Patent Office. I think it would not detract from the Senate, but be acting the part of prudence, to go to those who have special information before legislating upon such projects."[29] In fact, as Leonard White explains, "the reorganization of the General Land Office in 1836 was based on a bill drafted by Commissioner Ethan A. Brown."[30] Legislators solicited and even followed the expertise of specialists in administrative agencies, but they wrote the laws themselves. Thus during this period legislators followed the British model in which agencies could propose legislation but the final vote would take place in the legislature—a process that James Landis would later endorse during the New Deal.

A Spoils System? Appointment and Removal
Powers in Jacksonian America

The two great features of the Jacksonian period, historians explain, are the extension of the suffrage and the rise of patronage politics, where victorious political parties appoint loyal supporters to federal jobs. Henry Clay famously stated after Jackson's inauguration that "Among the official corps here there is the greatest solicitude and apprehension. The members of it feel something like the inhabitants of Cairo when the plague breaks out; no one knows who is next to encounter the stroke of death; or which, with many of them is the same thing, to be dismissed from office."[31] This description of the practice of appointment and removal during the Jacksonian period is largely accurate, though Leonard White has noted that many areas of administration were not subjected to the theory of rotation in office: "the statistics show that the number of removals, although unprecedented, was small in terms of percentage."[32] While the Jacksonian period confirmed the power of the president to make removals and to populate federal agencies with his own appointees, many Whigs dissented from the practice and a system of competitive examinations for filling office arose by the 1850s. The Whigs' attempt to establish independent administrative power, by opposing the president's constitutional power to remove officials, launched an instructive debate on the constitutional status of administrative offices.

Appointments During the Jacksonian Period

From 1828 to 1860 the president's power to appoint administrators was largely undisturbed. If anything, presidents complained consistently of the incessant barrage of patronage seekers that resulted from their exclusive possession of the appointment power.[33] In practice, however, the executive was respectful of requests regarding specific offices that came from the Congress, in large measure due to the strength of party organizations. The most significant developments during this period related to the methods for appointing inferior officers, and the development of a system of competitive examinations for certain administrative offices.

The Constitution clearly specifies that all officers of the United States must be appointed in accordance with an Appointments Clause that distinguishes between principal and inferior officers. Principal officers, according to the Constitution, must be nominated by the president and appointed by the president through the advice and consent of the Senate. By contrast, Congress may designate either the president, the heads of departments, or the courts of law to appoint inferior officers. However, the Constitution provides little guidance regarding the distinction between principal and inferior officers. Some of the practical decisions of Congress during this period shed light on where this line was to be drawn. It was during this time that the business of the departments first became overwhelming and sub-delegation to subordinates was necessitated. Assistant secretaries were established in various departments, and they were typically considered inferior officers who could be appointed by the department heads themselves (though Congress classified the Assistant Secretary of the Treasury as a principal officer).

In 1848, for example, the Secretary of the Treasury called upon Congress to establish an Assistant Secretary of the Treasury who would undertake all actions not requiring the secretary's signature. This official, he proposed, should be appointed by the Secretary of the Treasury himself to ensure unity within the department. Congress enacted legislation establishing the office in accordance with the recommendation.[34] Lower officers housed in various collectors' offices were also appointed by the Secretary of the Treasury rather than the president.[35] In 1853 Congress established an assistant secretary in the State Department, appointed by the president but without the confirmation of the Senate.[36] In both these cases, then, the assistant secretaries were considered to be inferior officers, though the Congress chose different appointment methods from the options afforded by the Appointments Clause. As Leonard White summarizes:

> Formal authority to appoint *inferior* officers and clerks was usually vested in the heads of departments. . . . A customary practice to consult the president existed so far as the more important appointments were concerned, such as chief clerks. . . . Subordinate field officers and employees were usually nominated by the head of the local office—for example, the collector of customs or the postmaster in large towns—and after approval by the head of the department were formally appointed by the responsible field officer.[37]

Although assistant secretaries were usually considered inferior officers, the list of principal officers requiring presidential nomination and senate confirmation was extensive. These offices included judicial appointments, department heads, diplomatic officials, military officers, collectors of customs, district attorneys, marshals, land agents, Indian agents, and many others. Eventually Congress added to this list certain postmasters in large cities, and the Assistant Secretary of the Treasury.[38] Certain bureaus for patents and military pensions were eventually established within departments, but once they became freestanding areas of business their chief officers were elevated to principal status.[39] Subordinate officers such as route agents in the Post Office were still considered inferior officers and were appointed by the Postmaster General.[40]

In summary, the list of principal officers for whom the president took personal responsibility in appointing was significant. This was often justified in much the same terms as Hamilton and other Framers justified the theory of unity in the executive. President Polk, a particularly strong president, wrote that he acted "upon the general principle that the important subordinate public offices should be filled by persons who agreed in opinion with the President as to the policy to be pursued by the Government, and who would cooperate with the President in carrying out that policy."[41]

The Arrival of Competitive Examinations

The principle of unity in, and accountability to, the president as Chief Executive was compromised to some extent by a system of competitive examinations that first appeared during the Jacksonian period. Although the rise of a civil service based on competitive examination is associated with the progressive reformers' notion of an administrative state (as will be discussed in Chapter Five), competitive exams were used in a limited manner prior to the Civil War. The goal of these examinations, however, was very different. It was not to separate politics and administration based on a scientific elite, but to provide experience and stability in certain administrative offices where these elements were most needed.

While Leonard White is quick to explain that "The term 'career service' was not used either before or after 1829, nor were the advantages and handicaps of such an institution praised or criticized," he describes the rise of competitive examinations for selecting medical officers in the army and navy, naval engineers, and even to departmental clerks (although the system of exams for clerks "slipped through the Senate with bare notice, and through the House with almost none").[42] The Gilmer Committee on Retrenchment in 1842 proposed a system of competitive examinations, and some of the secretaries of departments joined the recommendation in 1851. Daniel Webster, however, did not agree with the proposal to establish competitive examinations—a significant fact given that Webster strongly supported a quasi-career system where removal would be a rare occurrence and even favored restrictions on the president's removal power.

The examination system for clerks was enacted by Congress in 1853. The legislation established four classes of employees and declared that "No clerk shall be appointed in either of the four classes until after he has been examined and qualified by a Board, to consist of three examiners, one of them to be the Chief of the Bureau or office into which he is to be appointed."[43] The other two examiners were appointed by the head of the Department that housed the appointment. Approximately 700 clerks were covered by the act, which exempted the Attorney General's office, the State Department, and some other departments from its reach.[44] Two important features also limited the impact of the bill: chief clerks were not included, and only persons who were nominated by the head of the department were eligible for the examination. Most examinations were conducted orally. Therefore the goal of the system was not to select the most expert clerk but to weed out incompetence and corruption.[45] Still, Senator George Pendleton made much of this system when he pressed for the establishment of a similar measure in the 1880s, as Chapter Four explains.

Proto-Progressives?
Whigs, Democrats, and the Removal Power Debate

The rise of patronage and the theory of rotation in office, which marked a shift from the tenure-based system that prevailed prior to 1828, provoked a response from prominent Whigs such as Henry Clay and Daniel Webster. These Whigs advanced a constitutional theory in favor of insulating administrative officers from presidential control by limiting the president's removal powers. While not all Whigs favored limiting the president's removal powers, many Whig arguments foreshadowed later attempts to establish independent administrative power outside of electoral control.

Beginning with the nomination of Andrew Jackson, as explained earlier, the removal of administrative officials on a partisan basis took on significance and heightened the perceived importance of elections. Contrary to popular opinion Jackson did not remove a large percentage of administrators, but the partisan nature of the removals established a precedent that led to the expansion of partisan removals by later presidents. Martin Van Buren, Jackson's successor, aggressively removed postmasters towards the end of his single term in office.[46] Although the Whig Party came into existence to curb presidential power, Whig presidents participated in removals with little reluctance. William Henry Harrison engaged in widespread removals and acknowledged that the Constitution gave the president control over the executive departments, including the Treasury—a fact that he lamented, but which he conceded was part of the constitutional design.[47] Harrison actually removed administrative officials at a higher rate than either of his Democratic predecessors.[48] The presidents of the 1840s and 1850s made wide use of removals at will, following the example set by Jackson, Van Buren, and Harrison.[49]

Each and every president from Andrew Jackson to James Buchanan, in other words, operated under the presumption that the Constitution gives exclusive removal powers to the president, and that the power to remove administrative officials could be exercised at will. The Attorneys General who advised these presidents offered legal advice that buttressed the presumption. Van Buren's Attorney General, Benjamin Butler, maintained that Congress could not require the president to provide reasons for the removal of administrative officers—though Van Buren voluntarily complied with requests for a list of the removals that he had made.[50] Even President Harrison's Attorney General Hugh Legare conceded that "it is now too late to dispute the settled construction of 1789. It is according to that construction, from the very nature of executive power, absolute in the President, subject only to his responsibility to the country (his constituent) for a breach of such a vast and solemn trust."[51] The consensus among presidents and Attorneys General, whether Whig or Democrat, was that the First Congress had construed the Constitution as providing the president with sole removal power, and that this construction of the Constitution was binding on future situations.

Prominent members of the Whig Party in Congress, however, were less emphatic about the president's removal powers, and they threatened to erode this presumption in favor of the president's exclusive power to remove administrative officials. While efforts to limit the president's removal powers occurred in 1830 and 1832, the most significant attempt to limit presidential removal powers occurred in 1835, when Senators John Calhoun, Henry Clay, and Daniel Webster sought to require the Senate's concurrence in all removals by the president. Speaking on behalf of a select committee investigating the subject, Senator Calhoun invoked the precedent of the Tenure of Office Act of 1820, which required that "all district attorneys, collectors, and other disbursing officers therein mentioned, to be appointed under the laws of the United States, shall be appointed for the term of four years."[52] The difficulty with this Act was that it actually *facilitated* removals because the president could simply fail to reappoint officers whose terms expired. Instead of affirmatively removing these officers, the president could simply appoint someone else to the position.[53] Therefore the Tenure of Office Act actually facilitated the goal of rotation in office espoused by President Jackson in his first annual message to Congress.[54] Thus, Calhoun noted, the extent of the patronage had been increasing consistently and substantially after the election of Jackson.

Calhoun warned that these developments posed a fundamental threat to the Constitution itself: "the assumption that executive patronage and influence should increase in the same ratio with the growth and population of the country . . . must finally prove fatal to our institutions and liberty." Patronage, he argued, affords the president a power "sufficient of itself, when made an instrument of ambition, to contaminate the community, and to control to a great extent public opinion."[55] It has "tended to sap the foundation of our institutions, to throw a cloud of uncertainty over the future, to degrade and corrupt the public morals, and to substitute devotion and subserviency to power in the place of that disinterested and noble attachment to principles and country which are essential to the preservation of free institutions."[56] Calhoun's chief remedy for patronage was to reduce the size of the government and its expenditures.[57] However, "yet other means must be added to bring it within safe limits." He proposed that the president be required to provide a list of all removals to the Congress on the first of January each year, along with "the reason for which said officer may have been removed."[58] This provision was passed in 1835, but it did not challenge the president's constitutional power to remove administrative officials unilaterally. It merely imposed publicity and transparency on the president's removals.

Senator Webster and other Whigs went even further, challenging the president's constitutional removal power itself. Senator Thomas Ewing declared that "the Constitution does not vest in the President alone the power of permanently removing any officer who is appointed by the President, by and with the advice and consent of the Senate."[59] He denied that Article II's Vesting Clause, which granted the executive power to the president, included the power of removal. The power to appoint, he noted, "being expressly vested elsewhere than in the President, would it not follow that the removing power, which seems, in its nature, to attach itself to, and form a branch of, the appointing power, should pass with it to the same department?"[60] This blending of legislative and executive power with regard to appointments must therefore extend also to the removal power.[61] The removal power, Ewing concluded, "is a mere matter of legislative provision, subject to be vested, modified, changed, or taken away, by the Legislature, at their will; and, if it is not regulated at all by law, it vests in the President and Senate, as a part of the appointing power."[62]

Two days later, Webster introduced a bill which, in his words, merely contained "two measures. One is to alter the duration of certain offices, now limited absolutely to four years, so that the limitation shall be qualified or conditional." Those accounting officers whose accounts were regular would be retained in office past their original four-year term. The second part of Webster's bill required the president to explain to the Senate his reasons for removing officers.

On the constitutional question of the president's removal power, Webster conceded that "I do not mean to deny, and the bill does not deny, that, at the present moment, the President may remove these officers at will, because the early decision adopted that construction, and the laws have since uniformly sanctioned it."[63] However, he promptly added that "after considering the question again and again, within the last six years, in my deliberate judgment, the original decision was wrong. I cannot but think that those who denied the power, in 1789, had the best of the argument."[64] Webster reached this conclusion by challenging the position that Article II's Vesting Clause granted more powers than the specific powers that followed in the rest of Article II. Just as the Congress only receives certain specified powers in Article I of the Constitution, so also in Webster's mind the president receives only certain specified powers in Article II. He argued:

After providing the mode of choosing [the president], it immediately proceeds to enumerate specifically the powers which he shall possess and exercise, and the duties which he shall perform. I consider the language of this article, therefore, precisely equivalent to that in which the Legislature is created; that is to say, I understand the Constitution as saying that "the executive power herein granted shall be vested in a President of the United States."[65]

Webster argued, in other words, that the Vesting Clauses of Articles I and II were essentially equivalent—they merely meant to state where power was being vested, rather than vesting additional powers not specifically mentioned elsewhere in those articles. Thus he added, by interpretation, the words "herein granted" to Article II's Vesting Clause, making it equivalent to that of Article I. Since many specific powers *are* enumerated which are executive in nature, such as the power to command the army and navy, it stands to reason that Article II's Vesting Clause is not a grant of general executive power, as it would render the specific powers granted in Article II redundant.[66] Webster concluded:

If this be true, the inference is manifest. If the power of removal, when not otherwise regulated by Constitution or law, be part and parcel of the power of appointment, or a necessary incident to it, then whoever holds the power of appointment holds also the power of removal. But it is the President and the Senate, and not the President alone, who hold the power of appointment; and therefore . . . it should be the President and Senate, and not the President alone, who hold the power of removal.[67]

Some Whigs dissented from their party's attempt to restrict presidential removal power. Charles Francis Adams, writing as "A Whig of the Old School" in 1835, called Webster's speeches "ominous to the stability of our institutions." Adams relied on the authority of the "Decision of 1789" and his own understanding of the separation of powers to defend the president's constitutional power to remove administrators. "Of all the questions made since 1789 to this day, not one can be cited," he argued, "which has received so thorough and labored examination . . . as that upon the removing power of the President; not one ever obtained a more decisive and concurring voice of confirmation from all departments of the Government."[68] Citing many of the Founders' own writings, Adams argued that his party was going against the settled theory and practice in favor of exclusive removal power in the president's hands.[69]

In addition to relying on the precedent of 1789 and the authority of the Framers, Adams called Webster's argument "tory doctrine." "The genuine old whigs have from the first maintained," he continued, "that the boundaries of executive power are plain. . . . It is acting power, and *not* deliberating power— both essential to good government, but essential when in separate hands."[70] After distinguishing legislative power and executive power as deliberating and acting power, Adams relied on the vesting clauses to support the president's constitutional removal power. These clauses were intended not only to name departments but also to serve the negative function of prohibiting other departments from assuming the powers granted. Since "The approval or disapproval of *removals* from office was *not* a power expressly granted by the Constitution to the Senate," he argued, "It remains with the executive power" due to the Vesting Clause.[71] Without an explicit exception granting an executive power to another branch (as with appointments and treaties), all executive powers such as the power to remove an administrator must belong to the president.

Adams's attack on his fellow Whigs did not persuade his party to abandon its attempt to restrict the president's removal powers. The report of the Morehead Committee on Retrenchment in 1844 continued to press for restrictions on the president's removal powers. The Committee report argued that patronage was "a new practice . . . the offspring of party, not of precedent. . . . Such a practice derives no support from the precedent of 1789—none from the opinions of Madison and Ames—none from the history of the first forty years of the administration of the Government."[72] The "Decision of 1789," in its view, "amounted strictly to this: that the President could remove those officers who derived their appointments from him with the co-operation of the Senate, *and* that he could remove them only for just cause."[73] And this, the Committee asserted, was the practice that was followed by the first presidents from Washington to John Quincy Adams. During that period "Removals from office occurred during every administration; but, from Washington to the younger Adams, inclusive, they were made, with few exceptions, for cause, not from caprice."[74] The Committee report, however, failed to state whether the early American presidents thought removal without cause was illegal as opposed to simply bad policy.

In light of its reading of these precedents the Committee proposed a joint resolution for Congress to enact declaring "That the power of the President to nominate, and, by and with the advice and consent of the Senate, to appoint, certain officers . . . does not, in terms nor in effect, convey a power to the President to remove persons from office without at least the concurrence of the advice and consent of the Senate."[75] The Morehead report did not add anything novel to the Whigs' attempts to restrict the president's removal powers in 1835. However, it did recommend statutory specification of the acceptable range of causes that would justify removal—a law "declaring the disqualifications or the reasons which will be considered in law sufficient to authorize the President, the heads of departments, and courts of law, to suspend, dismiss, or remove persons from office."[76] Thus, the Whigs' attempt to limit presidential removal powers continued even in the 1840s, after they had held the presidency and distributed the spoils to their comrades. However, the Whigs and their ideological successors, the Republicans, eventually acquiesced to the practice, eventually becoming more adept at it than the Democrats.[77]

Whigs also made other, more minor attempts to separate politics and administration. President William Henry Harrison, for instance, issued an order against party assessments and objected to administrators participating in political activity. He promised to dismiss heads of departments who issued assessments. These actions could arguably be seen as precursors to the Hatch Act that passed during the New Deal period. Harrison's attempt to de-politicize the administration is in keeping with his general reluctance to exercise executive power unilaterally (as explained in the next section).

The Whigs' attempt to limit the president's removal powers, to challenge the "Decision of 1789," and to de-politicize administrative offices may appear to place them in the same category as later Progressive reformers who sought to separate politics and administration. However, there are important differences in constitutional principle between the Whigs and the Progressives. The Whigs never denied two things later denied by the Progressives. First, the Whigs always insisted upon *political* accountability, even if they wished to include the Senate in the process of removals. In other words, they did not believe in independent administrative power based on scientific expertise, insulated from political accountability through such devices as "for cause" removal. Second, the Whigs objected to the idea of patronage on different grounds than later Progressives. The Whigs objected to patronage due to its corrupting effects and tendency to consolidate power in the executive branch. True to their name, they were wary of a restoration of monarchical prerogative. Progressives would later object to the removal power on different grounds, namely, that it inhibited administrators' insulation from politics as such, rather than purely partisan personnel practices. Thus while on certain legal issues the Whigs and progressives took similar positions, their respective arguments for restricting removals rested on fundamentally different foundations.

Pluribus or Unum? Unitary vs. Plural Executive Theory

Given their assault on the president's constitutional removal power, it should not be a surprise that Whigs were also skeptical of the concept of unitary executive theory, though as in removals it was unclear whether their opposition rested on practical or legal grounds. William Henry Harrison went so far as to declare that he would follow the majority vote of his cabinet with regard to all major policy decisions (with the president having one vote).[78] He also supported an independent Treasury Department whose officers could not be removed unilaterally by the president.[79]

Harrison died in office before his pledge could be tested, and his successor Tyler was a Whig in name only. When informed by Secretary of State Daniel Webster about Harrison's practice of submitting decisions to the Cabinet, Tyler reportedly replied that "I, as President, shall be responsible for my administration. I hope to have your hearty co-operation in carrying out its measures. . . . When you think otherwise, your resignations will be accepted."[80] Thus ended the experiment with Cabinet concurrence in presidential decisions, though President Buchanan was forced to abide by decisions arrived at by a majority of his cabinet towards the end of his failed presidency.[81] Although

Tyler decisively asserted his authority to make decisions independent of the vote of his Cabinet, he followed Harrison's call for "complete separation . . . between the sword and the purse."[82] He proposed an independent Board of Exchequer whose members would only be removable for cause, eliminating the president's ability to remove all administrative officers at pleasure. Like Harrison, therefore, Tyler began to argue for the existence of an independent administrative power in the realm of public finance. There were rumblings in favor of making the Treasury Department more independent of the executive and more reliant on the legislature at the Constitutional Convention and in the early years of the Republic, but Tyler's proposal went farther than any president before him—though nothing came of it.[83]

The Battle over the Bank Deposits

What prompted Harrison's proposal for a division of executive decision-making power was, of course, President Andrew Jackson's aggressive assertion of executive power with respect to the Bank of the United States. Prior to engaging in his war on the Second Bank of the United States, Jackson had personally intervened in administrative decisions. He assumed control of federal criminal prosecutions, directing his Attorney General to terminate condemnation proceedings that had commenced regarding jewels owned by the Princess of Orange.[84]

In addition, Jackson's Attorneys General offered legal advice that contradicted Monroe's Attorney General, William Wirt, on the constitutionality of presidential control of administrative decisions (Wirt's view is discussed in Chapter Two). His first Attorney General, John MacPherson Berrien, maintained that the president could direct the Secretary of the Treasury to set aside decisions of the Second Comptroller of the Treasury.[85] His second Attorney General, Roger Taney, maintained a similar position, declaring that "the district attorney" is "under the control and direction of the President . . . and that it is within the legitimate power of the President to direct him to institute or to discontinue a pending suit."[86] But the real test of Jackson's authority over administration came when he decided to exercise unilateral power in his war on the Bank.

Early in his second term, Jackson decided to direct his Secretary of the Treasury, William Duane, to remove the deposits of government funds from the Bank of the United States and transfer them to state banks. (Duane had recently been appointed Treasury secretary after his predecessor Louis Mc-Lane was "promoted" by Jackson to the office of Secretary of State for his refusal to withdraw the deposits.) The withdrawals would essentially terminate the Bank itself.

Congress, however, had vested authority over the Bank deposits in the hands of the Treasury secretary, not the president, using the following statutory language: "the deposits of the money of the United States . . . shall be made in said bank or branches thereof, unless the Secretary of the Treasury shall at any time otherwise order and direct."[87] Though Duane had appeared to Jackson to be a reliable secretary who would act in accordance with Jackson's wishes, he refused to remove the deposits, much to the surprise of the president. Jackson specifically directed Duane to remove the deposits, and Duane stalled and eventually refused. This raised the question whether Congress could grant discretionary administrative power to an officer other than the president of the United States. Initially even Jackson himself did not assert the authority to displace the independent judgment of his Treasury secretary. He merely notified Duane that he might wish to consider the president's "sentiments upon the subject."[88]

However, as it became clear that Duane understood the statute to require him to exercise independent judgment, Jackson summarily removed Duane from office. He defended this decision by embracing the unitary executive theory he had heretofore been reluctant to assert. He declared "that the entire executive power is vested in the President of the United States; that as incident to that power the right of appointing and removing those officers who are to aid him in execution of the laws . . . that the Secretary of the Treasury is one of those officers . . . [and] that in the performance of these duties he is subject to the supervision and control of the President."[89]

After Duane's removal Jackson searched for a reliable subordinate, and found one in Roger Taney. Jackson moved Taney from the office of Attorney General to Treasury secretary through a recess appointment that was eventually rejected by the Senate. Taney, with the assistance of Amos Kendall and Levi Woodbury, issued the order announcing the withdrawal of the deposits from the Bank, effective October 1, 1833. Whigs in Congress were furious in response to the action. The House of Representatives had just passed a resolution declaring the deposits safe in the hands of the Bank of the United States, and Whigs generally supported the continuation of the Bank on policy grounds.[90] Henry Clay introduced a resolution condemning the removal of Duane as an unconstitutional usurpation of power.[91] He alleged that the Secretary of the Treasury was an "agent or representative of Congress," which directly granted discretionary power to him, not the president. His allies, including Webster and Calhoun, refused to go this far, but Webster did assert the original Jacksonian position that the president could remove a cabinet officer but did not have "the power to control him, in all or any of his duties, while in office."[92]

In short, some Whigs denied presidential control over subordinates in the Cabinet, while others acknowledged the power to remove, but not the power to direct their actions. In either case, however, the Whigs' response to Jackson's behavior challenged the theory of the unitary executive. But the challenge failed decisively. When the resolutions passed Jackson published a "Protest" that forcefully asserted the theory of the unitary executive. According to Jackson, the Constitution made the president "responsible for the entire action of the executive department" and "the power of appointing, overseeing, *and controlling* those who execute the laws—a power in its nature executive—should remain in his hands."[93] Jackson connected the power to appoint, oversee, and control administrative subordinates with the long-standing arguments in favor of responsibility and the Vesting Clause of Article II: "The whole executive power being vested in the President, who is responsible for its exercise, it is a necessary consequence that he should have a right to employ agents of his own choice to aid him in the performance of his duties, and to discharge them when he is no longer willing to be responsible for their acts."[94] As a consequence, he concluded, "the entire executive power is vested in the President of the United States" and "in the performance of these duties [the Secretary of the Treasury] is subject to the supervision and control of the President, and in all important measures having relation to them consults the Chief Magistrate and obtains his approval and sanction."[95] Jackson's "Protest" made the traditional arguments—ranging from the text of the Constitution to the theoretical arguments in favor of responsibility—to support his claim that the president may not only appoint and remove those who exercise executive power, but also may control and direct their use of power.

The Whigs were incensed at Jackson's protest. Clay fumed that "The President speaks of a responsibility to himself. . . . This is altogether a military idea, wholly incompatible with free government. . . . All are responsible to the law, and to the law only, or not responsible at all."[96] While historians often portray Jackson's victory as inevitable, the Senate was dogged in its resistance. It voted not to receive the protest and refused to confirm most of Jackson's nominees for Bank directorships. Only after a financial panic gave Jackson momentum in the court of public opinion did the Senate yield.[97] Clay's resolution to censure the president passed but was expunged from the record after Democrats regained the Senate in 1836.

Jackson's war with the National Bank buttressed the constitutional presumption in favor of presidential control of all exercises of administrative power, establishing unified presidential control of decisions made by subordinates.[98] It is clear, furthermore, that Jackson deployed a sophisticated constitutional argument in favor of this position—an argument that drew upon a well-established tradition reaching back to the Constitutional Convention in favor of presidential control for the sake of energy, accountability, and responsibility.

However, to say that Jackson's argument decisively established this understanding of unitary executive power is a reach. In fact, two approaches prevailed during the Jacksonian period: a unitary executive model in which the president assumed personal control and responsibility for all administrative action, and a plural model in which the president shared decision-making authority with department heads and accepted the establishment of independent bodies in the realm of fiscal administration. While the former approach was more dominant, several presidents, and prominent senators such as Clay, Calhoun, and Webster, adopted the latter approach.

Finally, some of the later presidents' Attorneys General returned to the view of William Wirt, that the president could not "step into the shoes" of an administrator in order to veto or direct his decisions if Congress vested discretionary power in his hands specifically. Polk's Attorney General, John Young Mason, conceded that the president "has the power of removal, but not the power of correcting, by his own official act, the errors of judgment of incompetent or unfaithful subordinates."[99] Removal, rather than an official veto and replacement of the administrator's action, was the only method for ensuring unity in the executive that Mason's position would support. Mason's argument was repeated by other Attorneys General, including John Crittenden, who served under President Fillmore. Crittenden maintained that only department heads, not the president, could direct subordinate officers in their departments.[100] Other Attorneys General adopted the position that was defended by John MacPherson Berrien, Jackson's first Attorney General, that the president could direct subordinate administrators in carrying out the law.[101]

Opinions were mixed, therefore, on the ability of presidents to direct subordinate officers in their execution of the law when discretionary power was delegated to them by Congress. Though only a few prominent figures doubted the president's legal authority to remove administrators at will, others—including some presidents and attorneys general—believed that lower-level subordinates could not be overruled or vetoed by the president. Though their position could not gain adherence from a majority of the government for an extended period of time, it amounted to a substantial minority view in favor of independent administrative power. On the whole, however, as Leonard White explains, "The Democrats maintained the tradition that heads of departments were assistants to the President," not independent administrative actors. "No secretary from 1829 to 1861," he continues, "challenged the supremacy of the Chief Executive. The Whigs appeared at times to lean toward a type of cabinet government, but such a theory found lodgment nowhere. The President appointed, the President gave directions, and in case of necessity, he had the undoubted power to remove the department heads."[102] The firmest check on administrative power would not come in the form of independence and insulation from elected officials, but accountability to the law and to the courts.

A New Jurisprudence of Judicial Deference?
The Taney Half-Revolution

As the previous chapter indicated, in the first decades after the Constitution was ratified the judiciary confronted several important cases that began the development of a nascent administrative law, understood as the doctrines that courts employ in reviewing the legality of administrative action. Common law damage actions, the writ of mandamus in cases involving ministerial administrative action, and courts serving as administrators themselves, all allowed for the development of these doctrines. The Jacksonian period continued many of the doctrines devised in the early decades of the republic, and disrupted some others.

Common Law Actions against Administrators:
The Continuation of De Novo Review

The use of common law actions, involving de novo review by courts when they presented questions of law, was untouched by judges during the Jacksonian period. The principle that judges should construe legal issues without affording deference to administrators in such actions was not questioned even by those judges who wished to establish a more deferential posture in other areas of administrative law. Though the Taney Court attempted, with some success, to make inroads against officer liability, in cases where liability did apply the Court followed the principle of de novo review. For instance, when Amos Kendall, the Postmaster General, lost a suit brought by the firm of Stockton and Stokes for payment of a claim arising out of a contract to carry the mail, he was sued for damages due to his delay in paying the award. In *Kendall v. Stokes*, the Taney Court ruled that Kendall could not be held personally liable for an error in judgment such as the one that caused him to lose in *Kendall v. United States*.[103] Chief Justice Taney argued that an officer, "acting to the best of his judgment and from a sense of duty, in a matter of account with an individual," had not been traditionally held liable for errors, and that the Court would act in accordance with this well-settled doctrine. Taney's history, of course, was inaccurate: revenue officers and other federal officials had long been held liable for errors made in the course of carrying out their responsibilities, as the previous chapter explained. Jerry Mashaw argues that the Court "was attempting to work a dramatic change in the law under the guise of settled doctrine," and indeed *Stokes* threatened to nullify the concept of officer liability.[104]

Cary v. Curtis, also decided in 1845, followed a similar pattern in limiting the scope of officer liability.[105] In that case, Congress passed a statute requiring customs collectors to pay funds received to the Treasury immediately, rather than holding on to them in order to have funds available in case of a lawsuit. Congress's intention was to eliminate the ease with which customs collectors (such as the infamous Samuel Swartwout) could embezzle funds. But Justice Daniel, writing in *Cary v. Curtis*, suggested that the statute eliminated personal liability altogether. After all, collectors could not pay damages if they no longer held the revenue collected. Thus, Congress must have intended to relieve the collectors of liability, though this intention was not at all clear from the statute.

Justices Story and McLean wrote scathing dissents. Story argued that the case involved "doctrines and consequences which . . . I cannot but deem most deeply affecting the rights of all our citizens, and guaranteed to supersede the great guards of those rights intended to be secured by the constitution through the instrumentality of the judicial power."[106] The majority's aim, he alleged, as "a substitution of executive authority and discretion for judicial remedies."[107] The essential question, according to Story, was whether Congress could eliminate "from the citizens all right of action in any court to recover back money claimed illegally," and thereby "clothe the secretary of the treasury with the sole and exclusive authority to withhold or restore that money according to his own notions of justice or right."[108] By claiming that the Treasury secretary had the exclusive power to settle these disputes, without the possibility of judicial recourse, Story claimed that the majority had transformed the very nature of the government: "it seems to me to be not what I hitherto supposed to be; a government where the three great departments, legislative, executive, and judicial, had independent duties to perform, each in its own sphere; but the judicial power . . . is superseded in its most vital and important functions."[109]

This decision ran against both the common law and the Constitution's vesting of judicial power over all cases and controversies arising under the laws of the United States in the judicial department.

McLean noted that the statute "so far from taking away the legal remedy, expressly recognizes it." After all, it says that "The collector must pay over the money, and not retain it until the termination of a suit. Does this take away the right to bring a suit?"[110] Rather, he concluded, the statute expressly anticipates a suit, confirming personal liability for collectors. Even if Congress *had* intended to eliminate officer liability, McLean argued, "I will take higher ground, and say, that congress have no power to pass such an act as the statute of 1839 is construed to be by this decision."[111] "The right to construe the laws in all matters of controversy," he asserted,

> is of the very essence of judicial power. Executive officers who are required to act under the laws, of necessity, must give a construction to them. But their construction is not final. When it operates injuriously to the citizen, he may, by any and every possible means through which it may be brought before the courts, have the construction of the law submitted to them, and their decision is final.[112]

McLean's language was striking. He was claiming that judicial power entailed the power to give a final construction of the law when an executive construction of the statute "operates injuriously to the citizen." This, he claimed, was "of the very essence of judicial power." The majority's principle, by contrast, was "that throughout the whole course of executive action, summary, diversified, and multiform as it is, for wrongs done the citizen, all legal redress may be withdrawn from [the citizen]; and he may be turned over as a petitioner to the power that did the wrong. . . . In short, in every line of the executive power, wrongs may be done, and legal redress may be denied."[113] According to McLean, "no principle can be more dangerous than the one mentioned in this case. It covers from legal responsibility executive officers."[114]

The saga of *Cary v. Curtis* was ultimately resolved by Congress, which quickly passed legislation clarifying that it did *not* mean to eliminate customs collectors' liability under the law.[115] Thus the mistake of Justice Daniel was corrected and Justices Story and McLean were vindicated, but not without a struggle. In *Bartlett v. Kane* Justice Campbell interpreted the statute to ensure finality to administrative determinations of the value of assessed goods.[116] Campbell announced that "when power or jurisdiction is delegated to any public officer or tribunal over a subject matter," such as the power of collectors' determinations of the value of imported goods, "and its exercise is confided to his or their discretion, the acts so done are binding and valid as to the subject matter. The only questions which can arise . . . are power in the officer and fraud in the party," unless Congress specifically authorizes an appeal to a supervising body.[117] Thus while the Taney Court was forced to concede that collectors were personally liable for damages under the common law, it also sought to give binding effect to their valuations of property in order to protect them from litigation.

In other ways, however, the Taney Court maintained the tradition of de novo review in cases involving common law actions against administrators. In the case of *Decatur v. Paulding* (discussed in more detail shortly) Taney refused to grant a writ of mandamus overturning the Secretary of the Navy's interpretation of two pension statutes, but clarified that this deferential standard only applied in mandamus cases where the issue revolved around the ministerial nature of the action. In non-mandamus cases, "[i]f a suit should come before this Court, which involved the construction of any of these laws, the Court certainly would not be bound to adopt the construction given by the head of a department," Taney concluded. Rather, the court would look at the administrator's construction, and "if they supposed his decision to be wrong, they would, of course, so pronounce their judgment."[118] But in a mandamus case where the standard for issuing the writ requires that the act be ministerial, the court may defer to an administrative decision, even one involving statutory construction, where some judgment is required. In other words, Taney erected a deferential standard in mandamus cases but did not touch the de novo posture of courts in common-law cases involving review of agency action.[119] Even after *Decatur*, as described below, inaugurated a new era of deference in mandamus cases, the courts continued to exercise de novo review of administrators' legal interpretations.[120] When valuation was not central to a common law action, the Court's decision in *Bartlett* could not protect the collector from liability, and in many of these cases the Taney Court overturned the action. In *Converse v. Burgess* the Court allowed a jury to decide de novo the value of imported goods due to a procedural error made by the inspector.[121] It also upheld a common-law judgment against a collector in another case, rejecting several claims of statutory interpretation offered by the Treasury Department.[122] As Ann Woolhandler summarizes, "One can thus detect a brake on trends toward bureaucratization of remedies in the tenacity of the common-law remedies against officers. Courts after the Taney era appear to have been less animated by the idea that the branches could not control each other, and were less likely to read statutes in ways that would abrogate preexisting judicial remedies" under the common law.[123] In these aspects, therefore, even the Taney Court was not inclined to retreat entirely from review of administrative action.

Mandamus: Searching for Discretionary, Unreviewable Action

The use of de novo review in cases involving common law actions, putting the courts in an oversight role of administrators, was therefore largely sustained throughout Taney's leadership on the Court. However, in other aspects of administrative law Jacksonian judges began to press for greater judicial deference to administrative determinations. Jackson's appointment of Taney to Secretary of the Treasury in order to carry out his wishes eventually produced critical episodes in the development of administrative law. Taney eventually became Chief Justice of the Supreme Court, an office to which he was elevated after his initial appointment to the Court was blocked by the Senate. Replacing Chief Justice John Marshall, Taney sought to establish new doctrines of judicial deference to administrative power, a project greatly at odds with the approach of his predecessor. The Taney Court pursued this revolution in several stages.

The first case, *Kendall v. Stokes*, involved his old associate, Postmaster General Amos Kendall. Kendall refused to pay a claim for payment asserted by a group with which the Post Office contracted to transport the mail. Congress intervened in the situation by passing a private bill ordering the Treasury Department to pay the claim. Kendall refused to acquiesce, and the contractors received a writ of mandamus to pay the claim. The Supreme Court upheld the writ on the grounds that the payment was mandatory and that Kendall's action was merely ministerial and not discretionary.[124] In the words of the Court "The mandamus does not seek to direct or control the Postmaster-general in the discharge of any official duty, partaking in any respect of an executive character, but to enforce the performance of a mere ministerial act, which neither he nor the President had any authority to deny or control."[125] While some have suggested that this ruling undermined the president's power over subordinate administrative officials, the distinction drawn by the Court between ministerial and discretionary action suggests that the Court merely vindicated the power of the legislature to require the executive to take certain actions in authorizing statutes. Such actions would merely be exercises of ministerial decision making rather than exercises of discretionary executive power. Writs of mandamus could be vindicated in a court of law, putting the judges in charge of the administrators, only when the action the courts forced was clearly a ministerial action mandated explicitly by congressional enactment.

The Jacksonians' response to the *Kendall* decision is striking for its aggressive assertion of executive power against judicial oversight. As Stephen Calabresi and Christopher Yoo explain, Kendall eventually paid the contractors, but the administration unsuccessfully pushed Congress to strip the circuit court for the District of Columbia of its power to issue writs of mandamus. Even in this case, therefore, the Jacksonians attempted to keep the courts from meddling in what they saw as the executive's turf.

Subsequent opinions would mollify any concerns the Jacksonians had after *Kendall*. Taney wrote the Court's opinion in the subsequent case of *Decatur v. Paulding* that granted great deference to a seemingly ministerial action that Secretary of the Navy James Paulding refused to carry out.[126] The widow of the great naval officer Stephen Decatur filed for two separate pensions under two separate statutes: a general pension statute for which she was eligible, and a special bill passed by Congress specifically granting her a pension. Secretary Paulding declared that she could only apply for one pension—that granted by the general law, and Decatur's widow filed for a writ of mandamus to compel the secretary to grant both. The Circuit Court for the District of Columbia refused to grant the writ, and the Supreme Court affirmed. Writing for the Court, Taney argued that the secretary's interpretation of the two pension laws was not a "ministerial act" but an "executive duty" that was discretionary in nature.[127] Taney concluded that because the act was not ministerial, relying on Marshall's distinction in *Marbury v. Madison*, mandamus would not be appropriate. *Decatur* was shocking in one sense because Taney proclaimed that a secretary had the discretion *not* to grant a pension to a person seeking it "under a statute that granted it to her by name, amount, and term of years."[128] If this was not sufficient to classify an administrative action as ministerial for the purposes of mandamus relief, what *would* suffice?

Indeed, Taney's opinion in *Decatur* had far-reaching consequences. As Aditya Bamzai writes, "*Decatur* effectively closed any avenue for mandamus relief against executive officials for four decades. . . . The next time that the Court approved the issuance of a writ of mandamus to a federal executive officer was in 1880."[129] However, as indicated above, Taney distinguished between the deferential posture courts would take in cases involving statutory construction in mandamus cases and the appropriate approach to statutory interpretation in other contexts. While Jerry Mashaw concludes that the Taney court "was clearly committed to protecting executive action from judicial interference,"[130] Ann Woolhandler and others have noted that Taney did not eliminate judicial intervention in many contexts. Mandamus review was clearly limited and there was no general statute that gave the courts the power to review agency determinations, but the common law actions persisted. Woolhandler concludes that "early administrative law was at once more coherent and less deferential than is commonly realized."[131] Several models of judicial review operated in different spheres. One model, a de novo model in which the courts did not defer to administrative decisions, was dominant "in the early Republic, with its reliance on the courts as instruments of administration." Another model, which she calls a *res judicata* model, affords judicial deference to administrative determinations. This model did prevail in certain contexts, and the Court even moved "toward the more deferential and bureaucratic res judicata style" as the nineteenth century progressed, but the de novo model was never entirely abandoned.[132] "The nineteenth century cannot be viewed as a monolithic age of judicial deference to agency decisionmaking," she concludes, but the reviewing court would tailor its level of scrutiny in accordance with the nature of the case.[133]

Natural Law and Judicial Review, versus Positivism and Judicial Deference

In summary, as Chapters Two and Three have argued, courts highly scrutinized agency action in the early republic, and the courts were significantly involved in review of administrative action prior to the Civil War. The Taney court did make some attempts to shield administration from judicial review, but achieved nothing on the level of what was accomplished in later eras.

However, Masha writes that Taney "elevated these narrow rulings" described in the previous sections "into general principles of judicial deference to executive power."[134] In a telling passage from one case, Taney wrote that "when power or jurisdiction is delegated to any public officer or tribunal . . . and its exercise is confided to his or their discretion. . . . [t]he interference of the courts with the performance of the ordinary duties of the executive departments of the government would be productive of nothing but mischief."[135] These decisions and *dicta* from Taney presaged a more systematic set of doctrines for judicial deference to administrative power that would emerge in the Progressive and New Deal eras. As Ann Woolhandler explains, the more deferential model of review "hit its high-water mark during the tenure of Chief Justice Taney."[136]

But *why* would Taney and other Jacksonian judges be so eager to insulate administrative power from judicial oversight? What constitutional theories or doctrines would lead them to attempt such a change in the law? The answer to this question lies in Taney's legal positivism. As Mashaw explains, "[t]he

Taney court in particular was clearly committed to protecting executive action from judicial interference. . . . [D]eference to executive discretion followed from an understanding of electoral democracy in which the President was an authentic representative of the people."[137] In this conception of law, the legitimacy of a legal commandment came not from its conformity to natural law, but from its positive sanction by elected officials who represent the numerical majority. Consequently, the Constitution and the laws of the country could not be interpreted in light of higher law. Judges would have to confine themselves to enforcing the text of the Constitution and the laws rather than interpreting them in light of higher law and imposing that interpretation on other, democratically elected political actors.

Deference, in other words, was entailed by a conception of law as binding because of its positive enactment rather than its reflection of higher law principles. Without an understanding of majority rule checked by a higher and more fundamental law the grounds for judicial scrutiny of administrative action vanished. As Kenneth Holland has written, "Taney was the first legal positivist to serve as Chief Justice of the Supreme Court. . . . Whereas natural rights and natural law doctrines occupied a fundamental position in the decisions of Marshall and Joseph Story, they entirely disappeared from Taney's jurisprudence."[138] The consequence of rejecting the natural law doctrines undergirding positive law was to insist upon the inability of judges to interpret, or even to question the legality of decisions made by democratically elected political actors and codified in positive law. For Taney and many Jacksonians "the moral content of law arose essentially from its status as contract and not in its conformity with eternal standards of justice."[139] This position necessarily entails that the decisions of legislatures and executives should receive the deference of judges. Taney's deference jurisprudence, therefore, arose not from within the consensus established during the early republic, but in opposition to it.

Conclusion: The Administrator in Chief

Eventually, as with the removal power, the power of the president over administration was vindicated in the area of judicial review, as it was with the removal power. Congress's power to vest the responsibility for carrying out mandatory duties in the hands of subordinate administrative officers was upheld, but the president's power over officials' exercise of discretionary power was also vindicated. While presidents hesitated to confront the issue directly by asserting a power to displace the decisions of subordinate officials, the issue did not need to be addressed—the unfettered removal power was sufficient to guarantee subordinates would follow the will of the president.

Thus in practice, if not exactly in theory, the theory of the unitary executive prevailed over objections of prominent Whigs such as Henry Clay and Daniel Webster. As Attorney General Caleb Cushing would write to President Franklin Pierce, "no Head of Department can lawfully perform an *official* act against the will of the president; and that will is by the Constitution to govern the performance of all such acts. If it were not thus, Congress might by statute so divide and transfer the executive power as utterly to subvert the Government."[140] The idea of an energetic and responsible execution of the laws through a unitary executive continued to govern administrative practice, and executive power was heightened to such an extent that a jurisprudence of deference to administrative decisions began to emerge under the leadership of Chief Justice Taney.

APPENDIX A

Section 32. *And be it further enacted,* That when steamers are about to meet each other in the night, in narrow channels, or in fog, it shall be the duty of the pilot in the descending boat to keep the channel and stop his engine, and suffer the boat to float with only steam sufficient to give her steerage, until the following signals are given and answered, and a space properly cleared:

It shall be the duty of the pilot of the ascending boat, as soon as the other shall be in sight and hearing, to sound his bell once, if he shall wish to pass to his right; and it shall be the duty of the pilot of the descending boat to answer the same by one stroke of the bell; if not answered, the pilot of the ascending boat shall strike his bell again and again, at short intervals, until heard by the pilot of the other boat. But if the pilot of the ascending boat should wish to pass to the left-hand side, he shall strike his bell twice; and it shall be the duty of the pilot of the descending boat to answer the same by two strokes of his bell, and both boats shall be steered accordingly. The first call may be made by the pilot of either boat, and it shall be the duty of the other to answer as aforesaid; but if the first call cannot be complied with safely, a negative answer shall be given, by ringing the bell five or six times in quick succession, after which the call shall be reversed.

When boats shall be near meeting in a channel, or place too narrow to pass each other with safety, the one that may first be in the channel shall have a right to it, except in the rapids of the Upper Mississippi, and the other shall give way.

Should the pilot of either boat fail to make or to answer the signals required, or should a signal be answered wrongfully, both boats shall be immediately stopped, and, if requisite, backed so as to prevent collision.

It shall not be lawful for an ascending boat to cross a channel (unless in compliance with the foregoing signals clearly made and answered) within possible striking distance by a descending boat. These rules shall be observed both night and day. Should any pilot, engineer, or master neglect or willfully refuse to observe the foregoing regulations, any delinquent so neglecting or refusing, shall be liable to a penalty of $30, and to all damage done to any person or persons by such neglect or refusal; and no vessel shall be justified in coming into collision with another if it can be avoided.

Congressional Globe, 32nd Congress, 1st Session (1852), p. 1709.

CHAPTER FOUR

The Beginning of Bureaucracy?

Administrative Power after the Civil War

Although there is extensive scholarship on the administrative state, the term itself has eluded a precise definition. As a result scholars continue to debate the origin, constitutional significance, and nature of modern American bureaucracy. Many histories of the administrative state mark the 1880s as the decade when the administrative state was born.[1] In particular, many credit two decisions: the passage of the Pendleton Act in 1883, and the passage of the Interstate Commerce Act in 1887. The former established a system of competitive examination rather than patronage appointment for filling federal offices. The latter created the first federal regulatory commission, the Interstate Commerce Commission. In these first, albeit hesitant steps, the scholarly story goes, America put itself on the path towards the administrative state. Although the full-fledged administrative state was not completely in place until later, it was built upon the foundations established in this period.

This chapter presents a different view: the Pendleton Act and the Interstate Commerce Act did *not* reflect a commitment to the idea of an administrative state, nor were they intended to eventuate in the modern administrative state we have today. The debates on the ideas of civil service reform and national regulation in the 1880s do not reveal a strong attachment to progressive ideas, and the measures that were passed reflected a more traditional understanding of the constitutional principles inhibiting the creation of an administrative state. The administrative state arrived later, after 1900, when the progressive rationale for the administrative state finally penetrated American political thought.

The difference between the reforms of the 1880s and the reforms advocated by the progressives were well understood by many of their contemporaries. For instance, in his series of lectures subsequently published as *The Administrative*

127

Process, James Landis remarked that "in 1887 the powers granted to the Inter-state Commerce Commission were meager" and that "the objectives for which they had been created were of themselves limited." Of the factors account-ing for the limited extent of the ICC's power in 1887, Landis noted three in particular: "Political pressures, remnants of *laissez faire* economics, [and] the moneyed interests of the East."[2] Yet one factor Landis did not credit for limit-ing the authority of the ICC was a *constitutional* resistance. The main reasons for the limitation on this new bureaucracy were, in Landis's view, consider-ations of narrow political and economic interest.

This narrative regarding the development of the modern American state is typical: reformers seek to respond to new problems by developing state ca-pacity to address them, and these reformers are resisted by entrenched inter-ests who stand to profit from a preservation of the status quo. The period of resistance to the creation and expansion of federal administrative agencies is portrayed as a minor obstacle to the inevitable process of the power shift from the legislature to the bureaucracy.

The story neglects the importance of higher motives, such as a dedication to constitutionalism, which animated those who resisted the expansion of the powers of the ICC and other national administrative agencies. In neglecting the principled arguments of those who resisted the expansion of the national administrative state, scholars not only fail to depict the contest in an accurate light, they also overlook the possibility that these opponents of the modern administrative state might have something to contribute to the ongoing proj-ect of melding national administrative capacity and cherished constitutional principles and institutions.

The argument of this chapter raises at least three salient points. First, and most obviously, an adjustment in the historical timeline of the administra-tive state is needed. Locating the administrative state in the reforms of the 1880s neglects the significant theoretical difference between those reforms and the progressive reforms that occurred nearly a generation later. Second, not all agencies are created equal. Some federal agencies engaged in regulatory tasks, such as the original ICC, are not *necessarily* at odds with traditional constitutional principles. Thus we are not presented with a binary choice be-tween accepting the administrative state and denying the possibility of federal regulation at all. Third, the opposition to the administrative state, which was carefully presented in the 1870s and 1880s as these issues came to the fore, is not grounded in laissez-faire but in American constitutionalism. This com-mitment to American constitutionalism is not the product of mere economic thinking, nor is it devoted to reducing the state to an absolute minimum. Rather, it is dedicated to ensuring that federal regulation occurs within the constitutional framework that preserves liberty and the rule of law.

From 1860 to 1880: The Prevalence of the Old Way

From the Civil War to the early 1880s administrative power remained largely on the same trajectory of antebellum administration. Courts reviewed administrative action in accordance with the principles laid down prior to the Civil War and Congress refrained from delegating its powers widely. However, major inroads were made against the president's exclusive power over hiring and removing administrative officers, and Congress granted the courts additional jurisdiction to challenge the legality of administrative action.

An Expansion of Administration?

From 1860 to 1890 there was an explosion of administrative departments, suggesting the possibility that Congress began to delegate more and more authority to a burgeoning administrative state during this time. The Department of Agriculture was created in 1862 (and elevated to cabinet-level status in 1889), the Department of Justice was created in 1870, and the Department of Labor was established in 1888, although it did not achieve cabinet-level status until the twentieth century. Jerry Mashaw examines this period and concludes that Congress did not constrain administrative discretion through clear statutes because of a nondelegation principle. He writes, "while many federal officers may have been beholden to individual congressmen or party machines for their jobs, their authority was poorly circumscribed by either statutory specificity or congressional budgetary controls." In other words, Congress granted wide discretion to administrators, in Mashaw's account, and did not direct the activities of administration through specific statutes constraining the discretion of the administrators. Accounts of the administrative state that emphasize "historic democratic control of administration by Congress, through detailed statutory descriptions and close control over administrative expenditures," he concludes, "imagine a world that never was."[3]

These forceful comments suggest that delegation to the bureaucracy was widespread during the post–Civil War period. A closer look, however, calls this into question. Several of Mashaw's examples have less force than he attributes to them. For instance, the 1871 statute updating the regulation of steamboats, in Mashaw's words, actually "codif[ied] many rules previously adopted by the Board of Supervising Inspectors of Steamboats."[4] It also subjected the rulemaking powers of the local licensing boards—powers that the previous chapter argued were not legislative in nature—to approval by the Secretary of the Treasury, making the steamboat administration accountable through departmental-level control. A pre-ICC statute regulating railroads authorized the auditor of railroad accounts to make reports to the Secretary of the Interior, and to examine the railroads' books and accounts in order to render such reports. The statute also authorized the auditor "to prescribe a system of reports to be rendered to him by the railroad companies."[5] While Mashaw introduces this as evidence of the delegation of legislative power, the regulations authorized only relate to the "system of reports" railroads must submit, as opposed to a general power to enact rules governing railroad conduct. Few if any of the examples Mashaw cites amount to a serious delegation of legislative power by the Congress to administrative officers.

On the whole, Congress followed the basic principles of the nondelegation doctrine during the post–Civil War period by refraining from delegating legislative powers to agencies. While discretion was delegated to administrative actors, that discretion was inherent in executive power, not a part of legislative power unconstitutionally granted. The Civil Rights Act of 1871, for instance, did not create an administrative agency but relied (in line with traditional approaches to administration) on private citizens and litigation in federal courts. Any person deprived of rights, privileges, or immunities could sue for redress and liability was attached to the person responsible for the deprivation.[6] Most laws followed this pattern, hewing to the older approach to administrative power: reliance on courts for enforcement of clear legislative mandates as opposed to the creation of new and independent bodies with regulatory authority. As Stephen Skowronek has explained, "After the wartime crisis, American government moved ahead within its effective mode of operations bounded by court decisions and national party competition. . . . The postwar decades were to bring the rule of courts and parties to their fullest flower," not dethrone that regime in favor of a new administrative state.[7]

Andrew Johnson's Impeachment and the Tenure of Office Act

The major episode that threatened to disrupt the well-established principle that the president could remove administrative officers at will occurred immediately after the Civil War. Andrew Johnson, who assumed the presidency after the assassination of Abraham Lincoln, had a very different approach to post–Civil War Reconstruction than the Congress. Consequently Congress sought to insulate those administrators tasked with carrying out Reconstruction from the president's control. Congress was in recess until December 1865, and this allowed Johnson to assume control over Reconstruction. As commander in chief, presiding during the conclusion of a rebellion, Johnson assumed that he had the power to admit the Southern states back into the Union, with representation. In Congress's absence he issued a broad pardon to Southerners and began the process of readmitting states. When Congress returned in December 1865 it refused to recognize the delegations from the South.

The conflict escalated quickly. Congress passed the Civil Rights Act and a bill renewing the Freedmen's Bureau, both of which Johnson vetoed. Congress overrode his veto of the Civil Rights Act and talk of impeachment began. At this point Johnson turned to the removal power, replacing over a thousand postmasters for political reasons. Congress fought back by attempting to curtail the president's removal power, directly questioning the wisdom of the Decision of 1789. In 1867 it added a requirement that the Senate approve the removal of the General of the Army in an appropriations bill. Johnson protested but could not veto the measure because of the need for the appropriation.[8]

Finally, in the same year Congress passed the Tenure of Office Act, which required that all officers appointed through the advice and consent of the Senate hold office until their successors were confirmed by the Senate. This essentially required Senate confirmation for all removals of officers nominated through advice and consent: the third option presented when the First Congress confronted the removal power issue. Some members of Congress wanted to exclude cabinet secretaries from the law under the theory that the president must control them in order to preserve his own responsibility—arguments that echoed those voiced at the Constitutional Convention and throughout the first century of American history. The Senate exempted cabinet secretaries from its bill, while the House included them. In conference committee the Senate's exemption was eliminated, but a compromise provision was included stating that cabinet members should hold office "for and during the term of the President by whom they may have been appointed . . . subject to removal by and with the advice and consent of the Senate."[9]

Johnson, of course, vetoed the measure, resting on the continuous and traditional interpretation of the Constitution that had prevailed since its inception. He argued: "That the power of removal is constitutionally vested in the President of the United States is a principle which has been not more distinctly declared by judicial authority and judicial commentators than it has been uniformly practiced upon by the legislative and executive departments."[10] Congress once again overrode his veto.

Johnson sought to test the legality of the Act by removing Secretary of War Edwin Stanton, a Lincoln appointee and vociferous opponent of most of Johnson's policies. In his removal statement he declared that "the President is the responsible head of the Administration" and must be able to remove a department head when his opinions "are irreconcilably opposed to those of the President in grave matters of policy and administration."[11] (Franklin Roosevelt would later take the same position in attempting to remove a member of the Federal Trade Commission.)

The removal was summarily rejected by the Senate, by a 35–6 vote, and Stanton was reinstated. Anticipating the Senate's move, Johnson's strategy was to have the Senate refuse to accept the removal, but to direct Ulysses S. Grant, whom he had appointed to fill Stanton's slot, to stay in office and let the courts resolve the constitutional issue. Grant refused and Stanton returned to office. Johnson removed him again and replaced him with an interim Secretary of War, at which point Stanton refused to leave and had to be removed from the War Department (in which he had barricaded himself) by force.

These events precipitated the first presidential impeachment in American history. The House of Representatives rested its case on Johnson's repeated violations of the Tenure of Office Act. In the Senate, the impeachment trial took on the characteristics of a legal and constitutional debate. The loophole contained in the Tenure of Office Act clearly helped Johnson's cause. Because Stanton had been appointed by Lincoln, not Johnson, he was not protected from removal by the Tenure of Office Act. Nevertheless, Johnson relied not simply upon this loophole but upon the proposition that the Tenure of Office Act was itself unconstitutional. Johnson was ultimately acquitted by a single vote in the Senate. A majority, but not a supermajority, was willing to remove the president of the United States.

As the Johnson impeachment demonstrates, unlike earlier periods of American history, the principle of the unitary executive applied to officeholders was widely disputed during the post–Civil War period. Scholars draw different conclusions as to the significance of the Senate's acquittal of Johnson. Jerry Mashaw, critical of the principle of the unitary executive, writes that the episode "has ambiguous significance for our administrative constitution. The Senate vote is opaque concerning the grounds and hence tells us little concerning contemporary beliefs."[12] By contrast, Stephen Calabresi and Christopher Yoo maintain that "Johnson's acquittal . . . was due to his strong defense of the unitary executive and to several senators who agreed with Johnson's defense."[13] They argue that Congress's decision to pass "unconstitutional legislation that would tie Johnson's hands with respect to the removal power . . . would ultimately prove Congress's undoing," suggesting that the Tenure of Office Act was repudiated in the Senate's failure to impeach Johnson for violating it.[14]

Neither position is entirely correct. It is true that there were multiple grounds for refusing to impeach Johnson, and therefore his acquittal cannot be admitted as evidence that the Senate eventually accepted the president's constitutional power to remove administrators. However, the constitutional arguments made by Johnson clearly played a significant role in the contest. Some senators at least were concerned about reversing the long-established rule that the president has the constitutional power to remove subordinates. On the other hand, the Senate's insistence in enforcing the Tenure of Office Act, refusing to accept Stanton's removal by a 35–6 vote, indicates that a significant bloc existed in favor of restricting the president's removal powers. While Daniel Webster was in the minority as a Whig fighting against the Jacksonians' use of the removal power, Johnson's opponents in the House and Senate were a significant majority.

Moreover, although Andrew Johnson survived the impeachment proceedings, the Tenure of Office Act survived as well. When Johnson's successor, Ulysses S. Grant, assumed office, he criticized the Tenure of Office Act in his first annual message to Congress. The House of Representatives voted to repeal the law, but the Senate was reluctant to give up its institutional power over administration. Grant played hardball, threatening not to nominate anyone, and therefore to deny patronage to the Senate, until the law was repealed. He won a compromise measure that allowed the president to suspend an officer without providing reasons to the Senate, and nominate a successor to be confirmed upon the advice and consent of the Senate. In other areas, however, Grant accepted limits to the president's removal powers, particularly in accepting statutes that required Senate approval of removals of deputy postmasters—laws that would ultimately be declared unconstitutional in the 1920s. On the whole, then, the period beginning in 1867 saw major inroads against the president's constitutional removal power. The power of appointment would become even more hotly contested little more than a decade later, as this chapter discusses later.

The Rise of Equity Power in Judicial Review

While the Taney Court during the Jacksonian Period had established a regime of judicial review in which courts granted deference to administrators in mandamus cases, combined with de novo review in common law actions, a third category in which courts possessed a wide equity power to address the legality of administrative action was emerging. This equity power first arose in the context of land cases and was gradually extended to a much wider array of categories, granting the courts greater powers to review administrative activity. The Land Department is one of the earliest examples, and likely the most significant, of an administrative agency that had the power to adjudicate questions that affected the legal rights of various parties. As the government acquired more land and disbursed it to claimants, Congress constructed an administrative system for resolving rival claims to the same land rights. It transferred these responsibilities from the Treasury Department to the General Land Office in 1812, which was later placed within the Department of the Interior when the department was formed in 1849. Claimants would acquire a patent to land by following agency procedures, and the patent would protect the holder from other common-law claimants to the same property. These rival claimants would typically bring a suit in ejectment under the common law to displace the holder of the government patent.

Once two rival claimants were in court, the legitimacy of the agency's decision to grant the patent was a matter the court had to address. In these cases the Supreme Court would typically distinguish between issues of law and issues of fact. If it was alleged that the agency lacked jurisdiction, the Court would treat the issue as a legal question and would review it de novo.[15] However, if the issue turned on a question of fact, the agency's determination was generally regarded as conclusive.[16] Hence the Court would approach review of Land Department determinations much as an appellate court would examine a lower court's determination: on questions of fact, the lower tribunal is considered the most competent decider, but on questions of law, the reviewing court has the greater capacity to resolve the issue.[17] The scope of cases involving legal issues and de novo review by courts was rather narrow; judicial review was not generally available to those alleging an error in judgment by the agency.[18]

Although parties could not typically challenge the Land Office's determinations by appeal or on a writ of error, as Ann Woolhandler explains, "the Court often reminded the litigants that more plenary review of [land] title could be had in equity between private parties."[19] In the equity context judicial review was expanded. "Fraud and mistake were also considered," Woolhandler notes.[20] This general equity power, in which courts would review agency action beyond the simple legal and jurisdictional issues, began to expand in the 1870s, as courts scrutinized agency action more carefully.[21] The most significant case illustrating these developments is the 1871 case of *Johnson v. Towsley*.[22] Johnson and Towsley were rival claimants to the same land. Towsley was granted the patent to the land by the local officer in the Land Office, and the Commissioner of the Land Office affirmed the decision, but upon appeal the Interior Department decided in favor of Johnson. The Court noted that an 1858 statute provided that the commissioner's decision "shall be final, unless appeal therefrom be taken to the Secretary of the Interior." This provision declaring the finality of the agency's action might be taken to preclude judicial review, but the Court disagreed with this interpretation. The Court granted that, in general, "when the law has confided to a special tribunal the authority to hear and determine certain matters arising in the course of its duties, the decision of that tribunal, within the scope of its authority, is conclusive."[23] However, it rejected the proposition that any agency, regardless of its statutory mandate, could "by misconstruction of the law, take from a party that to which he has acquired a legal right." In these cases, the Court denied that "the courts are without power to give any relief."[24] In other words, even when a statute appears to declare that an administrative action is final, judicial review of the legality of the action remains because an individual's legal rights are at stake.

But the Court went farther than this, relying on a general equity power "to inquiry into and correct mistakes, injustice, and wrong in both judicial and executive action."[25] Thus while the Court granted that "when officers decide controverted questions of fact, in the absence of fraud, or impositions, or mistake, their decision on those questions is final," it also affirmed that it could inquire into whether fraud, impositions, or mistake have occurred.[26] This duty is, the Court declared, "of the very essence of judicial authority to inquire whether this has been done in violation of law and, if it has, to give appropriate remedy."[27]

Towsley therefore marked a departure from the Taney Court's attempt to remove administrative determinations from review in federal court. It was much more consistent with the Marshall Court's position that administrative action not in accordance with law could be legitimately brought to the judiciary for review. As Mashaw has written, the *Towsley* case "seemed to set up a new division of labor between the Land Office and the courts. Land Office determinations were generally conclusive, but could be upset by a court of equity when the Land Office had made a mistake of law."[28] While there was no statutory authority for this general equity power the Court claimed in *Towsley*, it is important to note that in other areas of law the equity model of review was statutorily required. In patent and copyright laws, postal acts, and revenue laws, Congress had granted the federal courts jurisdiction over all cases in law or equity arising under the laws of the United States in these areas.[29]

The federal courts' equity power to review administrative action gained considerable momentum in 1875 with the enactment of a general federal question statute.[30] This statute gave the circuit courts jurisdiction over "all suits of a civil nature, at common law or in equity . . . arising under the . . . laws of the United States." As a result litigants seeking to challenge administrative action no longer had to resort to mandamus or to a common law trespass or damages suit to get to the judiciary. But this was less a revolution in the scope of judicial review than a continuation of trends that were decades long. As one scholar writes, "the 1875 grant of jurisdiction is best interpreted as an authorization for federal equity courts to . . . continue applying the preexisting federal equity law" that had emerged in these statutes and more generally in cases like *Towsley*.[31] These cases, and the creation of a broad federal question jurisdiction for the courts to review administrative action, portended a rise in judicial review—which would trigger a reaction during the Progressive era a few decades later.[32]

From the Civil War to the 1880s, in summary, a few major changes in the constitutionalism undergirding administrative power emerged. Contrary to the Jacksonian vision of administrative law, advanced by Jacksonian presidents and the Taney Court, the executive's power over administrators was moderately curtailed through devices such as the Tenure of Office Act. And administrative decisions were no longer as insulated from judicial review as they were during the Taney Court. The judiciary was coming back into the picture.

By many scholarly accounts, the 1880s is where administrative law actually began. The history presented to this point suggests, however, that law and administrative power had developed well before the creation of the civil service and the Interstate Commerce Commission. In addition, as the following sections of this chapter will argue, it would be erroneous to conclude that the 1880s was the point at which the modern administrative state came into existence. The creation of a civil service system and a regulatory body to deal with railroad issues was actually much more in line with previous practice than scholars tend to imply.

The Civil Service System and the Republican Principle

Although the passage of the Pendleton Act in 1883 is typically noted as a watershed moment in the development of the administrative state, the battle over patronage and control of the federal administration was not new to the 1870s and 1880s. But the importance of control over administrative personnel grew dramatically as federal agencies were created and expanded. Employment in civilian administrative office at the national level grew exponentially during the post–Civil War period. Consequently the question of who would be in charge of these government employees became acute, and the idea of competitive examinations for holding federal office emerged well before the passage of the Pendleton Act in 1883. As discussed in the previous chapter, a small portion of the national administration was already covered by competitive examinations prior to the Civil War. Efforts to expand this narrow category began well before the Pendleton Act was enacted. Charles Sumner, a Republican from Massachusetts, introduced a bill in 1864 providing for competitive examinations for public office and a civil service commission.[33] Sumner's bill "became the first of a twenty-year series of sixty-four reform bills aimed at creating a merit system" according to one scholarly assessment.[34] Thomas Jenckes, Republican from Rhode Island, also introduced a similar measure in the House in 1867. The movement to curtail political patronage was thus underway by the middle of the 1860s.

The Constitutional Debate over Civil Service Reform

The debate continued to rage throughout the 1870s. Supporters of civil service reform established commissions to explore the possibilities for reform. In the wake of the Johnson impeachment and the struggle over the Tenure of Office Act, President Ulysses S. Grant supported the proposals of the civil service commission of 1871, a body established by an appropriations rider in 1871 and which advocated many of the ideas that eventuated in the Pendleton Act in 1883. The ideas advanced by the commission prompted a significant backlash, which rested on foundational constitutional ideas such as republicanism. Charles Merriam, a prominent progressive reformer, wrote decades later that "the chief popular consideration urged in defense of the spoils system" was not a defense of party, but "the fear of aristocracy, bureaucracy, or monarchy. The cry was raised that democracy was in danger of overthrow, if the proposed qualifications for office were set up."[35] In other words, foundational complaints against the civil service system were based not on self-interest but on a cherished constitutional idea, the idea that we should be governed by political officials chosen through consent rather than competitive examinations. This principle of lawmaking by elected representatives can be clearly traced back to the theory of republicanism advanced in *The Federalist*.

Opponents of the civil service system were quick to raise constitutional arguments against its establishment. Much of the scholarly attention has focused on the entrenched party interests that stood in the way of reform, and their role in resisting the move towards a non-partisan, scientific bureaucracy. This work reveals helpfully the tension between the civil service movement and the strong party system that dominated American politics in the late nineteenth century, showing that it was the party leaders who had most to lose with the passage of the Pendleton Act.[36]

However, the arguments of principled opponents of the civil service system should not be neglected. These principled opponents were not merely seeking to preserve the dominance of the political parties. They were defending what they understood as core constitutional principles. As Grant's Attorney General Amos Akerman argued in his 1871 report on the questions presented by the establishment of a Civil Service Commission, "The objection is substantially this: That a rule, whether prescribed by Congress, or by the President in pursuance of authority given by Congress, that a vacant civil office must be given to the person who is found to stand foremost in a competitive examination, in effect makes the judges in that examination the appointing power to that office and thus contravenes the constitutional provisions on the subject of appointment."[37] In response the Attorney General replied that competitive examinations could be understood as merely advisory, an arrangement would render the plan consistent with constitutional design: "The appointing power may avail itself of the judgment of others as one means of information. . . . But this has been done in its discretion. I see no constitutional objection to an examining board, rendering no imperative judgments, but only aiding the appointing power with information. [However,] A legal obligation to follow the judgment of such a board is inconsistent with the constitutional independence of the appointing power."[38] Although he admitted that this rule was not always followed prior to the 1870s, past practice is not controlling when the meaning of the Constitution is clear, as in this case. "It more concerns us to ascertain what is the constitutional rule than to learn whether that rule has always been followed. Nineteen violations of the Constitution do not justify a twentieth."[39]

Akerman's objection to competitive examinations for appointing officials to civil offices was not based on party interest but on constitutional principle. But it is key to note that he was not entirely opposed to a civil service commission, provided that the commission did not exercise authority that violated the Constitution's institutional design. An examining board, which pronounced a judgment on the quality of nominees, would be entirely consistent with the Constitution's distribution of appointment power. As he concluded, "the test of a competitive examination may be resorted to in order to inform the conscience of the appointing power, but cannot be made legally conclusive upon that power against its own judgment and will."[40] Although Akerman did not make this argument, one could also point out that only "officers" of the United States are covered by the Constitution's appointment provisions, and that it might be inappropriate to call every employee of the national government an "officer." Some positions might be made on the basis of a competitive examination if they did not wield the kind of authority that would make them officers.

The constitutional issues were echoed in the congressional debates on civil service reform in the early 1870s. Senator Matthew Carpenter of Wisconsin introduced a resolution in January 1872 which read that "any law or regulation which is designed to relieve the President, and in the cases pertaining to them the courts of law or heads of Departments, of the full responsibility of such nominations or appointments, is in violation of the Constitution."[41] Thus in both the Congress and the administration in the 1870s there was constitutional resistance to the idea of establishing a civil service system based on competitive examinations.

Yet it was not merely a strict adherence to the letter of the Constitution that animated many of the opponents of the system of competitive examinations. Rather, the opposition rejected the idea because of the inconsistency of civil service reform and the republican principles of the Constitution. Henry Snapp, Republican congressman from Illinois, explored this idea thoroughly in response to the civil service commission report of 1871. Snapp alleged that this commission gathered together for "inventing, some scheme whereby the people of these United States may be cheated out of a great and important privilege, to wit, of having and exercising a voice in determining who shall fill the subordinate offices of the country." Snapp argued that "such a scheme is anti-republican and inimical to our form of free government."[42] The opposition to civil service reform, in Snapp's view, was based on core constitutional principles, namely, the republican idea that the people choose their rulers by voting for them. For Snapp, free government and republicanism were at stake. "In the first place," he argued, "we must not lose sight of the one grand and established fact, the truth that the foundations of our Government are that the people govern, that the people rule. . . . The people make the laws. The people make the lawmakers."[43] Any law that "undertakes to thwart that principle by in any manner robbing the people of these United States of their right to use their voice in whatever concerns them . . . must be in violation of the great fundamental spirit of the Constitution."[44]

Snapp presented the argument against competitive examinations in basic syllogistic form, beginning with the core principle of republicanism. First, the republican principle places the people at the foundation of the government. They choose their own rulers and create the laws of the country. Second, this principle is thwarted by proposals to rob the people of their right to vote for their own rulers. Snapp argued that "this 'Star Chamber' called a commission propose that somebody else than the people shall fill these offices."[45] It proposed to rob the people of the right to fill the offices of the government. Therefore, these proposals for civil service reform violated the republican principle—"the great fundamental spirit"—contained in the Constitution. He deemed the attempt to establish a civil service to be "the biggest scheme to bind the people of this country hand and foot since the day when the Parliament of Great Britain declared the right to bind the colonies in all cases whatsoever."[46]

The next day, Matthew Carpenter denounced the idea of competitive examinations in a speech that was far more measured but nevertheless invoked similar constitutional principles. Carpenter suggested that in embracing the proposals of the civil service commission, President Grant "has surrendered principles which the people, when they come to reflect upon the subject, will determine ought to be maintained."[47] Carpenter's argument rested on separation of powers grounds as well as on republican principles. He argued, "The great principle upon which our Government rests, the philosophy which supports all free institutions, is that the powers of sovereignty should be so distributed among different officers and bodies that each department shall operate as a check upon all the others."[48] Carpenter argued that the Framers' solution was to ensure that "[o]f the three departments of our government the executive is by far the weakest."[49] "The great predominant power of the government is," by contrast, "as it should be, the legislative department."[50] The primary power retained by the president in the American system, Carpenter maintained, was the patronage power. In fact, the power of appointment "is the only power of the presidential office which connects the President with the people. . . . Take this away, and the President is only the high constable of the Republic, and practically as powerless as the constable of a ward in Milwaukee."[51] To take this last remaining power from the executive, which is already the weakest branch of the government, would disrupt the separation of powers and substantially undermine the president's role in upholding the separation of powers. "The Constitution imposes upon the President the responsibility, and confers upon him the influence and strength which result from the power to nominate," Carpenter concluded, and it is essential to the separation of powers to preserve this constitutional power.[52]

These objections from the early 1870s were similarly invoked during the debates on the Pendleton Act itself during the early 1880s. Of course, some of the opposition was based on purely political considerations rather than constitutional principles. Although Pendleton, a Democrat, sponsored the legislation, the Act was largely supported by Republicans and largely opposed by Democrats. This has led some to conclude that the Congress voted largely on political grounds—the Republicans wanted to entrench their own political appointees and exempt them from future presidents' control, while the Democrats wanted to retain patronage in order to oust the Republican appointees when they finally gained the reins of power. Some legislators noted this motivation, particularly Senator Joseph Brown from Georgia, who moved to call the measure "a bill to perpetuate in office the Republicans who now control the patronage of the government."[53]

Despite the many objections to the Pendleton Act on obvious short-term political concerns, some legislators objected to the establishment of the civil service on the same, principled grounds that were expressed in the early 1870s: republicanism and the separation of powers. As Senator John McPherson, a Democrat from New Jersey, argued, "I can not consent by any vote of mine that a legislative commission shall be appointed, irresponsible to the people, irresponsible in themselves, responsible to no power whatever, and give them all the authority necessary to determine what shall be done in respect to certain offices in this government."[54] The central issue for Senator McPherson was the principled concern that an "irresponsible" commission could have the authority to determine how offices should be filled and how officers would be continued in office. It was the lack of responsibility to the people that motivated McPherson to oppose the Pendleton Act.

Daniel Voorhees, Senator from Indiana, invoked the same principles in his opposition to the Pendleton Act. Like McPherson, and like Snapp and Carpenter a decade earlier, Voorhees rested on the principle of republicanism. He argued:

> This is a people's government, a representative government. We are sent here by the people who own this Government. . . . I am not ready to say that the people who pay the taxes, till the soil, do the work and the voting, shall not have the ear of their representatives and access to their presence anywhere and everywhere. A different system is growing up here to that in the days of our fathers. The sooner we return to the old principle that we are the servants of the people and not their masters, the better it will be for us and this country.[55]

Voorhees claimed that the establishment of appointment by competitive examination was fundamentally contrary to the nature of representative government. Representatives are sent by the people to represent their interests, and they are accountable to the people. Establishing officers who hold their positions by examinations contravenes this principle.

Thus, beginning in the early 1870s, opponents of the system of competitive examinations for filling offices made a constitutional case that such a system is anti-republican and erodes the accountability of government to the people. It is important to understand the passage of the Pendleton Act in this light, because it illustrates why the Pendleton Act's application was so narrow, and that the support for the Pendleton Act was not based on an embrace of a modern technocratic administrative state but, rather, a negative reaction to the abuses of the spoils system. The Pendleton Act's limited scope and effect were a product of the fact that its proponents envisioned it as a reaction to the spoils system rather than a revolutionary step in a different direction.

The Limited Justification and Effect of the Pendleton Act

Though many commentators take the passage of the Pendleton Act as one of the foundations of the modern administrative state, this must be qualified. The Pendleton Act may have enabled the eventual emergence of the scientific bureaucracy that is called for by progressivism, but this scientific bureaucracy was likely not the intention of those who passed the Act. In other words, the Pendleton Act did not launch the administrative state; it merely attempted to end the corruption of the patronage system. As Stephen Skowronek has argued, "the very concept of a merit *system* overstates the achievement of reform in these years. Between 1877 and 1900, the merit service as a whole failed to gain internal coherence or to establish its integrity within the federal government."[56] Rather, in his words, "The merit system was born a bastard in the party state. . . . The status of a merit civil service in the heyday of American party government remained uncertain at best."[57]

The goal of ending the spoils system is not peculiar to progressivism, and it is not necessarily indicative of progressive reform. In fact, it was rooted in the practices of the early republic. At least some of the members of the Congress were cognizant of this. Lyman Trumbull, Republican Senator from Illinois and one of the leaders of the reform movement, explicitly connected his aim with the practice of the early republic. After noting that Washington removed only nine officials in his two terms, John Adams removed only ten, and even Jefferson removed only thirty-nine, Trumbull excoriated Andrew Jackson for introducing the spoils system "which has poisoned our civil service system." Trumbull then quoted Henry Clay in the early 1830s, arguing that the patronage system "is a detestable system drawn from the worst periods of the Roman republic." For Trumbull, the idea of civil service reform was entirely consistent with the design of the founders, and the patronage system was a *departure* from the administrative policies of the early presidents.

Trumbull was quick to state that, despite his support of civil service reform, he was "not opposed to party organizations. . . . A political organization for the purpose of carrying out measures, I believe to be right and proper. I go further than that: I believe that when a political organization thus formed succeeds to power in the Government, it should make use of instrumentalities in harmony with it to carry out the great measures on which it was elected as to high officials vested with discretionary powers." However, he continued, "in the subordinate offices, where the duties are merely ministerial, there is no particular importance in a man's political affiliations."[58] In other words, Trumbull's argument in favor of the Pendleton Act was hardly the stuff of progressivism or the famous distinction between politics and administration advanced by Woodrow Wilson and Frank Goodnow. Those arguments, as the next chapter argues, came after the turn of the century. Trumbull merely argued that certain "ministerial" positions could be carried out by persons of any party. Any position with real discretionary power to make policy, he granted, should be controlled by a party organization using its instrumentalities to carry out its objectives. Trumbull and other supporters of civil service reform agreed that political parties are needed to organize and mobilize public opinion in support of political movements in a republican society. They were not seeking to eliminate the influence of parties, but to eliminate their worst abuses. Furthermore, Trumbull rightly noted that many of the early presidents, revered founders of the republic, operated under the same presumption in their approach to removals. One could reconcile this position with the Constitution's appointment clauses by simply noting that those who fill such ministerial positions are not "officers" covered by those clauses.

Supporters of civil service reform were not aiming to create a European-style impartial civil service. Senator Pendleton himself invoked the authority of Thomas Jefferson during the debates on the Pendleton Act: "Fidelity, capacity, honesty were the tests established by Mr. Jefferson when he assumed the reins of government in 1801." Pendleton argued that he was merely continuing the Jeffersonian tradition: "these elements were necessary to an honest civil service, and . . . an honest civil service was essential to the purity and efficiency of administration, necessary to the *preservation of republican institutions.*"[59] Pendleton referred to the preservation of republicanism as the chief goal of civil service reform. By eradicating the evils and abuses of the spoils system, republicanism could be improved, not circumvented. Pendleton and other supporters' arguments in favor of the Pendleton Act invoked traditional American principles rather than showing contempt for them.[60] Thus, both the opponents and the supporters of the Pendleton Act were animated

by their understanding of the requirements of republicanism. Even the supporters of civil service reform were not seeking to undermine traditional understandings of American constitutionalism in order to establish a modern
bureaucracy.

Accordingly, the immediate effect of the Pendleton Act was minimal. As
scholars are often quick to note, the Pendleton Act did not apply to most
federal civil officials until well after it was passed. In the beginning of 1884
only 11 percent of the executive civil service was covered by the new system,
and the positions were clerkships in various federal departments like the Post
Office and Treasury.[61] This avoided the constitutional question whether these
positions would be appointed in a manner inconsistent with the Constitution's process for appointing inferior officers, since clerical staff in agencies
could be considered support staff or employees but not "officers" of the United States wielding decision-making authority for an agency. The Act empowered subsequent presidents to determine how far the merit system would
extend by issuing executive orders. Thus, the Pendleton Act's protections initially eliminated a small fraction of the federal workforce from the republican
process of election and appointment, and those jobs that were removed were
arguably not within the constitutional definition of even inferior officers.

Significantly, the original Act's provisions limiting the president's power
to remove administrative officials were struck from the final legislation after constitutional objections were raised. Senator Warner Miller of New York
stated explicitly that the Pendleton Act "instead of creating a life tenure, leaves
it entirely within the power of the president or of the Secretaries or heads of
Departments to remove officers even at will."[62] The positions filled under the
new examination system could still be placed under the authority of political
officials such as the president through the exercise of the removal power. It
would hardly be consistent with the idea of a neutral, expert bureaucracy to
establish a system of competitive examinations but continue the practice of
removal at will by a political official.

In short, scholars are wrong to suggest that the Pendleton Act established
the progressive vision for the modern administrative state. Donald Moynihan has recently argued that the Pendleton Act resulted from an acceptance
of the basic tenets of progressivism: "By the time the Pendleton Act was
passed in 1883," he writes, "the need for competent administration became
clear. The spoils system had come under public attack for its perceived moral
and practical failings, and the parties accepted the need for the civil service
reforms championed by the Progressives," who "outlined the basic elements

of a new administrative doctrine, borrowed from European civil service systems."[63] The analysis of this chapter suggests this assessment is inaccurate.[64] The civil service reform movement may have opened the door for a modern, apolitical bureaucracy, but this was not on the minds of those who passed and supported the Act. As Paul Van Riper concludes, "the passage of the Pendleton Act of 1883 represented the *adaptation* of a British political invention to the constitutional and administrative needs of the United States."[65] The key word is *"adaptation"*—the Pendleton Act did not merely copy existing European merit systems but modified the system to conform to American constitutional principles. It "reflected the peculiarities of the American Constitution as well as those of the political tendencies of the times."[66] It was not the beginning of the administrative state's personnel reforms, which was to occur years later.[67]

The ICC and the Question of Bureaucracy

Just as the passage of the Pendleton Act appears in hindsight to mark the inception of a modern bureaucracy but appears on closer inspection to spring from very different ideas than those of the progressives, the passage of the Interstate Commerce Act did not mark the inception of the independent regulatory commission. Many scholars peg the beginning of the administrative state to the passage of the Act and the Interstate Commerce Commission, which it created. Cass Suntein's *After the Rights Revolution* lumps the passage of the Interstate Commerce Act in with the creation of the Federal Reserve in 1913 and the Federal Trade Commission in 1914. During this "pre–New Deal period . . . the country embarked for the first time on the large-scale development of a national bureaucracy."[68] Robert Rabin claims that "when Congress established the Interstate Commerce Commission, it initiated a new epoch in responsibilities of the federal government . . . regulation of the [railroad] industry was committed to an institutional mechanism that was virtually untested on the national stage, an independent regulatory commission. The modern age of administrative government had begun."[69] Both of these arguments, by prominent legal scholars, tell a story about the administrative state that begins with the creation of the ICC.

Since the ICC is the first significant federal administrative commission in American history, there is a surface plausibility to this idea. However, the debates surrounding the creation of the ICC, and the powers eventually granted to it, indicate that the authors of the Act were not intending to create a new administrative state based on progressive principles.

The Creation of the ICC and the Issue of First Principles

The railroad question was an extension of political battles over internal improvements subsidized by the federal government. With the advent of this new technology the focus shifted from roads and canals to rails. In this area, the only constitutional method for subsidizing transportation projects was for the government to grant federally owned land for the construction of railroad lines. In 1850 the government granted land to construct a railroad from the Gulf Coast to Illinois. The subsidy was defended on the grounds that it would increase the value of surrounding federally owned land, thus serving as an investment to improve the government's overall portfolio.[70]

Many of the problems caused by the expansion of the railroads, arguably, were therefore produced by flawed government policies. According to many observers, the overbuilding of railroad lines created a market failure that promoted inefficient competition.[71] As railroad transportation replaced wagons and steamboats, local markets were transformed into regional and national markets. In these new market conditions, the availability and the price of rail service were crucial to success. But long hauls could be completed along several different paths, resulting in cutthroat competition for long hauls where shippers had many alternatives from which to choose. This competition reduced charges for long hauls essentially to the level of cost. In many cases the cost of long hauls was reduced below short-haul costs, especially due to the minimal marginal cost of long hauls (i.e., due to the significant initial investment required for railroad construction, most railroad costs were fixed costs as opposed to marginal costs). In short, competition drove many competitors to cut prices below the level needed to repay creditors whose capital helped establish the enterprise in the first place. In this environment, many companies became insolvent and were placed into receivership, exacerbating the situation, since these companies did not have to pay a return on their own fixed capital costs.

To make a decent return in such conditions, many firms resorted to rate discrimination (offering a lower rate to some customers), sometimes through drawbacks and rebates to large-scale shippers as opposed to small farmers. In many cases short hauls (where competition was less severe) were priced higher than longer hauls. A second option was "pooling," where competitors would merge to minimize the destructive effects of such competition. These regional associations would require a uniform rate (higher than what the market would dictate) and would monitor all firms to ensure compliance, but evasion was common.

These issues—rate discrimination, pooling, and combination—were the primary targets of the Interstate Commerce Act. Prior to 1887, state commissions had been established to deal with emerging issues of railroad regulation. Different states established different types of commissions with different powers.[72] One type, found in Connecticut, New Hampshire, and Vermont, was empowered merely to inspect railroad accounts and report findings to the state legislature, thus separating the functions of inspection and legislation. Another type, found in Massachusetts and New York, was empowered to hear complaints as a sort of adjudicatory tribunal, but did not have authority to enforce its decisions. A third type, found in California, Alabama, and Iowa, had the full array of regulatory powers, including rate-setting powers. As might be expected, Eastern states tended to give less authority to railroad commissions than states further west, where the Granger movement was powerful.[73]

For twenty years Congress had considered national legislation to deal with the railroad issue: "Between 1868 and 1886 more than 150 bills were introduced in Congress providing for some variety of federal control over railroads."[74] The first bill to pass either chamber of Congress, the McCrary bill of 1874, would have "utilized common law principles as a basis of railroad regulation."[75] This approach, to rely on the common law rather than novel institutional arrangements, was consistently advanced by the House of Representatives, controlled by Democrats led by "Judge" John Reagan of Texas. Reagan was an ardent populist and in many respects a predecessor to William Jennings Bryan and Woodrow Wilson's New Freedom. True to their Jacksonian roots and distrustful of both big business and big government, the "Reaganites" believed that the best solution was not to legitimize corporate power by putting a commission in control of it, but to strike at its roots by outlawing certain practices and letting the courts enforce the law.

Reagan introduced a bill to regulate railroads without a commission every year from 1878 to 1886. His proposals simply forbade discriminations and rebates and contained a strong anti-pooling prohibition. In other words, they clearly outlined what was forbidden and imposed strict penalties for violating the law. The courts would remain in charge of adjudication.[76] Only by outlawing specified practices and enforcing the law across the board, the Reaganites believed, could the corrupt practices of the railroads be rooted out.

Ambiguity in the law, by contrast, would allow a regulatory commission to adjust the law, which was tantamount to enervating it. For instance, the Cullom bill of 1883 (introduced by Senator Shelby Cullom, of Illinois) was much more open-ended. It "set up much more generally stated standards" governing railroads' conduct and gave the commission discretion to apply these open-ended prohibitions.[77] In the view of House Democrats, this discretion would render the law a dead letter in the hands of captured railroad commissioners. Creating a commission would result in half-measures as concentrated interests watered down the commission's activities.

On the other hand, Reaganites argued, establishing a commission would be *more* radical than their own proposal because it would take the country into uncharted constitutional territory. The commission "would be far away in Washington, unlike the courts, which were close to the people and familiar to them."[78] Unlike the courts of common law, which were the House's enforcement mechanism, the commission would be an alien institution. The awesome discretion committed to the commission alarmed many opponents, who wanted to keep the commission as a merely executive body, one that merely carried out relatively clear and explicit regulations contained in a statute. As Representative Charles Grosvenor of Ohio argued, the commissioners "are to have more power than has the President of the United States—more power for evil or good than has the Congress of the United States."[79] James Campbell of Ohio claimed that:

> The absurdity consists in describing an offense, forbidding its practice, decreeing its punishment, and then serenely permitting it to be committed with impunity by the consent of a commission. . . . Nothing like it has been known since the sale of indulgences. . . . If this principle is to be ingrafted upon our jurisprudence it would be next in order to establish a commission to modify or annul the Decalogue and prescribe upon what times certain favored persons might steal, covet, and commit other offenses prohibited in that fundamental moral law.[80]

Reaganites argued that the commission was a novelty not only in terms of the scope of its power but also in terms of the type of power that was to be granted. Some assumed that the commission was a court, and lambasted it for not conforming to traditional notions of how a court should be structured (no tenure during good behavior, no need to wait on a "case or controversy," and no guarantee of a jury trial, for instance). Others understood that the institution could not be categorized anywhere, but was sui generis.[81] This feature of the commission—the novelty of its quasi-judicial functions—caused several leaders to be critical of the extensive powers vested in the commission. Even Charles Francis Adams and Albert Fink argued against vesting coercive power in the commission. In their view, the commission's purpose should be to promote publicity and moral suasion rather than to exercise coercive legal power.

If given judicial power under a broad delegation of authority that would allow them to make the law while applying it, Fink argued, the commission would be "law-maker, judges, and sheriffs," something "not to be tolerated in a free country."[82] Adams favored the Massachusetts example, which by appealing to the public managed to regulate the railroads quite well. Massachusetts's railroad commission did not have to use coercion because it could appeal to the reason of the public, which would act in response.[83]

The debate in the House largely centered around Reagan's legislation and a substitute bill resembling Cullom's proposal (introduced in the Senate) which emerged from the House Committee on Interstate Commerce (often referred to in the debates as the "committee bill" or the "commission bill"). Cullom's proposed legislation, after it was amended by the Senate Committee on Railroads, would have established a five-member commission empowered to inspect the books of railroad companies, request the submission of annual reports by the railroads, and investigate cases of rate discrimination by railroads either by its own initiative or upon the filing of complaints. In the process of investigating rate discrimination, the commission would be empowered to summon witnesses, conduct hearings, and administer oaths. If the railroad company would not comply with the commission's decision, a U.S. attorney could bring suit against the company in federal court.

The two alternatives the Congress faced, then, were to establish a commission for publicity, investigation, and adjudication of rate discrimination claims, or to establish statutorily proscribed activities and task the courts with enforcement of statutory mandates. As Stephen Skowronek explains, the two measures pitted "the advocates of administrative management" against "the supporters of strict judicial surveillance. . . . One vision implied an administrative reconstruction of power; the other, a judicial consolidation of power."[84] The crucial differences between these options were understood by at least some of the members of the House. "The great difference" faced by the House, one member remarked, was that the Cullom plan assumed Congress was unable to establish "a complete code of railroad regulations." By contrast, the Reagan plan for codifying the proscribed activities assumed that the issues were "completely within [Congress's] grasp." Thus, the Reagan plan would "lay the mailed hand of political power upon the most complicated and sensitive business adjustments of modern times."[85] In other words, the Reagan bill would have made Congress the source of proscribed railroad activities, while the Cullom plan would entrust a commission to determine what would be illegal.

This was the crucial difference between the plans. During the congressional debates, Reaganites focused on the quasi-judicial nature of the proposed commission's powers. Democratic Senators Augustus Garland of Arkansas and Thomas Bayard of Delaware attacked the Cullom bill on the grounds that it vested judicial power outside of the judicial branch of government.[86] The most forceful condemnations came from Reagan, who proclaimed that Americans were "not accustomed to the administration of the civil law through bureau orders."[87] By contrast, as Poindexter Dunn, a Democratic supporter of the Reagan plan explained simply, all the Reagan bill attempted to do was "declare what is right and enforce it; declare what is wrong and prohibit it."[88] Dunn did not deny Congress's power of "that timely and wholesome control which will preserve the just right of all."[89] "Most certainly [the railroad companies] have rights," Dunn continued, "and it is not proposed by those who think as I do that any of these corporations shall lose one particle of their property or have any of their just rights impaired. But the people also have rights and powers, and hence the apparently impending conflict."[90] Though there may be a surface similarity, Dunn's suggestion that there was a conflict between the rights of the corporations and the rights of the public was not an expression of a modern approach to regulation, in which the public interest must override private interests. This issue—the use of property that affects the public interest—was a foundation of regulation from the first years of the American republic up to the 1880s when Dunn invoked it.[91] Dunn acknowledged that "the right of public control" of certain corporations "is a well-settled doctrine of the law." According to this doctrine, "whoever invests his money in any business affected with a public interest thereby agrees to accept public control and regulation of that business. No principle of the law is more definitely settled."[92] Furthermore, as Reagan noted, the railroad corporations derived their charters from grants of the state legislatures. In this sense they resembled other common carriers and corporations such as banks, which from the very beginning of the republic were regulated through the granting of specific charters.[93] The issue for Reagan, Dunn, and others was not the regulation of railroads in the first place, but how the regulation was to be crafted and who would be doing the regulating.

Therefore, like many of the advocates of the Reagan plan, Dunn believed that federal regulation of railroad corporations was legitimate; but the creation of a commission to do the job confronted insuperable objections. He expressed "the opinion that the bill of the committee *with all the provisions for a commission stricken out* would be the wisest step to take."[94] The reason Dunn preferred this course—of proceeding without a commission for regulating railroads—was that it "seeks first to declare certain rights, and also to declare certain things to be wrong. It seeks to enforce those rights and prohibit those wrongs. That is, perhaps, as far as legislation ought to go."[95] The best legisla-tion, in this view, does not delegate lawmaking discretion to commissions but merely establishes the law clearly in its own terms.

Dunn went on to state the crux of his opposition to the concept of a commission:

> I believe that the correct principle in government was asserted when the courts, state and national, were ordained and created to enforce rights and prohibit wrong. . . . If we have come upon a time when any law that we enact declaring rights and prohibiting wrongs can not be administered through their agency, then indeed have we reached the end of free government. . . . I will never give my consent in this country to place any body of men, any commission, between the suitor and the court in which his rights are to be adjudicated. No man, no set of men shall ever, with my consent, stand between the citizen and justice, and hold the power to say whether his rights shall be adjudicated or not. Let no petty autocrat stand between the citizen and justice.[96]

The commission, Dunn argued, would be a violation of constitutional prin-ciples because it would replace judicial justice, administered in courts, with commission-style justice. The power of adjudication would be possessed not by courts, implementing a law that clearly outlined what was proscribed, but by commissioners who would "stand between the citizen and justice."

Dunn's objection was echoed by Reagan. Reagan claimed that "The greatest defect in the committee's bill is that for many injuries to individuals it does not give an adequate legal or equitable remedy, but refers such matters to a rail-road commission which is to determine questions between the wrong-doing railroad companies and the Government, while in many cases no remedy is provided for wrongs done to individual citizens."[97] Reagan believed that the use of a commission was a fundamental defect, because it transformed private injustices between individuals into public injustices against the state, and in doing so transferred the authority to deal with these injustices to this new kind of institution. The proper alternative in Reagan's view was to establish "complete legal and equitable remedy without delay through the ordinary courts of the country."[98] The alternatives thus advanced by House members such as John Reagan and Poindexter Dunn did not seek to prevent regulation of railroad corporations, but to use legislatures and courts rather than commis-sions to deal with abuses.

In response to these challenges, supporters of the commission bill in the House clarified that the commission would only have limited powers and would not have legislative or judicial powers. Most of the powers would be investigatory in nature: "to examine into every complaint, to cause the production of books and papers, and thus to get at all the facts surrounding each and every transaction."[99] James Hopkins, Democrat from Pennsylvania, concurred with this assessment of the powers proposed to be granted to the ICC: "The clauses in this bill creating a commission and prescribing its power and functions are, as I understand it, merely auxiliary to the general purpose. The rights and remedies of individuals can not be impaired by the commission."[100] Another member, putting it more colorfully, concluded, "If this is not an ornamental board, and of as little use as the fifth wheel in a wagon, I have been unable to understand any of the provisions of this bill."[101] In short, even supporters of a commission believed that the Interstate Commerce Act was not creating a powerful administrative bureaucracy, and that the commission established would not be a leviathan.[102]

The passage of the Interstate Commerce Act, viewed in this light, cannot be understood as a deliberate embrace of a progressive-style administrative bureaucracy. Rather, it was a cautious reform aimed at providing for expertise in investigating abuses, without doing damage to established constitutional principles. As a result of the congressional debates and expert testimony from figures such as Fink and Adams, Hiroshi Okayama has noted, supporters of the commission "had to be careful in determining the amount of authority it would have and how it would operate so as not to infringe the judicial power."[103] The final legislation that established the ICC possessed quasi-judicial authority not *in spite of* constitutional concerns, but *because* of those concerns.[104] Several crucial features of the ICC resulted from these constitutional concerns:

- Section 9 of the Act clarified that the law did not disturb the right to bring a suit at common law. Rather than bringing a dispute to the ICC for decision, parties could take their case directly to the courts through the common law. Complainants were required to choose one enforcement method or the other.[105]
- The ICC had no enforcement power to back its decisions. Section 16 clarified that the commission could merely ask the appropriate U.S. Attorney to file suit in the courts of law to enforce its decisions. Section 14 announced that the ICC's determinations would be prima facie evidence in courts of law (i.e., courts would assume them to be correct unless refuted).

- The Act forbade certain practices, such as rate discrimination, rebating, pooling, unjust and unreasonable rates. However, it did not grant the ICC the power to set railroad rates. The Commission could merely declare, in response to complaints properly filed, find certain specific rates to be unjust and unreasonable. Thus, the Commission's rate power was not generalized and prospective (like a legislative power) but specific and reactive (like a judicial power). While this was not explicitly clarified in the law, the Commission itself interpreted the just and reasonable rate provision in this manner.

These adjustments carefully constructed the commission's powers so that Cullom and others could call them "quasi-judicial" rather than actually judicial. Cullom claimed that the commission possessed "a quasi power of arbitration" and noted that it lacked "any absolute power whatever so far as the finality of any finding that they may make."[106] Senator Orville Platt of Connecticut similarly stressed that the legislation was "carefully drawn so as to avoid the exercise of judicial powers by these commissioners, so as to deprive it of any constitutional objection."[107] And it was in this context, importantly, that the power of publicity and moral persuasion rather than legal coercion re-emerged as central to the ICC's purpose. Echoing the concerns of Fink and Adams, John Sherman of Ohio argued that the commission's strength would come not from legal authority but from the "moral power of the people of the United States," and that therefore there would be no "occasion to invoke the aid of a court."[108] Even this quasi-judicial power would not need to be invoked if the primary authority of the commission was moral rather than legal. These limits indicate the extent to which the ICC was deliberately shaped to conform to constitutional norms, rather than the extent to which the ICC crossed a constitutional Rubicon, taking the first step towards the modern administrative state. It was hoped that the ICC would work alongside the judicial system, not in place of the judicial system, in remedying some of the most egregious abuses practiced by the railroads. This aim was entrusted to Thomas Cooley, chosen by President Cleveland to serve as the first chairperson of the commission.

Cooley and the Ambiguity of "Constitutional Limitations"
That the ICC was not a radical step towards a new, modern administrative state is exhibited by the important fact that the ICC was not at its inception an independent commission. As Marc Allen Eisner notes, "the ICC was not independent, nor had Congress intended to give it complete independence.

Indeed, in the legislative debates there was no discussion of the commission's independence" from political influence.[109] For the first few years after its creation, the Interstate Commerce Commission was located in the Interior Department and operated under the supervision of the Secretary of the Interior. Two years after its creation, at the request of the secretary, it was granted independence from the Department of the Interior. The decision to insulate the ICC from political control was not the result of progressive thought but was "largely a historical accident. Congressman John Reagan . . . feared that President Benjamin Harrison, a former railroad attorney, would use his control of the Department of the Interior to undermine railroad regulation."[110] The removal of the ICC from political supervision was not the result of an acceptance of the theoretical distinction between politics and administration, such as is found in Woodrow Wilson or Frank Goodnow. Rather, it was the predictable result of normal political struggle. Reagan, the great opponent of bureaucracy in the debate over the Interstate Commerce Act, was the prime mover in establishing the independence of the commission from a Republican president.

Furthermore, as the debate over the creation of the ICC amply demonstrates, those who favored the commission were not deliberately choosing a progressive-style independent regulatory commission. As Eisner further explains, "the mixture of legislative, executive, and judicial powers that makes the independent commission so novel was a product of institutional evolution driven by conflict. The debates surrounding the passage of the Interstate Commerce Act revealed little concern with the precise nature of the delegated powers, although there was some speculation as to whether the ICC would be given legislative and judicial powers." The deliberate acceptance of a true independent regulatory commission, combining all the powers of government, did not come with the ICC but, rather, occurred much later, as Chapter Five will discuss.

In accordance with this picture of the creation of the administrative state, the original ICC was weak in comparison to modern agencies. The commission had the powers to gather data and conduct investigations on railroad abuses. It also required railroads to file annual reports with the commission, and gave the ICC subpoena power to monitor the structure and management of the railroads. The commission was finally empowered to issue cease and desist orders when its investigations revealed that a complaint was legitimate. But the courts were still required to enforce cease and desist orders by injunction, and the courts reviewed the commission's factual as well as legal determinations. Thus, the reviewing courts essentially tried all ICC-related cases de novo, as if they originated in the judicial branch. As Thomas Merrill notes, the provision establishing ICC findings "prima facie evidence" in judicial proceedings did not establish judicial deference to the ICC. Rather, "the inference ran in the opposite direction. By making ICC findings only prima facie evidence, the Act was read as endorsing the practice of taking additional evidence in court and having the court determine whether the prime facie evidence had been rebutted."[111] The end result of the Interstate Commerce Act, in short, was a weakened ICC and a substantial role for the courts—much like the opponents of the Act preferred.

The one substantial lawmaking power that the ICC may have claimed under the Act—the power to set maximum railroad rates—was only ambiguously granted by the Act. The Act required that railroad rates be "reasonable and just." Although this appears to be an open-ended grant of discretion, however, the phrase "reasonable and just" had a well-defined meaning in law that constrained the discretion of implementing agencies and courts. Thus, it was not an open-ended delegation of power to the agency, as it often appears today to be. Furthermore, the statutory requirement that railroad rates be reasonable and just did not specify that the commission was to establish rates in advance. Rather, the commission recognized that it could only declare specific rates to be unreasonable in response to specific complaints, and that it was ultimately a judicial determination whether a rate was reasonable. Therefore, judicial review of the commission's rate determinations would be available.[112]

The novelty, and ambiguity, of the Interstate Commerce Commission meant that the decisions of the commission in its first years would both be highly scrutinized and carry precedential significance. When Thomas Cooley, widely known as a defender of limited government and economic liberty, was appointed to the commission and accepted the post, this ensured that the initial years of the commission's work would be entrusted to someone with a keen understanding of the legal and constitutional, as well as the economic issues, surrounding railroad regulation. Cooley's administration of the ICC was an important episode in the development of modern administration.

Cooley is known today primarily as the author of the legal treatise known by its shorthand name *Constitutional Limitations* (originally published in 1868). As its name implies, Cooley's treatise was largely concerned with the constitutional limits on government power. As a result, he is considered by most scholars today as a powerful exponent of laissez-faire constitutionalism, a movement which increasingly gained traction in the post–Civil War period.

Yet Cooley's role with the ICC introduces an obvious dilemma. Why would a chief advocate of laissez-faire head up the first major federal regulatory commission? Cooley's leadership of the ICC in its early years produced mixed and ambiguous results. Many of his decisions reflected a sincere concern for constitutional principles and a desire to keep the commission within the bounds of constitutional authority. In other respects he pushed the boundaries of the agency's authority aggressively.

Born in the midst of the transition to the Jacksonian era, Cooley carried fundamental tenets of Jacksonian thought with him throughout his political and legal career. Alan Jones has argued that Cooley "approached the administrative task of implementing the Interstate Commerce Act with values and beliefs which had their source in the Jacksonian persuasion of the first three decades of his life."[113] This Jacksonian tradition in legal thought emphasized equal rights for all and special privileges for none.[114] Central to this philosophy was opposition to regulation that appeared to promote one class of interests over another. According to this tradition, free market or laissez-faire thought was connected not to ideas of natural law but to the idea of political neutrality and a fear of government power that would promote inequality by granting artificial advantages. As John Rohr explains, "Unlike the framers of the Constitution, Cooley did not hold a theory of natural rights. Indeed, he explicitly rejected this theory in his treatise on torts and adhered instead to the view that rights were created by law through history."[115] Cooley adhered to the theory of equal rights, not the theory of natural rights.

The core of Cooley's opposition to certain forms of regulation, in short, was a Jacksonian fear of special interest legislation that would result from government interventions that established monopoly or monopoly-like advantages for certain economic actors. One significant illustration of Cooley's Jacksonian philosophy comes from perhaps his most famous opinion as Chief Justice of the Michigan Supreme Court, in which he declared a Michigan statute unconstitutional because it used the state's taxing power to subsidize railroads, which he argued was the use of a public power for private purposes. In that opinion Cooley declared: "The state can have no favorites. Its business is to protect the industry of all, and to give all the benefit of equal laws." He continued, "when the State once enters upon the business of subsidies, we shall not fail to discover that the strong and powerful interests are those most likely to control legislation, and that the weaker will be taxed to enhance the profits of the stronger."[116]

This vision of "neutral" regulatory policy led Cooley to transform his ideas about regulation after the Civil War, as industrialization and new modes of transportation changed economic conditions dramatically. Under these new conditions, laborers and small shippers such as farmers were (in Cooley's view) no longer autonomous and self-sufficient. By the late nineteenth century, new conditions made them much more dependent on circumstances beyond their control. In these new circumstances, the Jacksonian emphasis on neutrality and equality might require positive government interventions to equalize the power of those whose autonomy and independence were threatened by new conditions. After the Civil War, as laborers agitated for new economic policies, Cooley sympathized with the laborers' cause, though he condemned some leaders' violent tactics.[117]

Cooley's evolving economic and policy views reflected an ongoing ambivalence about corporate power, in line with his Jacksonian sentiments. However, they also reflected new influences, namely, those from progressive academics surrounding him in Ann Arbor, where Cooley lived from the Civil War to the mid-1880s. Cooley became a law professor at the University of Michigan in 1859, and in 1864 he was elected to the Supreme Court of Michigan, where he served as Chief Justice from 1864 to 1885. In this academic community that was to become a hotbed of progressivism, Cooley slowly gravitated towards German historicism. While in Ann Arbor Cooley became close associates of Andrew Dickson White and Charles Kendall Adams, two men who were trained in German universities and believed strongly in the historical approach to law and politics.[118] Both the Jacksonian and progressive influences on Cooley's thought gave rise to Cooley's increasing concern about labor relations and corporate power while America was industrializing. In his lectures at the University of Michigan he denounced the "financial tricks of Wall Street" and called the practice of special grant and subsidy to railroads "illegitimate," "unjust," and "corrupt."[119] He was vocal about the legitimacy of labor interests and the moral duties that corporations must fulfill. This led him to the conclusion, like Charles Francis Adams and others, that the best method for regulating the railroads was one based on moral persuasion and publicity.[120] Thus, while Cooley was a believer in the need for regulation he retained his Jacksonian hesitation about the potential for government intervention to become a tool for the powerful to dominate the weak.

Cooley's views on the question of railroad regulation were generally viewed as balanced. He was not hostile to regulation now that the nation had industrialized, but he was still a constitutional conservative. His *Constitutional Limitations* had earned him a national reputation as a defender of limited government, yet his openness to regulation was apparent to scholars and jurists who knew him well. He wrote a response to the *Munn v. Illinois* decision upholding regulation of property "affected with a public interest" in which he denied that an unlimited police power was compatible with free government.[121] Yet a few years later he also published an article explicitly supporting state legislation upon excessive business profits.[122] Whether this balance was due to nuance or inconsistency in principle was irrelevant; it made Cooley a choice acceptable to multiple parties and interests. Thus when he was appointed to the ICC by President Grover Cleveland, "[h]is appointment was recognized universally as an eminently fit one, and both railroad managers and the public felt secure."[123]

As the ICC's first chairperson, Cooley was no stand-patter. He actively pursued the ICC's mission and even expanded it beyond its governing statute in important ways. This posture was easily foreseeable. Not only had he indicated a willingness to exercise regulatory power over railroads as explained above, he also presented his views on federal regulation of railroads in response to the Cullom committee's request during the 1886 congressional debates. Cooley stated that a railroad commission "would neither be unphilosophical nor out of accord with the general spirit of our institutions," if it were constructed in a specific manner with certain specific powers. Prior to receiving his appointment Cooley responded to a reporter that an "able and conservative" commission could "accomplish much good and remedy some serious abuses."[124]

In many respects Cooley pushed the commission's authority to its outer limits—and perhaps beyond them. Three decisions indicate Cooley's expansion of the ICC's power. First, in the second year of the ICC's existence a disturbing railroad strike occurred involving the Burlington railroad, which drastically affected all railroad traffic in Chicago. The ICC had no direct authority to investigate, adjudicate, or intervene generally in labor disputes involving railroads. Yet Cooley contemplated intervening and attempted to persuade the other commissioners to take action. He confided to his wife that he believed the commission could act whenever any labor dispute involving railroads threatened interstate commerce.[125] An episode of poor health cut Cooley's efforts short, yet when he regained health he managed to persuade his fellow commissioners into supporting a request to both sides in the dispute to submit the facts of the dispute (as they respectively framed them) to the commission.

John Rohr cites this action as evidence that Cooley sought an aggressive expansion of the commission's powers, and certainly he is correct that Cooley was relying on a power about which the commission's statute was entirely silent.[126] Yet the power to investigate a labor dispute, for which Cooley advocated, says nothing about the steps Cooley felt empowered to take once all of the facts were laid bare. If anything, such a power would conform nicely to the emphasis that Cooley and others placed on the non-coercive powers that the commission ought to wield, rather than legal coercion. Other decisions by Cooley (discussed below) reinforced his emphasis on publicity and moral influence rather than legal coercion as head of the ICC.

Second, the issue of Due Process hung ominously over the commission in its early years. As is well known, by the end of the nineteenth century some courts had invoked the Fifth Amendment to limit the acceptable range of powers and procedures that could be employed by the federal government. The central question with regard to due process and the ICC was whether judicial process alone could satisfy the requirements of the Due Process clause. That is, the issue was whether procedures offered by the agency could suffice for due process. If only the courts could provide due process, then every regulatory decision rendered by the agency would simply be heard anew when appealed to the courts. Such an outcome, Cooley believed, would not only cripple regulation; it was based on a fundamental confusion about the procedural requirements associated with the rule of law. Cooley countered by insisting that administrative agencies could satisfy the requirements of due process, and that due process was not the same thing as judicial process. In rendering findings of fact, he asserted, the ICC was not deciding questions of law but merely applying the law to its facts, a practice that involved questions of administration rather than of law.

Although Cooley's response to the courts seems forceful and suggests a dangerous lack of checks and balances, it must be understood that Cooley sought to compensate for diminished judicial review by establishing thorough procedures for ICC determinations, going well beyond what was required by statute. Thus, while he consistently asserted that due process did not require judicial process, he also sought to establish regular procedures to ensure that the ICC followed the rule of law. Paul Carrington goes so far as to suggest that "Cooley's major contribution as chairman . . . [involved] the creation of an administrative style and process that would guide future national institutions."[127] Cooley proposed a conception of administrative due process, a set of protections that would afford affected parties notice and the opportunity to be heard in the agency's decision-making process, a formal record on which the agency's final decision must be based, and the opportunity to comment on agency actions. Thus, even while Cooley pushed back against those who insisted that administrative process could not satisfy due process, he also limited the discretion of his own agency by establishing regular procedures that would promote the rule of law.

Finally, although the Interstate Commerce Act only authorized the ICC to declare certain rates unjust and unreasonable, Cooley inferred an implied power to set just and reasonable rates. As earlier indicated, the first section of the Act established that "All charges made" by railroads for transporting or storing goods "shall be reasonable and just" and declared unlawful "every unjust and unreasonable charge." These phrases in the ICC's organic statute suggested a passive authority limited to apply this language in specific cases to certain rates, rather than a blanket authority to set rates prospectively. Cooley, however, found a power by implication to set reasonable rates in advance. In July of 1890, for example, the commission reduced grain rates on all railroads in the Midwest.[128]

This is probably the most difficult decision to square with Cooley's conservative approach to the ICC's authority. After all, the power to set rates has always been understood in American jurisprudence to be a rulemaking activity, rather than an adjudicatory function. In other words, by inferring a rulemaking power alongside a quasi-judicial power, Cooley arguably transformed the ICC into an institution that combined legislative, executive, and judicial functions. On the other hand, perhaps Cooley's expansion of the ICC's power to set rates positively can be justified under common-law principles, of which Cooley was fond.[129] In this light, the ICC was not setting rates for future cases so much as it was announcing principles that had emerged through the litigation of particular cases. However, Cooley did not attempt (as far as I am aware) to reconcile this interpretation with constitutional principles.

Just as these three decisions pushed the outer limits of the commission's power, Cooley also made several decisions as chairperson to keep the ICC within constitutional boundaries. The first involved perhaps the weightiest issue the commission was forced to confront in its early days regarding the regulation of long- and short-haul rates. Section 4 of the Interstate Commerce Act made it unlawful to charge more for a shorter rather than a longer distance over the same line "under substantially similar circumstances and conditions." Herein lied an ambiguity. What conditions would allow carriers to depart from the requirements of Section 4 and impose different rates?

Cooley addressed this issue head-on in an early decision with a clear and unambiguous interpretation of the "short-haul" clause that limited the ICC's discretion and gave clear guidance on the law's meaning to regulated entities. In essence, Cooley's opinion established that exceptions to the short-haul provision would only be granted on the basis that the short-hauls entailed a higher cost to the carrier, and that the burden of proof was on the railroads. Competition, in other words, would not entail sufficiently different circumstances and conditions allowing carriers to circumvent the requirements of Section 4. The most important aspect of this decision, however, as observers then and now have noted, is that Cooley sought clarity and predictability by constraining the discretion of his agency. As Carrington concludes, "Cooley's approach was a self-limitation of administrative discretion making his administrative *law* indeed law in the conventional sense."[130] Such an approach to administrative discretion was radically different from the approach of New Deal–era practitioners such as James Landis, "all of whom argued in favor of broad administrative discretion in the exercise of economic regulation."[131] Cooley therefore sought to establish a model of administrative practice that would limit agency discretion as much as possible rather than reserving unlimited discretion to executive tribunals.

A second decision Cooley made illustrated his refusal to transgress constitutional limitations even when an implied power to do so might be inferred. In its first year the commission was pressed to award damages to complainants who received a favorable initial decision by the ICC. In writing the ICC's first annual report Cooley maintained that Congress had not granted the power to award damages to the agency, and even if it did so, the Seventh Amendment's requirement of trial by jury in suits over twenty dollars would seem to forbid the practice. Soon after, Congress gave the ICC the power to award damages, but Cooley still refused to exercise the authority out of respect for his constitutional principles. In his last annual report before leaving the commission Cooley explained that in such cases "it was deemed proper to leave it for determination in the courts."[132]

This decision to avoid awarding damages is indicative of Cooley's most significant course of action as ICC chairperson, namely, his general focus on non-coercive methods of regulation. In addition to his hesitations regarding specific remedies such as awarding damages, Cooley eschewed the coercive approach more generally in his leadership of the commission. As he confided to his wife, "The less coercive power we have the greater, I think, will be our moral influence," and it was the ICC's moral influence that Cooley wished to deploy.[133] Cooley's view (at least in the commission's early years) was "of the Commission as educator of public sentiment, exercising moral influence rather than coercive power, insisting on equal rights for railroad property and the public."[134] As a result, Cooley focused more on the task of moral persuasion, particularly by speaking directly to railroad men and calling them to higher moral standards. As Carrington notes, "Cooley's preaching was not without effect. Even later critics have acknowledged that the Commission was at first relatively effective in securing voluntary compliance with its policies by many roads."[135] Both Cooley and Henry Carter Adams, the head of the ICC's statistical bureau, "believed that the method of administrative interpretation, public education, and statistical analysis was a better beginning approach to the railroad problem than one based on 'criminal procedure.'"[136] This approach emphasized voluntary compliance with moral standards rather than the use of coercive government power to regulate and control economic activity. Where another chairperson might have been tempted to expand his office's political and legal powers, Cooley was content to rely on the least coercive method that would prove effective.

Cooley's record as chairperson of the ICC, like his regulatory philosophy in the years prior to his leadership of the agency, exhibits a mixture of restraint and assertiveness. In some decisions Cooley carefully limited the agency's powers. In others he aggressively expanded them. Two of his most important decisions expanding the ICC's powers—the power to set rates and the ability to satisfy due process—brought Cooley into a direct confrontation with the Supreme Court. The Court pushed back against Cooley's decisions in an attempt to keep the commission within the limits of constitutional principles.

Cooley, the ICC, and the Court

If reformers had hopes that the Interstate Commerce Commission would become a harbinger for a new administrative state, the Supreme Court would leave them greatly frustrated over the first decade of the agency's existence. Cooley sought to substitute administrative process for the due process of law and to assert the agency's power to set rates prospectively rather than passively. The Court had a very different view of the agency's role in setting railroad policy.

In the commission's early years it ran into judicial decisions reserving the power to review administrative fact finding de novo, as well as decisions requiring reviewing courts to take original testimony upon appeal from ICC decisions. Because the commission had to go to court to secure injunctions to enforce its orders, the courts could allow for new evidence to be submitted by the railroads. This meant that railroads could save evidence for judicial proceedings, essentially turning the administrative proceeding into a useless production. In the first case appealed to the courts, a federal circuit judge refused to accept the ICC's findings of fact and ordered a complete review of all of the ICC's determinations.[137] In *ICC v. Alabama Midland Railway Co.* the Supreme Court upheld this practice of allowing the submission of new evidence.[138] In the course of the opinion the Court rejected the agency's argument that courts should grant deference to its factual determinations, asserting the power to review factual as well as legal determinations made by the ICC.[139] In dissent Justice Harlan predicted that the decision would "make that commission a useless body for all practical purposes."[140]

If the courts were allowed to review the agency's findings of fact de novo, it stood to reason that the judiciary could also employ this standard of review for the commission's interpretations of law. In the Import Rate case in 1896 the Court employed this standard of review in rejecting the commission's interpretation of the Interstate Commerce Act.[141] The commission had interpreted the Act's prohibition of "unjust discrimination" to protect American-made goods against competition from foreign goods by requiring rates that would equalize shipping costs for shipping American goods and European goods that had reached American ports. Railroads could not charge less for goods imported from Europe and shipped on the same route as domestic goods, in the commission's interpretation. Rejecting this interpretation of an ambiguous statutory mandate (prohibit "unjust discrimination"), the Court substituted its own interpretation allowing for reduced rates for imported goods.

The battle between the fledgling agency and the Supreme Court came to a head when the ICC exercised a prospective rate-setting power. In 1897 the Court decided the Maximum Rate case in which it declared that as a quasi-judicial and not a legislative body, the commission could only issue judgements about past rates rather than set prospective rates in the future.[142] This was an evisceration of even a limited rate-setting power, and it fundamentally crippled the agency. As Justice Harlan, again writing in dissent, argued, "Taken in connection with the other decisions defining the powers of the Interstate Commerce Commission, the present decision, it seems to me, goes far to make that commission a useless body for all practical purposes. . . . [I]t has been shorn, by judicial interpretation, of authority to do anything of an effective character."[143]

In this showdown between the ICC and the Supreme Court, Stephen Skowronek argues, "The consistent line . . . is the commission's struggle for authority over national railroad regulation."[144] Yet it was precisely this authority which the Court denied it. The constitutional opposition had moved from the legislative to the judicial branch, where it prevailed in the early years of the commission's existence. "In 1887, the ICC seemed an unpredictable institutional anomaly in the state of courts and parties; by 1900 it had become a mere irrelevance," Skowronek concludes.[145] It "had effected no change in the established mode of governmental operations or in the business conditions of the country."[146] As a result of the original weakness of the ICC, and the judicial decisions interpreting the Act narrowly, the ICC was "reduced . . . to a mere statistics-gathering agency. There was to be no redistribution of institutional power to the administrative realm," Skowronek writes.[147]

This fact was not lost on railroads and politicians, of course. Richard Olney, the attorney general under President Grover Cleveland, candidly wrote to a friend in the railroads that "The Commission, as its functions have now been limited by the courts, is, or can be made, of great use to the railroads. It satisfies the popular clamor for a government supervision of railroads, at the same time that the supervision is almost entirely nominal."[148] In short, the ICC was not intended to be, nor was it in its initial practice, a powerful independent regulatory commission in the progressive sense. While some attempted to transform the commission into a powerful new tool for national regulatory policymaking, Congress did not intend to grant it such powers, and it was forbidden by the judiciary from obtaining such powers.

Conclusion: A Constitutionalized Administration

What many scholars treat as the first steps towards the creation of a full-throated federal administrative state in America—the creation of the civil service and the first independent regulatory commission in the 1880s—appears on full investigation to be much more complicated. The creation of the ICC was not the result of an ascendant progressivism. Rather, in Marc Allen Eisner's words, "the policies of the period can be seen to have in common the use of the market as a benchmark."[149] This leads to a further question: is the federal administrative state, by necessity, a tool of progressivism? In other words, is it possible to have federal regulation, involving administrative agencies, without buying into the core principles of progressivism?

Many of those who were involved in the creation of regulatory programs during this early period were not committed progressives. Moreover, many of those who opposed the creation of modern federal agencies were not entirely opposed to all forms of federal regulation. They merely disagreed about the structural, institutional principles surrounding many of these agencies. This suggests the possibility that the modern administrative state does not present us with a binary choice: either federal regulation, with the administrative state, or no federal regulation at all. Rather, these debates at the birth of the administrative state reveal the possibility of a different kind of regulatory regime, one that allows for regulation at the federal level without the abandonment of cherished constitutional principles.

Gradually, as Chapter Six explains, Cooley's emphasis on moral persuasion and publicity gave way to a new regulatory approach at the ICC. Commentators today generally conclude that the ICC was weak and ineffectual in its early years, and only after the commission was salvaged by the progressives was it able to achieve lasting reforms. Yet many important contemporaries of Cooley saw matters differently. Perhaps most prominent was his close colleague Charles Francis Adams, who became dismayed with the direction of the ICC after 1900. As Thomas McCraw explains, "the growth of coercive regulation dismayed [Adams] deeply. As the Interstate Commerce Commission grew more powerful, less temperate in its judgments, and much more prejudiced against railroads in favor of shippers, Adams became increasingly querulous and irascible. Repeatedly he tried to explain why regulatory policy was going wrong in substituting the principle of coercion for that of simple exposure."[150] As the ICC moved in a new direction, so did the American administrative state. Some elements of Cooley's example as the first chairperson of a modern regulatory agency remain prominent, most notably the emphasis on administrative procedure. But most have receded into history, as the following chapter will describe.

CHAPTER FIVE

A New Science of Administration

Progressivism and the Administrative State

In 1900, the state of administrative law had remained relatively static for over a century. Some significant changes had occurred during the Jacksonian era, and the national government had established small pockets of independent administration. There were new institutions such as the Interstate Commerce Commission, but they were not as revolutionary as they might appear at first glance. The courts exercised a modest degree of judicial review, particularly through common-law actions and when questions of legal interpretation arose. But a new, modern, administrative state had not emerged.

To illustrate, it is noteworthy that three years after the Congress supposedly launched the inaugural modern regulatory agency, it passed the Sherman Antitrust Act, which provided for no independent administrative power at all. It merely contained a statutory provision declaring "every contract, combination in the form of trust or otherwise, or conspiracy, in restraint of trade or commerce" to be illegal. No commission was established to implement the law. Prosecutions were brought by the attorney general in the federal courts, which were charged with applying and interpreting the law to apply to particular cases. As Marc Eisner writes, "By casting competition policy as law enforcement, Congress gave the courts a central role in defining policy."[1]

A sea change in administrative law and American constitutionalism was on the horizon, however. In both parties, a budding progressive movement promised to establish a new arrangement of powers on a new theory of administration. Both theoretical and political developments conspired to set the country on this new trajectory in the first part of the twentieth century. By the 1930s, progressive reformers had set in motion many of the changes they hoped would bring a new science of administration to the nation. The first step in this process, they understood, was to construct new doctrines of judicial review that would prevent the judiciary from being meddlesome.

Those Meddlesome Courts

In the 1890s, while the Court was busy checking and curtailing the powers of the ICC (see Chapter Four), it was also invalidating a host of state regulatory laws on substantive due process grounds. In administrative law the federal courts had consistently reserved for themselves the power to receive new evidence and take new testimony once an ICC decision had been appealed to it. This made the original agency proceeding more of a formality, a prelude to the judicial proceeding where the full evidentiary record would be produced. In the overwhelming majority of cases where the ICC was reversed by federal courts they had considered new evidence that was not part of the record in the agency proceeding.[2]

Furthermore, as a result of the broad category of "equity" jurisdiction that had developed in the nineteenth century, buttressed by the 1875 grant of federal question jurisdiction to the federal courts, the judiciary continued to engage in relatively broad review of administrative action into the twentieth century.[3] In the famous case of *American School of Magnetic Healing v. McAnnulty* the Court allowed the School to sue a local postmaster to obtain judicial relief for an illegitimate order from the Postmaster General.[4] Justice Peckham, writing for the Court, declared that when "an official violates the law to the injury of an individual the courts generally have jurisdiction to grant relief." Without the implication of this power, even when a statute is silent on the issue of reviewability, "the individual is left to the absolutely uncontrolled and arbitrary action of a public and administrative officer, whose action is unauthorized by any law, and is in violation of the rights of the individual."[5] *McAnnulty* suggested that courts possessed a general equity-type power to remedy injuries done by agencies to individual rights, regardless of statutory provision. This power was questionable prior to 1875, but the courts were much more confident in assuming the power once Congress granted federal question jurisdiction.

While the courts were exercising authority to overturn agency action on constitutional grounds, and the Supreme Court was limiting the power of the ICC in a set of major decisions, the judiciary was also exerting a broader power that amounted to what John Duffy has called "Administrative Common Law."[6] However, the judiciary was tilting at windmills. Events over the following decades would place the courts on the defensive, as a new political theory and a powerful political movement sought to remodel the political system to accommodate a new kind of administrative power.

A New Science of Administration: Progressive Political Thought and Administration

The American Progressive movement has been a subject of intense scholarly examination for decades, in large part because the Progressive era ushered in fundamental reforms to the American political system and the size and scope of the national government. Progressive reformers refashioned institutions, eliminating the indirect election of U.S. senators, attacking the party-based nominating convention system for the selection of candidates for office, undermining the strong Speaker of the House of Representatives in the famous Revolt of 1910 against Joseph Cannon, and advocating for the initiative, referendum, and recall to produce a purer and more direct democracy. At the same time, these reformers sought to construct regulatory institutions and new national programs to curtail growing economic and corporate power. They therefore challenged predominant views both of the purposes of government and the means by which government should promote those purposes.

While scholars debate whether the Progressive movement was based on a coherent philosophy, most accept that it challenged prevailing conceptions of American constitutionalism.[7] The principles of republicanism, separation of powers, and the rule of law through an independent judiciary, were replaced with a new understanding of the relationship between administration and constitutionalism. Not all progressives agreed with this transformation, however. Some, such as Ernst Freund and Louis Brandeis, found themselves more wedded to old notions such as the rule of law than their progressive counterparts and began questioning the wisdom of their proposals.

Republicanism and Progressive Democracy

Progressive reformers questioned the republican foundations of administrative law that had been in place for over a century. Republicanism, understood as the theory of government by consent through elected representatives, was seen by progressive reformers as undemocratic and outmoded. It was also attacked as antithetical to an administrative state that rested on expertise rather than political accountability. Given the pace of technological and political progress, progressives argued, a modern administrative state needed to put experts in charge who would employ scientific expertise as opposed to following public opinion. Therefore, as Charles Merriam explained, "[t]he direct action of the voters in the affairs of government was both widened and narrowed in [the Progressive] period."[8] Herbert Croly, who addressed the relationship between progressivism and democracy more thoroughly than any other reformer, concurred with this assessment: "[t]he relation between the old mechanism of democracy and the new is not as simple as either the friends or the opponents of the new democracy claim."[9] By this Croly meant that the Progressives rejected the idea of representative government in favor of a new understanding of democracy, which had a complicated understanding of the proper scope of popular involvement in the policymaking process.

As Croly's comment indicated, Progressive political thought on democracy proceeded along two paths that existed in some tension with each other. On the one hand, their rejection of representative government was based on the view that the people should rule more directly, as opposed to indirectly through elected representatives who make decisions on their behalf. Many if not all of the Progressives believed that representative government would necessarily betray the interests of the people in favor of the interests of the few. "It is just beginning to be understood that representative government of any type becomes in actual practice a species of class government," wrote Herbert Croly.[10] "The first thing which must be set aside," he claimed, "is the method of representation which has passed in this country under the name of representative government."[11] Croly argued that while representative government might have been good for a time—"prescribed by fundamental economic and social conditions," particularly the existence of "states chiefly devoted to agriculture, whose free citizens were distributed over a wide area"—"these practical conditions of political association have again changed, and have changed in a manner which enables the mass of the people to assume some immediate control over their political destinies."[12]

Therefore, during the Progressive era many reforms were intended to attack the principle of representation in favor of the principle of direct democracy, such as the direct primary, the initiative, the referendum, and the recall. Many even attempted to institute elections for the judicial branch but were unsuccessful at the national level.[13] These reforms were lauded by the Progressives as moving in the direction of direct government. After laying out the changes in American society, Croly wrote, "[t]he adoption of the machinery of direct government is a legitimate expression of this change."[14] In modern circumstances, he continued, "only in this way can the nation again become a master in its own house."[15]

The Progressives' emphasis on a greater degree of direct popular government was based on the premise that history is progressing towards a state of things in which the people are more unified and capable of ruling in accordance with reason.[16] In his theoretical writings Woodrow Wilson, for example, equated the idea that it would be dangerous to make policy by the direct expression of popular will to "childish fears" which must be "outgrown." He argued that historical progress has brought about an enlightened community that does not govern for the sake of interest but for communitarian purposes. This is why Wilson claims that "this democracy—this modern democracy—is not the rule of the many, but the rule of the *whole*."[17] Croly added to the Wilsonian optimism about democracy the argument that direct popular government will become a self-fulfilling proposition, for the more direct government we inject into the system of American government, the more invigorated and public-spirited the citizens will become. He argued, "the adoption of the machinery of direct popular government . . . corresponds, if you please, to the application of a faith cure to a patient the root of whose ailment had been an infirmity of will."[18] This "faith cure," he argued, would ensure that a more democratic government would produce policies that would benefit everyone, as opposed to a system in which each voter looks out for his or her immediate interest.

Subordinating the Democratic Machinery to the Democratic Purpose
By rejecting the idea of representative government, therefore, Progressives sought to bring about a more purely democratic political system. However, at the same time, their second conception of democracy, namely, the delegation of power to an unaccountable bureaucracy, tended to the opposite effect. Periodically the Progressives acknowledged that the transfer of power to administrators insulated from political (and therefore public) control was in tension with democracy as traditionally understood. Merriam admitted, for example, that many opponents of the Progressives "believed that the reduction of the number of elective officers was equivalent to the diminution of the power of the average voter. . . . It was charged that the movement was aristocratic in its origin and purposes, and was inspired by those unfriendly to democratic government."[19]

Progressives responded to this objection by redefining democracy as an end rather than merely a policymaking process. For Progressives such as Herbert Croly, the issue of democracy was less about who rules than it was about who benefits from rule. While they sought to bring the people more directly into politics, they also sought to transfer much of policymaking authority to unelected and unaccountable public officials located in the bureaucracy. This was consistent, they argued, because democracy as a principle is about more than who is in charge of the government. A socially democratic society may actually transfer power away from the people for the sake of securing the best interests of the people, understood as a democratic set of outcomes.

This reinterpretation of the meaning of democracy was most forcefully advanced by Croly in his most famous book, *The Promise of American Life*. There, he wrote that "The subordination of the machinery of democracy to its purpose . . . demands both a reconstructive programme and an efficient organization."[20] As David Noble explains, "Democracy, [Croly] was sure, could not be defined in terms of machinery, but only as the expression of the sovereign will of the people toward the pursuit of an ideal purpose."[21] Merriam similarly explained that during the Progressive period "there appeared a new democratic movement differing in spirit and technique from any that had preceded it." This new democratic movement involved "the formulation of a specific and somewhat comprehensive social democratic program" rather than a simple program of democratization.[22] Following Croly, the Progressive political theorist John Dewey argued that "the gist of the matter lies in the question whether democracy is adequately described as the rule of the many, whether the numerical attribute of democracy is primary and causal, or secondary and derived."[23] He asserted that the reduction of democracy to a numerical, vote-counting definition of democracy was inadequate if it did not produce the proper social program.

But it was Croly who fully developed this new conception of democracy. In *Promise* he acknowledged that "Democracy as most frequently understood is essentially *and exhaustively* defined as a matter of popular government."[24] This view of democracy he characterized as "primitive American democracy."[25] In his other major work *Progressive Democracy* Croly criticized Woodrow Wilson's "New Freedom," because it "intrust[s] the future of democracy to the results of a cooperation between an individualistic legal system and a fundamentally competitive economic system."[26] Croly therefore equated primitive American democracy, with its narrow emphasis on popular government, to a foundation of individualism in law and economics.

The new, Progressive democracy, Croly maintained, must be defined not by who rules but by who the government is ruling for. In the opening of *Promise* Croly explicitly acknowledged his objective: to transform the idea of democracy "from a political system to a constructive social ideal."[27] In his view, the problem facing America followed from "the practice of an erroneous democratic theory" that needed to be updated.[28] His update to the traditional conception of democracy was simple: "a more highly socialized democracy is the only practical substitute on the part of convinced democrats for an excessively individualized democracy."[29] Croly's goal, therefore, was to change the way Americans think about democracy: "Americans are usually satisfied by a most inadequate verbal definition of democracy, but their national achievement implies one which is much more comprehensive and formative."[30] America must be "committed to the realization of the democratic ideal" rather than the democratic process; it must be "prepared to follow whithersoever that ideal may lead," even if that path leads to removing political authority from the hands of the people.[31] As David Nichols argues, "Croly wanted a system where political leaders would act decisively to create a genuine sense of community. Democratic procedures were not the hallmark of such a system. The hallmark of the system would be its ability to foster human brotherhood."[32]

The fostering of human brotherhood, in this view, may actually require a departure from traditional conceptions of a democratic political organization. In particular, Croly maintained, a Progressive democracy was one in which a new social ideal would be married to a strong, and even somewhat unaccountable, national administrative power: "The less confidence the American people have in a national organization, the less they are willing to surrender themselves to the national spirit, the worse democrats they will be."[33] Towards the end of *Promise* he maintained that "American democracy can, consequently, safely trust its genuine interests to the keeping of those who represent the national interest. It both can do so, and it must do so. Only by faith in an efficient national organization and by an exclusive and aggressive devotion to the national welfare, can the American democratic ideal be made good."[34] Developing this claim in *Progressive Democracy* a few years later, Croly wrote that a Progressive democracy will only be realized when the people are made to refrain from interfering with national administration: "If [the people] do not impose limits on their use of the instruments of direct government, based upon the conditions of their profitable service, it will prove to be a barren and mischievous addition to the stock of democratic political institutions."[35] Consequently, "The realization of a genuine social policy necessitates the aggrandizement of the administrative and legislative branches of the government."[36]

Progressive theorists were aware of the paradox presented by their conception of democracy. At the same time they were advocating for more direct control of government, and less direct control of administrative policymaking. Croly and Wilson sought to resolve this tension by placing public opinion in the role of superintendent. In this capacity public opinion would not interfere in the daily affairs of bureaucrats, but administrators would be aware and mindful of public opinion. As Croly argued, "[e]very precaution should be adopted to keep [bureaucrats] in sensitive touch with public opinion. . . . Progressive democracy recognizes the need of these instruments, but it recognizes the need of keeping control of them."[37] Once power is delegated to administrative experts, in Croly's vision, the newly invigorated and enlightened public would oversee the administration: "A clear-sighted, self-confident and loyal democracy will keep in its own hands the active control of all the agents and instruments of its own fulfillment."[38] In this Croly was perhaps influenced by Woodrow Wilson, who in his famous 1887 article "The Study of Administration" maintained that "[t]he problem is to make public opinion efficient without suffering it to be meddlesome. . . . Let administrative study find the best means for giving public criticism this [superintending] control and for shutting it out from all other interference."[39]

Progressives seeking to establish a new foundation for modern administration were confronted with the challenge of justifying a role for expert policymaking in an administrative system based on the principle of republican government. American constitutionalism had firmly established that all lawmaking had to be done by representatives who were elected by the people as a basic principle. Progressives saw that if lawmaking power were to be transferred to expert administrators, a new conception of popular government would have to supplant the old. They also recognized that the creation of an administrative state would challenge traditional notions of the separation of powers. Therefore they sought to challenge those traditional notions at the same time.

The Separation of Powers and the Rule of Experts

Many Progressives vehemently criticized the idea that the Constitution mandated a strong separation of powers. Modern government, they claimed, necessitated the combination of certain functions and a straightjacket understanding of the separation of powers would render government incapable of meeting modern needs. As Merriam summarized in a survey of Progressive political theory, "in relation to the division of governmental powers . . . the drift away from the Revolutionary theory is evident." "The generally accepted theory since the eighteenth century," he noted, "has been that all governmental powers may be divided into the legislative, the executive, and the judicial; that in every free government these powers should be carefully separated." This generally accepted theory of separation of powers, Merriam claimed, was explicitly rejected by Progressive reformers: "Viewing the situation from the standpoint of administrative law, however, a new line of division has been recently drawn by [Frank] Goodnow. . . . Goodnow criticizes the theory of the tripartite division of powers as an 'unworkable and unapplicable rule of law,' and proposes to substitute another classification in its place."[40]

Goodnow's work built on a famous distinction that Woodrow Wilson made in "The Study of Administration" between political and administrative functions. There, Wilson had asserted that "The field of administration is a field of business. It is removed from the hurry and strife of politics." Therefore, he wrote, "Most important to be observed is the truth . . . that administration lies outside the proper sphere of *politics*. Administrative questions are not political questions. Although politics sets the tasks for administration, it should not be suffered to manipulate its offices."[41] Though Wilson did not develop this theory in much detail, Goodnow spent much of his academic career explaining the relationship, and the division, between the two.

According to Goodnow, the true separation of governmental functions was twofold, not tripartite. He argued that, "political functions naturally group themselves under two heads, which are equally applicable to the mental operations and the actions of self-conscious personalities." These are either the "operations necessary for the expression of its will, or [the] operations necessary to the execution of that will." For Goodnow, the structure of government should correspond to the way that "self-conscious personalities" conduct their operations. This he understood as a twofold process, in which will is expressed or formulated, and then carried into effect.[42]

Furthermore, Goodnow distinguished between the theory of dividing the *powers* of government and the theory of dividing the *authorities* wielding those powers. The separation of governmental powers, he argued, did not necessitate that each separate power be given to a separate actor to carry out that function. As he explained:

> Montesquieu's theory involved, however, not merely the recognition of separate powers of functions of government, but also the existence of separate governmental authorities, to each of which one of the powers of government was to be entrusted. . . . This theory was, as to this point, carried much further than its author would have considered proper, and in its extreme form has been proven to be incapable of application to any concrete political organization. American experience is conclusive on this point.[43]

As a result of early Americans' flawed conception of the separation of powers, by formulating it as a tripartite separation mandating the separation of authority as well as the separation of function, Americans had rendered the separation of powers completely unworkable, Goodnow concluded: "[It] has been proven to be incapable of application to any concrete political organization."[44] As a result it ought to be revised into a principle that is capable of practical use.

Other Progressive theorists followed Goodnow's lead in questioning the separation of powers principle. In *Constitutional Government in the United States* Wilson famously criticized the Constitution as a manifestation of outmoded Newtonian physics, specifically criticizing the separation of powers on these grounds. He wrote that "The makers of the Constitution constructed the federal government upon a theory of checks and balances which was meant to limit the operation of each part and allow to no single part or organ of it a dominating force; but no government can be successfully conducted upon so mechanical a theory. Leadership and control must be lodged somewhere," and the Constitution should accommodate measures to provide leadership in the system.[45] Leadership seemed, in Wilson's view, to be best located in the administrative and not the political realm of the government. In "The Study of Administration" he clarified that the distinction between politics and administration "is not quite the distinction between Will and answering Deed, because the administrator should have and does have a will of his own in the choice of means for accomplishing his work. He is not and ought not to be a mere passive instrument."[46]

What Progressives specifically criticized was the division of powers into independent branches that would oppose each other. As described in Chapter One, the leading Framers sought specifically to separate the legislative branch from the executive, and to divide the legislative branch internally, in order to frustrate any attempts of the legislative branch to transgress its limits. They then attempted to give all of these institutions the constitutional means and personal motives to check and balance each other. The result would be a government where no one single authority possesses all of the functions of government, which could then be exercised in a tyrannical manner. The reason this was a problem, in the Progressives' view, was that such a scheme frustrates and enervates the engine of government power. As Ronald Pestritto has argued:

> As opposed to a democratic system that would quickly translate the current public mind into efficient government action, the separation-of-powers system, as [Woodrow] Wilson understood it, was designed to protect the people from themselves; it would accomplish this by throwing up as many obstacles as

possible to the implementation of the people's will. Such a system served only to impede genuine democracy.[47]

To get around the Founders' system of separation of powers, many of the Progressives envisioned the creation of a version of British cabinet government, where the legislative and executive branches act in a coordinated manner for the sake of making government more energetic in carrying out its growing list of functions. Wilson specifically advocated a system where the Congress would be able to appoint or otherwise oversee the officers of the executive branch, in a way that would make the executive dependent on the legislature.[48] In *Congressional Government* Wilson praised "Cabinet government" as "a device for bringing the executive and legislative branches into harmony and co-operation without uniting or confusing their functions."[49]

Other Progressives were less bashful in their efforts to secure a greater consolidation of powers in administrative agencies for the sake of promoting efficiency and expertise. Croly, who would later endorse Theodore Roosevelt's "New Nationalism" over Wilson's "New Freedom" because of its embrace of administrative power, praised the fact that "A commission which gives a specific expression of the general policy of the state . . . does not fit into the traditional classification of governmental powers. It exercises an authority which is in part executive, in part legislative, and in part judicial, and which must be sharply distinguished from administration in its conventional sense." He also writes that such a governmental agency "is simply a convenient means of consolidating the divided activities of the government for certain practical social purposes."[50] This new theory of administration, separated out from politics, would serve as a convenient means for consolidating power and allowing government to achieve practical purposes that the separation of powers simply does not facilitate. Achieving this kind of consolidation would produce a new understanding of administration very different from that of "administration in its conventional sense." Keeping this new power out of the realm of politics would be necessary to ensure its faithful use.

The Relationship between Politics and Administration

The relationship between politics and administration was, consequently, very complicated. While insisting upon a neat separation between politics and administration, as indicated earlier, Progressives also insisted that this new power would remain under political and popular control. Squaring this circle proved to be extraordinarily difficult for Progressive theorists. Wilson in particular struggled to clarify the proper role that public opinion would play in overseeing administration in "The Study of Administration." Now that America has advanced into the final stage of its political development and is attaching a well-developed administrative apparatus to its free constitution, Wilson argued, "What, then, is there to prevent?" His response: "principally, popular sovereignty. It is harder for democracy to organize administration than for monarchy. The very completeness of our most cherished political successes in the past embarrasses us. We have enthroned public opinion," but this fact "has made the task of organizing that rule just so much the more difficult."[51] Too much political influence, too much public opinion in administration and it loses that which makes it distinctive, namely, its expertise and efficiency. After all, he noted, "The bulk of mankind is rigidly unphilosophical, and nowadays the bulk of mankind votes. . . . And where is this unphilosophical bulk of mankind more multifarious in its composition than in the United States?"[52]

These sorts of statements suggest that Wilson was cynical about the role of politics in administration and sought to insulate bureaucratic experts from popular accountability. And indeed Wilson argued that we ought to avoid "that besetting error of ours, the error of trying to do too much by vote. Self-government does not consist in having a hand in everything, any more than housekeeping consists necessarily in cooking dinner with one's own hands. The cook must be trusted with a large discretion as to the management of the fires and the ovens."[53] But he was quick to clarify that this large discretion, insulated from the process of voting, did not eliminate all methods of holding administrators accountable. In fact, Wilson claimed that, ironically, the more discretionary power entrusted to administrators, the more accountable they were likely to be. "[L]arge powers and unhampered discretion seem to me the indispensable conditions of responsibility. Public attention must be easily directed . . . to just the man deserving of praise or blame. There is no danger in power, if only it be not irresponsible."[54] Here was Wilson turning the arguments for administrative responsibility through the president, which featured so prominently at the Constitutional Convention and in *The Federalist*, into an argument in favor of modern administrative organization.

Therefore Wilson envisioned "that public opinion shall play the part of authoritative critic," not by voting on measures or electing bureaucrats but by overseeing administration just as a housekeeper oversees a cook.[55] The cook is left free to devise his own recipes so long as his cooking does not threaten the house. Politics would remain in charge of administration, not in overseeing the details of administration but in the important matters. How to distinguish a mere detail of administration from a matter of importance was a question Wilson did not satisfactorily address.

The Challenge of the Rule of Law

While sympathetic to the need for a stronger and more centralized political system, many progressives balked at the attempt to strengthen and consolidate administrative power. These progressive dissenters tended to congregate in law schools. The most prominent among them were Louis Brandeis (discussed later in this chapter), Roscoe Pound (as explained in the following chapter), and Ernst Freund.

Freund was a German émigré who studied at the University of Berlin and Heidelberg University and who was deeply influenced by German liberal thought, particularly the teachings of Rudolph von Gneist. The conception of the *Rechstaat* (German for "state of law") was expounded in German universities and even, for a brief moment, enacted into Prussian law, a movement that profoundly influenced Freund's thought. In the *Rechtstaat* administrative rules could be promulgated but appeals to ordinary, independent courts would exist alongside this power, constraining the bureaucracy. As Philip Hamburger explains, this idea never took full root in Germany, which eventually "established appeals from administrative decisions to administrative courts" rather than establishing "accountability in the ordinary courts."[56] In his telling this was progress, but only a half measure for restoring the rule of law: it "allowed Germans to enjoy a law-like version of absolute power and thereby to come as close to law as was possible under extralegal rule" through administration.[57]

Others such as Friedrich Hayek were more optimistic about the ideal of the *Rechtstaat*. In *The Constitution of Liberty* Hayek praised "the most distinctive contribution of eighteenth-century Prussia to the realization of the rule of law," namely, its contribution "in the field of the control of public administration." Building upon earlier thinkers, nineteenth-century reformers insisted that "all exercise of administrative power over the person or property of the citizen should be made subject to judicial review."[58] Hayek explained that "the central aim of the liberal movement" in Prussia became "the limitation of all government by a constitution, and particularly the limitation of all administrative activity by law enforcible [*sic*] by courts." These theorists and reformers were particularly concerned about "the quasi-judicial bodies inside the administrative machinery which were primarily intended to watch over the execution of the law rather than to protect the liberty of the individual."[59] Hayek lamented that the ideal outcome, namely, relying upon ordinary courts to enforce administrative actions, was not established in Germany, which instead relied upon specialized administrative courts.[60] Rather, Germany implemented a scheme of independent courts staffed with administrative as well as judicial officers. Nevertheless, like Hayek, Freund viewed these administrative courts as "the most ingenious solution of the problem how to combine bureaucracy and self-government."[61]

Freund brought to America these ideas about subjecting administrative power to the rule of law. He taught administrative law at Columbia University, alongside Frank Goodnow. In various writings and correspondence with colleagues he laid out his alternative vision for an administrative state bound to the rule of law. In particular, Freund engaged in a decades-long debate with Felix Frankfurter over the appropriate understanding of administrative discretion. Though they disagreed vehemently on this question, they also respected each other deeply.[62] In 1953, speaking in a lecture series named for Freund, Frankfurter announced that "I don't think I ever met anybody in the academic world who more justly merited the characterization of a scholar and a gentleman than did Ernst Freund."[63] Still, as Daniel Ernst has written, "the two disagreed fundamentally on how law could both empower and constrain the administrative state."[64]

In several important articles Freund attempted to outline an alternative to the administrative state that was being constructed in America. The first, titled "The Law of the Administration in America," was published by *Political Science Quarterly* in 1894. In 1915 he published "The Substitution of Rule for Discretion in Public Law" in the *American Political Science Review.*[65] A final attempt to address these issues came in 1928 with the publication of *Administrative Powers over Persons and Property.*[66] His most famous books, *The Police Power* (1904) and *Standards of American Legislation* (1917) also dealt tangentially with the question of administrative power and the rule of law.[67]

Freund believed that "the two greatest modern republics, the United States and France, represent the opposite extremes of administrative organization." In this respect, like Woodrow Wilson had argued in "The Study of Administration," Freund asserted that America could profit from the study of foreign administrative arrangements: "As the science of administrative law is new and has been chiefly developed in France and Germany, it is natural that the attention of the American student should be turned to foreign law."[68] This turn to foreign sources, Freund argued, revealed the greatest contrast, and therefore the great defect, of American administrative arrangement: its democratic character. "In the European states," he noted, "the administration is constituted in such a manner that its organs appear as a distinct portion of the state and of the people." In this system "The chief executive stands as the representative of governmental power; he is the head of an army of officials who derive their functions and duties directly or indirectly from him." Such an arrangement, Freund argued, "may be designated as bureaucratic government." It proceeded on the supposition that government officers should operate within a hierarchical form of organization and that the government itself "appears as a distinct organization in the state." This approach to administration "is believed to be contrary to the American conception of popular government," Freund explained, which states that "not only are the people the source of governmental power, but they exercise that power themselves." Consequently, as Chapter Two explained, in American practice administrative officers were not hierarchically organized but derived their power from the people, and in many cases the people themselves were the administrators, whether through private enforcement or through the use of juries. In America, Freund concluded, administrative officers are "held together only through their common allegiance and responsibility to the people."[69] These features of American administration were augmented by the reluctance of legislatures to delegate their powers over to administrative officers, binding discretion and creating ministerial rather than discretionary responsibilities.

"The advantage of our system is clear," Freund explained. Because of the way in which administration is bound by law, "we may truly speak of a government by law and not by men. But we should also see the true defects of such a system. . . . This system compels the legislature to specify in detail every power which it delegates to any authority."[70] "Thus we arrive at the fundamental principles of our administrative system: no executive power without express statutory authority . . . minute regulation of nearly all executive functions, so that they become mere ministerial acts," and "the principle of diffusion of executive power." "In contrast to these we find in Europe executive powers independent of statute, discretionary powers of action and control vested in superior officers, and the concentration of the administrative powers of the government through the hierarchical organization of the executive department."[71]

While Freund favored the more centralized, bureaucratic method of organizing administration that had been arrived at in France and Germany, he noted that the American method of imposing legal control on administration had advantages. Every system of administration, he explained, requires "further control . . . to hold subordinate officers to the performance of their duties and to protect private rights." The two methods of doing this are "administrative control" and "judicial control." Subordinate administrative officers can be held accountable by their superiors, or by independent courts. While administrative control guards against "the danger of official neglect and misconduct," it "is liable to fail where questions of fact or law arise between the administration and private persons." In these cases, Freund claimed, "the issue between public interest and private right should be decided with absolute impartiality, and the administration may be expected to lean in favor of the public interest. In this class of cases, therefore, the impartial control of judicial tribunals is more appropriate."[72] This use of judicial control rather than administrative is emblematic of American administration, Freund argued: "the absence of administrative control in the states must be regarded as a deliberate principle of legislation. . . . The idea underlying our system is that every officer is responsible to the law, and that for the enforcement of the law the courts are sufficient. The judicial control must therefore serve both purposes."[73] In Freund's assessment "the extraordinary jurisdiction [of the courts] by means of prerogative writs constitutes a judicial control, which, in one respect at least, compares favorably with that of the administrative courts of France and Germany." In those countries "claims arising out of the administration are adjudicated by special courts, which are connected with the administration and . . . are not entirely independent."[74] "[I]t is perfectly proper," he asserted, "to demand that the administration should keep strictly within the bounds set to it by law, and therefore the most vigorous scrutiny of its action, from a purely legal point of view, should be invited rather than excluded."[75]

Still, Freund noted that the system of administrative appeal to administrative tribunals had certain advantages: "simple forms of action," "informal procedure," and avoidance of "the expense, delay and risk of litigation." "On this showing the means of control for the protection of private rights really appear ampler and more efficient under the European than under the American system," he concluded.[76] Perhaps most important, though, in Freund's mind was that the system of administrative appeal eliminates the "greatest drawback" of the American approach: that "it makes no provision for the review of discretionary action." Independent, judicial tribunals are not equipped to review the substance of discretionary action, and so it is inevitable that "the law will narrow as much as possible the sphere of discretionary action" to avoid this paradox.[77]

Thus in 1894 Freund described an American administrative system with advantages and defects. The American devotion to the rule of law allowed for the protection of private rights by judicial control of administration, but this inevitably led to the binding of discretion through statutes. Since the independent courts could only review the legality of administrative action, and not the wisdom of a discretionary act, the legislatures had to constrain administrative power in advance through statutory provisions. The constraining of administration, in a system where administrative control and appeal was unavailable to the citizen, produced weak and ultimately ineffective government, in Freund's view.

This raised the important question whether "the present administrative system of the American states will be able to retain its peculiar features. . . . Our present system is the product of an extreme democratic spirit, combined with a comparative simplicity of the conditions of government." But as these conditions grew more complex, Freund predicted, the need for administrative discretion would become overwhelming: "With a change of the conditions that have made the present organization possible, the organization itself is liable to undergo significant modifications."[78] Specifically, Freund foresaw that "in our system it is becoming necessary, for administrative reasons, to modify any exclusively self-governmental organization by an infusion of bureaucratic or professional elements."[79] The infusion of bureaucratic and professional elements would conflict with the underlying democratic principles of nineteenth-century American administrative law, and it would be imperative to defend the rule of law in these new circumstances.

The solution to this problem was not to give up on judicial control but to supplement it with the kind of administrative control that was developing in France and Germany, Freund argued. Reformers would be needed to cure the growing administrative state of its threat to the rule of law. They would have to bring the *Rechtstaat* to America. Freund's alternative vision for administrative law was complex but can be reduced to several core elements. First, he called consistently for clear standards contained in legislation, which would effectively limit the delegation of discretionary power to administrative officers. As Dan Ernst explains, Freund praised the Raines Law, a New York statute governing liquor licensing. That law replaced an open-ended power to grant licenses to those with "good moral character," as interpreted by local officers, with more concrete and specific criteria to guide the individual licensing decisions. This law "substituted rule for discretion," which is why Freund favored it.[80] Freund's *Standards of American Legislation*, published in 1917, was an attempt to guide legislators in how to substitute rule for discretion in regulatory statutes. And the Transportation Act of 1920, he happily observed, required the ICC to hold hearings, using procedure rather than rule to limit the discretion of administrators.

In addition to more carefully crafted legislation, Freund advocated incorporating the characteristics of the *Rechtstaat* to American administrative law. Such an approach would involve the creation of administrative law courts in which the legality of administrative action could be tested. Without necessarily doing away with judicial review by independent, Article III courts, Freund's vision would have established an administrative court system in which jurisdictional and other legal issues could be contested in an independent tribunal. These courts would cure American administrative law of what Freund called (as mentioned above) its greatest drawback, namely, that the citizen has no check upon discretionary action. Had Freund's vision been successfully imported, the American administrative state would have developed along a dramatically different trajectory. While regulation and administration would still have expanded during the Progressive era, it would have been more tightly constrained by the rule of law. The *Rechtstaat*, in other words, would not have constrained the growth of administrative action during the Progressive era, but it would have made administration more lawful.

In 1913 Roscoe Pound needled Freund about the work being done by "administrative law people" such as himself. Freund responded in defense of his occupation: "there are mighty few of us and of a very different type from what you imagine." "Administrative law stands not for administrative power but for control of administrative power," he maintained.[81] But Freund was fighting a losing battle within his own discipline. As Philip Hamburger explains, "Freund desperately sought to advance this ideal [of the *Rechtstaat*]. . . . But his efforts were of little avail." Consequently, "the liberal German version of administrative law, the *Rechtstaat*, was reduced to the progressive American vision of administrative power."[82] Dan Ernst has similarly noted that Freund was gradually eclipsed by Felix Frankfurter, whose lectures published in 1930 as *The Public and Its Problems* took a far different stance on the question of administrative discretion. In that work, Frankfurter called for the creation of a professionalized bureaucratic class that would be free to use their scientific expertise to solve broad social problems without being tied down by rule or procedure.[83] The day of enlightened administration had come, and Freund's vision for limiting administrative discretion faded into history.

A New Kind of Administration:
The Emergence of an Administrative State

At the same time that Progressive theorists were formulating a new theory that promised to alter significantly the constitutional principles undergirding administrative power, political changes were being advanced by reformers who sought to insulate administrative power from Congress and the judiciary. Theodore Roosevelt was the most important reformer responsible for expanding and insulating administrative power. His former ally and later adversary, William Howard Taft, sought to contain administration within a traditional understanding of American constitutionalism. But once Taft was no longer an obstacle, Roosevelt was confronted by a figure who was both a Progressive theorist and a reformer, who also presented an intriguing understanding of the relationship between administration and the American Constitution: Woodrow Wilson.

Theodore Roosevelt and the Restructuring of the Civil Service

The first critical step in Theodore Roosevelt's project to transform administration was to attack the old, party-based patronage system for filling administrative offices. The Pendleton Act, as Chapter Four argued, did not do this. But it provided the wedge that Roosevelt would use as president to, in Stephen Skowronek's words, "break the bonds that tied civil administration to local politics and to forge an executive-centered reconstitution of civil administration in its place."[84] Central to Roosevelt's project, and an issue that would be raised repeatedly in the early twentieth century, was the relationship of the presidency to this new kind of civil service. Foreshadowing his "New Nationalism" platform in 1912 and his cousin Franklin Roosevelt's project to place the New Deal administrative agencies under the president's control in the 1930s, Roosevelt initiated a series of rule changes within the Civil Service Commission to place the civil service "dependent in all its interests on executive officers and the President's commission."[85] The number of merit appointments was increased by Roosevelt through executive order, and merit employees were placed under the supervision and even the removal authority of their appointing officers.

After he won his own term of office in 1904, Roosevelt took further steps to professionalize the emerging bureaucracy and separate it from the influence of parties and Congress. He formed the Keep Commission, the first of what would be many attempts to reorganize the administrative state. The Keep Commission pushed for a reclassification of the civil service that would establish clear guidelines for salary and promotion. As Hamilton had written in *The Federalist* over a century earlier, "In the general course of human nature, a power over a man's subsistence amounts to a power over his will."[86] Just as salary protections were critical to ensuring, as Madison put it in *The Federalist*, "that each department should have a will of its own," the Keep Commission sought to ensure that the will of administrators would not be bound to political officials holding power over their salaries.[87]

Following many of the Commission's suggestions, Roosevelt restructured the Forest Service by executive order, placing it in the Department of Agriculture and more directly under the control of the president and more insulated from the Congress. When Congress specifically required that the Land Office sell off federal lands to the public, the administration refused, causing a major controversy in Roosevelt's second term. The backlash was severe. Congress rejected every proposal of the Keep Commission, refused to print its reports, and enacted an appropriations rider forbidding any future funds to be used for investigations into administrative reorganization.

While Roosevelt's reforms began to reduce the independence of administrators in general, it also freed them from the influence of parties. Roosevelt's goal, unlike many of the Progressive theorists, therefore, was to establish an executive-centered administrative state rather than one entirely independent of politics—though it was admittedly not ever entirely clear in the theorists' writings how administrative independence would be structured.[88] His successor, William Howard Taft, was much more restrained in his vision for administrative adjustment, which temporarily suspended the controversy over the civil service. But Roosevelt had gained some significant ground in the project to establish a different kind of administrative structure.

A New Kind of Commission: The Hepburn Act and the Transformation of the ICC

After achieving a modest revolution in the civil service system, Roosevelt proceeded to press for an expansion of administrative power, starting with the Interstate Commerce Commission. By 1900 a consensus had emerged that the ICC had not dramatically changed the operation of the railroad industry, and measures to strengthen the Commission were once again advanced. The first major effort to strengthen the ICC came with the Elkins Anti-Rebating Act of 1903. Senator Stephen Elkins had assumed the chair of the Senate Committee on Interstate Commerce and introduced this as a half measure that would not provoke widespread resistance from the railroads.[89] The Elkins Act passed unanimously in the Senate and with minimal resistance in the House. It provided for criminal penalties for railroads that deviated from the rates filed with the commission, with adjudication in federal circuit court. Retaining the traditional judicial process for adjudicating violations of the statute ensured the measure's passage with little opposition.

A much more dramatic and decisive debate would occur a few years later with the introduction and passage of the Hepburn Act in 1906. The Hepburn

Act accomplished, for the first time, the vesting of ratesetting and final adjudicatory powers in the Interstate Commerce Commission—and therefore was the major step in transforming the Commission from an administrative body performing adjudication that eventuated in judicial proceedings to a modern regulatory commission with consolidated powers. Sponsored by William Hepburn, the bill passed the House easily but stalled in the Senate where conservative Republican senators dominated proceedings.

For months the Senate debated the constitutional issues raised by the Act. The central issue was the extent of judicial review of ICC orders. Now that ICC orders were to be self-executing, the scope of review was critical, since parties would presumably go to court to get an injunction in the period before the order went into effect.[90] Proponents of a narrow standard of review were only willing to allow for judicial review of constitutional claims brought by parties challenging the ICC. Others, such as Nelson Aldrich, the leader of the Republicans in the Senate, insisted on broad judicial review. In Thomas Merrill's words, they "wanted to confer general jurisdiction on federal courts to enjoin rate orders before they took effect on any legal basis, including that the rate was set at an 'unreasonably' low level." This would be accomplished by a statutory provision "authorizing review by carriers by a bill in equity, and by providing that carriers could challenge rate orders as being unreasonably low."[91] The impasse between the advocates of narrow and broad review was clearly the fundamental issue, as many of the Senate speeches illustrate. Senator Rayner called the two proposals "as widely different as it is possible for two divergent propositions to be. The one is review under the Constitution[,] . . . the other is the broad statutory review, which permits the courts to try the cases de novo and in the same manner as if no such body as the Interstate Commerce Commission had ever existed upon the face of the earth."[92]

Roosevelt and the insurgent Progressive Republicans in Congress were initially unwilling to accept any type of broad review. But when a pure bill limiting judicial review failed to pass in the Senate, they were forced to compromise. Roosevelt finally accepted a statutory provision stating that "if upon such hearing as the [circuit] court may determine to be necessary, it appears that the order was regularly made and duly served, and that the carrier is in disobedience of the same, the court shall enforce" the order. Another provision stated that ICC orders would take effect within thirty days unless "suspended or set aside by a court of competent jurisdiction," without clarifying the standard of review in the statute. With these ambiguous provisions in place, the senators threw up their hands and passed the measure.

The central issue, however, was still the nature of judicial review of ICC decisions, and the ambiguous provisions adopted did not clarify that matter. Therefore, once the Hepburn Act was passed, the question was whether the Supreme Court would continue its earlier approach to administrative power, curtailing administrative discretion where possible and reserving the authority to scrutinize the substantive grounds of agency decisions. Early indications were that the Court was prepared to retreat from this position in the face of the political opposition Roosevelt had aroused against it.[93] In 1910 the Court decided *ICC v. Illinois Central Railroad Co.*, where it restricted the Court's power to review the Commission's findings of fact, leaving only questions of law for judicial scrutiny.[94] While the Court reserved the power to decide "all relevant questions of constitutional power or right," as well as "all pertinent questions as to whether the administrative order is within the scope of the delegated authority" given to the agency, once those questions regarding the legality of the agency's action were decided, the Court would not inquire into "whether the administrative power has been wisely exercised."[95] (The distinction between review of legal questions and review of factual questions would become critical during the New Deal, as the following chapter discusses.) However, the Court took a different approach only a few weeks later in *ICC v. Northern Pacific Railroad Co.* In the opinion Justice Holmes scrutinized the ICC's contention that no "reasonable or satisfactory through route" existed between two points a legal, not a factual question. Therefore, under *Illinois Central* it would be decided de novo by the Court, and the ICC's determination was invalidated.[96]

Ultimately, the Court settled into a position that provided for de novo review of legal questions; agencies would be granted deference on factual issues including the substantive reasonableness of their determinations. As Daniel Ernst writes, after 1910 "Although courts were to determine for themselves facts going to the constitutionality of the ICC's order or to whether the commission had acted within its jurisdiction, they were to defer to the commissioners on such vital matters as the reasonableness of the railroad rates."[97] *Illinois Central* became administrative law doctrine. According to Thomas Merrill, "In the course of a very few years immediately following the passage of the Hepburn Act, the Supreme Court jettisoned the nineteenth-century model of judicial review and stumbled onto the appellate review model" in which courts grant deference to agencies' determination of facts.[98] The passage of the Hepburn Act was therefore a major turning point, not simply because of the new powers afforded to the ICC but also because of the significant change in judicial review it ultimately produced.

Taft's Constitutionalism and the Ill-Fated Commerce Court
At the very time when the courts appeared to be retreating from their aggressive posture towards administrative discretion, a new proposal emerged under
the leadership of President William Howard Taft. As Stephen Skowronek
explains, "Taft looked at the railroad regulation issue as a problem of separating powers and compartmentalizing different governmental functions under
the appropriate constitutional authorities."[99] His concern about the expansion
of administrative discretion cannot simply be explained "in antidemocratic,
prorailroad terms" but was rooted in a deep appreciation for the constitutional
restraints on administrative power that had prevailed over the first hundred
years of American history.[100] As a result he advocated the creation of a new,
specialized, and independent railroad court that would supervise the exercise
of the ICC's expanded powers. This Commerce Court would be one of many
new specialized courts that would constrain the power of the new administrative state and ensure it remains bounded by law. Under the proposal for a
Commerce Court, appeals from the initial agency decisions would go not to
generalist federal circuit courts but to this new court with specialized jurisdiction. The Attorney General would bring the appeal, "thus strengthening
the hand of the executive in regulation and separating the tasks of investigation (ICC), prosecution (Attorney General), and adjudication (Commerce
Court)."[101] Important parallels can be drawn between the Commerce Court
notion and the ideal of administrative law courts that was central to the *Rechtstaat*, discussed earlier in this chapter.

Taft succeeded in ushering the Commerce Court through the legislative
process, but not without some compromises. Taft wished for the members of
the Court to be permanent, but the proposal was amended to limit the term
of the judges to five years, after which they would return to the circuit courts
from which they came. Ultimately the Mann-Elkins Act (which contained
the provisions for the Commerce Court) passed by a wide margin in 1910, but
the Court was quickly deemed a failure. The first Chief Justice of the Commerce Court, Martin Knapp, took an aggressive stance against the agency, "in-
delicately overturning one commission order after another."[102] Knapp asserted
the power to assert its own independent judgment on ICC decisions, bound
by the facts found but not the conclusions reached by the agency. This threatened to unsettle the Court's carefully drawn distinction between questions of
law and fact, crafted in *Illinois Central*.

The Supreme Court was not interested in revisiting its compromise and
thrusting itself back into a precarious political position. It regularly overturned
Commerce Court opinions on appeal, casting aspersion not merely on the

Commerce Court but on judicial intervention as a whole. By the time of the 1912 election, Taft's approach to administrative reform had been marginalized, setting up a debate between two Progressives who had very different visions for the administrative state. The Commerce Court was abolished in August 1912, and "Beneath the attack on the Commerce Court lay the disintegration of the Republican party," a development that would reach its full fruit in the 1912 presidential election.[103]

The Progressive House Divided: Freedom, Nationalism,
and Competing Visions for Administration

After a brief synopsis of some of the scholarly literature on Wilson's New Freedom, this section will first discuss the paradoxical fact that Wilson was roundly criticized by TR and other progressives as a conservative during the 1912 campaign—a fact which is perplexing given contemporary scholarly accounts of Wilson's thought and action. Then, it will lay out the contours of the New Nationalism, which essentially advocated a centralized administrative power to regulate American economic life in the wake of industrialization. The New Nationalism, like many other elements of Roosevelt's 1912 campaign, would have fundamentally transformed the constitutional system created by the Founders. The following two sections will examine Wilson and Brandeis's response, which Wilson called the New Freedom. The New Freedom was intended to preserve the constitutional system and obviate the need for centralized administration by offering an alternative approach to regulation. The final section will attempt to outline the alternative institutional structure anticipated by the New Freedom. Though Wilson won the 1912 election, as president he pursued a course remarkably similar to the New Nationalism that he denounced on the campaign trail. This begs the question: what would Wilson's New Freedom have looked like if he had translated its principles into action? How would regulation have differed? How would the administrative state have developed differently as a result? The argument will conclude by discussing some of these questions, through laying out the constitutional theory that undergirded the New Freedom. In particular, the paper will argue that the New Freedom would have regulated competition in a way that preserved the rule of law and the constitutional separation of powers. Standards would be clearly set forth in statutes or in common law, would be administered through the executive branch, and would be adjudicated in courts of law. This was a stark contrast to the plan of the New Nationalism, which was to consolidate authority in administrative commissions.

Sidney Milkis emphasizes the significance of the division between the New Freedom and the New Nationalism: "the split between New Nationalism and New Freedom . . . betray[ed] fundamental differences over the relationship between the individual and the state."[104] This split "cut to the core of the modern state that, ostensibly, the programmatic initiatives touted by [progressive] reformers appeared to anticipate."[105] The dispute, thus, was nothing less than "a philosophical dispute between Roosevelt and Wilson on the social contract—on the appropriate balance between rights and duties in American political life."[106] Milkis persuasively argues that the disagreement over how to regulate competition was not simply a policy dispute. Rather, it was a fundamental argument over the appropriate powers and structure of the modern state. It implicated core principles of accountability and self-government, as Wilson and Roosevelt's campaign speeches indicate.

Yet other scholars have wondered whether there was really much to the distinction between the New Nationalism and New Freedom. For instance, Robert Wiebe writes that "Wilson's New Freedom did not deviate greatly in approach from the New Nationalism. . . . [A]s the philosophers sketched it—such men as Charles Van Hise on behalf of concentration and Louis Brandeis on behalf of decentralization—the distinction dimmed. Both men believed in an outer ring of rules and an inner core of administrative management." "Though important questions of balance and emphasis did separate them," Wiebe concedes, "a common orientation . . . meant that bureaucratic reform would dominate the discussions to come."[107] Unlike Milkis, Wiebe suggests that the distinction between the New Freedom and New Nationalism was merely a disagreement about means to shared ends. Both sides agreed that reforms were needed, and they agreed about the ends of reform, in this view, but how to go about achieving these reforms divided progressives in 1912.

Thus there is a perplexing disagreement among both scholars and contemporaries over the significance of the division over the New Nationalism and the New Freedom. The progressive journalist William Allen White, who joined the Roosevelt forces in 1912, dismissed the division as a minor disagreement—tantamount to the distinction between Tweedle-Dum and Tweedle-Dee. Yet in noting this fact Charles Forcey also argues that "When Croly, Weyl, Lippmann, and others stood with Roosevelt at Armageddon that year, they believed that the decision between Roosevelt's welfare nationalism and Wilson's individualistic freedom held the country's fate."[108] And Louis Brandeis—who scholars typically credit as a major influence in the development of the New Freedom—wrote to Wilson that the difference was "fundamental and irreconcilable. It is the difference between industrial liberty and industrial absolutism."[109] Even the leading characters in the disagreement between the two sides disputed the extent of the chasm that divided them. As with today's scholars, among his own contemporaries there was little consensus over whether Wilson was at the vanguard of progressivism or whether he had become an apostate of the movement. When he wrote his autobiography, published in 1913, Theodore Roosevelt had little doubt which was the case.

The "Ultra-Conservative" Woodrow Wilson

On the campaign trail in 1912 Roosevelt criticized Wilson's proposals to break up monopoly as "rural toryism." It was based on a refusal to understand and accept the new conditions of an industrial economy in which large-scale enterprise is inevitable. Wilson's desire to break up monopolies rather than control them was "ultra-conservative," TR alleged. He even wondered in many of his campaign speeches whether Wilson secretly desired to abolish the Interstate Commerce Commission.

In his *Autobiography*, Roosevelt characterized the issue thus: "The men who first applied the extreme Democratic theory in American life were, like Jefferson, ultra individualists, for at that time what was demanded by our people was the largest liberty for the individual." However, "During the century that had elapsed since Jefferson the need had been exactly reversed. There had been in our country a riot of individualistic materialism, under which complete freedom for the individual—that ancient license which President Wilson a century after the term was excusable has called the 'New' Freedom—turned out in practice to mean perfect freedom for the strong to wrong the weak."[110] To be Jeffersonian in the twentieth century, TR alleged, meant embracing extreme democracy but melding it with the "Hamiltonian . . . belief in a strong and efficient National Government."[111] Unfortunately, he concluded, Wilson's conservatism prevented him from offering this combination of Hamilton and Jefferson during the 1912 campaign. (However, Roosevelt's ally Herbert Croly would happily announce a few years into Wilson's presidency that he had essentially abandoned the New Freedom for the New Nationalism).[112]

"One of the main troubles" with addressing the challenges of the new economy, TR charged, "was the fact that the men who saw the evils and who tried to remedy them attempted to work in two different ways, and the great majority of them in a way that offered little promise of real betterment."[113] According to Roosevelt most progressives—at least in 1912—supported Wilson's goal "to bolster up an individualism already proved to be both futile and mischievous; to remedy by more individualism the concentration that was the inevitable result of the already existing individualism."[114] The "more individualism" that Roosevelt identified was implicit in the policy of "destroying [combinations] and restoring the country to the economic conditions of the middle of the nineteenth century."[115] He then repeated his charge that this approach "really represented a form of sincere rural toryism."[116] In short, the core of Roosevelt's critique of the New Freedom was that it sought to destroy large business combinations, with the aim of returning America to a pre-industrial economic system of small enterprise. These combinations, Roosevelt implicitly charged, were ineradicable and the true progressive policy would accept this inevitability.

Roosevelt's charge that the New Freedom was based on quixotic notion of an unattainable halcyon era was repeated by the historian Charles A. Beard in the pages of the *New Republic*: "Agrarian democracy was the goal of Jefferson's analysis, just as the equally unreal and unattainable democracy of small business is Wilson's goal" in the New Freedom, Beard charged.[117] He argued that Jefferson's anti-capitalist, anti-industrialist, and anti-urban philosophy rendered it unsuitable for modern America. He concluded: "To-day nearly half of us belong to the 'mobs of the great cities'—sores on the body politic. What message has the sage of Monticello for us? What message have the statesmen and their followers whose political science is derived from Jefferson for a society founded upon 'the casualties and caprices' of trade?"[118] By characterizing Wilson's New Freedom as a Jeffersonian, populist enterprise, Roosevelt, Croly, and other allies writing in the pages of the *New Republic* put themselves squarely on the side of Alexander Hamilton as a symbol of expanded national power. Wilson, by contrast, was depicted as a stodgy conservative clinging to antiquated notions of government.

Roosevelt's depiction of Wilson is striking, for Wilson stands today as perhaps the exemplar of progressivism and faith in the modern administrative state. Many scholars today consider Wilson to be the progressive thinker par excellence, and most recent treatments of progressivism in the field of American Political Thought place significant emphasis on Wilson.[119] Yet according to Roosevelt, Wilson was an apostate of progressivism, who had sold out in 1912 and run as a moderate. Separately, in the field of public administration, Wilson is typically offered as the founder of public administration and defender of administrative centralization. Most of these accounts focus not on Wilson's New Freedom but on his seminal article "The Study of Administration," published in *Political Science Quarterly* in 1887. This article is widely credited with launching the discipline of public administration in America, and it defends bureaucratic autonomy and the separation of politics and administration.[120] Treatments of Wilson's view of bureaucracy in contemporary public administration scholarship focus almost obsessively on "The Study of Administration," without mentioning the New Freedom at all. Thus scholars have largely treated the New Freedom either as an outlier or as irrelevant to a full understanding of Wilson's philosophy.

The result is that the New Freedom has largely been relegated to obscurity. Historians, of course, discuss it in their accounts of the 1912 election and the first years of Wilson's presidency, but without considering the constitutional principles that underlay it.[121] As an alternative to the centralized administrative state that progressivism eventually came to embrace, and in light of the profound impact of that administrative state on the vitality of American civic life, the New Freedom merits a renewed consideration.[122] A careful consideration of the New Freedom must begin by examining its contrast—Theodore Roosevelt's New Nationalism.

"No Other Way Except by a Commission"

The only workable solution to the problems presented by industrialization, Roosevelt contended, was to govern large corporations through commissions: "This state of affairs demands that combination and concentration in business should be, not prohibited, but supervised and controlled. . . . The nation should assume powers of supervision and regulation over all corporations doing an interstate business."[123] A Jeffersonian solution that prohibited the expansion of centralized power and expertise would inevitably fail, in Roosevelt's estimation.

Roosevelt acknowledged in his *Autobiography* that during his presidency he did *not* follow the course of regulating monopoly (of course, today he is popularly known as a "trust-buster" rather than a "trust-regulator"). The reason for this, he argued in his *Autobiography*, is that when he was president the very authority for the national government to interfere in business combinations *at all* was challenged. "When I became President," he explained, "the question as to the *method* by which the United States Government was to control the corporations was not yet important. The absolutely vital question was whether the Government had power to control them at all."[124] Roosevelt's primary objective as president was to establish the principle that interference in business was within the scope of the national government's authority—not with adopting the perfect method for controlling business combinations.

TR explained that he achieved great success in establishing the national government's authority to regulate big business, but he acknowledged: "We had gained the power. We had not devised the proper method of exercising it."[125] The proper method for controlling business, he reiterated, was not found in breaking up monopolies but in using administrative tribunals to oversee them. "Monopolies can, although in rather cumbrous fashion, be broken up by law suits. Great business combinations, however, cannot possibly be made useful instead of noxious industrial agencies merely by law suits, and especially by law suits supposed to be carried on for their destruction and not for their control and regulation." In contrast to the "law suit" method for controlling monopolies by breaking them up, TR offered his alternative: "the inauguration of a system of thoroughgoing and drastic Governmental regulation and control over all big business combinations engaged in inter-State industry." "Here," he lamented, as president "I was able to accomplish only a small part of what I desired to accomplish."[126] Yet he remained convinced that "The true way of dealing with monopoly is to prevent it by administrative action," namely, "a Federal Commission which should . . . effectively control and regulate all big combinations." "Such a Commission," he continued, "would furnish a steady expert control, a control adapted to the problem; and dissolution is neither control nor regulation, but is purely negative; and negative remedies are of little permanent avail."[127] The commission TR envisioned in his *Autobiography* "would have complete power to examine into every big corporation engaged or proposing to engage in business between the states."[128]

Roosevelt's analysis of the solution needed to meet the problem of business combinations requires a close examination. He deliberately contrasts two approaches to regulation: the "law suit" method and the commission method. He admitted that the law suit method can succeed in breaking up monopoly, though he rejects such a method as overly "cumbrous." In contrast, he offers "a system of thoroughgoing Governmental regulation and control" over business. The instrument for achieving this comprehensive control is the commission, because administrative action would "furnish a steady expert control" rather than elimination of trusts. Whereas lawsuits to eradicate monopolies would serve the "negative remedy" of removing the evil, Roosevelt saw expert commissions as able to control the effects of monopoly through ongoing supervision and control. The difference between the two approaches is the extent of governmental power needed to achieve them. Eradication of a monopoly through lawsuits and judicial decisions does not require the construction of new governmental institutions. Moreover, the actions are discrete—once the decision is rendered and the monopoly broken up, the government's action in that particular case is completed. By contrast, Roosevelt's plan sought to create new governmental institutions that would permanently oversee business through ongoing supervision.

Roosevelt's characterization of the New Nationalism in his *Autobiography* closely approximated his defense of the creation of a powerful trade commission on the campaign trail in 1912. As his close advisor Charles McCarthy explained, in response to Wilson's opposition to expanding administrative power, the government can not provide equal opportunity "except by a commission. . . . In the hundred and one changing conditions of our modern life, this commission must make its rulings on the actual facts as they are found and they change from day to day." McCarthy's argument, as indicated here, hinged on the fact that the circumstances of modern economic life *precluded* the old methods of regulation—based on clear, settled standards of conduct clearly set forth in statutes or in common law. Since the facts of modern economic life change daily, what is forbidden will change frequently. Thus, the commission must be given the flexibility to render judgments not based on clear legal rules settled in advance but on the facts as they exist in the present moment. As McCarthy explained, the New Nationalism "simply means that when a particular case arises the case can be dealt with vigorously, *not by the courts, but by this economic commission.*"[129] Courts would not have the needed flexibility to adjust the rules governing economic activity that would belong to an economic commission, in this view.

Therefore, the centerpiece of the New Nationalism was the turn to an economic commission, rather than the traditional method of judicial enforcement, to regulate economic life. Roosevelt argued that new circumstances necessitated the new institutional arrangements. In other words, the form of government that would be used to regulate the economy was of paramount concern to Roosevelt. It was this turn to commission government—which, incidentally, was supported by both Roosevelt *and* Taft during the 1912 election—that Wilson objected to during the campaign.[130]

"Must We Fall Back on a Discretionary Executive Power?"

In comparison to some of his earlier statements in defense of administrative discretion—particularly in "The Study of Administration"—Wilson's campaign speeches seem to indicate a dramatic about-face. On the one hand, Wilson consistently affirmed that he was a progressive in his 1912 speeches. But he also expressed the desire to reform gradually, in stark contrast to Roosevelt's embrace of radicalism. In one of the more famous speeches of the campaign, Wilson explained:

> The modern idea is to leave the past and press onward to something new. But what is progress going to do with the past, and with the present? . . .What attitude shall progressives take toward the existing order, toward those institutions of conservatism, the Constitution, the laws, and the courts? Are those thoughtful men who fear that we are now about to disturb the ancient foundations of our institutions justified in their fear? If they are, we ought to go very slowly about the processes of change. If it is indeed true that we have grown tired of the institutions which we have so carefully and sedulously built up, then we ought to go very slowly and very carefully about the very dangerous task of altering them.[131]

Wilson attempted, therefore, to distinguish between progressivism and radicalism, to seek gradual change without uprooting ancient and tested institutions—or at least to uproot those institutions only after great consideration.

Wilson's remarks on the need to embrace progress through gradual reforms, particularly where institutions ("the Constitution, the laws, and the courts") were involved, foreshadowed his attacks on Roosevelt's turn to commission-style government later in the campaign. His criticism of this element of the New Nationalism was relentless. In a speech titled "Freemen Need No Guardians," Wilson placed himself firmly on the side of Jefferson against Hamilton, whom he deemed "A great man, but, in my judgment, not a great American," for "He did not think in terms of American life."[132] In particular, Hamilton rejected the idea that the common man could understand and therefore administer government. In reply, Wilson argued, "nothing could be a greater departure from original Americanism, from faith in the ability of a confident, resourceful, and independent people, than the discouraging doctrine that someone else has got to provide prosperity for the rest of us."[133] Remarkably, Wilson—the former president of Princeton University—was taking the side of the common man, chastising Hamilton (and by extension Roosevelt) for undermining the idea of independent citizens who govern and take care of themselves rather than relying on experts and elites.

His faith in the capacity of the common person to govern himself was what led to Wilson's rejection of Roosevelt's proposal for commission government. "I don't want a smug lot of experts to sit down behind closed doors in Washington and play Providence to me," Wilson declared. "I believe, as I believe in nothing else, in the average integrity and the average intelligence of the American people, and I do not believe that the intelligence of America can be put into commission anywhere. I do not believe that there is any group of men of any kind to whom we can afford to give that kind of trusteeship," he concluded. On the campaign trail Wilson rejected the idea that experts could be trusted to govern men. "God forbid that in a democratic country we should resign the task and give the government over to experts," he argued.[134] Regulation by the establishment of a permanent commission, Wilson implied, would fundamentally alter the government by destroying ancient and cherished institutions that supported self-government. It would place "a smug lot of experts" in Washington in charge of citizens across the country.

Wilson's rejection of government by experts cannot simply be dismissed as the moderation of a presidential candidate seeking election. For he had earlier indicated his opposition to reforms that would fundamentally alter the constitutional structure of the government. For instance, in 1908 Wilson asked rhetorically, "Must we fall back on a discretionary executive power?" Is consolidating authority in the hands of the executive, in other words, the only path to taming the trusts? Remarkably, he shuddered at this possibility: "The government of the United States was established to get rid of arbitrary, that is, discretionary executive power. . . . If we return to it, we abandon the very principles of our foundation."[135] Four years prior to his dramatic confrontation of Roosevelt, Wilson was condemning the impulse to expand discretionary executive power.

As Melvin Urofsky has recently explained, "Nothing could have been more repugnant to Wilson and Brandeis than the idea of accepting the great trusts and using government to regulate them. To the evil of monopoly would be added the evil of big government controlling the market. . . . Brandeis and Wilson feared big and ruthlessly efficient government as much as Roosevelt opposed excessive individualism."[136] Wilson rejected the New Nationalism because it sought to accept monopoly and regulate it through centralized and powerful commissions. This would combine two wrongs rather than set things right. "[T]he only thing that the third party proposes should be done," Wilson explained, "is to set up a commission to regulate [monopolies]. It accepts them."[137] But, he responded, "I take my stand absolutely, where every progressive ought to take his stand, on the proposition that private monopoly is indefensible and intolerable."[138] Wilson's critique of the New Nationalism, especially its acceptance of the inevitability of monopoly, was heavily influenced by the advice he received from Louis Brandeis throughout the campaign.

Louis Brandeis and the New Freedom

The influence of Brandeis in helping to form Wilson's New Freedom cannot be overstated. In fact, the New Freedom itself cannot be understood without a close examination of Brandeis's reaction to the growth of centralized administrative institutions. Though he originally supported the campaign of Robert La Follette, the progressive Republican from Wisconsin who was eventually eclipsed by Roosevelt in the 1912 campaign, Brandeis endorsed Wilson after their meeting at Sea Girt, New Jersey, in August of 1912.

Brandeis himself characterized the distinction between the New Freedom and the New Nationalism in a set of "suggestions" that he authored and sent to Wilson during the 1912 campaign. Wilson's New Freedom, Brandeis wrote, "insists that competition can and should be maintained in every branch of private industry; that competition can be and should be restored in those branches of industry in which it has been suppressed by the trusts." In short, he asserted, the core of the New Freedom is the use of government to *restore* genuine competition where it has been destroyed by combinations that can simply be declared illegal and broken up. By contrast, Brandeis continued, the New Nationalism "insists that private monopoly may be desirable in some branches of industry, or at all events, is inevitable; and that existing trusts should not be dismembered or forcibly dislodged from those branches of industry in which they have already acquired a monopoly but should be made 'good' by regulation." Roosevelt's position accepted the soundness of trusts and monopolies and sought to make them subservient to the state through centralized commissions, in Brandeis's view. As noted earlier, Brandeis believed (contrary to William Allen White and many contemporary scholars) that the difference was "fundamental and irreconcilable. It is the difference between industrial liberty and industrial absolutism."[139] His characterization of the fundamental difference—one side seeking to eliminate monopolies, the other using government to regulate and control them—thus closely mirrored Wilson's campaign rhetoric.

Brandeis's opposition to the New Nationalism was sufficiently pervasive that, as Charles Forcey explains, he "would have nothing to do with the *New Republic* during its early days, when the lines between the New Nationalism and the Wilson-Brandeis New Freedom were still fairly clearly drawn."[140] The aversion the two parties felt for each other illustrates the extent of the rift that the New Freedom and New Nationalism caused within progressive ranks. It reveals that the dispute between the two camps had to do with core principles having to do with the soundness of traditional American institutions in a modern context.

In fact, Brandeis was determined throughout his career to meld his progressive ideals about government's role in regulating economic life with his opposition to the centralization of governmental power. Even as late as 1935, when he cast a vote as Supreme Court justice to strike down the National Industry Recovery Act, Brandeis stood by this opposition to administrative centralization. As he boasted (prematurely, in hindsight) to Thomas Corcoran, one of FDR's top advisors, "This is the end of this business of centralization, and I want you to go back and tell the President that we're not going to let this government centralize everything. It's come to an end."[141] Brandeis thus viewed his vote in striking down central programs of the New Deal as a continuation of his struggle against the establishment of centralized administrative power—a struggle in which he engaged alongside Wilson in 1912.

Scholars have credited Louis Brandeis with some role in shaping Wilson's New Freedom, though they debate the extent of Brandeis's influence. Wilson biographer Arthur Link has argued that Brandeis was responsible for "all of [the] ideas that [Wilson] expressed during the presidential campaign."[142] Milkis, on the other hand, warns that "scholars should not exaggerate Brandeis's contribution to the New Freedom. After all, Wilson had been seeking to rally supporters to enlist in a campaign against monopoly since he was anointed in Baltimore." Thus "Brandeis helped Wilson clarify a direction in which he was already moving."[143] It is true that Wilson did not follow every element of Brandeis's analysis of monopoly. For instance, Brandeis argued consistently that the size of trusts is what made them harmful to society, whereas Wilson typically drew a distinction between large corporations and monopoly, denouncing only the latter.[144] However, Brandeis helped clarify Wilson's alternative to the New Nationalism and sharpened Wilson's thinking about the central issues of constitutionalism provoked by Roosevelt's proposals.

"Any Decently Equipped Lawyer"

If Wilson and Brandeis did not trust a centralized governmental institution staffed with experts to regulate the economy, how would the New Freedom go about the business of regulation? In other words, what did they formulate as an alternative to the New Nationalism, and how would it rest on a different institutional foundation?

Wilson and Brandeis both maintained that the Sherman Anti-Trust Act was sufficient to break up trusts. It did not need to be replaced, they claimed; it merely needed to be strengthened so that it could be effectively administered.

In particular, as Thomas McCraw notes, Brandeis laid out a series of measures to Wilson that would strengthen the Sherman Act by prohibiting the specific methods by which the trusts gained their advantages, as well as the creation of a commission that would assist with investigations and offer advice to the Department of Justice with regard to specific anti-trust proceedings.[145] The path towards effectively breaking up monopolies, in this view, was to specify the conduct that is forbidden by law, and then support vigorous enforcement by traditional administrative means.

Under Brandeis's proposals, which were substantially adopted by Wilson in 1912, the rules that would govern the conduct of business with regard to combination would be established clearly in a legislative statute and would be enforced by courts rather than commissions. Wilson in 1912 argued that "Any decently equipped lawyer can suggest to you the statutes by which the whole business can be stopped."[146] Whereas Roosevelt suggested that a commission was needed because the rules of conduct could not be set forth in advance, Wilson asserted that it was possible to articulate basic rules prohibiting the kinds of combinations that gave rise to monopoly. Once the rules were established, they could be enforced by the traditional method of lawsuits against violators.

A few years prior to the 1912 election, Wilson helped to draft a platform for the Democratic Party of Pennsylvania. He recommended "legislation which will define and forbid those acts and practices on their part, and those methods in the organization and control, which have proved destructive of free competition."[147] The standards of conduct that business must follow, in Wilson's proposal, would come from the law, which would clearly define those standards. Continuing this theme in an interview with the *New York Times* in 1911, Wilson said that the best way to stamp out "the methods by which the greater trusts have driven competitors out of business" would be to make them "criminal offenses."[148] This is what Wilson meant when he stated his preference for "legal regulation" rather than "executive regulation."

Legal regulation would come from clearly defined standards in legislation (or common law) and would be enforced by courts and executive officials. Executive regulation involved the consolidation of rulemaking, executive, and adjudicatory power in expert commissions to oversee big business. As Wilson put it in a 1908 piece titled "Law or Personal Power," unless the law is written to contain "precise terms of regulation" the turn to expert commissions would substitute arbitrariness for the rule of law, since the same institution would create the terms that must be followed and carry them out.[149]

It is important not to confuse Wilson and Brandeis's proposal for a trade commission with the core proposal of the New Nationalism to empower a commission to oversee business generally. The New Freedom approach favored by Wilson and Brandeis would have created a commission merely for administrative or executive purposes, rather than combining rulemaking, executive, and adjudicatory functions. The commission envisioned by the New Freedom would serve limited purposes associated with a traditional understanding of administration: investigation, information-gathering, and assistance in carrying out laws containing clear enumerations of forbidden actions. The alternative to the New Nationalism, therefore, was regulation that would co-exist with the traditional separation of powers that prevailed prior to the Progressive era. Laws would state clear rules, agencies would investigate, prosecute, and enforce these rules, and particular cases would be resolved in courts of law.

Brandeis and Wilson offered another alternative to the Progressive vision for a modern administrative state, one that was more traditionally American than Freund's *Rechtstaat*. Whereas Freund advocated the creation of administrative law courts, Brandeis and Wilson relied upon the traditional American combination of carefully written statutes that limit discretion and judicial enforcement through litigation. While they sought to expand dramatically the scope of activity that would be governed through this model, their institutional vision had roots in core principles of American constitutionalism. While, as mentioned earlier, Wilson may not have implemented this vision strictly upon becoming president, in important respects this vision was central to the creation of the Federal Trade Commission. It would also be revived by reformers such as Roscoe Pound during the New Deal.

The New Freedom and the Federal Trade Commission

As indicated in the beginning of this paragraph, the Sherman Anti-Trust Act sought to address the problem of economic combinations and trusts that threatened to undermine fair competition through a traditional administrative structure. The statute declared combinations in restraint of trade to be illegal and utilized existing institutions (the Department of Justice and the federal circuit courts) for enforcement of the statutory provisions. Yet according to Progressive reformers this approach was insufficient because it did not adequately clarify in advance what the law actually forbade. Congress itself did not understand what the Sherman Act actually meant, and even Wilson argued in the 1912 election that the law needed updating simply to clarify the illegal trade practices that the law forbade.

The challenge lay not only in defining the illegal activities in law, but more profoundly in assembling the political support necessary to enact appropriate legislation. The second obstacle proved to be more significant than the first. Members of Congress quickly realized that they had little interest in setting forth these rules in advance, and if they could create a commission that would follow the will of Congress, they could have it both ways. They could agree to place an open-ended definition of unfair competition in the law and influence the implementation of the law by rendering the Commission subordinate to congressional oversight. The critical portion of the FTC Act of 1914 reflected this impulse, providing that "Whenever the Commission shall have reason to believe that" an entity "has been or is using any unfair method of competition or deceptive act or practice . . . and if it shall appear to the Commission that a proceeding by it in respect thereof would be to the interest of the public," it could institute a proceeding charging the entity with a violation of the Act. While on paper this appeared to make the FTC arbiter of a wide swath of economic activity, with an open-ended mandate that it could interpret to its liking, Congress sought to avoid that arrangement by retaining political control over the Commission.

Thus even the Federal Trade Commission, with its extensive and open-ended powers, bore resemblance to the earlier approach to administration in a few critical respects. In spite of his academic pronouncements about the need to separate politics and administration, Wilson undermined some of Roosevelt's efforts to expand the merit system and insulate the bureaucracy from the spoils system. "[T]he significant thing about his first term," Skowronek writes of Wilson, "is the abandonment of the idea that administrative control required independent and imposing executive machinery."[150] Wilson sought to keep the administrative state within the control of parties, although the parties would now be made responsible and would be led by presidents with a new understanding of leadership. The Federal Trade Commission was not immune from these efforts. The legislation establishing the FTC clarified that its personnel would not be covered by the merit system, and Wilson succeeded in securing a provision authorizing the president to direct the Commission regarding specific investigations. In important respects, therefore, the Federal Trade Commission did not represent a truly independent regulatory commission at its inception. As a result, Skowronek concludes, "Wilson failed to place relations between party and bureaucracy on a new plane. His programmatic achievements remained personal and circumstantial and left this basic structural tension between party power and administrative modernization unresolved."[151] Thomas Merrill similarly explains that the core of the Federal Trade

Act "was hastily cobbled together at the last minute with little opportunity for legislative discussion."[152] It was not a momentous shift reflecting a new theoretical understanding of the administrative state, but a confused piece of legislation passed through a chaotic congressional procedure.

The Emergence of Judicial Deference

Progressive ideas mattered significantly for administrative law. Even in the first few decades of the 1900s they successfully curtailed the scope of judicial review of administrative decision making. As G. Edward White explains, during this time "the Court . . . promulgated some specialized administrative law doctrines that had the effect of limiting review, such as the 'negative order doctrine,' which insulated from review refusals of an agency to grant relief on the hearing of a complaint; limitations on the standing of potential claimants before agencies; and the distinction between agency rulemaking and adjudication, which limited judicial review only to the latter type of decision."[153] All of these doctrines set limits on the judiciary's ability to hear cases involving, and therefore to review, administrative decisions. (The creation of standing doctrine is discussed in the following chapter.)

Even when the courts granted review, moreover, they began deferring to administrative determinations that were previously reviewed de novo.[154] In *Bates v. Payne*, decided in 1904, the Court was confronted with another Post Office interpretation, this time of a periodical titled "Masters in Music." Masters in Music issues were collections of sheet music, with each issue featuring the works of a single musician. The Postmaster General interpreted these issues not as periodicals subject to second-class mail rates, but as sheet music classified as third-class mail. Justice Brown, writing for the Court, acknowledged that the question presented was legal and not factual in nature—therefore to be reviewed de novo by the Court. However, invoking Taney's reasoning in *Decatur*, he argued that the statute granted discretion to the Postmaster General, and "the exercise of such discretion ought not to be interfered with unless the court be clearly of opinion that it was wrong."[155] In spite of the fact that the courts had general jurisdiction to review administrative interpretations of law—a power the judiciary obtained decades earlier in 1875—Brown seemed to think that deference to the Postmaster General was required. Brown's opinion explicitly mentioned *Decatur* and indicated that the case should be decided similarly to mandamus cases, in spite of the change in the scope of review that the 1875 law had created.[156] The juxtaposition of *Bates* with *McAnnulty*, discussed at the opening of this chapter, was striking and revealed how quickly the courts were shifting to a deferential posture towards administrative power. Justice Harlan, writing in dissent, was quick to point out that *Bates* went against the long-standing approach of courts reviewing administrative constructions of statutes.[157]

This movement to deference was especially prominent with regard to the ICC, now strengthened by the passage of the Hepburn Act.[158] In early cases involving the ICC, as discussed in the previous chapter, the courts viewed it with a skeptical eye and routinely handed down decisions adverse to the agency. After the passage of Hepburn, however, the tide shifted. In the "Intermountain Rate Cases" in 1914 and the *Akron, Canton & Youngstown Railway* case in 1923 the Court granted deference to the ICC's exercise of its rate-setting power, signaling a retreat from the field. In 1918 the Court explicitly conceded that whether a rate is discriminatory or unreasonable was an issue "of fact . . . confided by Congress to the judgment and discretion of the Commission."[159] "By 1920 . . . the courts and the ICC seem to have settled their differences, and the judiciary placed itself in a considerably more deferential posture," writes Reuel Schiller.[160]

Respecting a variety of agencies, from the Post Office to the ICC, and spanning several doctrines, from standing to sue to review of ratesetting, the courts began to retreat from their earlier, less deferential posture towards the new administrative state. But this did not happen all at once, nor did it occur across every agency. The Federal Trade Commission, in particular, seemed incapable of satisfying the judiciary even in the 1920s. In spite of the fact that the FTC's statutory mandate—to prohibit "unfair methods of competition"—seemed just as discretionary as the ICC's determination of discriminatory or unreasonable rates, the Court consistently maintained that it was an issue of law to be decided by courts rather than the agency. In *Federal Trade Commission v. Gratz*, the Court determined that it would decide the meaning of this statutory term rather than defer to the agency, a precedent that Thomas Merrill writes "set the pattern for judicial review of FTC cease and desist orders for the next twenty years. The Supreme Court . . . freely indulged in defining the scope of 'unfair competition' itself" during this period.[161] Therefore, even as the era of judicial deference descended upon the administrative state, there remained pockets of the traditional approach to judicial review of administrative agencies.

The Arrival of the Administrative State

The first two decades of the twentieth century brought the administrative state to American politics. But in important respects the reform agenda had not yet been achieved. The issue of agency independence had not yet been fully addressed and the place of regulatory agencies in the constitutional system was still hotly debated. Even the Federal Trade Commission was not made independent of the president. Yet Progressive reformers had articulated the theoretical foundations and established critical precedents that would pave the way for the administrative state's expansion over the next century. While they acknowledged the tension that existed between their approach to administration and that of the Framers of the Constitution, they had succeeded in supplanting the older approach. Even the judiciary was beginning to back away from the scope of review of administrative action that had prevailed over the first century of American history. The tension between the basic principles of American constitutionalism and the modern administrative state would lead to a series of constitutional crises that reformers would have to confront later. The New Deal's expansion of bureaucratic power brought the crises to the fore.

CHAPTER SIX

The Crisis of Legitimacy

The New Deal Challenge to
American Constitutionalism

WHEN FRANKLIN ROOSEVELT assumed the Presidency in 1933 he found an administrative state that had achieved a foothold through the establishment of a handful of critical agencies such as the Federal Trade Commission and the Federal Power Commission. In addition, as Chapter Five explained, new theories of judicial deference to administrative decision making had been crafted by jurists and theorists aiming to entrench this new administrative state as an independent, expert body of policymakers.

During his first two terms in office Roosevelt worked to expand this administrative state dramatically and to insulate its decisions even further from judicial oversight. This prompted a backlash, first from the judiciary itself, then from Congress, and finally from the legal community and its allies in Congress. The Supreme Court attempted to limit delegation of legislative power to agencies and insulate them from the direct oversight of the president. Congress successfully resisted FDR's attempts to reassert presidential control over independent agencies. Later in the 1930s and into the 1940s, lawyers and skeptics of administrative power in Congress sought legislation that would constrain the burgeoning administrative state. The first manifestation of this effort, the Walter-Logan Act, failed to overcome the president's veto. However, Congress successfully resisted Franklin Roosevelt's attempt to reorganize the administrative state under his direct supervision, and eventually enacted the Administrative Procedure Act in 1946, a measure whose intent was very different from its practical effect.

The New Deal Administrative State and the Courts
As historians have noted for decades, the Great Depression prompted an unprecedented response from Franklin Roosevelt once he assumed office in

1933. Along with myriad new federal programs to alleviate the crisis came "the creation of scores of new administrative agencies to implement" these programs.[1] These agencies were granted immense power, but in a haphazard manner due to the hurried nature of the response to the crisis.

The two most sweeping delegations of power to administrative agencies came in the National Industry Recovery Act (NIRA) and the Agricultural Adjustment Act (AAA). These two initiatives, which Roosevelt called the pillars of the New Deal in a fireside chat, gave the government broad powers to plan and coordinate economic and agricultural activity and production. The NIRA gave the president the power to enact "codes of fair competition," a power that he frequently delegated to various boards and commissions such as the Petroleum Administrative Board. Industries and government worked cooperatively under the NIRA to draft and promulgate these codes. The AAA authorized the Secretary of Agriculture to manage agricultural production in order to ensure the stability of agricultural prices. The central idea of both of these programs was to bring industry and government leaders together to coordinate and plan their activities. As Adlai Stevenson, Jr., a lawyer for the government charged with implementing the AAA, maintained, "in essence we're creating gigantic trusts in all the food industries."[2]

In addition to these foundational measures, the New Deal introduced a plethora of regulatory programs, each delegating broad powers to a newly created or existing administrative body. The Securities Exchange Act of 1934 gave the new Securities and Exchange Commission (SEC) the power to prohibit the use of "any manipulative or deceptive advice or contrivance in contravention of such rules and regulations as the commission may prescribe as necessary or appropriate in the public interest." The following year Congress passed the Public Utility Holding Company Act of 1935, granting SEC the power to veto reorganization plans of public utility holding companies if they "will result in an unfair or inequitable distribution of voting power among holders of the securities." The National Labor Relations Act gave the newly established National Labor Relations Board (NLRB) the power to govern relations between employers and employees, including the institution of collective bargaining rights. The Federal Communications Commission was authorized to grant broadcast licenses to applicants "if public convenience, interest, or necessity will be served thereby." Dozens of other agencies received similarly expansive mandates. Discretion was vested far and wide.

In short, as Joanna Grisinger summarizes, "By the end of the 1930s, the bureaucrats were in charge."[3] The New Deal amounted to a sea change in the

structure of the political system: "Americans transformed the political relationships, institutional framework, and legal structure of the federal government as they placed ever more legislative, executive, and judicial authority in
executive agencies and departments and in a new 'fourth branch' of independent regulatory commissions."[4] While the Progressive era witnessed sporadic
efforts to construct regulatory institutions and establish a regulatory state, the
New Deal dramatically expanded the scope of the regulatory state and made
it the most distinctive feature of modern American government.

"Delegation Run Riot"

The frenzied establishment of myriad agencies and programs during the New
Deal ran into resistance in 1935. In January of that year, the Supreme Court
decided *Panama Refining Company Co. v. Ryan*, a decision that for the first
time struck down a statute for violating the nondelegation doctrine.[5] This
complicated case involved section 9(c) of the NIRA, which authorized the
president to prohibit sales of "hot oil" in interstate commerce. Hot oil was
defined as petroleum or products thereof that were in excess of the amount
permitted by state authorities. Chief Justice Charles Evans Hughes, writing
for the Court, argued that section 9(c) of the Act failed to declare any policy
or set any standard that would guide the president's discretionary use of this
power. The statute required no findings of fact by the president before acting.
As such, Hughes reasoned, it delegated the power to make law to the president, rather than merely requiring the president to carry out the decisions
made by the legislature in the statute.

A few months later, the Supreme Court handed down a harsher decision on
what would eventually become known as "Black Monday": May 27, 1935. In
Schecter Poultry Corporation v. United States, the Court struck down section 3
of the NIRA, again for violating the nondelegation doctrine.[6] That section authorized the president to establish "codes of fair competition," and the Schecter
Corporation was convicted for violating New York City's Live Poultry Code.
That code fixed the hours of work days and minimum wages and prohibited
certain practices said to constitute unfair competition. In a unanimous decision the Court ruled that section 3 failed to define "fair competition" in such a
way that the Act itself "established the standards of legal obligation." Because
the Act did not establish the standards of legal obligation, it "attempted to
transfer that authority to others," in violation of the Constitution's mandate
that all legislative powers be exercised by Congress. *Schecter's* most famous
passage, however, came from Justice Benjamin Cardozo's concurring opinion.

Cardozo was willing to allow broad delegation to administrative agencies; he had provided the only dissenting vote in *Panama Refining*. But the NIRA's delegation of power to industry groups, who typically collaborated with the president to establish these codes of fair competition, "is delegation run riot," he proclaimed.[7]

Panama Refining and *Schecter Poultry Corp.* were the first two cases in the history of the Supreme Court in which the nondelegation doctrine was used to strike down a federal statute. On the same day that the Court handed down *Schecter*, it struck a further blow at the president by upholding a statute that appeared to insulate the head of the Federal Trade Commission from FDR's power to remove administrative personnel.

The Mere Retreat to the Qualifying "Quasi"

Early in his first term in office Franklin Roosevelt asked for William Humphrey, a commissioner on the Federal Trade Commission appointed by Calvin Coolidge in 1925 and reappointed by Herbert Hoover in 1931, to tender his resignation. FDR reasoned that the work of the commission "can be carried out most effectively with personnel of my own selection." Humphrey refused Roosevelt's request and the president again insisted on Humphrey's departure: "I do not feel that your mind and my mind go along together on either the policies or the administering of the Federal Trade Commission, and frankly, I think it best for the people of this country that I should have full confidence."[8] Roosevelt's appeal connected confidence in the president with his responsibility for administration, and by extension the need to have control over administrative decision makers. This was the language of presidential responsibility, so widely used during the framing of the Constitution, applied to modern administrative agencies. It also revealed Roosevelt's understanding that the separation of politics and administration can have pernicious effects not anticipated by earlier Progressives.

In October 1933, several months after asking for Humphrey's resignation, FDR dismissed him. Humphrey filed for back salary in the U.S. Court of Claims, alleging that he was illegally dismissed from his position. Shortly after filing Humphrey died from a stroke and his executor took over the case. If the FTC Act only permitted dismissal of commissioners for "inefficiency, neglect of duty, or malfeasance in office," was that a violation of the president's constitutional removal power? If so, then the statute's limitations on the president's removal authority were unconstitutional, and Roosevelt would win the case. As explained in Chapters Two and Three, the "Decision of 1789," while not overwhelmingly decisive, had seemed to settle the constitutional matter: the president had the constitutional authority to remove administrators at will. Even dissenters from this decision such as William Smith and Daniel Webster acknowledged the question as settled.

And recently, in 1926, Chief Justice William Howard Taft had ruled in *Myers v. United States* that officers such as postmasters were subject to the president's removal power. After examining the "Decision of 1789" Taft claimed that "there is not the slightest doubt, after an examination of the record, that the vote was, and was intended to be, a legislative declaration that the power to remove officers appointed by the President and the Senate vested in the President alone." He also acknowledged that this was the prevailing view of the decision "until the Johnson Impeachment trial in 1868."[9] Since *Myers* had been so recently decided, and it had clearly declared that the president's subordinate officers must be accountable to the president, Roosevelt's lawyers believed that victory was inevitable. After all, Taft had explicitly written in *Myers* that the president's "cabinet officers must do his will. He must place in each member of his official family, and his chief executive subordinates, implicit faith. . . . The imperative reasons requiring an unrestricted power to remove the most important of his subordinates in their most important duties must, therefore, control the interpretation of the Constitution as to all appointed by him."[10]

However, in an oft-overlooked portion of Taft's opinion, he granted that "there may be duties so peculiarly and specifically committed to the discretion of a particular officer as to raise a question whether the President may overrule or revise the officer's interpretation of his statutory duty in a particular instance." In addition, he continued, "there may be duties of a *quasi*-judicial character imposed on executive officers and members of executive tribunals whose decisions after hearing affect interests of individuals, the discharge of which the President cannot in a particular case properly influence or control."[11] Even in a decision that affirmed the president's power to remove subordinate officers, therefore, Taft proved not to be a pure Unitarian. He granted that Congress could vest administrators with certain duties that cannot be controlled by the president. This indicated that Taft did not see constitutional problems with vesting discretionary responsibilities in subordinate officers insulated from presidential control. Even in *Myers* Taft distinguished unitary control of administrative personnel, which he agreed was required under the Constitution, from unitary control of administrative decisions.

When the Court announced unanimously in *Humphrey's Executor v. United States* that Humphrey had been dismissed illegally, upholding the FTC Act's limitations on the president's removal power, most experts were shocked. How would the Court justify this departure from the settled construction of the Constitution and the decision's apparent conflict with *Myers?* Justice Sutherland, writing for the Court, opened by announcing that the FTC "must, from the very nature of its duties, act with entire impartiality. . . . Its duties are neither political nor executive, but predominantly quasi-judicial and quasi-legislative. . . . Its members are called upon to exercise the trained judgment of a body of experts."[12] With this opening, seemingly based on Taft's subtle admission in *Myers*, Sutherland distinguished between "political" and "executive" officers, who are not required to "act with entire impartiality" and can therefore be held accountable to the President, and administrators who perform "quasi-judicial" and "quasi-legislative" duties. These duties, in contrast to those of the executive officers, require "the trained judgment of a body of experts," which would be undermined by holding independent agencies accountable to a political officer. Consequently, Sutherland reasoned, the commission must be "free from political domination or control" and remain "separate and apart from any existing department of the government."[13] Applying this distinction between executive and "quasi-judicial and "quasi-legislative" administrators enabled the Court to distinguish this case from *Myers*. "A postmaster is an executive officer restricted to the performance of executive functions," Sutherland wrote. Conversely, "The Federal Trade Commission is an administrative body created by Congress to carry into effect legislative policies embodied in the statute. . . . Such a body cannot in any proper sense be characterized as an arm or an eye of the executive."[14]

Sutherland's reasoning essentially entrenched the Progressives' theoretical distinction between politics and administration as a doctrine of constitutional and administrative law. The irony was that this principle was advanced by a Court seeking to protect the administrative state from the influence of a president who wanted to exert political influence to advance progressive policy objectives. *Humphrey's Executor* essentially created a new category of governmental institutions—those wielding not legislative, executive, or judicial power but those wielding "quasi-judicial" and "quasi-legislative" power—in constitutional jurisprudence. Less than twenty years later Justice Robert Jackson would criticize this new category: "Administrative agencies have been called quasi-legislative, quasi-executive or quasi-judicial, as the occasion required, in order to validate their functions within the separation-of-powers scheme of the Constitution. The mere retreat to the qualifying 'quasi' is implicit with confession that all recognized classifications have broken down, and 'quasi' is a smooth cover which we draw over our confusion as we might use a counterpane to conceal a disordered bed."[15]

"Black Monday" was understood by at least some of the Justices as a key turning point in the New Deal. Justice Brandeis, who two decades earlier had fought Theodore Roosevelt's "New Nationalism," lectured his cousin's closest advisors on the need to obey the rule of law. After summoning Benjamin Cohen and Thomas Corcoran to his chambers following the reading of the *Schecter* and *Humphrey's Executor* opinions, Brandeis informed them that "This is the end of this business of centralization. . . . I want you to go back and tell the President that we're not going to let this government centralize everything." "The President has been living in a fool's paradise," Brandeis concluded, and the Court was going to ensure that Roosevelt remained in the real world, where the administrative state would be bound by constitutional principles enforced by the highest court in the land.[16]

Brandeis's boast that the Court would "end this business of centralization" proved to be unfounded. Roosevelt's New Deal agenda would be slowed, and adjusted, by the opposition of the Supreme Court and other actors, but the administrative state's expansion would continue. As the New Deal progressed, statutes were crafted more carefully, requiring findings of fact and guiding administrative discretion through "intelligible principles" contained in authorizing statutes, and the Court's resistance abated.[17]

Reorganizing the "Headless Fourth Branch"

The Supreme Court's rebuke on "Black Monday" directly challenged Franklin Roosevelt's vision for administrative law. By placing limits on the extent of administrative discretion and insulating administrative decision makers from presidential oversight the Court sought to reassert its role in overseeing the administrative state while undermining the president's control over the bureaucracy. Roosevelt's response was to press for legislative solutions to these judicial challenges. If Congress would voluntarily give him the power to supervise the administrative state and guard against extending judicial review over administrative action, Roosevelt reasoned, the new programmatic activities of the federal government could be managed efficiently and shielded from potential legal challenges. In the end he got some but not all of what he sought.

Franklin Roosevelt's Administrative Theory

As previous chapters have shown, by 1900 administrative law had settled on a framework for judicial review in which administrative agencies would receive judicial deference when making factual determinations, but courts would reserve de novo review for questions of law. This ensured that courts would exercise review in the area of their peculiar expertise: legal interpretation. Agencies, which possess expertise on the facts and circumstances in their policy areas, would be entitled to judicial respect in their areas of competence.

This distinction between law and fact in determining the scope of judicial review of agency findings came under attack by Progressive legal thinkers prior to the New Deal. Progressives, as noted earlier, sought to restrict the scope of judicial review across the board, including review of agency interpretations of law. Attacking the distinction between law and fact would allow Progressives to collapse judicial review into a single category in which deference would be the default rule. Perhaps the most influential thinker to advance this project was John Dickinson, whose 1927 work *Administrative Justice and the Supremacy of Law in the United States* became a foundational text in administrative law. The book was widely acclaimed and earned Dickinson a promotion from lecturer in the Government department at Harvard to an appointment as full professor at the University of Pennsylvania's law school.[18] In *Administrative Justice* Dickinson famously advanced the notion that the distinction between law and fact, while tenable as an analytical matter, broke down quickly in practice. In his words, they "are not two mutually exclusive kinds of questions, based upon a difference of subject-matter. Matters of law grow downward into roots of fact, and matters of fact reach upward, without a break, into matters of law." In other words, he argued, "there is no fixed distinction."[19] As Thomas Merrill has explained, this critical attack on the distinction between law and fact laid the groundwork for a single, unified theory of judicial review based on the appellate review model, in which the court does not substitute its judgment for that of the agency but merely ensures that the agency followed a minimal standard of rationality.

Bates v. Payne, discussed previously in Chapter Five, gave Dickinson the opening he sought. *Bates* had set up a middle position between questions of law and questions of fact, called "mixed question[s] of law and fact." In these categories, the Court reasoned in *Bates*, the agency should receive deference equivalent to that which governs judicial review of factual determinations. Dickinson's argument, and his use of the *Bates* precedent, meshed perfectly with the dominant views in the Roosevelt administration regarding the appropriate judicial role in the administrative state. As Aditya Bamzai notes, "the dominant approach within the academy—and the Roosevelt Executive Branch—embraced administrative discretion." And Dickinson's argument entailed that "certain questions that had traditionally been deemed 'legal' could be reconceptualized as 'factual' where the principle being articulated was of insufficient abstraction to require intrusion by generalist courts into

the functioning of expert agencies."[20] Transforming questions previously understood to be legal into "mixed questions of law and fact" or purely factual
questions would ensure that the courts would defer to a greater number of
administrative determinations, keeping the meddlesome judiciary from undermining the goals of the administrative state.[21]

While it might have seemed unlikely that the federal judiciary would adopt
a more deferential posture towards the administrative state, given the developments of the previous few decades, some of Franklin Roosevelt's closest
advisors were optimistic that the courts would soon see the light. Rex Tugwell,
Felix Frankfurter, and James Landis all argued that the New Deal should be
premised on a conception of "government as a profoundly prescriptive entity. Experts would formulate policy, agencies would implement it, and courts
would stay out of the way."[22] These thinkers "rejected any role for the courts in
the policymaking process. . . . [T]he vision of the judiciary that went with the
prescriptive state was a profoundly minimalist one."[23] These thinkers acknowledged that the old common-law remedies existed as a possible avenue through
which regulation could be administered, but as Landis wrote, they believed
that courts were unable to "maintain a long-time, uninterrupted interest in a
relatively narrow and carefully defined area of economic and social activity."[24]
Therefore regulation "could not be achieved through the intermittent intervention of the judicial process."[25] Expert administrators, rather than common-law
judges, would have to be the agents of the modern administrative state. Even
judicial review of expert administrators would have to be curtailed; as Mark
Tushnet has written, Progressives such as Frankfurter and Landis "wanted to
insulate the modern administrative state from judges supervising the agencies
and imposing court-like procedures on them."[26]

In one important sense, however, FDR departed from the vision for administrative law offered by intellectuals such as Dickinson, Tugwell, Frankfurter,
and Landis. While these thinkers, following the arguments of earlier Progressives, had insisted upon the separation of politics and administration in order
to facilitate the implementation of policy by experts, Roosevelt saw practical difficulties with such an approach. As Sidney Milkis explains, "Reformers
during the Progressive era, especially Herbert Croly, had defended making
independent commissions the principal agents of progressive democracy." In
their view "independent regulatory commissions made possible the separation
of politics and administration, thus freeing experts in various policy spheres
'to do right.'" "This view of public administration," he argues, "held sway until
the middle of the 1930s," as illustrated by the broad grants of authority to

agencies such as the ICC and FTC in the early part of the twentieth century.[27] Even in FDR's own administration, thinkers such as James Landis continued to defend this vision of an independent administrative power where expertise, not politics, would guide the formulation of policy. However, as Milkis notes, "Roosevelt's attempt to seize control over the FTC early in his administration revealed that he was never comfortable with such commissions." In Roosevelt's view, the problem with the separation of politics and administration and rule by experts was that it prevented "meaningful accountability to the public" and was "too susceptible to the influence of interests that would eventually obstruct the development" of good policy.[28] Instead of an independent administrative power, in which the president's hands would be tied, FDR envisioned placing the president at the head of the administrative state, imposing accountability as well as the public interest on an apparatus that risked being unaccountable and infiltrated by organized interests. After the flurry of the first few years of the New Deal subsided, Roosevelt was able to turn to this objective, prompting a dramatic showdown with Congress over the appropriate structure of the administrative state.

The Brownlow Committee and the
Struggle over Executive Reorganization

Given the growth of the bureaucracy set in motion by the New Deal, Roosevelt was afforded the opportunity to implement his administrative theory within a few years of assuming office. As Sidney Milkis has explained, "By 1935, the administration was becoming a bewildering maze of autonomous and semiautonomous regulatory agencies, a state of administrative decentralization and fragmentation that offended Roosevelt's vision of a unified and energetic executive department."[29] Presidential management of this administrative state was impossible due to its unwieldy nature. This prevented the president from assuming responsibility for his administration, and after 1937 FDR attempted to push a reorganization bill through the Congress that would renew his supervisory authority over the bureaucracy.

Knowing that any attempt to reestablish presidential control over the bureaucracy would produce significant opposition in the Congress, FDR sought to couch his proposals as simply an extension of the many preceding attempts by previous administrations to streamline and make efficient the activities of the government. He could point to commission after commission that had previously attempted to reorganize administrative agencies to reduce inefficiencies, from the retrenchment committees of the 1830s and 1840s, to the Dockery-Cockrell Commission, Keep Committee, and the Commission on

Economy and Efficiency. The latter three commissions were created during the Cleveland, Theodore Roosevelt, and Taft administrations to improve the methods and practice of the executive departments.

But FDR's attempt to reshape the burgeoning federal bureaucracy was destined to run into greater resistance, both because of the increased scope of the administrative state and the fundamental nature of his project. The report of the president's Committee on Administrative Management, typically known as the Brownlow Committee (named for its chairman, Louis Brownlow), which "formed the nucleus of Roosevelt's recommendations to the Congress in early 1937," did more than recommend making the bureaucracy more efficient.[30] It raised fundamental constitutional questions that would influence the development of the administrative state for decades to come.[31]

FDR convened the Brownlow Committee in the spring of 1936 and presented his reorganization plan, based heavily on the Committee's work, in January 1937. In addition to expanding the president's personal staff in the White House (as opposed to staff in the executive departments), and expanding the protections of the merit system to more personnel, FDR recommended placing the increasing number of independent commissions, boards, and agencies within the major executive departments, where they would be more directly accountable to the supervision of the chief executive. This latter point—the elimination of the independent status of many agencies (facilitated by the Supreme Court's decision in *Humphrey's Executor*)—was the most critical as well as the most controversial. As noted in Chapter Five, Congress routinely conspired to place agencies in an independent position so that it, and not the president, could control the agencies' implementation of regulatory programs. Both the ICC and the FTC had been made independent, not simply because of Progressive theory in favor of separating politics and administration but also because of its own institutional interest. Congress wanted to retain control over the bureaucracy for political reasons.

In its most famous passage, the Brownlow Committee report attacked independent regulatory commissions using constitutional language. These agencies, the report argued, amounted to "a headless 'fourth branch' of government, a haphazard deposit of irresponsible agencies and uncoordinated powers."[32] The administrative state had "grown up without a plan or design like the barns, shacks, silos, tool sheds, and garages of an old farm."[33] By invoking the constitutional language of executive responsibility, the Brownlow Committee report appealed to constitutional principle to attack the independence of the bureaucracy from politics. There was considerable constitutional pedigree for this argument in favor of the president's constitutional responsibility for administration: as noted in Chapter One, presidential responsibility was a critical theme at the Constitutional Convention and in Hamilton's defense of the presidency in *The Federalist*.

While the president's proposal for executive reorganization was couched as another of the many attempts to streamline the bureaucracy, Congress was not fooled. FDR's opponents in the legislature immediately recognized that the proposal was a far-reaching attempt by the president to transform the administrative state into an arm of the executive. As Milkis argues, "Congress would have been abnegating its constitutional responsibility by forfeiting control of administrative organization just at a time in American political history when administration was becoming the center of government action."[34] And it certainly did not intend to do so. After a protracted battle the 1937 reorganization bill was scuttled in the House of Representatives in April of 1938.

Humbled by this defeat, FDR eventually proposed a more modest reorganization measure that was enacted as the Reorganization Act of 1939. The most important independent regulatory agencies were exempted from the reorganization power that the Act granted to the president, ensuring that the independent regulatory commissions would remain an independent arm of the political system. While still significant, especially for the eventual establishment of the Executive Office of the President, which subsequent presidents would employ to gain greater control over the administrative state, Roosevelt failed to achieve the critical objective of placing the entire federal bureaucracy within the executive departments, where they might be more easily and directly supervised by the president.

The battle over executive reorganization, which pitted FDR against Congress over political control of the administrative state, was followed by a different conflict between Roosevelt and the lawyers who sought to place the administrative state under legal constraints imposed through judicial review. These legal reformers would eventually produce a piece of legislation, the Walter-Logan Act, that would have substantially weakened—if not crippled—the administrative apparatus FDR had worked sedulously to create. As with the fight over reorganization, however, FDR managed to ensure the integrity of the administrative state.

Lawyers in Opposition

Roosevelt saw that the bench and bar, including lawyers serving in the Congress, formed the primary opposition to his efforts to expand and insulate administrative power. He did not retreat from the fight, as illustrated by his famous attempt to expand the Supreme Court with justices more sympathetic to the New Deal. The practical consequence of these developments was to continue the established deferential posture that courts assumed with respect to administrative agencies.

Therefore, Roosevelt's struggle with the organized legal community was an extension of the struggle between the courts and the administrative state that had reached a détente in the 1920s, with courts agreeing to back away from stringent oversight of the administrative state. The doctrine of standing, first developed in the 1920s and furthered during the New Deal, limited the scope of controversies that the courts would have to adjudicate regarding administrative decisions. However, while Roosevelt had managed to satisfy the Supreme Court's constitutional resistance to the administrative state, the American Bar Association and its allies in Congress were working diligently to limit further the discretion granted to the bureaucracy.

The Invention of Standing?

Many recent commentators, mostly on the left, have accused the Supreme Court of inventing the concept of standing in the twentieth century, implying that there is no doctrine of standing to be found in the original Constitution.[35] There is something of a surface plausibility to the claim that there was no doctrine of standing that limited courts in the early republic. As explained earlier in Chapter Two, courts and individual citizens were extremely active in prosecuting and adjudicating violations of regulations in the early years of the republic. The use of informers to ensure execution of the laws, in particular, suggests that individuals were not shut out of the courts simply because they had no immediate personal stake in the controversy.

However, Ann Woolhandler and Caleb Nelson have argued that "there *was* an active law of standing in the eighteenth and nineteenth centuries" that limited courts to deciding only cases between legitimate parties and involving public rather than private rights.[36] When public rights rather than private rights were at stake the courts typically did not require that the parties had a personal and particular interest in the outcome. However, "[i]n favoring a private-injury requirement for private litigation, their decisions were influenced by American ideas about the proper role of the judiciary, its relationship to the political branches of the state and federal governments, and the legitimate allocation of public and private power."[37] The reason why many legal scholars presume that the concept of standing was a twentieth century invention is that the precise term "standing" was not used prior to the twentieth century, but the concepts were present at the beginning of the republic.

The central distinction that governed standing to sue in the eighteenth and nineteenth centuries, Nelson and Woolhandler argue, was that between private and public rights. In cases of private harm and private litigation such as torts and contract law, the courts were careful to ensure that both parties had a claim to take their case to the courts; on the other hand, many crimes were considered to fall under the province of public law because they constituted a threat to the public welfare of the whole community. As they explain, "[w]hat distinguished crimes and misdemeanors from mere civil wrongs was that they are a breach and violation of public rights and duties, which affect the whole community, considered as a community. Thus, most early state constitutions affirmatively required each indictment to specify that the defendant's conduct had been against the peace and dignity of the State."[38] In short, the commission of some crimes was considered, from the beginning of the republic, to fall under the classification of public wrongs under the cognizance of public law. It was in *this* category of crimes that the courts allowed private citizens and informers to enforce the laws by accusing violators. However, many wrongs fell *outside* the province of public wrongs, and in those cases the courts applied reasoning intended to ensure that only proper parties brought such cases to the courts.

While the concept of standing, therefore, has a long pedigree in American legal thought and constitutional law, typically lumped in with the political question in our early history, the actual legal doctrine of standing is of more recent origin. During the early twentieth century Progressive jurists utilized standing as a concept to shield regulatory action from the courts, as part of their overall project of insulating administrative action from judicial oversight. As Maxwell Stearns has observed, "[a]n impressive cohort of legal scholars now identify Louis Brandeis and Felix Frankfurter as the architects of the modern standing doctrine, and link the rise of the Progressive regulatory state to this important doctrinal innovation."[39] "The New Deal Court," he explains, "developed standing as a means of insulating Progressive regulatory reform from attack in a conservative lower federal judiciary that it feared was committed to obstructing progressivism."[40] The rise of the modern administrative regulatory state gave subsequent rise to standing doctrine as a means of *insulating* bureaucratic activity from judicial review, particularly on constitutional grounds. New Deal judges saw standing as necessary to prevent the courts from meddling with the apparatus that was being expanded under Roosevelt.

Throughout the 1920s and 1930s, as deference set in and Progressives increasingly wrote the Court's opinions, judges fashioned the doctrine of standing to keep administrative controversies from spilling over into the judicial branch. In the 1936 case of *Ashwander v. Tennessee Valley Authority*, for instance, the Tennessee Valley Authority (TVA) sought to purchase transmission lines and other property from the privately owned Alabama Power Company.[41] This transaction was opposed by plaintiffs who owned preferred stock in the Alabama Power Company. Brandeis concurred in the judgment in favor of the TVA, but not on the merits; rather, he argued that the plaintiffs had no standing to bring the case in the first place. In Brandeis's view, "stockholders have no standing to interfere with the management. . . . Stockholders are not guardians of the public. The function of guarding the public against acts deemed illegal rests with the public officials."[42] Brandeis argued that the legality of the transaction cannot be challenged by private shareholders, and that only public officials could inquire into the legal issues, as it is their province to determine the legality of public acts.

More fundamentally, Brandeis continued, in cases where the constitutionality of legislation is challenged, the presumption should be in favor of the constitutionality of legislation, and the courts should be cautious about overturning that presumption. Brandeis's concurring opinion in *Ashwander* emphasized this position repeatedly:

> The Court has frequently called attention to the "great gravity and delicacy" of its function in passing upon the validity of an act of Congress, and has restricted exercise of this function by rigid insistence that the jurisdiction of federal courts is limited to actual cases and controversies. . . . On this ground, it has in recent years ordered the dismissal of several suits challenging the constitutionality of important acts of Congress.[43]

Brandeis noted that the challenge to the constitutionality of the law authorizing the contract between the TVA and Alabama Power Company was central to the plaintiff's argument, yet because it is not blatantly unconstitutional, the courts must presume the authority to hear the case. Similarly, in the 1927 case of *United States v. Los Angeles and Salt Lake Railroad Company*, Brandeis furthered his argument against judicial review of administrative activity that does not directly affect the rights of particular individuals.[44] His argument in this case was that the action of the Interstate Commerce Commission, which engaged in a valuation of the petitioning railroad, was unreviewable, since it was not a final agency action affecting the rights of the regulated entity. Brandeis acknowledged that the Hepburn Act established judicial review of

ICC decisions. However, in Brandeis's view judicial review did not apply in this case because of the peculiar nature of the agency's activity:

> The so-called order here assailed differs essentially from all those held by this Court to be subject to judicial review under [earlier] acts. Each of the orders so reviewed was an exercise either of the *quasi*-judicial function of determining controversies or of the delegated legislative function of ratemaking and rulemaking.

> The so-called order here complained of is one which does not command the carrier to do, or to refrain from doing, anything; which does not grant or withhold any authority, privilege, or license; which does not extend or abridge any power or facility; which does not subject the carrier to any liability, civil or criminal; which does not change the carrier's existing or future status or condition; which does not determine any right or obligation. This so-called order is merely the formal record of conclusions reached after a study of data collected in the course of extensive research conducted by the Commission through its employees. It is the exercise solely of the function of investigation.[45]

Brandeis posited that the ICC's act of valuing the railroad in this case was not an act that affected the rights of the railroad, and was therefore unreviewable.

Justice Brandeis's strongest formulation of the standing doctrine to insulate administrative agencies from judicial scrutiny came in 1923 in *Edward Hines Yellow Pines Trustees v. United States*.[46] The case involved an order of the ICC that charged a daily fine to any company that held lumber at reconsignment points, in order to force lumber to the market. The commission's policy was challenged by lumber carriers, and following an internal examination and hearing, the commission voluntarily eliminated its fine. In doing so, however, it reserved for itself the power to reinstate the fine if conditions changed. The plaintiffs, who benefited from the ICC's fine policy, sued to reinstate the fine. In other words, the plaintiffs sought standing to sue the ICC on the grounds that they were harmed by the recission of the ICC's earlier policy. They were suing to force the ICC to act.

Writing for the Court, Brandeis responded, "plaintiffs could not maintain this suit merely by showing (if true) that the commission was without power to order the penalty charges canceled. They must show also that the order alleged to be void subjects them to legal injury, actual or threatened. This they have wholly failed to do."[47] Rather, Brandeis argued, the plaintiffs' *actual* source for potential redress is not the courts, but the agency itself. Brandeis wrote, "[p]laintiffs' right is limited to protection against unjust discrimination. For discrimination redress must be sought by proceedings before the commission. Its findings already made, and the order entered, negative such claim in this connection."[48] Brandeis's argument was a clear assertion of judicial restraint. The proper source for seeking redress, in his view, is the commission itself. Unless there is an actual legal injury, the judiciary has no basis for reviewing an administrative act. This was a case in which one party had appealed to the agency and persuaded the agency to reverse its policy. By denying their opponents the opportunity to challenge the reversal in court, Brandeis was signaling that they would similarly have to seek redress from the commission.

The arguments of jurists such as Brandeis and Frankfurter were based on the premise that the courts should adopt a deferential stance towards the political branches, which is much more in line with the Progressive theory that informed their views. They argued that judicial power and administrative power were fundamentally different and incompatible, and that particular parties seeking a reverse of policy must work through the administrative process. This general argument in favor of judicial deference to administrative power also influenced the development of other doctrines, especially the scope of judicial review of agencies' legal interpretations.

Mixed Questions of Law and Fact: The Path to Deference
As mentioned earlier in this chapter, several of Franklin Roosevelt's closest advisors saw in the *Bates* decision a precedent for insulating agencies' interpretations of law from judicial review. Prior to 1900 courts drew a distinction between review of administrative fact-finding and administrative legal interpretation, and deferred to the former while deciding the latter category de novo. During the New Deal, administrative law moved further in this direction, muddying the distinction between law and fact in order to move more agency findings into a category where judicial deference would be granted. In this area, as with standing to sue, the New Deal further entrenched a jurisprudence of judicial deference to administrative power.

Two famous cases illustrated the shift away from the simple distinction between law and fact that reigned in pre-1900 administrative law: *Gray v. Powell* and *NLRB v. Hearst Publications*.[49] In *Powell* the Seaboard Air Line Railway Company sought an exemption from the coal tax levied by the Bituminous Coal Division of the Department of Labor. Under the Bituminous Coal Act, the Bituminous Coal Division could promulgate regulatory codes governing the coal industry. These codes were technically voluntary, but to induce compliance the Division could impose a 19.5 percent tax on any producer "upon the sale or other disposal" of coal it produced. Therefore, a regulated producer could avoid the code and tax if it met one of two conditions: if it was both a producer and a consumer of coal, or if it did not "sell" or otherwise "dispose" of coal.

Seaboard, as a coal-burning railroad, was clearly a consumer of coal. In order to classify itself as a producer of coal it leased coal lands with an exclusive right to mine those lands. It also leased the equipment needed to mine the coal on behalf of a contractor who actually mined the coal. The contractor was under an exclusive contract to deliver the coal to Seaboard. The agency, interpreting the term "producer" in the Act, determined that Seaboard was not a producer of coal and thus was subject to the tax. In reviewing this interpretation of the law, the Court deferred to the agency's legal interpretation rather than deciding the issue on its own.[50] Justice Reed wrote that "Where as here a determination has been left to an administrative body, this delegation will be respected and the administrative conclusion left untouched. . . . It is not the province of a court to absorb the administrative functions to such an extent that the executive or legislative agencies become mere fact finding bodies deprived of the advantages of prompt and definitive action." In this last sentence Reed seemed to acknowledge that the question was not merely factual. But if the courts decided anew all questions outside of the realm of factfinding this would "absorb the administrative functions" and make agencies "mere fact finding bodies deprived of the advantages of prompt and definitive action." Therefore, some issues outside of the category of factfinding would receive deference from the courts.

Dissenting from the decision, Justice Roberts saw that this reasoning departed from the established method of reviewing agency decisions, granting deference to a new category of issues. "There are limits to which administrative officers and courts may appropriately go in reconstructing statutes," he proclaimed, and "If the Director [of the Division] was in error his error was a misconstruction of the Act which created his office and that error . . . is subject to court review." To hold otherwise "is a complete reversal of the normal and usual method of construing a statute."

Justice Roberts would have a second occasion to object to the Court's new approach to administrative determinations three years later in *Hearst*. That case involved an interpretation of the National Labor Relations Act, which required employers to bargain collectively with "employees." Hearst Publications, publishers of four Los Angeles newspapers, contended that newsboys were not employees and thus were not protected by the collective bargaining provision. The newsboys paid for newspapers and sold them at a higher price than their purchase price, earning their wages through the profit margin at the sale. They did not work full-time and were not employed continuously. Under these conditions the publisher argued that the newsboys were more like independent contractors than employees. The locations at which the newsboys sold the papers were set by the district managers, and the publisher arranged transportation for the newsboys to the places where they sold the papers.

The legal question, therefore, was straightforward: does the term "employee" in the National Labor Relations Act include the newsboys who sold Hearst's papers? The NLRB had determined after hearings that they were employees, and that Hearst therefore had to bargain collectively with them. After determining through de novo consideration that the term 'employee' did not merely codify existing common-law definitions of the term, the Court considered whether these newsboys fit the statutory definition. In deciding this question the Court deferred to the NLRB's initial decision: "It is not necessary in this case to make a completely definitive limitation around the term "employee." That task has been assigned primarily to the agency created by Congress to administer the Act." "Hence in reviewing the Board's ultimate conclusions," Justice Rutledge wrote for the majority, "it is not the court's function to substitute its own inferences of fact for the Board's." "Undoubtedly questions of statutory interpretation . . . are for the courts to resolve," Rutledge conceded. "But where the question is one of specific application of a broad statutory term in a proceeding in which the agency administering the statute must determine it initially, the reviewing court's function is limited." According to the majority, there was a space between the distinction between law and fact where "the question is one of specific application of a broad statutory term." This "mixed" the issues of law and fact, much in the way that *Bates* had talked about the gray area between this distinction and Dickinson had questioned the distinction. Some questions are neither purely legal nor purely factual, but are questions of legal application. In these areas, the majority claimed, the courts should defer to the agency and not substitute their own judgment on the meaning of the law.

Once again, Justice Roberts saw this as a critical departure from the settled and traditional approach to judicial review of administrative legal interpretation. "The question who is an employee . . . is a question of the meaning of the Act and, therefore, is a judicial and not an administrative question," he protested. He then proceeded to engage in de novo review of the agency's legal interpretation and he concluded, independent of the agency's own analysis, "that the newsboys were not employees of the newspapers."

Gray and *Powell* illustrated the judiciary's continued retreat from the more aggressive stance towards administrative decisions that prevailed throughout most of the first century of American administrative law. Along with new doctrines of standing that insulated many agency decisions from being challenged in courts, the more deferential posture towards agency legal interpretation indicated that the courts were now willing to remove themselves from the administrative arena and let the experts, whom Congress designated to resolve these questions, decide them on its own. The courts would retreat to merely ensuring that the administrative state stay within a minimal threshold of reasonableness in its decisions.[51]

An illustration of the judicial retreat came in the important case of *Crowell v. Benson*, which addressed whether Congress could give administrative agencies the power to make final determinations of fact in cases where individual rights are adjudicated, or whether such determinations must necessarily be made by Article III courts possessing the "judicial power" of the United States.[52] The case involved a decision by Crowell, a deputy commissioner of the United States Employees' Compensation Commission, that an employee had been injured while he was in Benson's employ. Benson challenged the determination on the grounds that it violated the Fifth Amendment's Due Process Clause and Article III's vesting of the judicial power in the federal courts.

Writing for the Court, Chief Justice Hughes brushed aside the Due Process challenge. "The use of the administrative method, assuming due notice, proper opportunity to be heard, and that findings are based upon evidence, falls easily within the principle of the decisions sustaining similar procedure" in previous cases involving Due Process challenges, he wrote.[53] Hughes signaled that, as long as the agency follows procedures that resemble judicial proceedings, including notice, an opportunity for parties to be heard, and an on-the-record decision based upon the evidence, administrative process could substitute for judicial process. Hughes's argument anticipated later efforts, in the drafting of the Administrative Procedure Act and in the 1960s and 1970s (discussed in the following chapter), to restrain bureaucratic rule through the use of procedures.

The larger question in *Crowell*, though, was whether the law at issue violated the Constitution's vesting of the judicial power in the courts of law. Hughes granted that in the 1856 case of *Murray's Lessee v. Hoboken Land & Improvement Co.*, the Supreme Court announced that Congress cannot "withdraw from judicial cognizance any matter which, from its nature, is the subject of a suit at the common law."[54] Yet he noted that the statute preserved the right to appeal the agency's decisions to a reviewing court for an injunction, and that Congress did not "attempt to interfere with, but rather provision is made to facilitate, the exercise by the court of its jurisdiction" to review the legality of the agency's determination.[55] In other words, the right to challenge the legality of the agency's action in a reviewing court cured the arrangement of any constitutional deficiency.[56]

Because the agency's legal interpretations were subject to judicial review, Hughes concluded, Congress could permissibly delegate the decision to the administrator. Hughes's opinion therefore turned on the distinction between law and fact. The agency's factual determinations were final, but this was consistent with earlier precedents in which Congress granted the power to make such determinations to an administrative officer. Quoting again from *Murray's Lessee*, Hughes distinguished "between cases of private right and those which arise between the government and persons subject to its authority in connection with the performance of the constitutional functions of the executive or legislative departments."[57] In upholding the grant of power to the agency, Hughes drew a critical distinction between the adjudication of "private rights" and public rights. Public rights, in *Crowell's* words, involving cases between "the government and persons subject to its authority." The resolution of cases in the latter category need not be confined to Article III tribunals but could permissibly be transferred to administrative tribunals. Hughes's opinion enabled a wide swath of activity to be delegated to the administrative state and ensured that the judicial role would simply be to review administrative decisions that were challenged by parties. As the courts retreated from de novo review of administrative action in decisions following *Gray v. Powell*, they also refrained from demanding that decisions be made in judicial rather than administrative tribunals.

"The Legal Profession Has Never Reconciled Itself"

It should not be surprising that many lawyers and judges were opposed to the New Deal project of reducing judicial review of administrative decision making. In the eyes of much of the legal community, administrative power came at the expense of the judiciary, which previously decided many of the issues that were now being transferred to agencies. (As previous chapters have illustrated, they were right about these historical developments.) Chief among these opponents of the administrative state was Roscoe Pound, an influential progressive legal theorist who founded the sociological jurisprudence and legal realism movements in a series of influential articles published from 1900 to 1915.[58] Pound served for twenty years as dean of Harvard Law School. Yet in spite of his prominence and position Pound led the legal criticism of the New Deal, ensconced in the American Bar Association (ABA). Pound therefore continued the intra-progressive opposition to the expansion of administrative power, a tradition advanced especially by Louis Brandeis during the debates and campaign of 1912.

Beginning in May 1933, the ABA began to voice reservations about the expansion of administrative power during the New Deal.[59] That year, the ABA's Special Committee on Administrative Law advocated transferring the judicial power out of administrative agencies and into independent tribunals such as the courts. This proposal to separate administrative and adjudicative power persisted throughout the 1930s.[60] Eventually, the organization changed course and began to advocate review boards in every department that would be charged with reviewing all administrative action within the department they were tasked with supervising.[61] The opposition rose to a crescendo a few years later with the publication of Pound's report in 1938, which decried the "administrative absolutism" of the New Deal and proposed radical changes in the structure of administrative power. These proposals came to a head with the introduction of the Walter-Logan Act in 1939, which would have established these review boards and also granted substantial authority to the courts to hear cases involving private citizens and to overturn agencies' decisions.

Congress passed the Walter-Logan Act, prompting President Roosevelt to issue a veto message condemning some lawyers' opposition to the New Deal. Roosevelt claimed that while "the more progressive bar associations" accepted the need for the judicial branch to be "supplemented by the administrative tribunal . . . a large part of the legal profession has never reconciled itself to the existence of the administrative tribunal. Many of them prefer the stately ritual of the courts, in which lawyers play all the speaking parts, to the simple procedure of administrative hearings which a client can understand and even participate in."[62] The more progressive lawyers understood the need for the administrative process, but many other members of the legal profession, FDR noted, still longed for the elimination of these tribunals. They wanted, in Roosevelt's view, to retain the process that kept them in charge, where they could "play all the speaking parts," rather than adjusting to the need for expertise.

Many in the legal community were shocked that Roscoe Pound, a giant of Progressive legal thought, could oppose the New Deal so strongly. Most thought that the New Deal was simply an extension of Progressive political and legal theory. This has led many scholars to condemn Pound as an inconsistent thinker who became a reactionary by the 1930s. However, a careful reading of Pound's writings reveals that the traditional account is oversimplistic and even downright misleading. Roscoe Pound's writings reveal a remarkable consistency, in that he was always willing to accept "executive justice" or "administrative justice" as a temporary evil, but had a consistent vision of the future of the administrative process that was fundamentally at odds with the vision of Landis, Roosevelt, and many of his Progressive interlocutors.[63]

Throughout his entire career, including the period from 1905 to 1920 when he rose to prominence for his call for sociological jurisprudence, Pound dedicated his work to shaping law to serve both the purpose of setting forth universal or general rules and the need to secure justice in particular and individual cases. Pound's approach to this problem was critical to his famous attack on "executive justice." In 1922 he opened a series of published lectures on legal history by introducing what in his view was an intractable problem:

> How to reconcile the idea of a fixed body of law, affording no scope for individual willfulness, with the idea of change and growth and making of new law. . . . For, put more concretely, the problem of compromise between the need of stability and the need of change becomes in one aspect a problem of adjustment between rule and discretion, between administering justice according to settled rule, or at most by rigid deduction from narrowly fixed premises, and administration of justice according to the more or less trained intuition of experienced magistrates. In one way or another almost all of the vexed questions of the science of law prove to be phases of this same problem.[64]

The central problem to which Pound addressed himself throughout his writings was how law can be both "justice according to settled rule" but also compatible with the discretion magistrates need to do justice in particulars. In basic terms, Pound was referring to the tension between using universal and inflexible rules to decide particular cases and reliance on the wise use of a prudent magistrate's discretion.

Pound argued that the traditional American approach to law was formalistic and devoted to the rule of law, almost to a fault. We were obsessed with following the precept of Montesquieu and Locke that no person should be trusted with holding any combination of legislative, executive, or judicial power. In America, as a result, "[n]othing is so characteristic of American public law of the nineteenth century as the completeness with which executive action is tied down by legal liability and judicial review."[65] In particular, "an effective apparatus of judicial control over administration by mandamus, prohibition, certiorari, and statutory substitutes" was achieved in the nineteenth century by the implementation of common-law doctrines.[66] Executive action in America prior to the twentieth century, in Pound's view, was excessively restrained by judicial control. We have seen in previous chapters the common law doctrines that courts used to control administrative action in the nineteenth century.

Pound criticized this earlier approach because, in his view, it led to "judicial interference with administration. Law paralyzing administration was an every-day spectacle. Almost every important measure of policy or administration encountered an injunction."[67] Ill-advised judicial control of administration rendered government ineffective and inefficient, and in the twentieth century "the paralysis of administration produced by our American exaggeration of the common-law doctrine of supremacy of law has brought about a reaction."[68] These ill effects produced a swing to the opposite extreme, namely, the rise of the administrative state.

Because of these developments, as early as 1907 Pound was writing that "the recrudescence of executive justice is gaining strength continually and is yet far from its end." "Where, a generation ago, we were agreed to be proud of our peculiar doctrine of judicial power over unconstitutional legislation, that doctrine has become the subject of constant and even violent attack. . . . [W]e have actually traveled a long way from the notions of a generation ago as to the relation of courts and administration."[69] Even "the judiciary has begun to fall in line," Pound stated, and "powers which fifty years ago would have been held purely judicial and jealously guarded from executive exercise are now decided to be administrative only and are cheerfully conceded to boards and commissions."[70] These developments, Pound believed, indicated the rise, or recurrence, of a theory of executive justice. Executive justice characterizes the "attempt to adjust the relations of individuals with each other and with the State summarily, according to notions of an executive officer for the time being as to what the public interest and a square deal demand, unencumbered by many rules."[71] This rise of executive or administrative justice, Pound wrote in 1924, "is perhaps the conspicuous feature of our American law."[72] Thus, well before the New Deal Pound was concerned about the rise of executive justice and the decline of judicial power. Duties long understood to be judicial in character were being transferred over to administrative boards. Pound was concerned about the problem of executive justice even at the height of his contributions to Progressive legal thought, twenty years before authoring the ABA's report in 1938, a report that made him infamous.

"Administrative Absolutism": The Infamous 1938 ABA Report

Even so, the tone of Pound's 1938 "Report of the Special Committee on Administrative Law" for the ABA surprised many of his colleagues.[73] It denounced Roosevelt's "administrative absolutism" and even compared the New Deal to doctrines of "Soviet Russia." In the main section of the report, Pound exhorted the bar to check the rise of administrative justice that was reaching its pinnacle in the New Deal: "[t]he attitude of courts and of the profession toward administrative agencies and tribunals and the balance between the judicial and the administrative are of fundamental importance in the expanding administrative jurisdiction of today."[74] He focused his audience on the clear issue of the day—the expanding nature of administrative jurisdiction and its encroachment on judicial power, upsetting the tense balance between the two. He stated that "administrative bureaus and agencies are constantly pressing upon legislatures for increased jurisdiction, and for exemption from [judicial] review, and in the nature of the case encroach continually on the domain of judicial justice."[75] Thus there was a direct confrontation between administrative agencies and justice through the judicial system, and "except as the bar takes upon itself to act, there is nothing to check the tendency of administrative bureaus to extend the scope of their operations indefinitely even to the extent of supplanting our traditional judicial regime by an administrative regime."[76] In basic terms, "the pressure for administrative absolutism goes on and the profession must be vigilant to resist it."[77]

Pound thus argued that nothing short of regime change was occurring in the New Deal. A judicial regime was being supplanted by an administrative regime, and the bar was the last remaining line of defense. In a striking passage, Pound claimed that the administrative absolutism was like "the proposition recently maintained by the jurists of Soviet Russia that in the socialist state there is no law but only one rule of law, that there are no laws—only administrative ordinances and orders."[78] In turning to administrative absolutism, Pound concluded, the New Deal was taking America in the direction of Russia.

But Pound also reminded his audience that "the reasons" for the rise of administrative absolutism "are historical, growing out of a bad adjustment between courts and administration which was a legacy from the contests between common law courts and the crown in seventeenth-century England."[79] Pound thus repeated that "In the nineteenth century we had carried to the extreme a system of judicial interference with administration. Something very much like a paralysis of administration by judicial order" was taking place during that time.[80] Therefore, Pound argued in the report, the causes of our current crisis of administrative absolutism point the way to the solution. What is needed, Pound explained, is "to achieve a better adjustment between administration and judicially enforced law."[81] This can be achieved by reforming the judiciary away from the evils that produced judicial interference with administration and the turn to administrative justice.

Nothing in the ABA report was inconsistent with the warnings Pound gave as early as 1907 about the rise of executive justice and the need for courts and lawyers to respond appropriately. All of the same elements were present in the Pound of 1907 and the Pound of 1938: the argument and warning about executive justice, the argument that the courts were responsible for the rise of administrative justice because of their outdated jurisprudence, and the faith that the best response was to update the administration of justice. In Pound's view the ordinary courts would resume the functions being delegated to agencies, but they also needed to update their own principles to decide cases on sociological grounds rather than mechanically applying law to facts.

The Bridge to Nowhere: The Road to the APA and the Continuation of Deference

It was easy for lawyers to criticize the New Deal's shift to discretionary administrative power, but more difficult to discern the alternative. What was Pound's alternative to the New Deal? His ABA report called for reforms that would eventually work their way into the legislative process. The basis of many of these proposals was Pound's rejection of the faith in administrative expertise that characterized so many of his progressive allies and was particularly prominent in the writings of progressives such as Frank Goodnow and James Landis. In the ABA report Pound argued that independent regulatory agencies were more likely to be politicized than repositories of scientific expertise. "The postulate of a scientific body of experts pursuing objective scientific inquiries," Pound wrote, "is as far as possible from what the facts are or are likely to be in a polity where the administrative bodies are not protected in tenure by the Constitution as are the courts, and . . . are subjected to centralized executive control."[82] Courts with lifetime tenure, in Pound's view, would be *more* independent and insulated from political pressures than regulatory agencies controlled by the president.

Furthermore, Pound disputed the widely held notion that agencies would be superior policymaking organizations due to their expertise. "In many fields of administration there is no particular expertness," he claimed.[83] The assumption that all administration must be undertaken by experts overlooks the fact that much (or even most) of administration is handled perfectly well by in-expert judges who nevertheless impose the rule of law on otherwise arbitrary government activity. In the end, Pound thought it impossible to have a purely expert model of regulation and administration: "The professed ideal of an in-dependent commission of experts above politics and reaching scientific results by scientific means, has no correspondence with reality."[84] Controlled by the executive and subject to political pressure, the only means of protecting the people from a politicized administration is "the check of legal limitations en-forced by an independent tribunal."[85]

More specifically, in the ABA report Pound advanced three general propos-als reflected in the APA: an argument each for rulemaking, for public notice of rulemaking, and judicial review of administrative action. In the proposed legislation accompanying the report, Pound explained that the bill called for "the issuance and publication of rules and regulations implementing the stat-utes administered by governmental agencies."[86] This stood in sharp contrast to the accepted administrative practice of the time, which was to make policy through ad hoc adjudications rather than through general rulemaking.[87] If agencies would issue rules and regulations rather than using ad hoc adjudica-tions, Pound reasoned, agencies would have to follow generalized rules, a key component of the rule of law.

These rules, furthermore, would be accompanied by notice to interested and affected parties, allowing the public to know the rules in advance and to check agency abuse. "As to the objection that adequate argument is not assured," Pound wrote, "it ought to be possible to provide for notice of the application to the public authorities interested and to interested individuals."[88] If agencies proceed by making general rules, with comment to the public, rather than through ad hoc determinations, and their actions are checked by judicial re-view, the victory of administrative absolutism may be checked.[89] In general, then, the practical recommendations of the Pound report focused primarily on procedural checks on agencies enforced by the courts, combined with a robust role for judicial review of the substance of administrative decision making.

More radically, Pound envisioned that the judiciary would come to reassume many of the functions performed by administrative agencies in the 1930s, just as the agencies had assumed many functions previously carried out by courts.

In his view, although "there is an element of discretion in the judicial process and a function of adjudication in the administrative process," "the two processes are characteristically distinct. The one deals with each case as one of a type and seeks to determine it by a rule for cases of that type," while the other "tends to treat cases as unique and make *ad hoc* determinations."[90] Even when they perform a quasi-judicial function, agencies are established and disposed to decide cases based on procedures and principles that are fundamentally different from those of courts.[91] Preserving the administrative process, with the possibility for review by courts, does not resolve the issue. Decisions are still made in the first instance by the administrative process in which every case is dealt with on an ad hoc basis.

Therefore, because the administrative and judicial processes are irreconcilable, simply to transfer the judicial process to administrative agencies with the option for judicial review after the fact would not, in Pound's view, solve the dilemma. Such an approach would actually *entrench* the administrative process rather than undermine it by establishing a legal process for adjudication of particular cases according to very different rules and principles. The power to decide these particular cases was traditionally held by the courts in American law.

The yet-unsolved problem in Pound's view was "how a kind of administrative justice can be developed within the Anglo-American legal system."[92] While Pound confusedly combined multiple visions for the reform of the administrative state, ranging from stricter judicial review to independent administrative law courts and the restoration of judicial justice as opposed to executive justice, other scholars have sought to explain the significance of the analogy Pound repeatedly drew between the New Deal and the challenge of administrative justice faced in Britain in the sixteenth and seventeenth centuries. For instance, Bernard Schwartz has explained that in Britain the executive tribunals that arose temporarily, such as Chancery and the Star Chamber, eventually became judicialized and developed into independent courts. Pound's alternative to the administrative state, as Schwartz explains, was "for it to follow the pattern of the executive tribunals of three centuries ago" in Britain. Administrative tribunals "must become truly judicialized and administered by bodies possessing solely judicial authority. Such bodies will, in time, follow the example of Chancery and develop into courts. Our administrative law will then become as much a part of our ordinary law as did our law of equity after Lord Nottingham."[93] The critical move to begin this process would have been the adoption of proposals to separate completely the administrative and the adjudicatory functions of agencies, so that the agencies' judicial function would be exercised by tribunals that would begin to resemble common-law courts. "There seems to be little doubt," Schwartz explained, "that if this proposal were followed the judicial sections [of administrative agencies] would and should eventually develop into courts. Such has been the common historical development of tribunals endowed only with judicial authority."[94] The separation of administrative and judicial power within agencies would promote not only the separation of powers; it would ensure that administrative power would adopt the institutional structures and methods of Anglo-American constitutionalism.

A precondition of any attempt to construct this alternative administrative state, in Pound's view, was complete reform of the judicial branch. To deal with modern circumstances, modern courts would have to be developed. Pound thought that much of the reform would be organizational. In a paper written in 1909 that was incorporated into an earlier ABA report on preventing delay and cost in litigation, Pound argued that "The whole judicial power of the state . . . should be vested in one great court, of which all tribunals should be branches, departments or divisions. The business as well as the judicial administration of this court should be thoroughly organized so as to prevent not merely waste of judicial power, but all needless clerical work, duplication of papers and records, and the like, thus obviating expense to litigants and cost to the public."[95]

The focus would be threefold, on organization of personnel, of judicial business, and of administrative business. In a consolidated judicial system, we could have "specialized judges rather than specialized courts."[96] The organization of judicial business would remedy a similar problem, by preventing judges from hearing myriad cases involving myriad subjects simultaneously. Administrative organization would allow courts to have control of clerical officers, rather than choosing such personnel through election as was typical in Pound's day. If all of these changes would be implemented, "the court becomes not merely a machine for deciding cases formally presented, but a bureau of justice."[97] This bureau of justice would be the means by which the bench and bar would finally be updated to deal adequately with modern circumstances. Expert judges would be available for the resolution of particular cases, in accordance with traditional judicial processes but with a foundation in sociological jurisprudence. Progressive goals would be realized through this bureau of justice rather than the decisions of administrative experts.

Pound's proposal, then, was not to increase judicial review of administrative agencies but to reorganize the judicial branch to *replace* administrative agencies as we know them today. Pound argued that his proposals to reorganize the judicial branch "would enable the judicial department to do adequately the work which, in desperation of efficient legal disposition, we have been committing more and more to administrative boards and commissions, which are contrary to the genius of our institutions and often, at best, are mere experiments."[98] Administrative agencies would still exist, of course, but the administrative process would be replaced by an updated judicial process.

Pound's solution, therefore, was to recommend not greater judicial review of administrative agencies but a restoration of the tradition of courts as administrators by updating the judicial branch to meet the demands of modern government. The ultimate question, according to Pound, was whether certain powers were to be conferred on courts or agencies. The answer to this question would determine whether America would continue to be a nation based on the rule of law, or whether administrative absolutism would win the day.

Legal opposition to the New Deal helped give rise to the Walter-Logan Act, passed by Congress in 1939. Walter-Logan's specific provisions would have dramatically weakened the administrative apparatus that was constructed during Roosevelt's first term in office. Named after Representative Francis Walter and Senator Marvel Logan, the measure sought to enact several reforms. First, it would have required trial-type hearings for agency rulemaking and adjudication. In addition, it sought to provide intra-agency appeals boards where affected citizens could have recourse for challenging administrative decisions. Finally, the measure would have dramatically expanded judicial review of agency factfinding, and authorized reviewing courts to overturn agency actions on legal and jurisdictional grounds.[99] As mentioned earlier, the bill passed in both houses of Congress but fell to Franklin Roosevelt's veto pen.

Once it became clear that Roosevelt would not accept a measure like Walter-Logan, Congress was forced to consider a compromise measure that could survive the threat of a presidential veto. That compromise measure became the Administrative Procedure Act of 1946 (APA). In anticipation of the debate over administrative power and process, Roosevelt formed his own Committee on Administrative Procedure in 1939 to propose more moderate measures to curtail administrative discretion than those contained in Walter-Logan and advocated by the ABA. Finally published in 1941, the Committee produced a moderate majority report that largely served as the basis of the APA, and a minority report that pressed for more fundamental changes. The political goal of this committee, as revealed in the legislative debates, was to preempt attempts at more radical reform and to redefine the terms of the debate.

The Commission: "A Metaphysical Omniscient Brooding Thing"
During the legislative debates over the APA in 1946 there was general agreement on the problems that needed to be addressed. More radical members of
the Congress such as John Jennings of Tennessee described the bill as a first
attempt in "fitting a restraining legal strait-jacket on these people who have
been harassing the citizens of this country." In his view, "The chief indoor sport
of the Federal bureaucrat is to evolve out of his own inner consciousness, like a
spider spins his web, countless confusing rules and regulations which may deprive a man of his property, his liberty, and bedevil the very life out of him."[100]
Jennings explicitly connected the problem of the administrative state to the
doctrine of republican government: "It was never contemplated or intended
by the founders of this Republic that the power to legislate vested in Congress
should be usurped by a bunch of appointive officers here in Washington who
were never elected by any constituency and never could be."[101] Others invoked
the separation of powers. Samuel Hobbs of Alabama observed, "It seems to
me that the Constitution of the United States, has divided the powers of our
Government into three coordinate branches, the legislative, executive, and judicial. These have been swallowed up by some administrators and their staffs
who apparently believed that they were omnipotent. These have exercised all
of the powers of government, arrogating to themselves more power than ever
belonged to any man, or group. This has made necessary the enactment of
some such legislation as is now in process of passage."[102]

Senator Alexander Wiley of Wisconsin similarly proclaimed that there
is a "tendency in republics to what might be called barnacle growth such as
that found on the hulls of ships." "Unless we are alert," he claimed, "barnacle growth will endanger us, and the ship of state will become fouled, so to
speak, and our institutions will become endangered."[103] Francis Walter, whose
measure had received FDR's veto several years earlier, gave a critical speech
in the House supporting the bill, which opened with the recognition that
"for a generation Americans have been brought face to face with new forms
or methods of government, which we have come to call administrative law.
It is administrative because it involves the exercise of legislative and judicial
powers of government by officers who are neither legislators nor judges. It
is law because what they do is binding upon the citizen exactly as statutes
or judgments are binding."[104] And Senator Pat McCarran, who ushered the
measure through the Senate and called it a "bill of rights for the hundreds of
thousands of Americans" affected by bureaucracy, proclaimed that "We have
set up a fourth order in the tripartite plan of Government which was initiated

by the founding fathers of our democracy. They set up the executive, the legislative, and the judicial branches; but since that time we have set up a fourth dimension, if I may so term it, which is now popularly known as administrative in nature. So we have the legislative, the executive, the judicial, and the administrative."[105]

Others objected to bureaucracy not on separation of powers but on rule of law grounds. While these were the most prominent themes in political debates surrounding the administrative state, legal analysts also criticized the lack of transparency and consistency in the adjudicatory process. Prior to the APA, agency hearings were typically governed by trial examiners who did not have the power to render decisions. Consequently the agency heads, who decided cases for the agencies, were not the ones who heard the testimony and evidence at the hearings. Specialists within the agency often decided cases, which were then signed by agency heads who had not participated in the process. This dramatically diminished administrative responsibility and was denounced as contrary to basic notions of the rule of law. As Dean Acheson, chairman of the Attorney General's Committee on Administrative Procedure, remarked:

> The agency is one great obscure organization with which the citizen has to deal. It is absolutely amorphous. . . . There is someone called the commission, the authority; a metaphysical omniscient brooding thing which sort of floats around the air and is not a human being. That is what is baffling. . . . There is no idea that Mr. A heard the case and then it goes into this great building and mills around and comes out with a commissioner's name on it but what happens in between is a mystery. That is what bothers people.[106]

Regardless of their position on the ideological spectrum, the members of Congress believed that they were taking a first step towards regulating a large bureaucratic apparatus that had grown up over the past generation and that threatened basic principles of American constitutionalism. They were, in the words of these members, "barnacles" that threatened to foul the ship of state, a "fourth dimension" that disrupted the tripartite division of powers, and a spider spinning a web of regulations that bedeviled the citizenry.

The other point of consensus during the legislative debates was that the APA was the product of an extraordinary amount of careful study and beneficial compromise. McCarran announced that "I have one ambition in life, and that is that this bill, when enacted into law . . . will become a monument to the

Congress of the United States for its careful study."[107] He was continually interrupted during his lengthy remarks by members praising him for his efforts in studying and managing the details of the bill. Interestingly, several members announced that the reason for the failure of Walter-Logan was not ideological but, rather, that FDR merely wanted to delay reforms until the work of his Committee on Administrative Procedure was finalized. As McCarran explained, Walter-Logan "was vetoed by the President in 1940, partly on the ground that action should await the final report of [his] committee."[108] McCarran's statement was repeated by others during the debates, including Francis Walter himself.[109] For such an important measure, the legislative debates are striking for the extent of agreement and the degree of cordiality displayed by the members of both parties. Everyone seemed to agree that the APA would produce much-needed improvements in administrative law.[110]

When it came to particular provisions and proposals, however, the consensus appeared to erode. Four aspects of the Act in particular prompted discussion: the separation of executive and adjudicative functions, the standard of evidence in agency proceedings, access to judicial review, and scope of judicial review. Senator McCarran noted that the APA's separation of functions provision allowed for prosecutors and decision makers to be housed within the same agency and therefore was a moderate alternative to earlier approaches. Even the Brownlow Committee, he noted, sought "complete separation of investigative and prosecuting functions and personnel from deciding functions and personnel." "The pending bill," he acknowledged, "does not go as far as that 1937 recommendation."[111] While McCarran did not lament the failure to adopt the more strident separation of functions, others did. Representative Howard W. Smith admitted that "I introduced a bill which went farther than the present bill. I had hoped that certain features of it would go farther. I had hoped that we would have a more complete separation of the judicial and executive functions in this bill."[112] Walter agreed that "this section is of great importance because it is an attempt to deal with one of the most critical sectors of administrative operation. It does not provide for a complete separation of functions in the sense that hearing officers are entirely and physically separated from the agencies in which they operate," but, he argued, its "'internal' separation of functions" would still be an improvement.[113] Like Howard Smith, Representative John Gwynne said that this provision "is hoped to at least make a start, although I think it does not go as far as it should, in arriving eventually at a complete separation between the deciding functions and the prosecuting functions."[114] There was general agreement that some separation between prosecution and adjudication was imperative, but some members were unsatisfied with how far the APA went in this regard. Their clearly stated objective was to build upon the separation of functions provision of the APA and eventually to provide complete separation, in accordance with previous proposals.

The issue of admissibility of evidence also provoked considerable discussion. In the Senate McCarran couched the provision as a compromise. Prior to the APA, he noted, agencies could collect hearsay evidence and use it as the basis for its decision. While this increased the flexibility of the administrative process, it also threatened to undermine the rights of individuals confronted by an administrative decision. "So rather than curtail the agencies," he explained, "we sought an intermediate ground which we thought would be protective of the rights of individuals, and at the same time would not handicap the agencies."[115] This intermediate ground stated that the agencies could acquire secondary evidence, but the decision must be based on probative evidence or face invalidation by a reviewing court. In answering a series of questions McCarran affirmed that this requirement would increase the amount of evidence needed to sustain administrative decisions in court. And as Francis Walter argued in the House, the law "authorizes agencies to receive any evidence," but "no sanction may be imposed or rule or order be issued except on consideration of the whole record . . . and as supported by and in accordance with reliable, probative, and substantial evidence." Thus "the accepted standards of proof, as distinguished from the mere admissibility of evidence, are to govern in administrative proceedings as they do in courts of law and equity."[116] This was taken by many legislators to be an important advance in the fairness of administrative procedure.

Finally, the scope of judicial review of administrative decisions prompted considerable debate. McCarran's lengthy speech in the Senate was interrupted by a question from Senator McKellar of Alabama, asking whether "the principal purpose of the bill is to allow persons who are aggrieved as a result of acts of governmental agencies to appeal to the courts?" McCarran confirmed twice that this was the underlying purpose of the APA, although he reminded McKellar that where a statute precludes judicial review, the APA does not displace that provision.[117] Francis Walter reiterated in the House debate that "[e]very form of statutory right or limitation would thus be subject to judicial review under the bill." He acknowledged that the APA "exempts all matters so far as statutes preclude judicial review" but assuaged members that "Congress has rarely done so."[118] When the agency's organic statute is silent, he maintained, judicial review is assumed. Furthermore, while the APA explicitly exempted judicial review on matters "committed to agency discretion," Walter reassured the House that agencies do not have the discretion under the APA to be arbitrary, to willfully act or refuse to act, to ignore evidence or to violate statutes or the Constitution.[119] Such activities would be illegal under the APA and would not escape judicial review.

In the critical matter of the scope of judicial scrutiny of agency decisions, several members of Congress confirmed that the effect of the APA would be against the increasing tendency of courts to defer to administrative determinations. The reign of deference, they argued, would be undermined by the bill. Francis Walter made this point most forcefully. When an agency engages in adjudication and the underlying statute does not require a hearing, he explained, the APA is silent on the appropriate procedures because "the parties affected are entitled to try out the pertinent facts in court and hence there is no reason for prescribing informal administrative procedures beyond the [limited] requirements" of the APA. "The right of trial de novo in judicial review in cases where agencies do not proceed upon a statutory hearing," he continued, "will also be discussed later in connection with section 10."[120] That section, commonly known today as Section 706 or the scope of review section, clarified that "the reviewing court shall decide all relevant questions of law," and "interpret constitutional and statutory provisions."[121] Francis emphatically proclaimed that this provision "requires courts to determine independently all relevant questions of law, including the interpretation of constitutional or statutory provisions." The critical part of this statement was "independently"— courts were not to defer to legal interpretations offered by agencies under this standard. Other members of the House concurred with Walter's interpretation. Representative Raymond Springer told his colleagues that "under the scope of review set forth in the pending bill it will give every person the opportunity and right to have a fair, just, and impartial trial in the judicial proceeding, and a complete review of the case which has been conducted against him."[122] For these members of Congress, the scope of review provisions in the APA would increase the level of judicial scrutiny of administrative determinations, particularly defending the authority of reviewing courts to review agencies' legal interpretations independently. This would serve as a clear signal that recent, deferential Supreme Court decisions would not continue into the future.

The Limited Effect of a "Pioneer Effort"

In the end, these discussions and exchanges illustrated different approaches and interpretations of the APA's statutory provisions. But they were not indicative of a deeper disagreement over the utility of the bill itself. Everyone knew that the APA would pass; they merely sought to clarify how far it went and whether it was sufficient. There was a clear sense among many members that the measure was merely a first step and that further measures would be necessary. Representative Earl Michener concurred: "It is not perfect. It is a pioneer effort. It can be amplified as circumstances warrant."[123] His colleague John Robsion agreed that "This legislation is very necessary, and it is long overdue," but:

> It is not as comprehensive as it should be. It certainly is a step in the right direction, and as time goes on no doubt it will be perfected by appropriate amendments. . . . [T]he naked fact is that we do have these agencies and officials administering hundreds of acts of Congress, and in so doing they have issued orders, directives, and rules exceeding the powers granted to them by the Congress. In other words, they have assumed the function of making laws. The power to legislate and make laws rests alone in the Congress and not with the powers of any officer or any one of these agencies. These same officers of these agencies issue these orders, directives, and rules, and then they proceed to hail the citizens and business concerns before them for investigation, trial, and judgment. . . . They are the lawmakers, prosecutors, juries, and judges of their own laws.[124]

In the House, Clarence Hancock and John Gwynne announced that they would continue to push for further legislation building upon the foundation laid by the APA. Hancock endorsed the APA, not as "the final word, but it is a good beginning." "As far as I know," he continued:

> There is no opposition to the bill on this side of the aisle, although there are many of us who would like to have it stronger. Nevertheless, I think we are all prepared to go along with it because we feel it is the first important step in the direction of dividing investigatory, regulatory, administrative, and judicial functions in Government agencies. I have long favored reform of administrative procedure, legislation which would protect individual citizens against the abuses of delegated power, legislation which would separate the functions of investigator, prosecutor, judge, jury, and executioner.

"If weaknesses develop" in the legislation, he concluded, "the Congress can pass legislation to correct those weaknesses."[125] Gwynne similarly described the APA as "a start at least along the road that we must travel to regulate the many bureaus and tribunals that are now operating in the executive branch of the Government. Some of you who have been very much interested in this subject," he granted, "may read this bill with a certain amount of disappointment. You will regret that the bill does not go further. I am frank to say that I have those same feelings myself."[126] Nevertheless, he encouraged his fellow Republicans to support the bill and then to keep pressing for further measures afterwards.

This legislative history indicates several important conclusions. The first is that the APA was the product of a genuine consensus among members of Congress not only that the administrative state had grown out of control but that it also threatened basic principles of constitutional government—though some members expressed this point more forcefully than others. The most significant piece of legislation in administrative law was the product of a fundamental tension between the administrative state and American constitutionalism. Thus the modern administrative state is, in essence, defined by this tension. Second, many skeptics of administrative law saw the APA not as a definitive settlement of this tension but merely a first step on the way to restoring constitutional government. The APA, in their view, would need to be supplemented by additional legislation if constitutional government were to survive the administrative onslaught. This was a widely held and frequently expressed position during the debate and was repeated after the passage of the APA. As Pat McCarran, who labeled the APA a "bill of rights" for those controlled by the activities of the administrative state, proclaimed in 1948, "a set of improvements have been initiated with the adoption of the Administrative Procedure Act. . . . But now is the time to probe deeper into the general problem of regulatory government. We must do that, lest we become deluded into thinking that what we have done, or are now doing, marks the end of the road to which there is, in truth, no end."[127]

Third and finally, the APA was clearly understood to broaden the scope of judicial review, in terms of access to judicial review as well as the scope of judicial scrutiny. Agency factfinding was to be held to a more rigorous "substantial evidence" standard, agencies would be constrained in terms of the evidence that could be used to support a decision, and agencies' legal interpretations would be reviewed de novo by courts. Questions along these lines were repeatedly raised during the debates and both the statutory text and the legislative history supported this reading of the APA.[128] Although it was understood by members of Congress to be a "pioneer effort," they still expected the APA to change the level of judicial scrutiny of administrative action. Reiterating the consensus that prevailed on the floor of Congress, Sen. McCarran wrote an article for the American Bar Association's annual journal confirming that the

APA "simply and expressly provides that Courts 'shall decide all relevant questions of law.'" This provision in particular, he alleged, "cut down on the 'cult of discretion'" that had been produced "in the last decade or so."[129] Even John Dickinson, who had done more than anyone to erode the law/fact distinction that preserved de novo review of agencies' legal interpretations, conceded that the APA repudiated this project.[130] Dickinson granted that the APA required courts to decide questions of law "for itself, and in the exercise of its own independent judgment."[131]

These expectations turned out to be in vain. As Aditya Bamzai writes, "The revival of the independent-judgment rule that the APA appeared to augur did not occur."[132] In a few cases courts took a less deferential posture towards agencies' legal interpretations, but the APA did not decisively reverse the New Deal tendency towards deference. Two years following the passage of the APA, in *FTC v. Cement Institute*, Justice Black defended a doctrine of deference to administrative agencies' legal interpretations that resembled the pre-APA approach of *Gray v. Powell* and *NLRB v. Hearst Publications*.[133] Black wrote that "we give great weight to the Commission's conclusion [of law], as this Court has done in other cases." This made sense in light of "the express intention of Congress to create an agency whose membership would at all times be experienced, so that its conclusions would be the result of an expertness coming from experience."[134] In 1951 the Court decided *O'Leary v. Brown-Pacific-Maxon* by following essentially the same principles set forth in *Gray* and *Hearst*, deferring to an agency's legal interpretation on the grounds that it was a mixed question of law and fact.[135] In light of these and similar rulings, the influential administrative law scholar Kenneth Culp Davis proclaimed: "The doctrine of *Gray v. Powell* has survived the APA."[136] The APA's provisions regarding the proper scope of judicial review amounted to much sound and fury, signifying nothing.

Thus the New Deal era in administrative law began with a dramatic expansion of the administrative state, along with a further entrenchment of the judicial deference that had begun to emerge during the Progressive era. The New Deal prompted a significant backlash, particularly in the legal community, and even among progressives such as Roscoe Pound who believed that Roosevelt had enshrined "administrative absolutism." This backlash resulted in many proposals, including the Walter-Logan Act, but eventually produced the Administrative Procedure Act in 1946. The APA seemed to require a change of course in administrative law, bringing greater procedural requirements to agencies, separating functions within agencies, and especially bringing the courts back into the administrative process. But by the end of the 1950s the regime of judicial deference to administration was undisturbed by the APA. It was not until liberal reformers, wary of the bureaucracy, turned against deference that the courts began to reassert their influence, as described in the following chapter. The cult of deference continued, at least for a few more decades.

CHAPTER SEVEN

"A Surrogate Political Process"

The 1970 Administrative Law Revolution

THE FIGHT OVER the legitimacy of the administrative state subsided after the New Deal and the passage of the Administrative Procedure Act in 1946, but it did not vanish. Rather, that conflict shifted to a new arena: administrative law and judicial review of administrative power. From 1960 to the end of the 1970s, a revolution in administrative law brought the federal judiciary and interest groups into the struggle for control over administrative policy. By the 1970s it was obvious that the administrative state's challenge to fundamental principles of American constitutionalism was not going to be brushed aside easily. What was surprising was that it was liberal reformers who sought to use administrative law to control the bureaucracy.

This chapter describes the administrative law revolution and its effects on the administrative state. As presidents struggled to gain control over the bureaucracy, devising new techniques for "capturing" the administrative state, liberals became increasingly wary of the case for centralized, technocratic, and apolitical administration combined with judicial deference. New theories of administrative accountability, which loosely resembled but were very different from the older approach to republicanizing administrative power, became prevalent in administrative law. Legal doctrines governing the administrative state were devised in response to these new theories of participatory democracy, and courts and interest groups became major players in the administrative state's policymaking process.

The Post–New Deal Regime

FDR's limited success in establishing presidential control over the administrative state (discussed in the previous chapter) ensured that his successors would be continually frustrated in their attempts to establish their priorities over the bureaucracy. As he left office, Harry Truman famously predicted the difficulty that his successor, Dwight Eisenhower, would face in attempting to control the bureaucracy: "He'll sit here, and he'll say, 'Do this! Do that!' And nothing will happen. Poor Ike—it won't be a bit like the Army."[1] Truman was speaking from experience. At one particularly difficult juncture, in which he could not get the bureaucracy to move according to his wishes, he breathlessly complained, "I thought I was the President, but when it comes to these bureaucrats, I can't do a damn thing."[2] The growth of the bureaucracy, combined with the lack of a clear hierarchy leading up to the president, ensured that the "headless fourth branch" would remain difficult to guide.

These dynamics combined with another variable—congressional delegation—to complicate the president's role in administration even further. As David Lewis has shown, Congress often designs the structure and accountability of agencies to ensure that its preferences are secured, and not those of the president.[3] While "presidents have tremendous influence in the design of administrative agencies" through their use of the veto power, their ability to influence Congress, and their ability to create agencies through executive action, Congress is also equipped to override presidential influence when it wants to insulate an agency from presidential oversight, particularly after the *Humphrey's Executor* decision.[4] By the 1950s, in short, the government was a long distance from the principle of presidential responsibility that was so emphatically insisted on during the Founding period.

Of course, presidents would not be expected to accept responsibility for an administration they have little power to direct, and the growth of an insulated bureaucracy prompted reforms by presidents to regain control over the administrative state. As Lewis explains, "Presidents have responded [to these developments] in a number of ways, including increased public activities, the development of the Executive Office of the President, and attempts to politicize the bureaucracy and centralize its control in the White House."[5] Up against a Congress that could monitor agencies through a decentralized committee structure, and influence the bureaucracy through program authorization and the appropriation of money to agencies, presidents sought to equip themselves with other tools to extend their own control over the administrative state.

Social Regulation, Capture Theory, and the
New Politics of Administrative Design

At the same time that presidents struggled to gain control over the existing administrative state, a new political movement brought another wave of regulatory programs and administrative agencies, modifying significantly the scope and structure of the administrative state. The Progressive and New Deal approach to administration focused on the creation of economic regulation that controlled market activity to manage the economy. Agencies like the ICC, FTC, Federal Reserve, SEC, NLRB, and others aimed primarily at controlling "the price and supply of goods, the number of participants in certain regulated industries, and the conditions of entry into these industries."[6]

The new agencies created in the 1960s and 1970s were profoundly different in their objectives and structure. Instead of focusing on economic regulation, these new agencies engaged in social regulation. Their goal was not so much to ensure orderly markets as it was to promote broad-ranging public values like health, safety, nondiscrimination in employment, and environmental protection.[7] These new agencies—such as EPA, OSHA, NHTSA, EEOC, and CPSC—had much broader mandates that spanned the entire economy.[8] Consequently they were structured very differently. Instead of constructing regulatory commissions that would operate independently of the executive branch, these new social regulatory agencies were often housed within executive departments whose personnel were more directly accountable to the president through his removal powers.[9]

The attempts of presidents to gain control over the bureaucracy came to a head in the Nixon administration. Richard Nathan chronicled the challenges the Nixon administration faced in establishing an "administrative presidency" from an insider's perspective. When Nixon realized that Congress would not enact his "New Federalism" agenda, like many of his predecessors he sought to make policy through the bureaucracy. He established his Domestic Council in 1970, leaving the cabinet secretaries free to manage their departments and seeking to develop policy through his own personal advisors in the White House.[10] Nixon was forced into this strategy in part because he followed the traditional approach to cabinet appointments, in which the cabinet was envisioned "to be representative of a broad range of viewpoints as well as different professions and geographical areas."[11] Consequently, when he introduced his cabinet en bloc he emphasized that each appointee "is an independent thinker."[12] The creation of such a cabinet composed of independent thinkers undermined centralized presidential control of administration, a fact that Nixon lamented during his first term in office.

Nixon quickly found that directing the agencies was just as difficult as directing the Congress. Rather than serving as "spokesmen for the president" and his agenda, his own appointees were drawn "into the orbit of the program interests of their agency."[13] The "[f]orces that come into play after an appointment has been made" turned Nixon's own appointees against him.[14] They had to rely upon the expertise of the career bureaucrats in the agency, who knew much more about program details. Furthermore, "strong outside forces," particularly congressional committees and various interest groups, stymied efforts to impose the president's objectives on unwilling agencies.[15] These forces combined with restrictions on the president's removal power to undermine the president's control over the administrative state. Nixon's political appointees in the administration were coopted by the agencies and the various players that were oriented around them. This phenomenon prompted Nixon aide John Erlichman to remark at a press briefing about the administration's appointees: "We only see them at the annual White House Christmas party; they go off and marry the natives."[16] Eventually Nixon abandoned regular meetings with his domestic cabinet secretaries, as he found that they increasingly opposed him and brought their own programmatic priorities to him for support.[17]

Undaunted, Nixon devised an alternative to working through his political appointees in the executive departments. He attempted to use his personal appointees in the White House, housed in the Executive Office of the President. The Office of Management and Budget was reorganized and the Executive Office of the President was dramatically expanded. Nixon created "working groups" composed of White House officials and reliable personnel within the agencies themselves to circumvent the cabinet secretaries and establish direct relationships between the White House and policy implementers "well below the level of the Secretary." As Nathan explains, "Only the most astute Cabinet member could keep on top of this policy process" that developed outside of the executive branch hierarchy.[18] Yet this strategy, Nathan explained, was also unsuccessful due to the size and complexity of the administrative state.[19] Still, Nixon's "plot" (as Nathan describes it) caused great alarm among liberal reformers who now saw that their favored programs might be left in the hands of an ideological opponent and his political appointees. This forced them to rethink their approach to administrative law. Administration had become re-politicized. As a theoretical matter, the re-politicization of administration was a consequence of the rejection of the Progressives' faith in scientific administration. As Chapter Five explained, the Progressives rooted their faith in administrative expertise in the view that regulatory policy questions had an objectively right answer. The only desideratum was to ensure that administrators would be adequately trained to seek and devise that answer, and free to implement it.

This position was openly rejected by reformers of the 1960s and 1970s. In their view, the goal of regulatory policy is not to find the scientifically correct answer to policy problems, but to serve fundamental values that lie beyond the facts and calculations of administrators. As Richard Stewart explained in 1975, "Today, the exercise of agency discretion is inevitably seen as the essentially legislative process of adjusting the competing claims of various private interests affected by agency policy," rather than the pursuit of objectively right answers to policy problems.[20] Instead of the stark separation between politics and administration, these reformers insisted on the overlap between administration and politics. The issues to be decided by bureaucrats, in their view, "clearly do not turn on technical issues that can safely be left to the experts."[21] This position assumes "that there is no ascertainable, transcendent 'public interest,' but only the distinct interests of various individuals and groups in society."[22] In short, administration was now viewed as "the provision of a surrogate political process to ensure the fair representation of a wide range of affected interests in the process of administrative decision," rather than a technical process of devising the objectively best means to reach the ends set forth by Congress.[23]

But the politicization of administration presented a difficulty. Especially once Nixon had attempted to take control of the bureaucracy, liberals confronted the possibility that a chief executive could use the administrative hierarchy to *frustrate*, rather than to achieve, the ends that the modern administrative state was authorized to attain. As Harris and Milkis note, "public lobbyists learned about the pitfalls of politicizing public administration through the White House. Perhaps most important, it became clear that the Oval Office might not be occupied at all times by an individual of Franklin Roosevelt's vision and commitment to executive action. . . . More ominously, though, the chief executive might be hostile to the goals of public lobbyists."[24] Agencies were now increasingly seen as "captured" by the very firms they were empowered to control. One of the most prominent exponents of the new "capture theory" was Marver Bernstein, whose 1955 book *Regulating Business by Independent Commission* became a core text for liberal reformers in the 1960s and 1970s. He explained that many factors, not simply the potential antiregulatory leanings of a chief executive, bent administrative agencies in the direction of the firms they were charged with regulating. As the agency develops expertise, often drawn from experience working in the same firms the agency is supposed to oversee, "The commission becomes accepted as an essential part of the industrial system," working alongside the industry itself. It sees its task as helping to manage the industry, for the betterment of the regulated, rather than the public interest with which the agency interacts only minimally. As a result "the commission's standards of regulation are determined in the light of the desires of the industry affected" and the agency will not "be able to extend regulation beyond the limits acceptable to the regulated groups."[25] Thus even if an agency is structured to be independent of presidential oversight, reformers argued, it will still adopt a pro-industry posture. In fact, many argued that the independence of the commission from politics enabled and exacerbated agency capture.

In addition to the possibility of a hostile chief executive, and the natural industry bias that an agency accumulates as it manages an area of the economy, the very nature of the interests involved in regulation, capture theorists argued, ensured that an agency would be biased in carrying out its mandate. The interests affected by regulation have a deep and ongoing interest in monitoring and influencing agency action, while the interest of the public in regulation is diffuse and disorganized. As Roger Noll explained, "Most regulatory issues are of deep interest to regulated industries. . . . The stake of the general public may in the aggregate be even higher, but it is diffused among a large number of unorganized individuals."[26] Thus the outside pressures likely to be exerted on agencies will come disproportionately from organized interests, particularly those who are subject to the regulatory powers of the relevant agency, unless the diffuse interests of the public are organized and given tools to influence agency decision making.

As capture theory gained adherents even the most ardent defenders of the New Deal's reliance on administrative experts insulated from popular accountability entertained second thoughts about the wisdom of such an approach. Well before Nixon's attempt to coopt the federal bureaucracy, James Landis—of all people—lamented in a report to President-Elect John F. Kennedy that "Spectacular instance of executive, legislative, and industry interference with the disposition of matters before the agencies have been uncovered." Consequently, he reasoned, "A reappraisal of the various functions and activities of the regulatory agencies is thus desirable at this very critical period of our national life."[27] Not only capture theory but simple and base politics had played a role in distorting the administrative process. Because of the politics of agency design (explained above), he maintained, "No rational line has been pursued by the Congress in differentiating the 'independent' agencies from those embraced within some Executive Department."[28] Landis had become exasperated with the administrative state that he had played so instrumental a role in establishing a few decades earlier—though as Joanna Grisinger explains, Landis believed "that the problem of the independent commissions was more a management problem than a legal one."[29] In other words, Landis's frustration did not prompt him to rethink his core assumptions about the need to have expert agencies making policy independently of political oversight.

In short, the administrative state's "third wave" of expansion in the 1960s and 1970s, as Cass Sunstein has written, "differed both substantively and institutionally from that of the 1930s." It not only embarked on broader and more ambitious projects, it also "largely abandoned the New Deal faith in administrative autonomy. Bureaucracy was the problem rather than the solution. . . . Experience had shown that administrative autonomy often gave rise to precisely the risks of self-interested representation and factionalism that the original constitutional framework was designed to prevent."[30] Opponents of the New Deal such as Roscoe Pound predicted this result. But instead of heeding their earlier warnings and restructuring administration to return to an earlier understanding of American constitutionalism and administrative law, liberal reformers restructured the administrative state to increase judicial and interest-group oversight of the growing regulatory state. In one important respect, however, liberals looked to use the Constitution's Due Process clause to constrain administrative discretion to resolve questions affecting citizens' individual rights.

A Legitimate Claim of Entitlement

As indicated in previous chapters, since the early years of the republic, when administrators made determinations that affected the rights and interests of individual parties, there was a consensus that procedures should be in place to assure a fair opportunity for the individual to present his or her side of the story. During the Founding period one of the most frequently voiced objections was that officers were empowered by the British government to search citizens' property without warrants or hearings in advance. The idea of due process of law as a constraint against arbitrary administrative action was a well-established principle.

With the rapid expansion of administrative power in the early twentieth century, questions arose about the application of the Constitution's Due Process clauses to the exercise of administrative power. Two early cases in 1908 and 1915 addressed this question and drew different conclusions. The first, *Londoner v. City and County of Denver*, indicated that constitutional due process requires certain procedures to be followed when an agency engages in rulemaking—in this case, an assessment of a tax for paving city streets in Denver.[31] The Court determined that the landowners whose property was improved by the project, and who were assessed for the cost, were denied Due Process of Law under the Fourteenth Amendment because they were not afforded the opportunity to be heard. *Londoner* indicated that administrative decisions would have to follow a relatively sophisticated set of procedures to satisfy constitutional due process, but in 1915 the Court decided *Bi-Metallic Investment Co. v. State Board of Equalization of Colorado*, limiting the scope of the *Londoner* decision.[32] In that case the Court rejected a due process claim against a tax increase imposed by Colorado's Board of Equalization and distinguished *Londoner* because the latter case involved "a relatively small number of persons, exceptionally affected." When a more general decision by an agency affects a larger number of people, the Court implied, it would not be subjected to constitutional due process requirements.

Those cases seemed to indicate that the Due Process Clauses of the Fifth and Fourteenth Amendments would not offer citizens much hope when challenging administrative action. But in the 1960s and 1970s, liberals revived due process as an important tool that could be used to impose procedural checks on administrative power. In some ways, their concerns echoed those of early administrative law, but to bring due process to bear on the modern administrative state liberals first had to broaden the scope of interests protected under the concept of due process.

That project was advanced in several landmark cases, which indicated liberals' growing concern with arbitrary administrative power and their turn to the courts to protect individuals from the bureaucracy. In *Goldberg v. Kelly* the Supreme Court interpreted the Due Process Clause of the Fourteenth Amendment to require a state to provide an evidentiary hearing prior to terminating welfare benefits.[33] The decision was noteworthy for at least two reasons. First, the Court noted that welfare recipients are at the mercy of a vast bureaucracy and, without procedural protections, could be harmed by an arbitrary decision maker. In other words, instead of presuming that the administrators were acting in the public interest, the Court shifted to presuming that individuals needed to be protected from the bureaucracy. This applied especially to those on the edge of subsistence: "For qualified recipients, welfare provides the means to obtain essential food, clothing, housing, and medical care. . . . Since he lacks independent resources, his situation becomes immediately desperate. His need to concentrate upon finding the means for daily subsistence, in turn, adversely affects his ability to seek redress from the bureaucracy." The Court was now focusing on the individual, trapped inside a bureaucratic web, as opposed to the ability of unfettered experts to promote the public interest.

Second, the Court assumed that there was no difference between a traditional right and positive rights bestowed upon individuals by government programs, such as welfare. Both categories of rights, the Court argued, were protected by the Due Process Clause. "The constitutional challenge," Justice Brennan explained in the majority opinion, "cannot be answered by an argument that public assistance benefits are a privilege and not a right." Rather, Due Process is triggered when an individual "may be condemned to suffer grievous loss." The deprivation of property through civil penalties and the deprivation of a welfare benefit both impose a grievous loss on the individual, according to the Court, and therefore both types of deprivations can be inflicted only if due process is afforded.

In a certain respect, therefore, liberals who turned to the Due Process Clause to check administrative power were departing from the original understanding of the clause's protection of "life, liberty, [and] property." However, with the advent of the modern state and its expansion of government programs and benefits, liberals were arguably adhering to the original intention of the clause: to prevent individuals from being subjected to arbitrary government power. The rationale underlying *Goldberg* was extended in another landmark case, *Board of Regents of State Colleges v. Roth*.[34] The case involved a different kind of government benefit, namely, government employment as a professor at a state university. David Roth alleged that he was deprived of his public employment without an opportunity for a hearing. While the Court ruled against Roth, it did so by reaffirming that it "has fully and finally rejected the wooden distinction between rights and privileges that once seemed to govern the applicability of procedural due process rights." Rather, the Court explained, the state may provide individuals with entitlements to certain benefits. As long as these benefits are adequately "grounded in the statute[s] defining eligibility for them," the Court reasoned, beneficiaries have "a legitimate claim of entitlement" to them, and such benefits cannot be taken without affording due process. Otherwise, a government official could deprive people of claims that significantly affect the daily lives of individuals. "It is a purpose of the ancient institution of property," the Court announced, "to protect those claims upon which people rely in their daily lives, reliance that must not be arbitrarily undermined."

In short, liberals began to use the Due Process clause to open up an avenue for challenging administrative action in the judiciary. Instead of advocating deference to agencies, and condemning efforts to constrain them in the exercise of their powers, liberals turned to an old remedy but in a new bottle. Due process would not be used merely to protect traditional negative rights to liberty and property from arbitrary government interference—it would now be used to protect the positive rights that individuals acquired from statutes creating entitlements to specific benefits from the government, an awkward new institutional configuration. Yet this liberal turn against the bureaucracy

in the context of due process was merely the beginning of a much larger and
more significant revolution that would transform administrative law.

Democratizing the Administrative State:
The 1970s Procedural Revolution

Beginning in the 1960s and extending into the 1970s, federal courts radically
altered the administrative process. As a result of the expansion of the administrative state and the fear of agency capture, courts came to accept a different
view of their relationship to agencies in the modern administrative state. Instead of ensuring basic procedural fairness and substantive reasonableness as
directed by law, judges expanded their oversight of the administrative state
to grant interested parties greater influence in the direction of administrative
policymaking. Settled doctrines of administrative law were modified to extend judicial oversight of the growing bureaucracy.

With regard to the procedures for administrative rulemaking, federal
courts worked assiduously to expand the meager notice-and-comment procedures that the Administrative Procedure Act (APA) mandates. This set
of developments led to the famous *Vermont Yankee* case in 1978.[35] The Supreme Court also eased standing requirements to allow interested groups to
challenge administrative agencies in court. In both cases it was liberals who
began to experience "buyer's remorse" regarding the administrative state.
Their remedy, however, was not to return to the earlier, nineteenth-century
approach to regulation and administration but, rather, to use procedural requirements and new standing doctrines to democratize the administrative
state by giving courts and interest groups an active role in supervising administrative agencies, preventing them from being captured and turning from the
public interest. While these contests were important to policy development,
they were also rooted in an ongoing concern about the relationship between
administrative power and American constitutionalism. Administrative law,
in other words, became the forum in which the relationship between the
administrative state and American constitutionalism would continue to be
debated and worked out.

The Road to Vermont Yankee

As explained in the previous chapter, the APA established three basic requirements for agencies engaged in informal rulemaking: a notice of proposed
rulemaking containing "the terms or substance of the proposed rule or a description of the subjects and issues involved," an "opportunity to participate in

the rule making through submission of written data, views, or arguments with or without opportunity for oral presentation," and "a concise general statement" of the basis and purpose of the rule.[36] The procedural requirements for formal rulemaking were more extensive, but that category had become irrelevant by 1980, for two reasons. First, it was clearly unsuited to the legislative activity of rulemaking. As then-Professor Antonin Scalia wrote, "The inappropriateness of the judicialized procedures for the sort of quasi-legislative activity understood by the term "rulemaking" should be obvious. . . . The formal rulemaking provisions have in fact been applied to very few programs of general rulemaking, where they have had predictably inefficient results."[37] The inefficiency of adjudication and formal rulemaking was believed to be inapplicable in the new administrative state, where agencies would engage in broad and prospective rulemaking rather than case-by-case adjudication to regulate. Beginning in the 1960s, as the administrative state's workload expanded, a "flight to rulemaking" took place. Agencies such as the FTC, which traditionally operated by individualized "cease-and-desist" orders, discovered that they could use prospective and general rules to regulate more efficiently. This made the work of agencies more manageable, and so the period of the 1960s and 1970s witnessed "the constant and accelerating flight away from individualized, adjudicatory proceedings to generalized disposition through rulemaking."[38] In sum, agencies began regulating through rulemaking rather than adjudication as a result of the expansion of their responsibilities.

Second, the Supreme Court ruled in *United States vs. Florida East Coast Railway* that formal rulemaking procedures would only be required when the magic words "on the record after opportunity for an agency hearing" appear in the agency's organic statute.[39] Previously, the presumption was that if an agency was required by statute to conduct a "hearing" before acting, this indicated Congress's intent to require formal procedures. Thus at the very time that agencies were engaged in a "flight to rulemaking," they were also engaged in a flight from formal to informal rulemaking.

However, the reduction of agencies' procedural requirements cut against the prevailing liberal understanding of the administrative state. As mentioned above, in the 1960s and 1970s capture theory fundamentally changed the stance of courts towards administrative agencies. The earlier paradigm of administrative law described in the previous chapter was challenged by liberals who, influenced by the emerging capture theory and newly distrustful of large-scale bureaucratic organizations, distrusted agencies and sought to control them by extending judicial review, as well as ensuring participation from the public in the administrative process. Both of these objectives could be achieved in part by adding to the agencies' procedural requirements. Because of the *FECR* decision, however, administrative agencies' procedural requirements were diminishing, affording less ground for judicial oversight of the rulemaking process. As Gary Lawson explains, "At the same time that agencies were exercising ever-increasing authority under ever-decreasing procedural requirements, confidence in agency decision making among scholars, judges, and participants in the administrative process was reaching a new low."[40] Capture theory demanded that the procedural constraints on agencies be increased, not diminished. Therefore the federal courts went on a crusade to expand these procedural requirements.

Because it, and not the Supreme Court, was responsible for crafting most federal administrative law, the DC Circuit was the engine of reform.[41] From the late 1960s to the early 1970s, the DC Circuit essentially created a type of procedural category called "hybrid rulemaking," which went beyond the rather bare requirements of the APA's informal rulemaking category. As it was doing this, the DC Circuit acknowledged periodically that hybrid rulemaking was not based on the APA but, rather, the recognition "that basic considerations of fairness may dictate procedural requirements not specified by Congress."[42] Eight years earlier, in 1966, the DC Circuit announced, "This Court has indicated its readiness to lay down procedural requirements inherent in the very concept of fair hearing for certain classes of cases, even though no such requirements had been specified by Congress."[43] Thus sometimes the DC Circuit created procedural requirements simply to impose its own understanding of fairness on agencies.

At other times the DC Circuit expanded procedural requirements under the guise of interpreting the APA's requirements for informal rulemaking. The APA's requirement that agencies issue a notice of proposed rulemaking was broadened to mandate that the agency disclose all of the relevant data supporting the proposed rule, as well as provide the actual rule being proposed rather than a general description of the issues under consideration. In *Portland Cement Association v. Ruckleshaus* (1973) Judge Leventhal criticized the EPA for issuing an emission standard through informal rulemaking without disclosing in its notice the methodology it employed in tests that supported the final rule.[44] In remanding the rule to the agency, Leventhal lectured the agency that "the cause of a clean environment is best served by reasoned decision-making," and asserted that "It is not consonant with the purpose of a rule-making proceeding to promulgate rules on the basis of inadequate data, or on data that, [to a] critical degree, is known only to the agency."[45] *Portland*

Cement was ultimately interpreted to mean that agencies would have to provide all of the relevant studies and data supporting the proposed rule at the beginning of the rulemaking process in order to survive judicial review.[46] The DC Circuit also expanded the requirement that agencies provide a "concise statement of . . . basis and purpose" when issuing final rules. In 1968, for instance, in *Automotive Parts & Accessories Association v. Boyd*, the DC Circuit argued that "it is appropriate for us . . . to caution against an overly literal reading of the statutory terms 'concise' and 'general'" in the APA's "concise general statement of . . . basis and purpose" procedural requirement.[47]

It is important to note the fervor with which the DC Circuit engaged in its project of creating this hybrid rulemaking process for the sake of ensuring a fair administrative process. Many of the judges on that court took up their pens and wrote law review articles defending and explaining themselves to the legal public.[48] And Congress followed the DC Circuit's lead by regularly adding to procedural requirements for specific agencies through new and amended organic statutes. For example, the Environmental Impact Statement (EIS) process established by the National Environmental Policy Act (NEPA) of 1969 ensured maximum participation through greater procedural controls on agencies. Under section 102 of the act, as Jim Rossi explains, "all federal agencies, proposing actions that will significantly affect the environment must prepare an EIS and make copies available to the public" for public participation.[49] Any agency that undergoes this process must hold hearings when there is a controversy or even when there is substantial interest. Moreover, the final EIS produced after comments are received and hearings held must respond to all legitimate opposing viewpoints.

In summary, by the 1960s and 1970s the earlier paradigm of deference to administrators had sharply declined. As Robert Kagan notes, by "the late 1960s and early 1970s welfare rights lawyers used litigation to drive state and local governments toward higher standards of *procedural* justice," a movement that "had genuine substantive consequences."[50] These procedural hurdles would have been unthinkable to the Progressives and New Dealers. For instance, in 1938 James Landis wrote, "I have seen as little as twenty minutes elapse between the drafting and promulgation of a permissive rule where the exigencies of the situation called for quick action."[51] One can imagine the kind of procedural laxity that would be necessary to produce such hasty rulemaking activity. However, the flexibility granted to experts to deal with broad problems—a concept central to the Progressives' understanding of the administrative state—was substantially eroded not by conservatives but by liberals.

The Relaxation of Standing and the New Private Enforcement

The doctrine of standing declares that the judicial branch can only hear specific cases that involve particular parties personally involved in the dispute in question. It is ultimately connected to the idea that the purpose of courts is not to decide on the merits of legislation in the abstract sense but only as applied to particular cases. Judgment, not will, is the virtue of the judicial branch—to paraphrase *Federalist 78*—which means that some doctrine must ensure that judges only exercise judgment in particular cases by applying the law made in other branches.[52] As a practical matter standing doctrine limits the number of cases that courts can decide. In the context of administrative law, the doctrine of standing limits the extent to which the courts can review decisions made by the agencies of the administrative state.

From this perspective, standing therefore has a profound impact on the relative authority of the executive and judicial branches. The more standing is broadened, the more cases involving an agency decision the courts are empowered to decide, which increases the power of the courts and reduces that of the agencies; and vice versa. As Shep Melnick writes in the context of welfare law, "Aggressive judicial review almost always raises the cost of welfare programs. The rules of standing and jurisdiction almost virtually ensure this: the vast majority of cases are brought by recipients who argue they were denied benefits promised by the statute; taxpayer suits are not accepted by the federal judiciary."[53] The question of who gets to sue the agency has a dramatic effect on the outcomes of agency decision making. The more judicial review that is permitted, the more that interested parties can influence through litigation the direction of regulatory policy.

The shift to looser standing requirements fits the long-term trends of political strategy that developed in the twentieth century. As courts began to be viewed more favorably by those on the left, in light of the growing distrust of agencies, liberals began to push for laxer standing thresholds, allowing more interest groups to influence the administrative process through courts sympathetic to their purposes. This development on the left was a shift away from the earlier Progressive approach that called for judicial deference to agencies—a position reflected in the standing cases discussed in the previous chapter.

The APA directly addressed the question of who has standing to sue an agency: "A person suffering legal wrong because of agency action, or adversely affected or aggrieved by agency action within the meaning of a relevant statute, is entitled to judicial review thereof."[54] The kinds of "legal wrongs" cognized by the APA were the traditional injuries that were sufficient to satisfy standing requirements in other areas of law. As the previous chapter explained, the authors of the APA believed they were expanding access to judicial review, even though this was not the immediate effect of the Act.

The right to sue in court may come from a constitutional or a statutory source. Article III of the U.S. Constitution declares that the federal judiciary has the power to decide "cases and controversies." These cases and controversies would arise either from constitutional provisions or from instances where statutorily protected interests are implicated. Congress can, either explicitly or implicitly, grant access to the courts to specific parties by creating protected interests in a statute.[55] Therefore, many cases involving standing in the administrative law context are centered around whether standing can be derived from the positive benefit set forth in the positive law.[56]

At the time of the passage of the APA in 1946, standing to sue did not include generalized injuries or distress and was confined to legal wrongs under the definition provided by common law. The common law's definition primarily restricted legal wrongs to economic and property interests. Therefore, in short, the state of statutory standing in 1946 insulated much agency action from judicial review. Moreover, the text of the APA cited above referring to a "relevant statute" meant special review statutes that were frequently passed by Congress to grant statutory standing to particular parties. Congress, therefore, could expand upon the common law's approach to standing by granting statutory standing, but not without limits.[57]

This relatively limited scope of standing had begun to expand in the 1960s as liberal judges became more skeptical of administrative agencies. In two circuit court decisions—*Scenic Hudson Preservation Conference v. Federal Power Commission*[58] and *Office of Communication of United Church of Christ v. FCC*[59]—the courts began to shift to a generalized notion of injury. In addition, these cases also moved from an economic definition of injury towards one that granted standing to "ideological" interests. In the former case, the 2nd Circuit noted that standing for ideological interest groups, such as the Scenic Hudson Preservation Conference, would ensure "that the Federal Power Commission will adequately protect the public interest in the aesthetic, conservational, and recreational aspects of power development."[60] In language similar to the partnership notion employed by the DC Circuit in the context of procedural review, the 2nd Circuit argued that the FPC could not be trusted to make policy without the guidance and oversight of interest groups, through interventions in the judicial branch. In *United Church of Christ v. FCC*, the DC Circuit argued that members of the general public, the "listening audience," have a sufficient stake in the decisions of the FCC to bring suit against decisions of that agency that affect them adversely. Thus in this case as well the DC Circuit sought explicitly to move away from the idea of economic interest as the basis for standing and incorporate an approach more friendly to generalized and ideological interests.

In 1970 the Supreme Court, in *Association of Data Processing Service Organizations v. Camp*, suggested that the question of standing concerns "whether the interest sought to be protected by the complainant is arguably within the zone of interests to be protected or regulated by the statute or constitutional guarantee in question."[61] With this phrase, the Court crafted "zone of interests" standing, which grants standing to sue to any party that is within the general zone of interests "protected or regulated" by the statute.[62] In that case, the Court shifted from looking to see whether the Constitution or Congress had clearly established standing and instead signaled that the primary question is whether the party seeking review falls under the general zone of interests of the statute.

Two years later, in *Sierra Club v. Morton*, the Sierra Club sought to challenge a decision by the Department of the Interior (in particular, the U.S. Forest Service) which allowed for the development of a Disney ski resort in a valley near Sequoia National Park.[63] In order to establish standing to sue, Sierra Club had to demonstrate that it was injured by the decision. The Sierra Club relied on the relevant language of the APA to establish the basis for judicial review, but because it had not demonstrated that any of its members were actually affected by the decision, the Court ruled against the group. Yet in doing so, the Court reiterated the "zone of interests" standard and explained that it was a broader standard than the constitutional requirements for standing. As Justice Stewart, writing for the Court, explained:

> Early decisions under this statute interpreted the language as adopting the various formulations of "legal interest" and "legal wrong" then prevailing as constitutional requirements of standing. But, in *Data Processing Service v. Camp* . . . we held more broadly that persons had standing to obtain judicial review of federal agency action under . . . the APA where they had alleged that the challenged action had caused them "injury in fact," and where the alleged injury was to an interest "arguably within the zone of interests to be protected or regulated" by the statutes that the agencies were claimed to have violated.[64]

The Court spent the remainder of its opinion explaining how this was an expansion of access to the courts to review administrative action, which the

Court endorsed,[65] while maintaining that an actual harm or injury was still required to trigger standing to sue.[66] Therefore, while Sierra Club lost this battle, it ultimately won the war; for the Court implicitly recognized that non-economic or property interests—"ideological" interests—can be sufficient to establish standing, at least for purposes of the APA's provisions concerning judicial review.

These developments culminated in the 1973 case of *United States v. Students Challenging Regulatory Agency Procedures* (SCRAP).[67] SCRAP was a group of five law students at George Washington University who organized to challenge instances of agency capture through litigation. The students challenged a rate change made by the Interstate Commerce Commission on the grounds that its implementation would substantially harm the environment and therefore their interests. The students contended that they were "adversely affected" or "aggrieved" within the meaning of the APA for purposes of standing and therefore the courts could hear their case. In ruling for the students, Justice Stewart (the author of the Court's opinion in *Sierra Club v. Morton*), argued:

> Here, by contrast [to *Sierra Club v. Morton*], the appellees claimed that the spe-
> cific and allegedly illegal action of the Commission would directly harm them in
> their use of the natural resources of the Washington Metropolitan Area. Unlike
> the specific and geographically limited federal action of which the petitioner
> complained in Sierra Club, the challenged agency action in this case is applicable
> to substantially all of the Nation's railroads, and thus allegedly has an adverse
> environmental impact on all the natural resources of the country. Rather than a
> limited group of persons who used a picturesque valley in California, all persons
> who utilize the scenic resources of the country, and indeed all who breathe its
> air, could claim harm similar to that alleged by the environmental groups here.[68]

Therefore, the Court sided with the students: "The District Court was correct in denying the appellants' motion to dismiss the complaint for failure to allege sufficient standing to bring this lawsuit."[69] In short, the Court argued, agency decisions that affect the entire country, no matter how attenuated the connection, render anyone who asserts an injury a proper party to bring suit against the agency in the judicial branch. Some statutes, of course, create a very wide "zone of interests," and sometimes the zone is large enough to include the entire population of the United States. *SCRAP* was the Court's endorsement of this interpretation of the zone of interests. As Stewart explained, by the middle of the 1970s courts were "willing to imply legal protection to an interest from the structure and purposes of the statute," regardless of the statute's explicit statement on standing. "Given the vague, general or ambiguous nature of many statutory directives, and given the pervasive role of government in a developed economy, there appears to be no logical limit to this expansion of standing rights."[70] If such broad interests are protected by statute, in other words, and statutory protection can be construed by the courts as an implicit grant of standing to those seeking to protect those interests, almost any public interest advocacy group will have standing to sue an administrative agency.

As in the procedural realm, Congress followed where the courts led. Just as new regulatory statutes created "hybrid rulemaking" procedures that were more robust than those required by the text of the APA, they also granted citizen standing to buttress the legal doctrines that the courts were crafting. The Clean Air Act contained a citizen standing provision, as well as intervenor funding to pay the attorneys' fees of organizations who successfully challenged agencies in court.[71] As Marc Allen Eisner explains, "The goal of all of these provisions is clear: to democratize the regulatory system and guarantee advocacy groups a continuous presence in policy implementation."[72]

These developments indicated a revolution occurring in the administrative state in the 1970s. Dramatic expansion of the APA's procedural requirements for agency rulemaking, combined with an expansion of standing to sue agencies, ensured that interest groups with a stake in administrative policymaking would have the ability to influence these decisions. Both of these developments, therefore, advanced an understanding of democracy as applied to administrative power. Scholars even began talking of a "Representative Bureaucracy," demonstrating the ongoing commitment to principles of American constitutionalism while radically reinterpreting them. As Stewart explained, proponents of public participation in the administrative process claimed that such participation "will not only improve the quality of agency decisions and make them more responsive to the needs of the various participating interests, but it is valuable in itself because it gives citizens a sense of involvement in the process of government."[73] This justification suggested that the administrative process, without extensive procedures and broad standing to challenge agency decisions, risked sacrificing core principles such as accountability and civic participation.

These legal changes also triggered an explosion of interest group activity in the administrative state. Organizations like the Environmental Defense Fund, Natural Resources Defense Council, Consumer Federation of America, and other groups were organized to engage in public interest litigation. Contributors to these organizations could gain access and influence in the administrative process through new legal avenues that the federal courts had opened up in this new administrative law revolution. Therefore the twin pillars of democracy and capture theory led courts to the same conclusion: courts and interest groups must have enhanced powers to challenge and overturn administrative action. American constitutionalism continued to play a profound role in the development of the administrative state, through administrative law doctrines seeking to democratize it.

Liberals Take a Hard Look at the Administrative State

The same reasons that led liberals to expand procedural requirements and loosen standing to sue agencies in court led them to advocate greater scrutiny of the substance of agency decisions. As a result judicial review of agency legal interpretation and policymaking discretion became more searching, expanding judicial intervention further. As E. Donald Elliot explains, "In the 1960s and 1970s courts reviewing agency action were typically quite aggressive in reviewing 'questions of law.' How a court should interpret an agency's governing statute was a prototypical question of law for the court."[74] During this period the judiciary began to view agency action with greater skepticism, imposing its interpretation of governing statutes on agencies and reviewing agency decisions to ensure they were made properly.

Consequently, power shifted *within* agencies to the lawyers who offered legal advice on the meaning of statutes and how reviewing courts would scrutinize an agency's interpretation. As Elliot explains, during the 1970s the EPA's lawyers in the Office of General Counsel (OGC) would declare to their colleagues: "the statute means this. There is only one meaning to the statute. We in OGC are the keepers of what the statute means. The statute speaks to every question, and you must follow what we in OGC tell you is the correct/best interpretation of the statute or you will lose in court."[75] As judges became more skeptical of and less deferential to agencies' interpretations of law, lawyers within the agencies became more powerful in dictating decisions to agency personnel.

The political effects of heightened judicial scrutiny were profound. For example, courts influenced the implementation of the Education for All Handicapped Children Act of 1975 (EAHCA), to the agitation of many conservatives. The Act created a statutory right for disabled children to a free and appropriate public education. What this required in practice was unspecified. The key institutional question was whether the agencies or the courts would determine what constitutes a free and appropriate public education. Does it require integration of handicapped and non-handicapped children in the same classroom? Do handicapped children have to learn the same things as non-handicapped children? Does discipline by suspension and expulsion deny the handicapped child an appropriate education? These questions and a host of others were left to be worked out in contentious battles between courts and agencies (with Congress and interest groups playing a major role from the margins).

Courts were aggressive in defining the content of a free and adequate public education and signaled to the bureaucracy that if it failed to comply, its actions would be set aside. Shep Melnick has chronicled the interaction between courts and agencies in this area and noted that the scope of judicial review was much greater than it would likely have been thirty or forty years earlier during the New Deal. Actions of various school districts were commonly overturned by federal courts. In two cases federal courts reinstated handicapped students who were expelled for disrupting school activities and for physically abusing other students and teachers.[76] The Supreme Court eventually took the side of the lower courts, with Justice Brennan declaring that Congress intended the law to prevent schools from unilaterally (i.e., without judicial permission) expelling disruptive handicapped students.[77] In this area the courts were quick to substitute their own judgment for the judgments of public educators when it came to expelling students.

The courts were equally assertive in specifying what constitutes an appropriate education. The courts dictated to school administrators how to comply with this aspect of the law. In this context, during the late 1970s, the EAHCA's statutory ambiguity did not entail deference to administrative interpretations of the Act, according to legal scholars; rather, "judges and hearing officers" should "take an active role in the intimate details of educational decision-making." In doing so, courts would determine the meaning of various ambiguities in the statute: "courts have risen to the challenge of turning vague language into meaningful guidelines for conduct," rather than agencies.[78] This marked a sharp departure from the Progressives' approach, where broad grants of discretion were understood to be a signal to let bureaucrats solve social problems without judicial interference.

By the early 1980s, there were indications that the Supreme Court had enough. In one case a deaf student named Amy Rowley was placed in a regular class by her school, and given daily tutoring, a hearing aid that allowed her to hear much of what was said in class, and weekly speech therapy. Yet, when the school declined to provide her with a sign language interpreter for class, the Rowleys went to court and had that decision overturned by a district court, which was upheld by the Second Circuit Court of Appeals. This time, the Supreme Court finally resolved to take a stand against judicial scrutiny of school administrators. Writing for a 6–3 majority overturning the Second Circuit, then-Justice Rehnquist argued that the ambiguity in the statute counseled judicial restraint, rather than a court substituting its judgment for that of administrators. Rehnquist wrote that "Noticeably absent in the statute is any substantive standard prescribing the level of education to be accorded to handicapped children." Therefore, the language of the statute is "by no means an invitation to the courts to substitute their own notions of sound educational policy for those of the school authorities which they review."[79] For Rehnquist, the absence of a clear standard in the statute was a signal to the courts to defer to administrative agencies' interpretation of the law, filling in the statutory gap. The principle Rehnquist employed in *Rowley* was judicial restraint, the idea that courts should be disinclined to substitute their judgment for that of administrative agencies.

The Supreme Court's command to lower courts to restrain themselves when reviewing school administrators was not heeded, and lower courts simply continued to exercise independent judgment about whether school administrators had provided an adequate education after the *Rowley* decision. But *Rowley* signaled a potential backlash—a potential realized just a few years later, as the next chapter will describe.

Judges intervened in other areas of administrative policy as well, as illustrated by the *Adams v. Richardson* litigation involving Title VI of the 1964 Civil Rights Act. That provision declared that "No person in the United States shall, on the basis of race, color or national origin, be excluded from participation in, be denied the benefits of, or be subjected to discrimination under, any program or activity receiving federal financial assistance." The suit in *Adams* maintained that the Office of Civil Rights within the Department of Health, Education, and Welfare was required to interpret this principle to mean that previously segregated schools must assign students selectively to different schools in order to maintain racial balance.[80] The impetus behind this litigation, in Jeremy Rabkin's words, was "the frustration of civil rights advocacy groups with OCR's failure to sustain the expectations generated by an extremely activist administrative policy" after the Civil Rights Act was passed.[81] In other words, advocacy groups were no longer content with allowing the agency to interpret a vague statutory mandate such as the requirement to eliminate discrimination. Now, fearing inaction from the agency, the groups turned to a litigation strategy in which the courts would impose their own interpretation of the law against that of the agency. This trend had significant political ramifications; as the agencies were perceived to be "captured" because they were not pursuing sufficiently liberal policies, many on the left turned to the courts to review agency policymaking and influence it in a liberal manner.[82]

Taking a "Hard Look"

As the Progressives' consensus on the enlightened character and knowledge of bureaucrats faded, courts became more involved in the administrative process. As just described, one area where this took place was in statutory interpretation, where courts interpreted congressional enabling statutes de novo rather than deferring to the agencies' interpretations. At the same time federal courts also expanded their scrutiny of administrative policy decisions that were not related to statutory interpretation. This second category of substantive (as opposed to procedural) review was ostensibly rooted in a provision of the APA which declares that a reviewing court shall "hold unlawful and set aside agency action, findings, and conclusions found to be . . . arbitrary, capricious, an abuse of discretion, or otherwise not in accordance with law."[83] This has become known as the "arbitrary or capricious" standard.

The APA provides little guidance on how to determine if an agency decision is arbitrary or capricious. Consequently, the scope of judicial scrutiny under this standard will vary based on prevailing conceptions of the administrative process. For judges during the Progressive and New Deal eras, when the faith in administrative expertise was at its apex, it was very difficult to prove that an agency's action was arbitrary and capricious. After all, the agency might have some insight that is unavailable to non-specialized judges. What looks like an arbitrary action might be necessary to promote the public interest.

However, as capture theory began to dominate the thinking of administrative law practitioners, judges became increasingly suspicious of agency action and devised more extensive tests for agencies seeking to prove that their decision did not run afoul of the arbitrary and capricious standard. The hard look standard of review requires courts to ask whether the *agency* took a hard look at all of the relevant factors before rendering the decision under review. Agency actions are understood to be arbitrary or capricious if they do not follow the proper process or procedures that characterize non-arbitrary and non-capricious decisions.

As with the other areas of judicial review, the DC Circuit took the lead in expanding arbitrary or capricious review. In Gary Lawson's words, "By the

1960s and 1970s, the original understanding of the arbitrary and capricious standard was no longer acceptable to courts. The search was on for an interpretation of [the APA] that permitted a greater degree of judicial control of agency policymaking."[84] But this raised the following dilemma: what serves as evidence that an agency made an arbitrary or capricious decision? Is it the lack of procedures that the agency followed? The failure to give reasons for the final decision? The substance of the decision itself? Depending on the answer to this question, "hard look" review would emphasize either the procedures an agency followed in reaching its decision or the substance of the decision itself.

In the end, the DC Circuit sought to have it both ways. It would scrutinize the agency's procedures for signs of arbitrariness, as well as the reasons the agency gave for its final decision. The first sign of this development came in 1970 in *Greater Boston Television Corp. v. FCC*, in which judge Leventhal announced that "The function of the court is to assure that the agency has given reasoned consideration to all the material facts and issues. This calls for insistence that the agency articulate with reasonable clarity its reasons for decision, and identify the crucial facts." "[I]f the court becomes aware," he continued, "that the agency has not really taken a 'hard look' at the salient problems, and has not genuinely engaged in reasoned decision-making," the reviewing court must intervene under the arbitrary and capricious standard.[85] This "hard look" standard was interpreted by the DC Circuit four years later in *Industrial Union Department AFL-CIO v. Hodgson*. There, the DC Circuit argued, "What we are entitled to at all events is a careful identification by the Secretary, when his proposed standards are challenged, of the reasons why he chooses to follow one course rather than another."[86] This interpretation of the requirements of arbitrary and capricious review further ensured that agencies would have to consider, on the record, input received from those affected by an agency decision. If they did not address criticisms received from affected interests, agencies would face the possibility of having their decision overturned as arbitrary. As Stewart explained, by the mid-1970s "courts have imposed upon agencies an affirmative duty to consider all the relevant interests affected by agency policy."[87]

All of the legal doctrines described in this chapter—procedural requirements for rulemaking, standing to sue, review of agency legal interpretation, and review of agency decision making under the arbitrary and capricious standard—were linked to a new vision of the administrative state. This new vision emphasized not agency expertise, judicial deference, and scientific administration but participatory democracy, judicial oversight, and the increased

influence of interest groups in administrative decision making. Shep Melnick
has explained the practical significance of this development for agencies:

> The purpose of [hard look review] is clear: requiring agencies to uncover more
> information produces better policy; requiring them to offer clear explanations
> encourages full public debate; and requiring them to hear a variety of viewpoints
> discourages administrators from bowing to the nearest interest group. . . . Con-
> sequently, these doctrines too have increased participation by those previously
> excluded from agency deliberations.[88]

The practical effect of the hard look doctrine has been to force agencies to
open up the administrative process to the public, to ensure that they will have
taken a hard look at the issues they decide.

Legitimizing the Administrative State?
Courts and Agencies in Partnership

As Marc Allen Eisner has written, "The late 1960s and the 1970s saw the
emergence of a new regulatory regime."[89] This new manifestation of the administrative state was different both in the ends it pursued and in the legal
means by which those ends would be attained. Instead of expert administrators making policy free from legal constraints imposed by judicial and private
actors, the new administrative state would be participatory, and interest groups
and courts would be empowered to supervise the administrative process. In
the words of one recent assessment, liberals critical of the older approach
maintained "that to save democracy there would need to be greater access
to administrators and new forms of participation in government as well as
the means to force the bureaucracy to become more responsive to public demands."[90] These changes in administrative law "have unquestionably had a
major effect on national politics and policy. . . . Nearly every federal agency
has been touched by the 'reformation' of American administrative law."[91] These
legal developments dramatically limited bureaucratic discretion through oversight from courts and (by extension) interest groups and rested in large part
on the theory of deliberative democracy. The theory was eventually integrated
into administrative law as a means of expanding democratic participation in
the administrative process, and courts would be in charge of ensuring that the
administrative state more closely conformed to democratic principles.

While they have not linked these legal developments to the emergence of a
new theory of democracy, scholars have noted the emphasis on participation

that animated these attempts to democratize the administrative state. This emphasis on participatory democracy was central in the minds of many reformers in the "New Left" during the 1960s and 1970s.[92] In a significant break with progressive and New Deal reformers, those who supported the democratization of the administrative state were highly distrustful of bureaucracy. Participatory democracy was viewed as a means to re-engage citizens who were alienated by the rise of massive centralized agencies. The solution, Richard Harris and Sidney Milkis explain, was simple: "The key to achieving any measure of participatory democracy was acquiring an ongoing presence in regulatory institutions."[93] By ensuring representation for advocacy groups in the administrative process, the administrative state could be made legitimate because citizens would use it to engage in a process of deliberative democracy.

Having explained these developments in some detail, we are now prepared to understand the theoretical foundations of liberal reformers' expansion of judicial review in the 1960s and 1970s. Liberals have advocated for "proceduralizing" the administrative state for two reasons related to American constitutionalism. First, extensive procedures will make the administrative state more rational, because more comments, facts, and studies will prevent administrative agencies from making decisions based on base politics. Second, procedures help to democratize the administrative state by allowing the public to become involved in the process of making administrative policy. In the case of *American Medical Association v. Reno*,[94] the DC Circuit connected the APA notice-and-comment procedures to both rationality and democracy, explaining that the procedures "serve important purposes of agency accountability and reasoned decision-making" and that they "impose a significant duty upon the agency."[95] These arguments merit further exploration.

Liberals tend to believe that procedures inherently serve to enhance the rationality of agency decision making. The more procedures an agency must undergo, the more its decision will be based on science rather than politics. As Robert Kagan explains (critically) "legal demands for careful study and evaluation before public action reflect the ideal of *comprehensive rationality*." Yet, "the ideal of comprehensively rational analysis rarely can be fully achieved." The problem is that "the law demands comprehensive rationality, including the filing of scientific findings," and "[a]ny private advocacy organization . . . can challenge it in court."[96] The law governing procedures, Kagan notes, is designed to increase the rationality of agency decision making, based on the idea that more procedures mean more studies, which entails greater expertise and rationality.

This follows immediately from the idea of capture theory. If agencies are no longer trustworthy, the courts must enter into a partnership with the agencies to ensure that they do not stray from the requirements of their organic statutes. As Mark Seidenfeld has argued,

> By demanding that agencies publicly justify their rules, however, judicial review can discourage the adoption and interpretation of rules preferred by special interest groups. Increasing the likelihood that a rule will be upheld by relaxing the requirements that an agency explain its decision to a court might, by the same token, increase the proportion of rules driven by pressure from special interest groups or an agency agenda that is at odds with the general public's desire for regulation.[97]

Seidenfeld argues that "without the influence of aggressive judicial review, proposed rules and the analyses that accompany them to the agency tend to reflect the perspective of the program office within the agency" that initially drafts and proposes the rule. Since "[t]he perspective of the lead office, however, may be very parochial or biased towards special interests," judges need to be highly involved in oversight so that the final rule does not reflect the wishes of these narrow interests.[98]

The purpose of judicial review, in this view, is to ensure that agency decisions are made rationally, on the basis of facts, as opposed to private interests and political concerns. In this model, judges are perceived to be the guardians of the administrative process. They are above the petty influences of parochial interests. Therefore, they are uniquely positioned to identify whether the procedures or decision-making process of an agency produce scientific rationality rather than reliance on political bias. Courts can use their searching review of the procedures employed by an agency to ensure that the administrative process is rational. Seidenfeld writes, "judges are experienced in spotting weaknesses in factual support and soft spots in logical reasoning. Hence, courts are geared to ensure that an agency's decision is well thought out."[99] This argument rests not only on a distrust of agencies but also a sharp distinction between private interests and the public interest. Procedures are necessary to avoid private interests from driving administrative policy, by allowing public interest groups to oversee the process.

Procedural review demonstrates how this idea is translated into administrative law. The fewer procedures, the more likely private interests will drive the administrative process. The more procedures, the more likely public interest groups will be able to drive the administrative process. The interesting fact of note here is that for contemporary liberals, the separation of politics and administration is a threat to the public interest. Politicizing administration through litigation, in order to offset politicization through the executive, is the solution. Richard Harris and Sidney Milkis explain that the "public lobby regime" of the 1960s and 1970s "continued this thrust of politicizing public administration," from the New Deal, "although obviously the emphasis has shifted from securing presidential control to widening the opportunities for citizen participation in regulatory politics."[100] In other words, while liberals continued to insist that private interests and politics ought not be allowed to corrupt the administrative process, they did not assume that the means to achieve this consisted in separating administrators from oversight.

Citizen participation in the administrative process was not only conceived as a new means to the old end of ensuring impartial and scientific administration; it was also understood to be an end in itself. Greater procedural requirements for administrative agencies meant that citizen participation in the administrative process would be enhanced. The notion of participatory democracy could be more fully realized, according to these theorists, by a democratic administrative state rather than the traditional representative institutions of the Founders' Constitution.[101] Enhancing the procedures of notice-and-comment rulemaking legitimizes the administrative state by making it more accountable, in the eyes of these theorists. As Jim Rossi explains, "Standard justifications for broad-based involvement in agency decisions regard participation as serving purposes of accountability and oversight, minimizing the potential for capture of the process, and counteracting myopia by improving information available to agency decision makers and citizens. Citizen involvement in agency decisions also reinforces proceduralist goals and helps to create and affirm citizenship."[102] Rossi's description here captures all the rationales explained thus far—checking potentially captured agencies, granting more information to enhance agency expertise, and involving citizens in the administrative process that furthers participatory democracy. Rossi even goes so far as to say that the administrative state is *itself* a model of representative government: "Representative democracy is widespread before administrative agencies to the extent that individuals themselves do not appear before agencies, but instead participate by virtue of their voluntary membership in interest groups, such as unions, environmental organizations, corporations, or public interest groups."[103] By ensuring greater procedural requirements that facilitate citizen involvement in the administrative process, the argument goes, the administrative state can be democratized and therefore legitimized.

These arguments in favor of democracy and rationality were equally critical in animating liberal reformers' attempts to expand standing to sue agencies in court. Of course, one obvious reason liberals pressed for wide standing was political: when courts and citizen groups are more liberal than agencies, giving them more authority in the administrative process will yield more liberal policy. This relies upon a very different view of the judiciary than that shared by earlier progressives, when courts were viewed as backwards-looking and too interested in adhering to constitutional scruples. By the 1970s courts were regarded by the left as the most trustworthy branch, as the one branch of government where their interests are viewed most favorably. As Hudson Henry writes, in embracing the "public law" model that regards the court as public enforcer of regulatory policy (as opposed to merely the protectors of private rights), liberals view "the role of the court as a vindicator of public values."[104] The argument of many liberals, in short, was that the courts are more reliable and should be enlisted to press regulatory agencies forward in carrying out their responsibilities.

However, liberal legal scholars make the arguments for rationality and participatory democracy in the standing context as well. If private citizens, organizing and mobilizing through citizen groups, can bring suit against administrators in court, this advances popular participation and collaboration in the administrative process. Earlier Progressives explicitly rejected this approach, but today's liberal scholars appear to endorse it wholeheartedly.

In their important study of the evolution of administrative law, Richard Harris and Sidney Milkis have noted this connection between democracy and standing. They write, "The ideal of participatory democracy also provided the basis for revamping legal institutions. Undoubtedly, a major success was the establishment via case law and legislation of standing to sue for 'interested parties' in environmental controversies."[105] "This new role for the courts," they repeat, "must be counted as an extremely important institutional change advancing the new regulatory idea of participatory democracy."[106] As Richard Stewart similarly noted in his seminal treatment of the evolution of administrative law, "participation, it is claimed, will not only improve the quality of agency decisions and make them more responsive to the needs of the various participating interests . . . but is valuable in itself because it gives citizens a sense of involvement in the process of government."[107] The participatory democracy argument in favor of greater procedures and standing is that, regardless of whether it improves agency decision making, it is intrinsically beneficial to involve more interest groups in the administrative process, because that gets us nearer to our democratic ideals.

For many on the left, allowing public interest groups to challenge bureaucracies in court is a means of promoting democratic purposes, which is a means of legitimizing a regime where most policy is made by unelected officials. This is distinctive of American administrative law in comparison to other industrialized nations. As Robert Kagan notes, "In most democratic countries officials are held accountable . . . primarily by administrative supervision and political oversight. . . . But far more than other democracies, the United States employs an additional accountability mechanism: litigation."[108] In particular, "[b]ecause of the unusually broad American rules concerning 'standing to sue,' virtually any interested party—including the world's widest array of public interest lawyers, acting as self-appointed 'private attorneys general'—can bring lawsuits against alleged violations of public law."[109]

Another argument employed by many legal scholars on the left in favor of wide grants of standing is based on their view of private versus public interests. Liberal legal scholars advocate loose standards for standing because it allows interest groups that claim to represent the public to challenge agencies that might be captured by private interests. Ideological standing, for instance, prevents court challenges from being brought solely by economic interests, which would enhance private interest influence on administrative policy. This amounts to the shift from courts as protectors of individual rights to the courts as vindicators of public values, and also allows for more people to be involved in the decision whether a particular administrative decision is allowed to stand. Those who are active in groups such as Sierra Club, Paralyzed Veterans, and the Natural Resources Defense Council can now participate in the administrative state by challenging bureaucracies in court. For those interested in "legitimizing" the administrative state, this is seen as a way of recapturing some of the democratic elements lost in the shift to bureaucratic decision making.

Mark Seidenfeld and Lisa Schultz Bressman are two administrative law theorists who advance this position. In Seidenfeld's view, administrative law cannot rely solely on political oversight from within the executive branch to control bureaucratic discretion, because that oversight will be dominated by special interests. He writes that "[r]eliance on political oversight alone also raises the prospect of agency rules driven by immediate political concerns."[110] The purpose of judicial review is to ensure that agencies are not captured by special interests: it should "prompt the agency to think creatively about

regulatory approaches that will adequately respect all affected interests."[111]
Bressman similarly argues that denying standing to interest groups is based on
a flawed model of "presidential control" of the bureaucracy, which emphasizes
the need for accountability of agencies (through the president) but overlooks
the potential for arbitrary action stemming from the President's hijacking administration to promote private interests. Bressman argues that we need to
design administrative law to prevent "arbitrary" administrative decision making, and that scholars have been too focused on making administration more
accountable. Arbitrary administrative action, she explains, "often results from
the corrupting forces that the constitutional structure is designed to inhibit:
private interest and governmental self-interest."[112]

Bressman claims that the purpose of the Founders' constitution was to
thwart private interest in favor of the public interest. The problem, she notes,
is that "[b]road delegation of lawmaking authority facilitates both private interest and governmental self-interest." Therefore, administrative law needs to
close the opening for private interests to hijack the administrative process.
Presidential control, which involves giving the presidency the power to control administration (and thus curtailing the influence of courts and interest
groups), is "insufficient to prevent arbitrary administrative decisionmaking,"
according to Bressman.[113] Thus, courts must be employed to prevent the president from turning agencies away from the public interest and in favor of
private interests.

The relationship between public interest and private interest—and its relationship to administrative law, particularly in the area of standing—has been
capably discussed by Jeremy Rabkin. As he shows, the idea behind expanding
access to the courts for public lobby groups was to establish an idea of public
law that would promote public values and not the private interests or rights of
any particular individual.[114] Ultimately, this view "celebrates a vision of courts
free to enforce duties that do not correspond to the rights of anyone in particular"; that is, it promotes a vision of courts as vindicators of public values,
by holding agencies responsible for carrying out their statutory mandates.[115]

These public values may, and often do, stand in opposition to private rights
and interests, which is why courts in particular must cooperate with public
interest groups to protect them from being captured. The ironic result is that
private individuals are enlisted by administrative law to serve as protectors
of public values, with the predictable result that administrative law becomes
captured by private citizens acting on their private preferences, in the name of
the public interest.[116] Thus, "While public law litigation is designed to make
public policymaking more responsive to neglected interests and values, it often

ends up *privileging* special interests and values over the general interest."[117] As Rabkin explains:

> Allowing courts to enforce public values makes an open-ended range of program goals, operating principles, or administrative concerns into values that *must* be honored [through the binary and adversarial legal process] in abstraction from the rest of public policy. But, then, still more incongruously, this scheme leaves it to private litigants, in the first instance, to determine which goals, principles, or concerns do qualify for this treatment and to determine when and how they should be so treated. This is a very odd approach to safeguarding the moral integrity of government. But it is a natural consequence of confusing public values with personal rights.[118]

The idea of wide participation in the administrative process, through procedural requirements and wide grants of standing to public lobby groups, is central to the "civic republicanism" defense of the administrative state currently pressed by scholars. For instance, Cass Sunstein writes that participation is designed not only to limit the possibility of capture and factional influence; "it is also a vehicle for the inculcation of such characteristics as empathy, virtue, and feelings of community."[119] Granting participatory power to groups such as the Sierra Club, then, is necessary to improve the social and communitarian outcomes of the administrative process, not only in terms of results but also in terms of an active citizenry. Thus the expansion of standing, like the expansion of procedural requirements, is justified in constitutional terms, as a restoration of the democratic basis of our political system. The administrative process will be democratized by the public's increased access to and participation in agency decision making.

To summarize, liberals promote the expansion of standing to sue administrative agencies for three reasons. These reasons are based on the idea that agencies are no longer representatives of the public interest, and that they are captured by private interests. First, liberals believe that the judiciary is friendlier to their preferred policy outcomes than the executive branch. Second, they believe that wide grants of standing to sue promote participatory democracy. Third, they view public lobby groups and courts as representatives of public and community interests, which have greater moral standing than private and pecuniary interests in their mind. These reasons are essentially identical to the rationale in favor of expanding agencies' procedural requirements, a goal that liberal reformers argue will also enhance democracy and rationality. What is noteworthy about these developments is that liberal reformers of the

administrative state have appealed to constitutional principles like citizen participation, participatory democracy, and the public versus the private interest.
They have sought to use administrative law reforms to advance these principles from within the administrative state, shoring it up from inside. And perhaps most surprisingly, it was liberal reformers, not conservatives, who turned
on the bureaucracy in the 1960s and 1970s.

The Ongoing Crisis of Legitimacy

The revolution of administrative law in the 1960s and 1970s demonstrated
that, in spite of the earlier attempts to overcome the constitutional objections
to the modern administrative state, core conceptions of American constitutionalism would continue to be employed in questioning the legitimacy of the administrative process. What *was* distinctive, however, was the method by which
these constitutional principles would be brought to bear on questions of administrative power. Whereas in the first century of American history American
constitutionalism was understood to preclude certain administrative arrangements, now the principles of American constitutionalism would be imported
into the administrative state through administrative law. Administrative law
would make the new state accountable, approximating the checks that republicanism imposed on the exercise of political power.[120] Now more than ever, liberals understood the challenges that modern administrative government posed
to cherished ideals such as democratic accountability, the rule of law, and the
separation and checking of political power. But the traditional approaches to
these questions were still unpalatable. They therefore turned to administrative
law to vindicate these principles within the new administrative state.

Consequently, these liberal critics of the Progressives' and New Dealers' administrative state produced a very different set of institutional arrangements.
This new configuration of power has been called the "public lobby regime" by
Richard Harris and Sidney Milkis. In this new configuration public interest
groups would be organized "to ensure that the public interest would not be
sacrificed or co-opted as policy concerns . . . shifted from legislation to administration. . . . In the view of public interest advocates, the only remedy to this
situation was to maintain a permanent watchdog presence with independently operated organizations funded from the grass roots."[121] In their telling, it
was "ideas—suspicion of the establishment and participatory democracy" that
"helped to shape the public lobby regime and distinguished it as a unique historical episode in the development of federal regulation."[122]

The practical consequence of putting courts and interest groups in a new position of power over the bureaucracy was to entrench a "politics of partnership"

between courts and agencies to advance administrative policies, as Shep Melnick has explained. Given new tools with which to exert influence over the bureaucracy, courts increasingly forced agencies to regulate, even when their supervisors in the executive branch sought to rein in regulation. Agency personnel and the congressional subcommittees that supervised them were generally pleased to be "forced" to regulate by judicial fiat, as they gained freedom from the chief executive and blame could be placed at the feet of unelected judges.[123] Courts, agencies, and interest groups eventually became regulatory partners operating outside the supervision of the president and party leaders in Congress who might impose a broader, national interest on the decisions of local and specific interests represented by the particular representatives on congressional subcommittees and the interest groups that supported them. Instead of the familiar "iron triangles" composed of subcommittees, agencies, and interest groups, Melnick argued that "it is tempting to speak of an 'iron rectangle' instead," adding the judiciary to the mix.[124] The critical difference between the issues advanced by iron triangles and these new programs was that "the costs of many of these programs" expanded through the new model of administrative law "have grown too large for outsiders to ignore." Still, it was clear by the end of the 1970s that, whereas "New Deal politics was high visibility, breakthrough politics," the new political dynamic was "complex, low visibility, administrative politics" driven by courts and interest groups.[125]

Perhaps most interesting of all was the conservatives' response to the emerging liberal criticism and reformation of the administrative state. As courts and interest groups became more active in countering the unchecked administrative power that Progressives and New Dealers had constructed, conservative judges and thinkers began to defend the earlier regime. Taking on the arguments of the Progressives and the New Dealers, ironically, conservative administrative law scholars and jurists advocated deference to administrative power through a return to earlier doctrines such as reduced procedural requirements, deference to agencies' legal interpretations and policy decisions, and heightened requirements for standing to sue. The resemblance between the conservative and Progressive arguments in administrative law, as the next chapter describes, was startling and uncanny.

CHAPTER EIGHT

The Conservative Counterrevolution?

The Rise of a Jurisprudence of Deference

THE PREVIOUS CHAPTER discussed the revolution in administrative law led by liberal reformers in the late 1960s and 1970s. The legal and political developments in this period pointed to two conclusions. First, the administrative state was transformed profoundly as the Progressives' faith in administration eroded. Capture theory and the general decline of faith in technocratic expertise led reformers to construct new agencies on very different legal and institutional principles. Instead of independent regulatory commissions, agencies were once again housed in the executive departments, and there was a return to single-headed administrative units (similar to what happened under the Articles of Confederation two centuries ago). Instead of judicial deference, and rule by elite experts, the administrative process became heavily supervised by courts and interest groups under a new theory of participatory democracy. Scientific administration had given way to a politicized bureaucracy under the influence of organized interests.

Second, the administrative state's critical challenge to cherished principles of American constitutionalism—representative government, the separation of powers, and the rule of law—ensured that the battle over the administrative state's legitimacy would not end quickly or quietly. However, the forum in which the relationship between administrative power and American constitutionalism would be worked out shifted heavily to judicial review. It was here that principles of democratic accountability and the legality of administrative action would be tested and legal doctrines devised in light of these considerations.

As the "Reagan Revolution" established new political dynamics surrounding the administrative state, a curious reversal of institutional allegiances emerged in response to the liberal administrative law revolution. Conservatives began to advocate a policy of judicial deference to agency policymaking. The unspoken assumption was that conservatives were willing to acquiesce in the administrative state, giving up their constitutional objections, as long as they could influence administrative policy by keeping the liberal courts out of a presidentially directed bureaucracy. From an institutional perspective, conservatives appeared indistinguishable from early Progressives such as Theodore Roosevelt, Woodrow Wilson, Frank Goodnow, Felix Frankfurter, and James Landis, who also consistently sought to force the courts to defer to the determinations of administrative agencies. The irony of this development was noted by Shep Melnick: "A principal feature of the current dispute over the role of the courts . . . is the reversal of the New Deal's institutional patterns. For three decades liberals have championed the judicial activism that Roosevelt and his allies condemned. Conversely, in the 1970s and 1980s conservatives called for greater deference to the executive—a stance they bitterly opposed" during the Progressive and New Deal eras.[1] Cass Sunstein has also described this feature of administrative law:

> In a surprising reversal of New Deal alliances, those who were critical of the effects of regulation in the 1980s were frequently insistent on administrative autonomy . . . whereas critics seeking to bring about greater regulatory protections saw administrative independence and autonomy as the problem rather than the solution.[2]

This chapter describes this "conservative counterrevolution" in four now-familiar areas of administrative law: agency procedures, standing to sue administrative agencies, judicial review of agencies' legal interpretations, and judicial review of agency policymaking decisions. While many scholars have concluded that conservative judges such as William Rehnquist and Antonin Scalia successfully reversed much of the liberal administrative law revolution of the 1960s and 1970s, the reality is more complicated. Today, administrative law is situated between the liberal paradigm of judicial scrutiny of administrative decisions and conservative judicial deference to administrative action. And the principles of American constitutionalism continue to play a central role in administrative law opinions. Importantly, however, conservative judges failed to re-establish meaningful constitutional limits on administrative power. They avoided revisiting questions concerning delegation of legislative power to agencies, and the insulation of administrative power from presidential control.

The Road from *Vermont Yankee*

As discussed in the previous chapter, liberal reformers in the 1960s and 1970s successfully expanded procedural requirements with which agencies had to comply under the Administrative Procedure Act. Whereas these procedural requirements were originally understood to be minimal, administrative law precedents pushed them to their outer boundaries. Led by Justice William Rehnquist, the Supreme Court pushed back against the lower courts leading this charge, with limited success.

Vermont Yankee's Failure:
The "Ossification" of Administrative Rulemaking

The movement to establish "hybrid rulemaking" and its greater procedural constraints on agency policymaking was denounced with unusual vigor by then-Justice Rehnquist in the 1978 case of *Vermont Yankee Nuclear Power Corporation v. Natural Resources Defense Council* (NRDC).[3] *Vermont Yankee* concerned a licensing question involving the Vermont Yankee Nuclear Power company, which had applied to build a new plant. In particular, the NRDC mounted a procedural challenge to a rule that had been used to determine the environmental impact of the nuclear fuel cycle in the process of considering Vermont Yankee's application for a license.

The DC Circuit, following its standard practice during this period, determined that the procedures in making the rule were inadequate due to the lack of discovery or cross-examination during the rulemaking process. On appeal, the Supreme Court reversed in a scathing opinion, reached by a unanimous vote.[4] Justice Rehnquist leveled some unusually harsh criticism of the DC Circuit's reasoning. The thrust of Rehnquist's opinion was that lower courts are not free to add to the procedures required by the APA for informal rulemaking. Congress entrusted the agencies with discretion to fashion the procedures they deemed necessary to carry out their assigned functions; courts should not feel authorized to add to those procedures without congressional sanction.

The tone of the opinion was as noteworthy as the ruling. Rehnquist argued that the Court thought it was "worth noting" that "we find absolutely nothing in the relevant statutes to justify what the court did" in the case.[5] Lacking legislative authorization to overturn agency decisions based on procedural considerations, he continued, "To say that the Court of Appeals' final reason for remanding is insubstantial at best is a gross understatement."[6] Because there was no statutory support for what the DC Circuit did, Rehnquist accused the DC Circuit of playing politics: "Administrative decisions should be set aside in this context, as in any other, only for substantial procedural or substantive reasons as mandated by statute, not simply because the court is unhappy with the decision reached."[7] As if to twist the knife further, Rehnquist quoted approvingly a petitioner's claim that the DC Circuit was practicing "judicial intervention run riot,"[8] a reference to the famous phrase coined by Justice Cardozo in the *Schecter* decision.[9]

Given that the decision of the Court was unanimous and the opinion so strident, one might expect that the DC Circuit would have been humbled into submission. However, it fired back four years later, in *Connecticut Light and Power Company v. Nuclear Regulatory Commission,* announcing that it would continue on the path on which it embarked prior to *Vermont Yankee.*[10] The DC Circuit upheld the agency's decision (perhaps in order to insulate itself from review by the Supreme Court) but in doing so explained that it would continue to require rigorous procedures based on the notice and comment procedures associated with informal rulemaking. Therefore, the DC Circuit reasserted its authority to interpret the APA to impose substantial procedural burdens for administrative agencies' rulemaking activities.

Since *Connecticut Light and Power*, the DC Circuit has emerged victorious in the struggle over the proper procedural requirements for informal rulemaking. As Jack Beermann and Gary Lawson have observed, today administrative law operates with many "important administrative law doctrines that do seem to fly squarely in the face of all but the most unreasonably narrow understandings of the Vermont Yankee decision."[11] The signal from *Vermont Yankee*, that administrative law was heading in the direction of weaker procedural requirements for agencies, turned out to be a false sign.

With regard to the notice of proposed rulemaking (NPR), the first step in the APA's process for informal rulemaking, several challenges are still available to those seeking to overturn agency rules because of insufficient procedure. If the agency does not release all of its data and information in its notice, the rule that emerges from the process may be set aside.[12] Moreover, if an agency makes a rule that concerns a subject not adequately flagged in the NPR (i.e., if the subject of the final rule is only tangential to the original proposed rule), the rule may be struck down.[13] Further, the "logical outgrowth" doctrine, which posits that any rule that is substantially different from the originally proposed rule must be "renoticed," unless it is a logical outgrowth of the proposed rule, is still applicable law.[14] This implies, of course, that under any other circumstances courts will require the entire process to be redone. Finally, current administrative law doctrine necessitates that every time an agency promulgates a final rule, the statement of basis and purpose includes a response to all meaningful or substantial comments introduced in the comment process.[15]

Ultimately, for a variety of reasons,[16] the Supreme Court's effort to force the DC Circuit to stop adding procedural requirements for agency rulemaking failed. This resulted in a widespread phenomenon known as "ossification,"[17] which describes the extreme delay in agency rulemaking as the agency attempts to jump through the substantial procedural hoops grafted by the courts onto the APA. The analytic burden placed on agencies by courts who expect a full evaluation of all the arguments introduced during the comment process has led to a situation in which agencies take years to promulgate rules. As Thomas McGarity wrote in 1992, years after *Vermont Yankee* was decided, "During the last fifteen years the rulemaking process has become increasingly rigid and burdensome. An assortment of analytical requirements have been imposed on the simple rulemaking model, and evolving judicial doctrines have obliged agencies to take greater pains to ensure that the technical bases for rules are capable of withstanding judicial scrutiny."[18]

The agencies' response to ossification has been to seek other avenues for making policy, turning to informal mechanisms such as interpretative rules and guidance documents. Rather than formulate a new rule, replete with the procedural requirements required for doing so, agencies have preferred to make policy through other means. The APA exempts "interpretative rules" and "general statements of policy" from the notice-and-comment procedures established in that provision.[19] Under this general category, agencies often issue guidance documents that outline in some detail how the agency interprets a particular provision of its organic statute or one of its existing rules. The abuse of these exceptions allows agencies to make policy through interpreting the law they made without going through the onerous procedural requirements now associated with informal rulemaking.[20]

Interpretative rules, similarly, may interpret either the agency's organic statute or one of its existing rules and regulations. Agencies have, at times, used this exception to the APA to promulgate vague rules and then modify them through interpretative rules that do not require extensive procedures. As one might expect, given the history of agency-court interaction in this area, the DC Circuit has attempted to eliminate the advantage gained by the agency through this approach by striking down interpretative rules on procedural grounds. In a series of cases the DC Circuit crafted what became known as the "Paralyzed Veterans" doctrine, named after the DC Circuit's decision in *Paralyzed Veterans v. D.C. Arena*, which stated that when an agency seeks to revise its previous interpretation of its own regulation, it must do so by notice-and-comment procedures.[21] In 2015 the Supreme Court put an end to this doctrine in *Perez v. Mortgage Bankers Association*, ruling that it was incompatible with *Vermont Yankee*.[22]

In short, the Supreme Court has sought to avoid adding procedural requirements not set forth in congressional statutes to the rulemaking process. This effort has been spearheaded by the conservative members of the Court. The DC Circuit, by contrast, animated by capture theory, distrust of agencies, and the pursuit of participatory administrative processes, has fought back, continuing to overturn agency actions that seek to circumvent the informal rulemaking process. In this struggle liberals have mostly (but not entirely) emerged victorious. On the whole, the procedures required for notice-and-comment rulemaking remain far more extensive than originally anticipated in the APA. However, this has driven agencies to make policy through processes even less transparent and procedurally robust than informal rulemaking.

Standing

As described in the previous chapter, during the 1960s and 1970s and in keeping with the general trend of administrative law towards greater judicial scrutiny of administrative agencies, standing to sue was dramatically expanded. This cut against the Progressive and New Deal eras approaches to administrative law, which emphasized the need to insulate administrative decisions from review.

A backlash occurred in 1992 in *Lujan v. Defenders of Wildlife*.[23] In *Lujan*, the Defenders of Wildlife sought to challenge a Department of Interior rule interpreting the Endangered Species Act (ESA). The agency's rule declared that the statute only applied within the United States and on the high seas. In ruling in favor of the Interior Department purely on the standing question, Justice Scalia set up a three-pronged test to determine whether a party has standing to bring a case to court. First, a party must have suffered an injury-in-fact. Second, the injury must be caused by the conduct complained of in the suit; it must be traceable to the action being challenged. Third, a positive decision in the courts must be likely to redress the injury. Scalia also maintained that the injury-in-fact must be concrete, imminent, and particularized, meaning that it "must affect the plaintiff in a personal and individual way."[24] In *Lujan* a majority of the Court was not persuaded by the affidavits of some plaintiffs who speculated that they might return to the areas affected by the Interior Department's decision as sufficient to establish injury.

Six years later the Court interpreted the injury prong loosely, deciding (with Scalia dissenting) that Congress could create a general right to obtain information about political contributions governed by the Federal Election Campaign Act of 1970, and that agency decisions which insulate that information from public scrutiny can be challenged by citizens.[25] In 2000, *Lujan*'s limits on standing were further eroded in *Friends of the Earth v. Laidlaw Environmental*

Services,[26] which interpreted the injury and redressability prongs of the *Lujan* test broadly. *Laidlaw* involved the Clean Water Act (CWA), which requires businesses that discharge pollutants into waters of the United States to receive a National Pollutant Discharge Elimination System (NPDES) permit from the EPA. Laidlaw Environmental Services had a NPDES permit but it repeatedly exceeded the limits imposed by the permit: it violated the daily limit on mercury discharges into the North Tyger River in South Carolina on 489 occasions between 1987 and 1995. Friends of the Earth (FOE) filed suit to prosecute noncompliance with the NPDES permit, seeking an injunction and civil penalties against Laidlaw.

The Court agreed that FOE had satisfied the injury and redressability requirements. Friends of the Earth, heeding the signals from *Sierra Club v. Morton* and *SCRAP* (discussed in the previous chapter), collected statements from members who lived near the river and who claimed that they used the river until Laidlaw polluted it. However, scientific analysis revealed that there was no actual harm done to the environment from the mercury discharge violations. Thus the injury to the members of FOE was purely psychological in nature. Nevertheless, Justice Ginsburg, writing for the Court, claimed that this was sufficient to demonstrate injury. In short, according to *Laidlaw*, injury is established by inquiring not whether actual injury had taken place but whether perceived injury had taken place. This clearly served as an expansion of the injury-in-fact requirement, since it is much easier to allege injury than to demonstrate one.

The second question concerned redressability. Laidlaw contended that civil penalties would not redress any injury to Friends of the Earth, since the penalties are paid to the government, not to the plaintiffs. Again, the Court sided with FOE, because its injury would be indirectly redressed through the deterrent effect of the civil penalties. As the Court explained, "a sanction that effectively abates that conduct and prevents its recurrence provides a form of redress."[27] This ruling similarly expanded the requirement for redressability by stating that penalties paid to a third party can still redress an injury done to one of the two parties, if there is a deterrent effect that would reduce the probability of the injury occurring in the future.

On the whole, therefore, *Laidlaw* signaled a significant retreat from the comparatively restrictive approach to standing established in *Lujan*. It is no coincidence that Justice Ginsburg wrote the majority opinion in *Laidlaw*, while Justice Scalia authored a harsh dissent. Scalia's dissent implicitly evoked the method of administrative enforcement that prevailed in the early years of the American republic. In his view, *Laidlaw* was revolutionary: he asserted that the Court "has promulgated a revolutionary new doctrine of standing that will permit the entire body of public civil penalties to be handed over to enforcement by private interests." Handing over the enforcement of public laws to private actors, of course, was widely practiced in the early years of American history, as Chapter Two of this book describes. Thus the *Laidlaw* case presented an intriguing dynamic. Ginsburg was returning a doctrine of administrative law to where it stood during the early republic, while Scalia was denouncing his colleague for doing so.

Substantive Review of
Agency Legal Interpretation and Policymaking

The previous section questioned whether the attempted counter-revolution was successful in the areas of procedural review and standing to sue administrative agencies. In both cases, an early landmark decision—*Vermont Yankee* and *Lujan*, respectively—signaled a shift back to the Progressive and New Deal patterns of administrative law. Yet subsequent cases, such as *Connecticut Light and Power* and *Laidlaw v. Friends of the Earth*, demonstrated that the conservatives' efforts to restore judicial deference had not entirely succeeded.

Even more noteworthy was the nature of the institutional allegiances. Whereas during the New Deal era progressive-leaning judges sought to insulate administrative agencies from judicial scrutiny, fearing aggressive review by conservative courts, now conservative judges sought to insulate administrative agencies from judicial scrutiny, and progressive-leaning judges sought to preserve judicial review to ensure the vigorous administration of regulatory programs and requirements.

Substantive review of administrative decision making mirrored these developments. As the Presidency became increasingly perceived as a conservative institution, the suspicion that agencies would not regulate in the public interest also increased. This led to an impulse among progressives and liberals in favor of greater judicial scrutiny of agencies' legal interpretations and exercises of policy discretion. These trends were accelerated by an important executive order issued by Ronald Reagan that promised greater presidential control over agency rulemaking.

Reagan's Administrative Revolution?
The Rise of Presidential Regulatory Review

 Early in his first term in office Ronald Reagan issued an executive order establishing White House review of "major" rules promulgated by executive agencies, undertaken by the Office of Information and Regulatory Affairs

(OIRA).[28] Executive Order 12291 required agencies to submit their rules to OIRA along with a positive cost-benefit analysis which showed that the costs of the rule were outweighed by its benefits. This process has been renewed by every subsequent president.

Though OIRA review has enhanced the president's control over agency rulemaking to an extent, scholars have shown that it was not a game-changing innovation.[29] Because the legal authority for OIRA review comes from an executive order, it applies only to executive agencies. Independent regulatory commissions are exempt. Furthermore, it is legally and practically unclear how conflicts between OIRA and administrative agencies are resolved.[30] The Office of Legal Counsel's opinion in 1981, when Reagan issued the original executive order establishing OIRA review, was that the president may "consult with those having statutory decision-making responsibilities . . . as long as the President does not divest the officer of ultimate statutory authority." For a variety of reasons OIRA review's effect has been diminished and it is still difficult to hold the president accountable for the administrative state.[31]

Regardless of its practical effect, Reagan's attempt to extend greater control over the administrative state prompted a reaction against judicial deference to administrative determinations. The new regulatory review process, even if it lacked the teeth necessary to make it a game-changer, seemed to signal the politicization of administrative rulemaking, and therefore gave rise to a new dynamic in administrative law. In two areas of substantive review—agency legal interpretations and agency policymaking choices—battles were fought over the appropriate scope of judicial review. The scope of judicial review of agency legal interpretation became the most significant and controversial arena of administrative law.

The Rise and Fall of Chevron

The consistent expansion of judicial scrutiny of administrative legal interpretation in the 1960s and 1970s, while arguably more in keeping with the intent of the APA, triggered a backlash beginning with what has become the most famous administrative law case in American history: *Chevron v. Natural Resources Defense Council (NRDC)*.[32] At issue in *Chevron* was an interpretation of the Clean Air Act's (CAA) language pertaining to stationary source pollution output. The EPA interpreted the statute to permit its "bubble policy" by which an emissions increase in one portion of a stationary source could be permissibly offset by the cumulative effect of lowering emissions for the entire source. Opposing the use of the bubble policy, the NRDC challenged the EPA's interpretation of the Act in court.

Following the standard mode of proceeding during the 1960s and 1970s, a
federal appeals court undertook "de novo" review of the CAA and overturned
EPA's interpretation, assuming that the agency is entitled to no deference in
its interpretation of the statute. The Supreme Court reversed on appeal. In his
opinion for the Court, Justice Stevens explained that:

> When a court reviews an agency's construction of the statute which it admin-
> isters, it is confronted with two questions. First, always, is the question whether
> Congress has directly spoken to the precise question at issue. If the intent of
> Congress is clear, that is the end of the matter; for the court, as well as the agency,
> must give effect to the unambiguously expressed intent of Congress. If, however,
> the court determines Congress has not directly addressed the precise question at
> issue, the court does not simply impose its own construction on the statute, as
> would be necessary in the absence of an administrative interpretation. Rather, if
> the statute is silent or ambiguous with respect to the specific issue, the question
> for the court is whether the agency's answer is based on a permissible construction
> of the statute.[33]

Justice Stevens was merely offering a brief explanation of how reviewing
courts traditionally reviewed administrative determinations of law. However, his
statement has become known as the *Chevron* "two-step"—at step one, courts
discern whether the language of the statute is ambiguous; if it is, then at step two
courts must defer to any reasonable or "permissible construction" of the statutory
ambiguity. While Stevens had not necessarily intended to do so in *Chevron*, the
case was used as a precedent for agency control of legal interpretation at an age
where courts were increasingly active in substituting their own interpretations
of statutes. Through subsequent decisions invoking Stevens's two-step formulation in *Chevron* as doctrine, the case became known for shifting control of the
administrative state back to the bureaucracy: a shift encouraged (as also in the
Rowley case discussed in the previous chapter) by conservative jurists.[34]

Yet *Chevron* has not turned out to be as significant as it appeared by the late
1980s. One scholar has recently suggested that "today *Chevron* applies less often
and is cited by the Court far less frequently."[35] The Supreme Court has retreated
away from *Chevron* consistently in recent years, signaling a shift back to the
judiciary as an important player in the administrative state. Until very recently,
conservatives defending *Chevron* sought to buttress it by appealing to several constitutional principles, demonstrating the ongoing relevance of American
constitutionalism to contemporary administrative law, as well as the consensus
among many who seek to accommodate the modern administrative state.

Does Chevron Apply At All?

Courts have, without overturning it, undermined *Chevron* in a variety of ways, restoring judicial primacy over agencies in interpreting the laws. In one set of cases, the Court has limited the category of cases in which *Chevron* applies in the first place. While some have argued that the doctrine should apply to any attempt by an agency to interpret a governing statute, others have said that the underlying rationale for the decision means that it only applies when an agency decision can be connected to that rationale.

The Court originally based *Chevron* on three principles—the agency's expertise, its accountability through the president, and Congress's intent to grant interpretive power to the agency.[36] Therefore, for some, it follows that *Chevron* should only apply when the agency's expertise is the basis of the interpretation, the agency's decision is derived from an accountable officer, or Congress has clearly granted to the agency the power to fill in the statutory ambiguity. Legal doctrine has evolved to include this threshold step in the *Chevron* inquiry, namely, the "initial inquiry into whether the *Chevron* framework applies at all."[37] This battle has been fought in several recent cases. Where the different justices stand in each case, and the arguments they deploy against their interlocutors, illustrate the ongoing importance of American constitutionalism in administrative law as well as the curious shift in institutional patterns. Prior to these decisions the Court failed to address the threshold question of whether *Chevron* applies.[38]

In *Christensen v. Harris County*, the Court did not apply *Chevron* deference to an interpretation of the Fair Labor Standards Act (FLSA) by the Department of Labor's Acting Administrator of the Wage and Hour Division, because it was advanced in an opinion letter promulgated outside notice-and-comment rulemaking.[39] Justice Thomas, writing for the Court, declared that *Chevron* does not apply to "[i]nterpretations such as those in opinion letters . . . policy statements, agency manuals, and enforcement guidelines, all of which lack the force of law."[40] While Scalia agreed with the outcome of the case, he wrote separately, maintaining that *Chevron* "established the principle that a court may not substitute its own construction of a statutory provision for a reasonable interpretation made by the administrator of an agency."[41] The following year the Court decided *U.S. v. Mead Corporation*, refusing to defer to a tariff classification ruling by the U.S. Customs Service.[42] In an 8–1 vote, with Scalia alone dissenting, the Court determined that an agency's interpretation only "qualifies for *Chevron* deference when it appears that Congress delegated authority to the agency generally to make rules carrying the force of law, and that the agency interpretation claiming deference was promulgated in the exercise of that authority."[43] Both of these cases signaled that agencies would only receive *Chevron* deference in a limited set of cases, particularly when engaging in activity such as adjudication or rulemaking where the decision carries the force of law. (This threshold inquiry to determine whether *Chevron* applies at all is generally known as "*Chevron* step zero.") When an agency fails to receive *Chevron* deference, a lower level of deference known as "Skidmore" deference applies.[44]

Writing for the majority in *Mead*, Justice Souter conceded that "Underlying the position we take here . . . is a choice about the best way to deal with an inescapable feature of the body of congressional legislation authorizing administrative action."[45] Those who supported the Court's limitation of *Chevron*'s scope decided that, given the inevitability of congressional delegation of power to the administrative state, it is best to impose conditions upon granting deference to agencies' interpretations of the laws they implement. The judiciary should serve, in this view, as a check on administrative power. Scalia's denunciation of *Mead* also made a constitutional argument. He wrote that "The doctrine of *Chevron* . . . was rooted in a legal presumption of congressional intent, important to the division of powers between the Second and Third Branches. When, *Chevron* said, Congress leaves an ambiguity in a statute that is to be administered by an executive agency, it is presumed that Congress meant to give the agency discretion, within the limits of reasonable interpretation, as to how the ambiguity is to be resolved."[46]

In short, for Scalia *Chevron* rests on implied congressional intent and the proper division of power between (in his words) "the Second and Third branches." The assumption is that every statutory ambiguity results from a congressional decision to delegate the resolution of that ambiguity. Furthermore, Scalia's rationale for *Chevron* assumes that delegations are best left to be worked out in the "Second branch," rather than the "Third." Congressional intent, paired with the necessary division between executive and judicial power, forms the rationale for the expansive interpretation of *Chevron*.

Substituting Judicial Interpretation for Agency Interpretation

In limiting the scope of cases in which *Chevron* applies, *Mead* signaled a substantial move away from judicial deference to administrative interpretations of law. Other developments involving "step one" of *Chevron*—whether a statute is clear, thus triggering judicial deference to the agency—similarly undermined *Chevron*'s impact. One way to interpret step one is to say that the statute is clear only if its meaning is obvious without extensive interpretation. This would diminish the number of cases in which the statute is deemed to be clear by a reviewing court, and therefore would increase the impact of *Chevron*. An alternative way of interpreting step one is to say that the statute is clear even if it requires extensive interpretation to discern its meaning. This, of course, would allow courts ample latitude for employing techniques of statutory interpretation to unearth the meaning of the statute and impose that meaning on agencies. In other words, even if *Chevron* applies, courts could overturn agencies' interpretations of law if they allowed for a robust judicial role in step one of the *Chevron* inquiry.

In many cases the Court has used a robust interpretation of step one to overturn agencies' interpretations of their statutory mission. In *MCI Telecommunications Corp. v. AT&T* the Court ruled that the Federal Communications Commission impermissibly interpreted the statutory term "modify."[47] Interestingly, it was Justice Scalia who wrote for the Court, overturning the agency's interpretation of the statute. In a more prominent case, *FDA v. Brown & Williamson*, the Court determined that FDA had impermissibly interpreted the Food, Drug, and Cosmetic Act's use of the term "drug" to include nicotine— an interpretation FDA used to impose regulations on the tobacco industry.[48] The Court decided that the Act was clear, and that the statute clearly forbade interpreting nicotine as a drug. In that case, the Court set up a clear statement rule: if Congress had intended to delegate authority on matters of critical importance to society, it must do so in clear and unmistakable language. Because the Congress had refused on multiple occasions to modify the Act to give the FDA clear jurisdiction over tobacco, the Court reasoned, the statute clearly does not define nicotine as a drug.[49]

This clear statement rule was used in *Rapanos v. U.S.* to overturn the Army Corps of Engineers' interpretation of the Clean Water Act (CWA).[50] The CWA governs the "navigable waters" of the United States, a term that the Army Corps had interpreted to include tributaries of such waters and wetlands adjacent to navigable waters. Justice Scalia wrote for the Court, rejecting this interpretation as incompatible with the clear meaning of the statute. Relying on the clear statement principle, he argued that "We ordinarily expect a clear and manifest statement from Congress to authorize an unprecedented intrusion into traditional state authority."[51] Thus even Scalia was willing to enforce a judicial interpretation of a statute against an agency's, on the grounds that the statute was clear.

The Limited Impact of the Chevron Doctrine

As the foregoing cases demonstrate, even within the *Chevron* framework, courts have found ways to engage in a relatively extensive review of agencies' interpretations of statutes, as opposed to deferring to agencies. According to

Chevron's original formulation, the question for the Court to decide at step one was whether "Congress had directly spoken to the precise question at issue," or in shorthand, whether the statute was clear. In order to make that determination, however, courts have assumed that one must look beyond the statute to the institutional competency of the agency and the court in each particular case. Application of step one of *Chevron* has therefore produced an ad hoc approach that is tailored to the specific decision under review in each case.

This resembles how courts have applied "step zero" of *Chevron*. Based on the underlying premise of *Chevron*, namely, that Congress had decided to delegate the authority to the agency to fill in any statutory gap, the step zero inquiry asked whether Congress *would have wanted* the agency to have the discretion to interpret the statute. In step zero, this question was decided based on whether Congress had delegated power to the agency to act with the force of law; if so, Congress clearly wanted to delegate significant interpretive power to the agency, but if not, Congress must have wanted the courts to resolve any statutory ambiguity. Similarly, at step one the courts have asked whether Congress would have wanted to give authority to an agency to resolve a particular statutory gap based on the expertise involved and the accountability of the agency. The statute is considered by the courts to be clear if the Congress would have wanted the court to resolve any statutory ambiguity—having considered the type of decision being made. In each instance, the question is "one of constructive congressional intent," rather than the meaning of the statute. And this gives the court ample room to apply the law in an ad hoc, arbitrary manner, yielding different results depending on the policy context of each decision.[52] As one commentator has characterized the step one inquiry, courts must "determine whether the statutory language is sufficiently ambiguous that *Congress would have intended the agency to fill the void.*"[53] One sees how the step one inquiry has evolved from a question of the meaning of the statute to the question of whether, from the courts' point of view, the agency decision at issue should be granted deference. In such a scheme, clearly the courts have retained the flexibility and authority, even while not expressly overturning *Chevron*, to be the arbiters of statutory meaning in the administrative state.

The way in which the courts approach their ad hoc role at step zero and step one further demonstrates the challenge the administrative state poses to traditional constitutional principles. Under the combined influence of step zero and step one, *Chevron* becomes fundamentally about whether a court or an agency should interpret the vague laws that Congress passes delegating power to some other institution. According to one recent commentary:

The question of deference posed in *Chevron* is fundamentally about "the choice of the appropriate interpretive institution—the agency or the court. Every statutory interpretation case becomes a separation of powers case." And because Congress does not generally indicate its preferred interpreter explicitly, the job falls to the courts to weigh the institutional factors that militate in favor of or against deference at Step One.[54]

Each decision under *Chevron* analysis is about *who*, given the unique circumstances of each individual case, should make law, now that the Congress has delegated to some other institution.

Chevron itself pointed to two possible factors that would help courts determine whether they or agencies should fill in the statutory gaps created by Congress: expertise and political accountability. Clearly, the courts will defer to agencies at step one if they believe that the statute ought to be filled in with the expertise of administrative agencies. There is empirical evidence that suggests the courts use *Chevron* in precisely this manner.[55] Conversely, the courts may conclude at step one that the statute constitutes an ambiguity meant for the agency to resolve if that agency is more accountable than others—if it is an "executive" as opposed to an "independent" agency. As it has been argued, "courts might decide that Congress would be more likely to delegate interpretative authority the more politically accountable an agency is."[56] This was, in fact, the approach advocated by then-Dean of Harvard Law School Elena Kagan.[57] Thus the controversy over who should be in charge of the administrative state has now shifted to the arena of administrative law, where competing constitutional principles are invoked to justify judicial scrutiny or deference.

The Pitfalls of Deference

As conservatives have first defended and then rethought some of the assumptions of the *Chevron* doctrine, the pitfalls of deference have become increasingly evident. The assumption that Congress can delegate to agencies the ability to interpret statutes to shore up gaps or ambiguity allows agencies to "update" statutes to deal with problems never anticipated by the authors of the original legislation. Although Justice Scalia was a committed textualist and partially defended *Chevron* on that ground, the doctrine actually undermines textualism by allowing agencies to update statutes by creative interpretation.

Chevron allows the meaning of statutes to evolve as agencies reinterpret their own authority, typically to expand their authority. As E. Donald Elliot writes, "the increased ability of the law-making system to adapt to new conditions without legislation may in turn help to account for the relative paucity of significant environmental legislation since 1990. . . . [L]egislation is less necessary today because of the Executive Branch's post-*Chevron* powers to update and adapt existing legislation to meet emerging problems."[58] For example, although Congress failed to pass the Lieberman/Warner Climate Security Act of 2007, which would have given the EPA power to regulate greenhouse gases, this very objective was realized simply by interpreting the Clean Air Act to have already given the agency that authority.[59] The EPA has initiated the rulemaking process to provide for regulation of carbon dioxide through the authority contained in the CAA. Similarly, in the wake of the recent defeat of the legislation to "bail out" the auto industry, the Secretary of the Treasury simply looked to accomplish its objective by using the Troubled Assets Relief Program funds that had been granted to him by Congress in earlier legislation.[60] By reinterpreting the statute, administrators can assume authority that may have been defeated in the legislative branch even very recently. And if the courts are to defer to agencies' statutory interpretations, there is little that can be done about this.

This explains why some legal scholars on the left such as Cass Sunstein defend the *Chevron* doctrine. Sunstein writes that "the Chevron approach may be defended on the ground that the resolution of ambiguities in statutes is sometimes a question of policy as much as it is one of law." In fact, *Chevron* itself "nicely illustrates this point," for Sunstein, because *Chevron* dealt with a question and a problem Congress failed to foresee when it wrote the law. Rather than requiring Congress to amend the statute to bring it up to current exigencies, *Chevron* seems to say that agencies can do the work that would otherwise have been left to Congress, which is a good thing in Sunstein's view. He writes:

> Sometimes regulation is made more difficult because of the problem of changed circumstances. New developments involving technological capacity, economics, the international situation, or even law may affect regulatory performance. Congress is unable to amend every statute to account for these changes, a situation that creates a genuine problem for those who must apply the statute. Here as well, administrators are in a far better position than courts to interpret ambiguous statutes in a way that takes account of new conditions.

"The result," Sunstein concludes, "is to confer a power of adaptation on institutions" allowing them to update the law without the difficulties associated with congressional involvement.[61]

The Re-emergence of Conservative Distrust

Therefore, by 2009, when President Barack Obama took office, the institutional patterns surrounding agencies' interpretations of law had become largely entrenched. Conservative judges would defend the agencies' ability to interpret statutes relatively free from judicial scrutiny, and liberal judges would search for possible means for circumventing the deference rule pronounced in *Chevron*. It was inevitable, however, that the inauguration of a more Progressive president would test the allegiance of both sides to these institutional allegiances. And the Roberts Court has, indeed, revived the controversy over the very legitimacy of the rule pronounced in *Chevron*—revealing a potential shift among conservative justices on the Supreme Court over the legitimacy of the entire *Chevron* framework.

Recent cases illustrate this potential shift. The first, *City of Arlington v. FCC* (2013), raised the question of whether *Chevron* applies when an agency is interpreting its own jurisdiction.[62] In a 6–3 decision, with Justice Scalia writing for the majority, the Court answered that it does. However, the three dissenting justices in the case were Kennedy, Alito, and Chief Justice Roberts. Roberts wrote a vigorous dissent in which he argued that *Chevron* only applies if Congress intended to grant interpretive authority to the agency—thus sticking to the original rationale for the framework—and "the question whether an agency enjoys that authority must be decided by a court, without deference to the agency." In Roberts's view, the legal question at *Chevron* step zero is a pure question of law for courts to decide de novo, thus allowing courts to determine whether *Chevron* applies in the first place. More interesting than Roberts's logic was his tone. He warned that "the danger posed by the growing power of the administrative state cannot be dismissed" and argued that "the authority of administrative agencies" to interpret statutes should be considered in light of the fact that we now have "hundreds of federal agencies poking into every nook and cranny of daily life." Roberts seemed to be suggesting that *Chevron*'s reach needs to be limited in light of the extensive power that the administrative state has accumulated over the past decades.

The opinions of Roberts and others on the right side of the Court in cases such as *Perez v. Mortgage Bankers* and even *King v. Burwell*, in which the Court upheld the IRS's interpretation of the Affordable Care Act allowing the federal government to award subsidies to individuals who purchased health insurance on federal exchanges rather than exchanges "established by the states" (as the statute read), indicate an increased willingness to ignore or circumvent *Chevron* on the right. In *Burwell* Roberts interpreted the Affordable Care Act without any deference to the agency at all. While the IRS's interpretation was upheld, Roberts interpreted the statute de novo. Many commentators, including Cass Sunstein, expressed astonishment that Roberts paid no attention to *Chevron*, even while upholding a strained interpretation of the statute by the IRS.[63]

These recent cases suggest that we may once again be on the cusp of a shift in institutional allegiances in administrative law. At least one member of the Court—Justice Thomas—appears ready to move past the *Chevron* doctrine. In *Michigan v. Environmental Protection Agency* the Court overturned the EPA's mercury pollution rules in a decision written by Justice Scalia and in which the agency lost in spite of the application of *Chevron* deference.[64] While that result would be enough to demonstrate the decline of *Chevron* among conservative justices (who voted with the majority), Justice Thomas went further in a concurring opinion to voice his "serious questions about the constitutionality of our broader practice of deferring to agency interpretations of federal statutes. . . . [W]e seem to be straying further and further from the Constitution without so much as pausing to ask why. We should stop to consider that document before blithely giving the force of law to any other agency 'interpretations' of federal statutes."[65]

It is impossible now to know whether this reversion to Progressive-era institutional patterns, in which progressives defend the executive and conservatives defend judicial review of administrative decision making, is a temporary response to a unique political configuration or a more permanent rethinking of the constitutionality of the administrative state. What is clear in 2016, however, is that the *Chevron* doctrine of judicial deference to reasonable agency interpretations of law is on thin ice. In this context it is critical to understand what preceded the *Chevron* doctrine's approach in order to predict how the administrative state may function in a post-*Chevron* context.

How Hard a Look?

Administrative agencies frequently make discretionary policy choices that do not interpret statutes. In these cases, the appropriate level of judicial scrutiny—as described in Chapter Six—is indicated by Section 706 of the APA, frequently referred to as the "arbitrary and capricious" standard. As the previous chapter explained, the DC Circuit translated this standard into the concept of "hard look" review in a set of important cases in the 1970s.

"Hard look" review gained the sanction of the Supreme Court in the 1983 case of *Motor Vehicle Manufacturers Assn. v. State Farm Mutual Automobile*

Insurance Co.[66] The case involved the rescission of an earlier rule by the Department of Transportation requiring the use of passive restraints in new automobiles. In reversing the rescission and reinstating the rule, the Supreme Court endorsed the DC Circuit's creation of the "hard look" test and grounded it in the arbitrary and capricious standard of the APA. The Court declared that an agency acted arbitrarily if "the agency has relied on factors which Congress has not intended it to consider, entirely failed to consider an important aspect of the problem, offered an explanation for its decision that runs counter to the evidence before the agency, or is so implausible that it could not be ascribed to a difference in view or the product of agency expertise."[67] The Court therefore laid out a four-part test, and any agency action that failed one of the prongs of this test would be set aside.

In keeping with the liberals' approach to administrative law issues since the 1960s, "hard look" review was considered to be a salutary antidote to agency "capture." In the view of those who pressed for thorough hard look review, the longer agencies looked at a particular decision, the less likely the ultimate outcome would be clouded by the particular interests of those groups likely to capture the agency. A corollary to this principle is the "swerve" doctrine, which states that agencies should take an *especially* hard look at any decisions to change or rescind a rule or interpretation. The presumption is that the rescission of rules is likely due to political pressures placed on agencies by interest groups as opposed to a disinterested pursuit of the public interest. In the words of Mark Seidenfeld, "The doctrine helps to ensure that agency decisions are determined neither by accommodation of purely private interests nor by surreptitious commandeering of the decision-making apparatus to serve an agency's idiosyncratic view of the public interest."[68] Therefore, when an agency "swerves" from its typical course of action, like the NHTSA did in the *State Farm* case, heightened judicial scrutiny will apply: "If an agency route veers from the road laid down by its precedents, it must justify the detour in light of changed external circumstances or a changed view of its regulatory role that the agency can support under its authorizing statute."[69]

The connection between this corollary and progressivism is clear. It supposes that agency regulations promote the public interest, and that deregulation is contrary to the public interest, and is intended to benefit a private or particular interest. Therefore, regulations are the product of neutral, disinterested expertise, while rescissions of regulations are evidence of agency capture. The hard look doctrine therefore fits neatly with the approach of liberals who seek to push for greater regulation.

The conservative justices' response to the "hard look" doctrine and the conception of legitimate decision making it advanced is noteworthy. In a fascinating (partial) dissent in the *State Farm* case, Justice Rehnquist argued that the Court had erred in asserting that the "hard look" test nullified an agency change in policy produced by a change in administration. In Rehnquist's view, the courts should leave such policy choices to the agency:

> The agency's changed view of the standard seems to be related to the election of a new president of a different political party. It is readily apparent that the responsible members of one administration may consider public resistance and uncertainties to be more important than do their counterparts in a previous administration. A change in administration brought about by the people casting their votes is a perfectly reasonable basis for an executive agency's reappraisal of the costs and benefits of its programs and regulations. As long as the agency remains within the bounds established by Congress, it is entitled to assess administrative records and evaluate priorities in light of the philosophy of the administration.[70]

Rehnquist implicitly accepted that agencies are entitled to make policy by whatever means deemed appropriate "[a]s long as the agency remains within the bounds established by Congress." He defended the discretion of an elected administration to adjust administrative priorities because it can be held accountable through the president, who is responsible for the actions of the agency. More fundamentally, Rehnquist's defense of deference to agency policymaking assumed that Congress can legitimately delegate discretion to the agency in the first place. The delegation of legislative power to agencies is the basis for Scalia's *Chevron* opinion as well as Rehnquist's dissent from the "hard look" doctrine.

Deference therefore derives in part from an acceptance of the need for congressional delegation of lawmaking power to agencies. For both Scalia and Rehnquist, the idea of judicial deference to administrative agencies is based on accountability, particularly the distinction between political branches (Congress and the president) and non-political branches (the judiciary). Thus, when power is transferred from one political branch to another, it still is preferable to have that political branch make policy rather than have the non-political branch guide administrative policymaking.

There are two difficulties with this position. First, the distinction between political and non-political branches is an oversimplification of the constitutional system. Considering the separation of powers, it is clear that accumulating all of the powers of government in one set of hands would be problematic, regardless of whether that branch is political or not. In other words, it is likely that the Constitution's Framers would not have considered the accumulation of all powers in a single, political branch as preferable to checking a political branch with a non-political one. In fact, as noted in Chapter One, the courts were often used as a check against arbitrary administrative power during the early republic.

Second, the distinction between political and non-political branches does not adequately describe the character of administrative agencies. It assumes that administrative agencies are political, which implies that they fall under the traditional tripartite system of government devised by the Framers. Yet it is clear that administrative agencies have always been considered, at least in part, to be apolitical. They were certainly designed by the Progressives to be separate from politics (as explained in Chapter Five), and they have retained this character, at least in part, particularly after the Supreme Court's decision in *Humphrey's Executor* insulated them from presidential removal. Viewed from this perspective the argument that judges should defer to agencies because they are part of the political branches of government loses its force.

Thus there are serious constitutional difficulties with the Rehnquist-Scalia position in favor of judicial deference to administrative agencies. Having given up on the critical question of congressional delegations of power to administrative agencies, the retreat to judicial deference seeks to replace the original constitutional approach to administrative power with a weaker set of checks and balances. Accountability through the president and Congress's intent to delegate interpretive power to administrative agencies have replaced the original checks on administration imposed by the principles of republicanism, the separation of powers, and the rule of law. This attempt to meliorate the challenges posed by the modern administrative state through the framework of administrative law is the subject of the following section.

Retreating from American Constitutionalism

Having described the developments in these four areas of administrative law—procedural review, standing, agency legal interpretation, and agency policymaking—it is worthwhile to explore the broader implications of the "conservative counterrevolution" in some detail. The debates surrounding these administrative law doctrines are indicative of two important aspects of the administrative state: the extent to which basic ideas of American constitutionalism still resonate in administrative law today, and the curious shifting of institutional alliances in contemporary administrative law.

Even the defenders of the administrative state have experienced buyer's remorse and have sought to temper the effects of the turn to bureaucracy. The Progressive and New Deal era faith in unfettered experts firmly entrenched in administrative agencies, free from the bounds of public opinion, was replaced by the idea that the courts ought to take a more active role in overseeing the administrative process. Of course, the courts that adopted this position towards administrative agencies were more liberal than the administrators, and so they used judicial oversight to push policy in a more liberal direction.

Having abandoned the original constitutional constraints on the use of government power, when they built the administrative state, its defenders have opted for a second-best method of control: administrative law. In the words of Thomas Miles and Cass Sunstein, "a central point of judicial review, was to respond to the open-ended delegation of discretionary power by ensuring a firm check on agency decisions. . . . On this view, the hard look doctrine might be seen as a second-best substitute for the original constitutional safeguards against the uncontrolled exercise of discretion."[71] The buyer's remorse about giving up the Founders' checks on arbitrary government led to a faith in administrative law to step into the breach. Reformers sought to import the principles of American constitutionalism into the administrative state through administrative law, shoring it up from within.

Meanwhile, in response, conservative jurists began to oppose the meddling of the courts in the business of the administrative agencies. This put many conservative judges and legal theorists in the awkward position of defending the original setup of the administrative state, derived from Progressive political and legal theory, against the liberals' advocacy of judicial review of the administrative process. The broader constitutional implications of these developments are profound. Across the spectrum of administrative law is a consensus accepting the administrative state, and using administrative law to cure its constitutional defects. As Robert Schapiro explains:

> The administrative deference that *Chevron* mandates can be understood as ensuring the vitality of the modern activist government. . . . As part of its validation of the New Deal, the Court desisted from enforcing the nondelegation doctrine, thus allowing Congress broad discretion to allocate legislative power. . . . Deference thus ensures that Congress, not the judiciary, will have the primary role in allocating lawmaking power.[72]

Rather than confronting the administrative state, the conservative counter-revolution made its peace with bureaucracy and sought to leave it to executive politics. As Richard J. Pierce has written, whereas "by 1980, it appeared that a majority of the Supreme Court Justices were prepared to outlaw large por-tions of the administrative state by holding that Congress cannot delegate major policy decisions to 'politically unresponsive administrators,'" in *Chevron* "the Supreme Court unanimously stepped back from that abyss and instead took a major step toward legitimating and democratizing the administrative state."[73] Justices Scalia and Rehnquist—on a variety of grounds including con-gressional intent, deference to expertise, and political accountability—chose to validate the administrative state and seek to improve it through administra-tive law. This accommodation is evident first, in their opinions upholding the constitutionality of the administrative state, and second, in their rationale for deference in both procedural and substantive review of administrative action.

Détente with the Administrative State

The most obvious and prominent area in which the administrative state's le-gitimacy continues to go unchallenged concerns the nondelegation doctrine. With the exception of Justice Thomas, no one on the Court has expressed an interest in questioning the legitimacy of the very delegations that empower the bureaucracy in the first place.[74] Rather, led by Justice Scalia, conservatives on the Court have sought to accommodate the administrative state when dele-gation challenges reach their chambers. In *Mistretta v. United States*, the Court upheld the Sentencing Guidelines set by the U.S. Sentencing Commission as valid, in spite of a claim that they violated Article I, section 1 of the Consti-tution that vests legislative power in Congress.[75] In a straightforward majority opinion, Justice Blackmun first noted that "Congress simply cannot do its job absent an ability to delegate power under broad general directives" and that the Court has "upheld, again without deviation, Congress' ability to delegate power under broad standards." After noting that the broad directives set forth in the Sentencing Reform Act were no more vague than those contained in many other authorizing statutes, Blackmun easily concluded that the statute was within the established precedents applying the nondelegation principle.

Although he dissented from the decision, Justice Scalia conceded that "while the doctrine of unconstitutional delegation is unquestionably a funda-mental element of our constitutional system, it is not an element readily en-forceable by the courts. Once it is conceded, as it must be, that no statute can be entirely precise . . . the debate over unconstitutional delegation becomes

a debate not over a point of principle but over a question of degree." With
that statement, Scalia concluded that the Sentencing Guidelines involved "a
pure delegation of legislative power" and therefore was one of the few cases in which a court could enforce the principle. Yet Scalia refused to insist
upon the nondelegation principle in subsequent cases. In *Whitman v. American Trucking*, writing for the Court, Scalia brushed aside the nondelegation
question, even quoting *Mistretta*'s pronouncement that "we have almost never
felt qualified to second-guess Congress regarding the permissible degree of
policy judgment that can be left to those executing or applying the law." Scalia's posture represented the predominant attitude among conservatives on the
Court after 1980: accommodate the administrative state and the precedents
that give it constitutional legitimacy, but dissent when the Court goes beyond
those precedents to uphold more dramatic departures from the traditional
constitutional structure.

The predominant attitude is evident in a second critical area in which conservative justices have failed to overturn the long-standing consensus in favor
of the administrative state: the insulation of administrative officials from the
president's removal power. Since *Humphrey's Executor* deprived Franklin Roosevelt of the authority to remove the heads of independent regulatory commissions (described in Chapter Six), presidents have struggled to gain control
over administrative policymaking—a far cry from the responsible executive
envisioned at the Constitutional Convention. Roosevelt deemed the decision
to be illegitimate, and the Brownlow Committee condemned the "headless
fourth branch" of government that it entrenched. Even after 1980, in the midst
of the alleged conservative counter-revolution, the Supreme Court refused to
challenge the precedent set by *Humphrey's*. In *Morrison v. Olson* the Court upheld the Ethics in Government Act's provision restricting the Attorney General from removing independent counsels, who were in charge of essentially
executive functions such as investigation and prosecution.[76] Had the Supreme
Court applied the reasoning in *Humphrey's*, namely, that administrators vested with "quasi-legislative" and "quasi-judicial" authority are not executive and
therefore can be insulated from presidential removal, the independent counsel
would not have been safe, since the functions of that office were executive in
nature. But the majority in *Morrison* extended the range of offices to which
Congress could attach good cause restrictions on removal to the independent
counsel as well.

It was this aspect of the decision, that prompted Scalia to dissent from
the majority in *Morrison*. In his words, "Governmental investigation and

prosecution of crimes is a quintessentially executive function." Since *Humphrey's*, he argued, "it has been established that the line of permissible restriction upon removal of principal officers lies at the point at which the powers exercised by those officers are no longer purely executive." Instead of applying this precedent, he lamented, "*Humphrey's Executor* is swept into the dustbin of repudiated constitutional principles." In other words, Scalia objected not to *Humphrey's*, but to the Court's unwillingness to apply it faithfully. Perhaps Justice Scalia was willing to reconsider the principle in *Humphrey's* itself, but there was no prospect of such a reconsideration during his tenure on the Court. As with the nondelegation doctrine, while conservative academics and theorists openly questioned the constitutional validity of *Humphrey's*, the challenge never made it from the ivory towers and thinktanks into the courtrooms.

The unwillingness of many conservative justices to press for reconsideration of *Humphrey's* has produced curious opinions in recent years. A leading example is *Free Enterprise Fund v. Public Company Accounting Oversight Board (PCAOB)*.[77] In that case the Court, in an opinion written by Chief Justice Roberts, struck down provisions of the Sarbanes-Oxley Act that granted protection to the PCAOB, which could only be removed for cause by members of the Securities and Exchange Commission, who are also protected from removal except for cause. Roberts's opinion asserted that such an arrangement "is contrary to Article II's vesting of the executive power in the President," invoking a core constitutional principle of executive responsibility. The difficulty with the opinion was that it overlooked existing precedents that clearly undermined the principle of executive responsibility. After summarizing the precedents set by *Humphrey's Executor* and *Morrison*, Roberts explained that "The parties do not ask us to reexamine any of these precedents, and we do not do so."

As for why the second layer of removal protection crosses a constitutional line not transgressed by a single layer, Roberts merely asserted that it produces "a Board that is not accountable to the President, and a President who is not responsible for the Board. . . . The President therefore cannot hold the [SEC] fully accountable for the Board's conduct, to the same extent that he may hold the Commission accountable for everything else that it does." Roberts never explained why the removal protections for PCAOB transformed the SEC's accountability to the President for its supervision of the Board, when the point of giving the *SEC* for cause removal protection was to insulate it from presidential supervision in the first place. The curiosity in the opinion was that Roberts was willing to make the constitutional case for the responsible, unitary executive, but unwilling to apply it against precedents that clearly failed to conform to the principle. It seemed clear that while many justices on the Court were uneasy about the rise of the administrative state, they were only willing to limit its expansion rather than consider overturning precedents that provided for its foundation. Instead of making the constitutional case against the administrative state, they crafted rationales for accommodating it and keeping the courts from intervening in its operation.

The Rationale for Judicial Deference to Administrative Action

Justice Rehnquist's defense of agency discretion to determine appropriate procedures, forcefully announced in *Vermont Yankee*, was in part justified on the basis of congressional intent. Justice Rehnquist's rebuke of the DC Circuit was so scathing because the DC Circuit flaunted the Supreme Court's persistent statement that Congress, not the courts, is responsible for determining the appropriate procedures for administrative rulemaking. The ultimate position rested on judicial deference to the legislature. This was also the underlying rationale for judicial deference to administrators in the *Chevron* case. In both instances Congress's intent should control the courts, according to the conservatives.

One of Rehnquist's arguments in *Vermont Yankee* was that if agencies are required to use greater procedures to produce an adequate record, they "simply will have no choice but to conduct a full adjudicatory hearing prior to promulgating every rule." This would, in Rehnquist's words, "seriously interfere with that process prescribed by Congress."[78] In his lengthy article discussing the *Vermont Yankee* decision, then-Professor Scalia noted that the APA is not procedural charter into which the DC Circuit was attempting to make it. Regardless of "the virtue or vice of legislative activism in the area of administrative procedure," which is a separate issue for Scalia, "[w]hat is unquestionable," is that "such activism cannot coexist with fundamental legislation of the sort the Court's opinion in *Vermont Yankee* pronounces the APA to be."[79] In other words, procedural "activism" or adding to the procedural requirements of administrative agencies may or may not be beneficial, but it is certainly not what the Congress intended the APA to do. For Scalia, this is an important consideration in determining whether Congress has intended the APA to support the kind of administrative procedure envisioned by the DC Circuit.

However, Rehnquist also advanced a separate argument from the one grounded in congressional intent. He argued that agencies *ought to* have this discretion because of their unique character. In Rehnquist's opinion for the

Court in *Vermont Yankee*, he argued that the Court had "for more than four decades emphasized that the formulation of procedures was basically left within the discretion of the agencies."[80] In general, the discretion of the agencies to perform their duties must be unfettered by the courts, according to Rehnquist: "Absent constitutional constraints" such as the Due Process Clause, "or extremely compelling circumstances the 'administrative agencies' should be free to fashion their own rules of procedure and to pursue methods of inquiry capable of permitting them to discharge their multitudinous duties."[81]

In making this argument Rehnquist quoted liberally from *FCC v. Pottsville Broadcasting Co.*, a 1940 opinion written by Justice Frankfurter. The original opinion quoted by Rehnquist is a striking assertion of the Progressives' view of the relationship between courts and agencies:

> To the extent that a federal court is authorized to review an administrative act, there is superimposed upon the enforcement of legislative policy through administrative control a different process from that out of which the administrative action under review ensued. The technical rules derived from the interrelationship of judicial tribunals forming a hierarchical system are taken out of their environment when mechanically applied to determine the extent to which Congressional power, exercised through a delegated agency, can be controlled within the limited scope of "judicial power" conferred by Congress under the Constitution.
>
> Courts, like other organisms, represent an interplay of form and function. The history of Anglo-American courts and the more or less narrowly defined range of their staple business have determined the basic characteristics of trial procedure, the rules of evidence, and the general principles of appellate review. Modern administrative tribunals are the outgrowth of conditions far different from those. . . . These differences in origin and function preclude wholesale transplantation of the rules of procedure, trial, and review which have evolved from the history and experience of courts. Thus, this Court has recognized that bodies like the Interstate Commerce Commission . . . should not be too narrowly constrained by technical rules as to the admissibility of proof, should be free to fashion their own rules of procedure and to pursue methods of inquiry capable of permitting them to discharge their multitudinous duties.[82]

Frankfurter's defense of allowing agencies to determine their own procedures, own form of proceeding, and own rules of evidence was predicated on the fact that administrative agencies represented an altogether new institution suited for new economic and social conditions. He argued that these agencies are vested "with power far exceeding and different from the conventional judicial modes for adjusting conflicting claims." They are intended to perform a judicial-like function but are entirely different from traditional Anglo-American courts, and should therefore not be bound by outmoded rule of law procedures. This is the opinion which Rehnquist quoted in *Vermont Yankee*, now defending administrative agencies from the DC Circuit's grafting of additional procedural controls onto the administrative process. In essence, then, as his reliance on Justice Frankfurter suggests, Rehnquist's defense of minimal administrative procedure in *Vermont Yankee* stems from an unwillingness to preserve the traditional Anglo-American judicial model in the wake of administrative justice as carried out by expert agencies.

Rehnquist's argument in *Vermont Yankee* that agencies should be free to use their own discretion in crafting their procedures was an acceptance of the administrative state and a desire to accommodate it properly. Once Congress has delegated considerable discretionary power to a modern administrative agency, judicial restraint seems to demand deferential treatment of that institution. This approach is also illustrated by Justice Scalia's writings on *Vermont Yankee*, which offer fascinating observations about the relationship between procedures and administrative justice. He writes, "legislators cannot be unaware that the prescription of procedure profoundly affects an agency's political capabilities, *i.e.*, its ability to reach decisions not solely on the basis of science and reason but also on the basis of what is acceptable to the most potent interest groups involved."[83] The more procedures that are required, the more difficult it is for agencies to make policy in the way that a legislature would. If an agency like the FCC is required to make decisions on a record produced by substantial procedures, he continues, "it becomes virtually impossible for the Commission to negotiate, among the principal contending interest groups . . . a political accommodation of the sort the Congress itself would produce if the issue were resolved there."[84] Implicitly, for Scalia, agencies ought to do what Congress does, namely, make policy by fashioning political compromises and accommodations. "[T]he fashioning of such political accommodations," he continues, "is one of the appropriate functions of administrative agencies, at least when they are operating under a legislative directive no more specific than to serve 'the public interest, convenience, and necessity.'"[85] Extensive procedures prevent agencies from making decisions based on political accommodation. And, importantly, for Scalia, agencies should be in the business of making political arrangements of this sort, since Congress has permissibly delegated power to them.

The retreat from constitutional objections to the administrative state, and the shift to judicial deference, demonstrate the consensus that emerged in administrative law. They imply a willingness to accept and accommodate an administrative state, seeking to prevent judges from interfering in the administrative process, and ensure that agencies have wide discretion to carry out the obligations delegated to them by the legislative branch.

Who Enforces the Law?
Standing and Deference to Administrative Agencies

In keeping with their views on the appropriate role of the courts in administrative law, conservative jurists have argued for more stringent requirements for standing to sue, which resembles the position taken by earlier progressives—in particular, Justices Brandeis and Frankfurter. This is not to suggest that they take this position for the same reasons as the Progressives. The conservative argument for restrictions on standing stems not from the presumption of the constitutional validity of administrative action, or the idea that courts should defer to experts in the bureaucracy. Rather, it rests on the idea that standing is a product of a proper understanding of the separation of powers, particularly who is given the authority to enforce the laws. The conservative position on standing is also informed by the argument on behalf of majoritarianism.

In a key article staking out his position on standing, then-Professor Scalia argued that standing doctrine is "an Essential Element of the Separation of Powers."[86] In Scalia's view, standing is necessary to restrain courts to their properly delegated authority, namely, authority to decide cases between particular parties based on legal principles, as opposed to making political decisions based on general theories, enforced by decisions brought by general parties.

Scalia's emphasis on the distinction between private and public law, which undergirds his argument for standing, is based on this separation of powers argument. In *FEC v. Akins*, discussed earlier in this chapter, Scalia's dissent emphasized this principle. Although the injury—lack of access to information possessed by the FEC—was generalized, the Court ruled that the voters who sought the information had standing to sue. Scalia argued that this amounted to a switch from a private law to a public law model, which is an affront to the separation of powers:

> When the executive can be directed by the courts, at the instance of any voter, to remedy a deprivation which affects the entire electorate in precisely the same way . . . there has occurred a shift of responsibility to a branch not designed to

protect the public at large but to protect individual rights. . . . This is not the system we have had, and it is not the system we should desire.[87]

In Scalia's view, the separation of powers entails the "private law" approach to standing, since the proper role of the judiciary is not to vindicate public rights but to protect individual rights. Similarly, in dissent in *Laidlaw*, Scalia lamented that "[t]he undesirable and unconstitutional consequence of today's decision is to place the immense power of suing to enforce the public laws in private hands."[88]

Scalia's argument is buttressed not only by the "cases and controversies" language of Article III of the Constitution, but also, in his view, Article II. According to that Article, the president has the duty to "take care that the laws be faithfully executed." For Scalia, this means that the executive branch necessarily has the discretion to choose how to prosecute and execute the law, including the authority to prioritize among various enforcement objectives. To allow any party to bring suit against federal agencies in court, to compel enforcement of a particular law, would deprive the executive of its constitutionally delegated authority. In short, therefore, the separation of powers rationale behind standing doctrine means that courts should be restrained not only because of their particular role and responsibility but also to protect the executive branch.

Scalia also presents a second argument on behalf of standing, namely, that it is necessary to support the majoritarian character of the U.S. Constitution. In his arguments in favor of standing doctrine, Scalia reveals his views about the anti-democratic character of the judicial branch. He writes that judges are "selected from the aristocracy of the highly educated." Moreover, they are "removed from all accountability to the electorate." To allow for private groups of citizens to use the courts to enforce the law in the absence of bureaucratic support for enforcing the law, Scalia argues, would allow courts to impose enforcement where popular support for enforcement does not exist. He argues, "Where the courts, in the supposed interest of all the people, do enforce . . . policies that the political process itself would not enforce, they are likely (despite the best of intentions) to be enforcing the political prejudices of their own class."[89] For Scalia, standing should be a legal doctrine that prevents judges from enforcing their own counter-majoritarian political preferences. It therefore "restricts courts to their traditional undemocratic role of protecting individuals and minorities against impositions of the majority, and excludes them from the even more undemocratic role of prescribing how the other two branches should function in order to serve the interest of the majority itself."[90] To use standing to "prescrib[e] how the other two branches should function" would be "even more undemocratic" than protecting the rights of the minority from majority tyranny, Scalia argues. In short, the role of the judiciary is fundamentally different from the role of the other branches, for Scalia. Judges must confine themselves to protecting minority rights and implementing private law. Standing doctrine secures this aim.

For the sake of democracy, then, judges should curtail access to courts in order to allow the political branches to represent the people. Interestingly, Scalia noted in dissent in *Laidlaw* that the Court's decision meant that "[e]lected officials are entirely deprived of their discretion to decide that a given violation should not be the object of suit at all, or that the enforcement decision should be postponed."[91] The "[e]lected officials" to which Scalia refers are those of the EPA, who can bring suit themselves in the courts if they deem necessary. In Scalia's view, then, when private groups have standing to bring suit, the elected officials of the EPA no longer have discretion to bring suit themselves.

In his majoritarian arguments for standing, therefore, one sees Scalia's heavy emphasis on the idea of democracy as tantamount to majority rule. He admits that judges have a legitimate antidemocratic role, but he seeks to limit the scope of that role as much as possible. This will allow the executive branch wide leeway to execute the law, which in turn will allow for social change in line with the will of the majority. Thus, in the context of standing, as in other doctrines, a strong majoritarian impulse is at work in Justice Scalia's approach.

The Flawed Constitutionalism of Deference

On substantive review, especially the nature of judicial review of agencies' legal interpretations and policy choices, conservative judges have traditionally emphasized the link between a particular understanding of the constitution and the need for judicial deference. Justice Scalia, in particular, has been a stalwart defender for a broad application of *Chevron* deference. His arguments for doing so appear to be grounded in the view that the courts should refrain from meddling in the decisions of administrators. This view is more appropriately connected to the progressive argument that courts should stay out of the administrative process because of the expertise of administrators as opposed to judges. It is impossible to disaggregate entirely the arguments for judicial restraint and the Progressive argument for expertise. As E. Donald Elliot explains, "*Chevron* represents a culmination of the vision articulated by the first generation of administrative lawyers in the 1930s that 'expertise' should play a greater role than 'legalism' in our law."[92] The reasons might be different, but the kind of administrative process that results is the same.

In the handful of prominent public pronouncements Scalia has made regarding the *Chevron* doctrine, his acceptance of the administrative state is evident. Scalia has emphatically denied the proposition that judges should defer to agencies based on their expertise, which was one of the underlying reasons for deference in the *Chevron* opinion authored by Justice Stevens. He argued, "that is not at all the reason that we give deference to the agency's interpretation. Rather, our deference has something to do with the allocation of power among the branches of government. Where Congress chooses not to be specific in a statute . . . the general principle is that the filling-in of those interstices has been left to the agency."[93] In short, Scalia argues, judicial deference to agency legal interpretations through the *Chevron* doctrine is not based on the agency's superior expertise; rather, it is based on the separation of powers—in particular, the idea that the courts should not interfere in congressional delegations of lawmaking power to agencies. The *Chevron* doctrine, for Scalia, follows logically from the abandonment of the nondelegation doctrine. If Congress can delegate power to agencies, courts should stay out of the agencies' business, since Congress wanted agencies to have the authority to make whatever decisions were delegated to it by the legislature. Judicial deference to agencies is based on judicial deference to the legislature.

Justice Scalia explained this rationale in detail. He has remarked, "the theoretical justification for *Chevron* is no different from the theoretical justification for those pre-*Chevron* cases that sometimes deferred to agency legal determinations":

> [The justification is] ultimately a function of Congress's intent. . . . An ambiguity in a statute committed to agency interpretation can be attributed to either of two congressional desires: (1) Congress intended a particular result, but was not clear about it; or (2) Congress had no particular intent on the subject, but meant to leave its resolution to the agency. When the former is the case, what we have is genuinely a question of law, properly to be resolved by the courts. When the latter is the case, what we have is the conferral of discretion upon the agency.[94]

This distinction admits that Congress can place an ambiguity in a statute and have "no particular intent on the subject." Even from the Founders' perspective, of course, agencies will have discretion, but not discretion conferred upon them by an open-ended congressional statute where the legislature had no intent. Rather, the kind of discretion agencies will have is intrinsic to the nature of executive power; it comes from the nature of their office, not from Congress. To suggest that Congress can confer discretion on executive agencies, having no intent on how that discretion is used, and from which discretion can emerge rules and adjudications that have the force of law, is to say that Congress can simply tell the courts that administrative agencies should make law over a wide area of policy unfettered by judicial review. Again, to reiterate, this is precisely the kind of argument Progressives like Wilson, Croly, and Goodnow employed to achieve strong judicial deference to New Deal administrative agencies. The tables have turned in administrative law.

Indeed, after laying out the aforementioned distinction between statutory gaps where Congress had an intention (not requiring deference) and statutory gaps where Congress had no intention, other than to confer discretion on agencies (which triggers deference), Scalia states that one can judge on which side a particular statute falls by considering:

> Such frequently mentioned factors as the degree of the agency's expertise, the complexity of the question at issue, and the existence of rulemaking authority within the agency. All these factors make an intent to confer discretion upon the agency more likely. *Chevron*, however, if it is to be believed, replaced this statute-by-statute evaluation (which was assuredly a font of uncertainty and litigation) with an across-the-board presumption that, in the case of ambiguity, agency discretion is meant.[95]

After *Chevron*, courts must now assume that all statutory gaps are signals to courts of Congress's intent to authorize agencies to fill in those gaps, without judicial interference. Indeed, Scalia continues:

> [This] is a more rational presumption today than it would have been thirty years ago—which explains the change in the law. Broad delegation to the Executive is the hallmark of the modern administrative state; agency rulemaking powers are the rule rather than, as they once were, the exception; and as the sheer number of modern departments and agencies suggests, we are awash in agency expertise.[96]

For Scalia, the distinction has collapsed, reasonably, since Congress regularly delegates broad rulemaking authority to agencies and generally wants the experts to figure out how to make policy in the modern administrative state. Scalia not only does not object to the modern administrative state; he wants to *facilitate* its operation by giving the congressional decision to delegate broad power to agencies the sanction of judicial deference. Scalia's defense of applying *Chevron* across the board is that today Congress is, reasonably, more willing to delegate power to agencies because of their expertise and the complexity of modern government.

Additionally, with regard to administrative policymaking, centered particularly around the famous *State Farm* decision, Justice Rehnquist has defended judicial deference to administrators in part with the argument that such an arrangement promotes accountability because the judiciary is a non-political branch. As Michael Herz has written, each of Rehnquist's prominent opinions in administrative law "reflects a hands-off conception of judicial review of agency action."[97] The administrative state is more accountable and democratic, Rehnquist seems to argue, if the president (rather than the courts) sets the agenda. Having given up on truly representative government, Rehnquist appears to argue that a more accountable bureaucracy is the second-best option. But as Chapter One argued, the Framers' conception of representation requires more than indirect accountability. Judicial deference to administrative power simply produces a more powerful bureaucracy, with fewer checks on its plenary policymaking authority. As Bernard Schwartz has stated, under his leadership the Rehnquist Court became "the most pro-executive and administrative agency Court in over half a century."[98] In the final analysis, Rehnquist's approach to the administrative state was to get the courts out of the way—identical to the Progressives' agenda—rather than to entertain any serious challenge to its fundamental institutions.

On a practical level this response is sensible, because liberal policy has most often been advanced (at least recently) from outside the administrative process—from courts and liberal interest groups through litigation. However, this agenda does not advance the longer term project of seeking a way out of the administrative state and in fact further entrenches the administrative state by giving it sanction and legitimacy. The flawed constitutionalism of judicial deference emphasizes congressional intent rather than the separation of powers, and democracy rather than representation by elected lawmakers. It is not a suitable substitute for the constitutional design for administration that prevailed in the first century of American history.

CONCLUSION

The Ongoing Crisis of Legitimacy

THE PRECEDING CHAPTERS have provided a broad overview of the development of American administrative institutions from the Revolutionary War to
the present day. As the first three chapters demonstrated, prior to the Civil
War American administrative law was tightly constrained by basic principles
of American constitutionalism, particularly accountability through electoral
representation, decentralization of power, separation of power, the rule of law,
and nondelegation. Binding rules were derived either from legislative statutory enactments or the common law. Administrators carried out relatively
clear instructions contained in these legislative and judicial sources. At the
state and local levels accountability was non-hierarchical; administrators were
accountable to legislators rather than superiors within the executive branch.
At the national level, there was some contention about whether administrators
were accountable to the president or to Congress, but most agreed that the
principles of American constitutionalism demanded executive responsibility,
which could only be attained through a unitary executive. Judicial review of
administrative action, outside of mandamus review, was broad—and access to
the courts on administrative issues was similarly broad.

Experience over a century demonstrated that regulation could be attained
through a competent administrative power without sacrificing the basic tenets
of constitutional government. But this consensus would unravel in the 1900s,
as Progressive reformers sought to restructure the constitutional system in
order to advance a new conception of administrative power. As Chapter Four
argued, the administrative state did not arrive in America in the period from
the Civil War to 1900. It is true that the Interstate Commerce Commission
was created, and the merit system established, in the 1880s, but the legislative

debates surrounding these actions and the actual provisions of these measures were not indicative of a modern administrative state. Rather, the effort to construct an administrative state was first articulated in theory by reformers such as Woodrow Wilson, Theodore Roosevelt, Frank Goodnow, Herbert Croly, and James Landis. It was then advanced during the presidency of Theodore Roosevelt and (ironically) in the contest between TR and Woodrow Wilson in 1912. There, the intra-Progressive dispute about the administrative state was resolved, and the Progressive dissenters who rejected the model of an administrative state were defeated. Judicial deference to administrative decisions began to emerge as the new conception of independent administrative power took hold in American politics.

The New Deal brought the greatest opportunity to establish a comprehensive administrative state, and as Chapter Six explained, Franklin Roosevelt worked diligently to set up an administrative state where power would be consolidated rather than separated, and where the president would bridge the gap between politics and administration by keeping the new bureaucracy within his control. Judicial review would need to remain deferential in order to keep this system of consolidated power in place. The greater number of checks on the bureaucracy, the greater the dispersion of power from the president to other political actors.

Yet at the end of the New Deal era the backlash, both from Progressives and conservatives, had risen to a crescendo. First the American Bar Association, then the Walter-Logan Act, and finally the Administrative Procedure Act sought to reintroduce constitutional checks on a bureaucracy that was increasingly viewed as a threat to basic principles such as representation, the rule of law, an independent judiciary, and the separation of powers. Even defenders of the administrative state who nevertheless sought to introduce these checks described it as a fourth branch of government that needed to be brought back into the constitutional fold. The Administrative Procedure Act, in their view, was a first step in this process, and it demanded a greater role for courts in scrutinizing administrative action as well as a greater separation of functions within administrative agencies.

This "buyer's remorse" increased in the post–New Deal period, as Chapter Seven describes. In this case, liberal and progressive reformers saw the downfall of consolidating administrative power in an unconstrained bureaucracy. These pitfalls became especially apparent as the White House became increasingly hostile to their political agenda, and as the White House devised new techniques for extending presidential control over the bureaucracy.

Their solution was to reintroduce judicial review as a means of promoting democratic participation as well as a check on administrative discretion. Even those who defended bureaucracy and an enlarged administrative state, in other words, appealed to constitutional principles to check it through revised administrative law doctrines. For the first time since the Progressive era, those who favored governmental action were against the bureaucracy and in favor of the courts reviewing administrative decisions. In all of the critical areas of administrative law: standing to sue, procedural review, review of agency legal interpretations, and review of agency policymaking, these reformers radically altered the structure of the administrative state through doctrines of judicial review.

The response by conservatives, chronicled in Chapter Eight, was to defend administrative discretion and curtail the scope of judicial review. In critical cases in administrative law, such as *Vermont Yankee*, *Chevron*, *State Farm*, and *Lujan*, they sought to keep the courts out of the business of administrative agencies. Like the liberal and progressive reformers they opposed, they too appealed to principles of American constitutionalism to justify judicial deference. Political accountability, congressional intent, the proper role of the courts versus the political branches, and other principles animated their own efforts to supplant the new era in administrative law and the return to the Progressive and New Deal era approach. As we have seen, their efforts had important but limited effects, and today administrative law is situated somewhere between the aggressive judicial review model and the hyper-deferential model.

The Challenge of the Administrative State

Through this historical survey three important conclusions can be drawn. The first is that in spite of contemporary scholarship insisting that no tension exists between the administrative state and American constitutionalism, American bureaucracy poses a serious challenge to core principles of our constitutional order. Throughout American history, from the beginning of the nation to the present day, political thinkers and actors have understood that the creation of an independent bureaucracy threatens representative self-government, the separation of powers, and the rule of law that serve as the foundation of the constitutional system. Franklin Roosevelt called the bureaucracy a "headless fourth branch of government." James Landis admitted that the Constitution may forbid rulemaking by administrative agencies and that something like congressional ratification of administrative rules might be needed to remedy the defect. Across the entire political spectrum, during the debates over the Administrative Procedure Act, representatives called our attention to the threat that bureaucracy poses to our political system. Even prominent progressives such as Louis Brandeis, Roscoe Pound, Ernst Freund, and (surprisingly) Woodrow Wilson rejected the notion that the administrative state was perfectly compatible with American constitutionalism.

These hesitations about the administrative state ensured that administrative power would be constrained for well over a century of our history, which is apparent from the debates over the Steamboat Act in 1852 and the debates over the Interstate Commerce Act and the Pendleton Act in the 1880s. In other words, contrary to the claims of many contemporary scholars that hesitation over bureaucracy in America is an extremist position, it seems to be a hallmark of American constitutionalism.[1]

Second, the generally recognized and long-standing tension between American constitutionalism and the administrative state has led to the use of administrative law as a means of solving the dilemma. Administrative law has been seen as the method by which we can have it both ways: the possession of a powerful administrative apparatus along with our Constitution's checks on power. Administrative law, it is believed, steps into the breach to remedy the threat bureaucracy poses to self-government. By ensuring that agencies follow proper procedures before making decisions, base their determinations on the record, provide for public comment and input in their rulemaking process, separate functions within their organizations, and are checked by judicial review, we can allow agencies to make policy without worrying about the constitutional implications. The Progressives who first constructed the administrative state, admittedly, did not harbor any reservations about it and therefore did not see administrative law as critical means of curing a constitutional defect. However, by the time of the New Deal, reformers on both the left and the right were frantically searching for administrative law doctrines that would restore representation, the separation of powers, and the rule of law.

This turn to administrative law as a cure for the illness of bureaucracy is a clear indication that the tension just described between bureaucracy and American constitutionalism indeed exists. It also illustrates that administrative law is not simply a forum in which bureaucracies defend their decisions before judicial tribunals. Administrative law is now the forum in which the principles of American constitutionalism are repeatedly tested, formulated, and applied. Along with major actions by Congress (such as the enactment of legislative vetoes) and presidents (such as OIRA review), litigation provides the means by which we seek to defend and restore constitutionalism to an institution that necessarily resists the formalism of law. In short, the Constitution and its core principles have a significant effect on how the administrative state functions in America as opposed to other nations. As Herman Belz explains, "In the United States the bureaucratic state has been adapted to the political culture. It has been democratized, politicized, and fragmented." This is because constitutionalism "has a configurative effect . . . in providing the forms, rhetoric, and symbols by which politics is carried on."[2] The principles of American constitutionalism have configured the administrative state differently in America. Thus we have to understand bureaucracy in America as something different from bureaucracy in other nations.

Yet it is also clear that, in spite of reformers' faith in the ability of administrative law to solve the problem of bureaucracy, administrative law has failed to provide us with a satisfactory set of doctrines that allow for administrative power to coexist with constitutional principles. If anything, the consensus in favor of the administrative state is in decline. Recent opinions by Chief Justice John Roberts and Justice Clarence Thomas have questioned whether the administrative state can be reconciled with the Constitution's framework.[3] At the same time, the decline of faith in administrative agencies among progressives and liberals reveals that both sides are dissatisfied with the way that bureaucracy functions. Just as the faith in bureaucracy has eroded over the past century, it is starting to appear as if the faith in administrative law to cure bureaucracy's defects is also dwindling. The crisis of legitimacy is back, though in many ways it never left.

Institutional Reversal

This leads to the third important conclusion of this survey, namely, the curious shift in institutional patterns. Prior to the New Deal, and throughout the nineteenth century, those who opposed the construction of centralized bureaucracy viewed the courts as critical to a proper administration of the laws. Whether the courts were applying clear statutory rules in specific cases, crafting common-law rules to facilitate a well-regulated society, or reviewing the actions of administrators, they were viewed as a bulwark against bureaucracy. As the Progressives and New Dealers sought to establish the administrative state in America, they pushed increasingly for judicial deference to administrators. Both sides, in other words, saw the courts as an obstacle to the administrative state.

This changed dramatically beginning in the 1960s, as Chapters Seven and Eight explain. As progressive and liberal reformers increasingly questioned their alliance with administrative power and revived more stringent standards of judicial review, conservatives ironically retreated to Progressive and New Deal era arguments and doctrines shutting the courts out of the administrative process. In what was likely a short-term calculus designed to keep increasingly liberal judges out of increasingly conservative administrative decisions, conservative judges made their peace with the administrative state as long as they could remove the courts from the equation. The result was a consensus in favor of the administrative state's legitimacy but an ongoing struggle for control over how it would be structured and held legally accountable.

All of these conclusions taken together point us towards an inescapable fact: reformers have worked for a century to construct, refine, and incorporate a bureaucratic system within our constitutional framework, but this effort has largely failed. The institutions that have been created over the past century have not provided us with sufficient institutional means to govern effectively and have not increased the average citizen's faith in the capacity of the political system to work properly. This raises serious questions about the future of constitutional self-government. Yet again, there are reasons to believe that this consensus and these short-term institutional patterns may once again be in flux. However, the consequence of this should not be a simple reversion to Progressive and New Deal era institutional patterns. This merry-go-round approach to the institutional configurations of the administrative state does not address the long-term, constitutional challenges that earlier reformers understood and explained clearly. Consequently these short-term calculations are unlikely to produce any stable settlement of the questions of legitimacy that continue to swirl around the administrative state. A more serious response would reevaluate the administrative state alongside other options for ensuring that the administration of law, including regulatory programs, remains within the boundaries established by the principles of American constitutionalism.

The Future of Constitutional Government

For this reason it is worthwhile to examine carefully the alternative administrative structure that existed in America prior to 1900, as the first several chapters of this book sought to do. That system relied extensively on specific legislative rules contained in statutes, along with judicial resolution of cases and controversies arising out of such rules. The administrative apparatus needed to execute the law was extensive, but it was also limited to investigation, prosecution, and enforcement.

There is a myth that this approach was emblematic of a laissez-faire society in which natural rights were used as trumps to prevent the government from carrying out critical and basic functions. As this book and other scholarship has demonstrated, that myth is utterly false. The alternative to the administrative state is not laissez-faire but a constitutional administration. Constitutional administration is in the service of representative and judicial institutions that ensure republican government, the separation of powers, and the rule of law. Through accountability to the chief executive a constitutional administration enables presidential responsibility and the efficient, uniform, and predictable enforcement of law. It guarantees a responsive and energetic government that effectively responds to majorities while respecting the legal rights of parties who are affected by regulation. These virtues are not attained by the modern administrative state, which values expertise over representation, consolidation of power over checks and balances, and ad hoc decision making rather than stability and predictability.

David Rosenbloom writes in an oft-cited text on administrative law, "American constitutionalism embraces a radically different set of values from those of managerially focused public administration."[4] This book has chronicled the development of American administrative power to show that there is a deeply rooted tension between core tenets of American constitutionalism and the rise of the modern administrative state (which, as Rosenbloom notes, "embraces a radically different set of values"). Reformers have attempted to use administrative law to remedy this tension, and as a result, Rosenbloom acknowledges, "judicial decisions have required broad changes in administrative values, decision making, organization, processes, and policy implementation. The legal dimension began to develop in the 1950s, became a major force by the 1970s, and continues to expand incrementally."[5] The administrative state has been defined by American constitutionalism, as interpreted by administrative law and applied to administrative decision making.

Rosenbloom frequently describes this development as "the judicial effort to constitutionalize public administration."[6] Has it been successful? As G. Edward White writes in his history of the New Deal and the American Constitution, the conventional view of the administrative state "tends to juxtapose constitutional objections to agencies against . . . extraconstitutional arguments on their behalf." In this telling "the constitutional objections reveal themselves to be rigid and outmoded, and they are gradually overcome or modified out of existence."[7] This view of the administrative state pits the reasonable defenders of the administrative state against its opponents, who adhere to "rigid and outmoded" constitutional doctrines. This is a conventional view of administrative law: it has overcome the objections to the administrative state and relegated its opponents to the margins. As this book has explained, however, this is an overly optimistic assessment. In the first place, it overlooks the genuine contributions that American constitutionalism has made to the development of administrative law. Without American constitutionalism, and indeed without those who opposed the creation of the administrative state, it would not operate in the manner that it does today. More fundamentally, however, the concerns about the compatibility of modern administrative government and core principles of American constitutionalism have not been "overcome or modified out of existence." These concerns are ongoing, and they are rooted in serious constitutional considerations. Attention to these considerations will be critical in shaping the future of bureaucracy in America.

NOTES

Introduction

1. *City of Arlington v. FCC*, 569 U.S. ___ (2013) (Roberts, C.J., dissenting).

2. Arthur Bestor, "The American Civil War as a Constitutional Crisis," *American Historical Review* 69 (1964): 329. I thank Johnathan O'Neill for directing me to Bestor's argument.

3. Charles J. Cooper, "Confronting the Administrative State," *National Affairs* 25 (2015): 96.

4. See especially Jonathan Turley, "The Rise of the Fourth Branch of Government," *Washington Post*, May 24, 2013 (accessed December 3, 2015); George Will, "Battling the Modern American Administrative State," *Washington Post*, November 27, 2015 (accessed December 3, 2015). See also a series of articles in *National Affairs* on the administrative state, including Christopher DeMuth, "The Regulatory State," *National Affairs* 12 (2012): 70–91; Adam J. White, "Reining in the Agencies," *National Affairs* 11 (2012): 42–58; and Cooper, "Confronting the Administrative State," 96–108.

5. James Freedman, *Crisis and Legitimacy: The Administrative Process and American Government* (New York: Cambridge University Press, 1980).

6. Daniel Ernst, *Tocqueville's Nightmare: The Administrative State Emerges in America, 1900–1940* (New York: Oxford University Press, 2014); Joanna L. Grisinger, *The Unwieldy American State: Administrative Politics since the New Deal* (New York: Cambridge University Press, 2012); Anne M. Kornhauser, *Debating the American State: Liberal Anxieties and the New Leviathan, 1930–1970* (Philadelphia: University of Pennsylvania Press, 2015).

7. John A. Rohr, *To Run a Constitution: The Legitimacy of the Administrative State* (Lawrence: University Press of Kansas, 1986); Jerry L. Mashaw, *Creating the Administrative Constitution: The Lost Hundred Years of Administrative Law* (New Haven: Yale University Press, 2012).

8. Theodore Lowi, *The End of Liberalism: The Second Republic of the United States*, 2d ed. (New York: W. W. Norton, 1979).

9. Philip Hamburger, *Is Administrative Law Unlawful?* (Chicago: University of Chicago Press, 2014).

10. Philip Hamburger frames this question in terms of "subdelegation." Ibid., 377–402. In particular, he writes, "By means of the Constitution, the people delegate power to government . . . the question is not whether the principal can delegate the power, but whether the agent can subdelegate it" (377).

Chapter One
An Improved Science of Administration:
Administration and the American Founding

1. Judith Best, "The Presidency and the Executive Power," in *The Framing and Ratification of the Constitution*, ed. Leonard W. Levy and Dennis J. Mahoney (New York: Macmillan, 1987), 210.

2. Oscar Theodore Barck, Jr., and Hugh Talmage Lefler, *Colonial America*, 2d ed. (New York: Macmillan, 1968), 238.

3. A few colonies, such as Pennsylvania and Georgia, possessed unicameral legislatures. In these instances the governor retained a council, but it exercised no legislative powers.

4. Barck and Lefler, *Colonial America*, 240.

5. Forrest McDonald, *The American Presidency: An Intellectual History* (Lawrence: University Press of Kansas, 1994), 106.

6. See Barck and Lefler, *Colonial America*, 238–40.

7. See Oliver Morton Dickerson, *American Colonial Government 1696–1765* (Cleveland: Arthur Clark, 1912), 159–60. McDonald notes, however, that the governors had the power to impound appropriations of funds and fix the salaries of public officials, powers that limited the impact of the elected assemblies' power of the purse. See McDonald, *The American Presidency*, 106.

8. Barck and Lefler, *Colonial America*, 243–44.

9. Nelson, *The Americanization of the Common Law: The Impact of Legal Change on Massachusetts Society, 1760–1830* (Cambridge, MA: Harvard University Press, 1975), 14–15.

10. L. Kinvin Wroth and Hiller B. Zobel, eds., *Legal Papers of John Adams* (Cambridge, MA: Harvard University Press, 1965), I:xxxviii–xliv, provides the material from which I draw for this description of the colonial Massachusetts judicial system.

11. McDonald, *The American Presidency*, 105. In South Carolina, for instance, the colonial governor complained in 1748 that "Almost all the places of profit or of trust are disposed of by the General Assembly" rather than by his decision. As a result, he concluded, "the people have the whole of the administration in their hands." Quoted in McDonald, *The American Presidency*, 109.

12. Barck and Lefler state that a justice of the peace's "court was regarded as a 'people's court,' for it was readily accessible to anyone who sought a hearing, the decisions were prompt, and court costs were reasonable." *Colonial America*, 246.

13. Wroth and Zobel, *Legal Papers of John Adams*, xxxix.

14. Barck and Lefler, *Colonial America*, 246.

15. Wroth and Zobel, *Legal Papers of John Adams*, xl.

16. Nelson similarly explains that "Sessions was, in effect, the county government; the only significant regulatory power it lacked was that of control over public health procedures, especially over the licensing of smallpox inoculation hospitals and the imposition of quarantines for smallpox." Nelson, *Americanization of the Common Law*, 15.

17. Wroth and Zobel, *Legal Papers of John Adams*, xlii.

18. Nelson, *Americanization of the Common Law*, 16.

19. Ibid., 17.

20. As Paul Moreno writes, "Most colonial government took place at the local level, in the townships and counties, and there the courts were the *de facto* administrative agencies. . . . Local courts and justices of the peace dealt with licensing, taxation, poor relief, internal improvements, and the range of what would later be called 'the police power'—regulation to protect the public health, safety, welfare and morals." Paul D. Moreno, *The Bureaucrat Kings: The Origins and Underpinnings of America's Bureaucratic State* (New York: ABC-Clio, 2016).

21. Nelson, *Americanization of the Common Law*, 17.

22. Ibid.

23. Moreno, *The Bureaucrat Kings*, 5.

24. Bruce Newman, *Against that "Powerful Engine of Despotism": The Fourth Amendment and General Warrants at the Founding and Today* (Lanham, MD: University Press of America, 2007), 2.

25. Ibid., 7.

26. Hamburger, *Is Administrative Law Unlawful?* 186.

27. John Adams, "Abstract of the Argument Against Writs of Assistance," April 1761, Founders Online, National Archives: founders.archives.gov/documents/Adams/05-02-02-0006-0002-0003.

28. Ibid.

29. John Adams, "Letter to William Tudor, March 29, 1817," Founders Online, National Archives: founders.archives.gov/documents/Adams/99-02-02-6735.

30. Hamburger, *Is Administrative Law Unlawful?* 189.

31. Samuel Adams, "A List of Infringements and Violations of Rights," in *A Report of the Commissioners of the City of Boston, Containing the Boston Town Records, 1770–1777* (Boston: Rockwell and Churchill, 1887), 3:100. Emphasis original; minor corrections made to spelling.

32. Edmund S. Morgan, *The Birth of the Republic*, 3d ed. (Chicago: University of Chicago Press, 1992), 90.

33. Nelson, *Americanization of the Common Law*, 18. My discussion of colonial administrative law in these paragraphs relies heavily on Nelson's analysis.

34. Ibid., 3.

35. Ibid.

36. Ibid., 30.

37. Ibid., 34.

38. Ibid., 35.

39. Barck and Lefler, *Colonial America*, 92.

40. See Henry William Elson, *History of the United States of America* (New York: Macmillan, 1904), 2:214–16.

41. *Dedham Recs.*, 3:53; cited in Kenneth A. Lockridge and Alan Kreider, "The Evolution of Massachusetts Town Government, 1640 to 1740," *William and Mary Quarterly* 23 (1966): 551.

42. Barck and Lefler, *Colonial America*, 93.

43. See Nelson, *The Americanization of the Common Law*, 14.

44. Morton Keller, *America's Three Regimes* (New York: Oxford University Press, 2007), 20.

45. Thomas Jefferson, *Writings* (Ford), 1:112.

46. James Madison, "The Federalist No. 48," in Alexander Hamilton et al., *The Federalist*, ed. Jacob E. Cooke (Hanover, NH: Wesleyan University Press, 1961), 333.

47. James Wilson, *Works*, 1:357.

48. Fletcher M. Green, *Constitutional Development in the South Atlantic States: A Study in the Evolution of Democracy* (Chapel Hill: University of North Carolina Press, 1930), 40.

49. Green, *Constitutional Development in the South Atlantic States*, 40.

50. Ibid., 42.

51. Alfred Billings Street, *The Council of Revision of the State of New York* (Albany: William Gould, 1859), 203.

52. Ibid., 204.

53. Ibid., 205, 207.

54. Ibid., 215.

55. Ibid., 217.

56. Veto Message, October 9, 1780, in C. Z. Lincoln, ed., *Messages from the Governors* (Albany: J.B. Lyon, 1909), 2:113–14. Jay's alliance with Clinton on the Council in defense of independent executive power should not be surprising, for Jay learned early about the defects of weak executive authority. As Edward Rutledge wrote to Jay in November of 1776: "your country, I think, will be safe; provided you establish a good government, with a strong executive. A pure democracy may possibly do, when patriotism is the ruling passion; but when the State abounds with rascals, as is the case with too many at this day, you must suppress a little of that popular spirit. Vest the executive powers of government in an individual, that they may have vigour, and let them be as ample as is consistent with the great outlines of freedom." Rutledge to John Jay, November 24, 1776.

57. *Town Papers, Documents and Records Relating to Towns in New Hampshire*, 846.

58. Ibid., 847.

59. Green, *Constitutional Development in the South Atlantic Colonies*, 90.

60. *Pennsylvania Archives*, Fourth Series (1900), 3:762.

61. Harry Alonzo Cushing, *History of the Transition from Provincial to Commonwealth Government in Massachusetts* (New York, 1896), 177.

62. Cushing, *From Provincial to Commonwealth*, 178.

63. Samuel Otis to Elbridge Gerry, Nov. 22, 1777, in J. T. Austin, *Life of Elbridge Gerry*, 1:266.

64. *Massachusetts Archives*, 156:131.

65. Jefferson, *Notes on the State of Virginia*, in *Writings* (Ford), 3:225.

66. Jerry Mashaw, *Creating the Administrative Constitution: The Lost One Hundred Years of American Administrative Law* (New Haven: Yale University Press, 2012), 32.

67. McDonald, *American Presidency*, 136.

68. Jay Caesar Guggenheimer, "The Development of the Executive Departments," in *Essays on the Constitutional History of the United States during the Formative Period, 1775–1789*, ed. J. Franklin Jameson (Boston: Houghton, Mifflin & Co., 1889), 119.

69. Guggenheimer, "Development of the Executive Departments," 120.

70. Ibid., 147–49.

71. Marshall, *Life of Washington*, 2:299–300, quoted in Thach, *Creation of the Presidency*, 56.

72. Ibid., 57.

73. Quoted in McDonald, *American Presidency*, 139.

74. Guggenheimer, "Development of the Executive Departments," 150.

75. Hamilton, *Works*, 1:129.

76. Jerry Mashaw, *Creating the Administrative Constitution: The Lost One Hundred Years of American Administrative Law* (New Haven, CT: Yale University Press, 2012), 33.

77. Ibid., 30. In fairness, Mashaw follows this claim by granting that several of the Constitution's provisions directly address questions of administrative structure and organization. However, in the end he emphasizes "the Constitution's silence on most matters administrative," suggesting that few issues concerning administration were resolved at the time of the Constitution's framing and ratification. Ibid., 31.

78. Max Farrand, *The Records of the Federal Convention of 1787* (1911), 1:21. In some instances throughout this chapter I have made minor corrections to spelling and grammar in the *Records* for the sake of clarity.

79. Ibid., 65.

80. Ibid.

81. Ibid.

82. Ibid.

83. Ibid., 66.

84. Ibid.

85. Ibid., 67.

86. Ibid. Emphasis added.

87. Ibid.

88. Ibid., 68, 69.

89. Ibid. 86.

90. Ibid., 85.

91. Ibid., 88.

92. Ibid.

93. Ibid., 88–89. Pierce's notes also state that "Butler was of opinion that a unity of the Executive would be necessary in order to promote dispatch; —that a plurality of Persons would never do." Ibid., 92.

94. Ibid., 96.

95. Sherman, for instance, said that an executive independent of the legislature "was in his opinion the very essence of tyranny if there was any such thing." Ibid., 68.

96. Ibid., 97.

97. Ibid., 2:343.

98. Ibid., 343–44.

99. Ibid., 367. It should be noted that the Committee's proposed Privy Council added in the legislative and judicial officers Ellsworth included in his proposed council.

100. Saikrishna Prakash, "Hail to the Chief Administrator: The Framers and the President's Administrative Powers," *Yale Law Journal* 102 (1993): 1005–6.

101. Farrand, *Records*, 2:542.

102. This suggests an alternative interpretation from that of Jerry Mashaw, who maintains that there is "extremely modest textual support for the notion that all administration was to be firmly and exclusively in the control of the President." Mashaw, *Creating the Administrative Constitution*, 31. The debates over the number of executives, as well as the consistent rejection of proposals for an executive council, all pointed to the need for unity in the executive to secure accountability. These arguments were also made consistently during the ratification debates, as this chapter later discusses.

103. Farrand, *Records*, 2:538–39.

104. Ibid., 539.

105. Though it might be noted that Sherman—the most prominent *critic* of executive power at the Convention—seconded the motion. See ibid., 627.

106. Ibid., 627. Emphasis added.

107. Guggenheimer goes so far as to claim that this proposal "was not seriously considered for a moment." Guggenheimer, "Development of the Executive Departments," 174.

108. Herbert Storing, "What the Anti-Federalists Were For," in *The Complete Anti-Federalist* (Chicago: University of Chicago Press, 1981), 1:49.

109. Murray Dry notes that "during the ratification debate no Anti-Federalist objected to the single executive. The only qualification came in the form of a frequently made argument for a council of appointment." Murray Dry, "The Case against Ratification: Anti-Federalist Constitutional Thought," in *The Framing and Ratification of the Constitution*, ed. Leonard W. Levy and Dennis J. Mahoney (New York: Macmillan, 1987), 285.

110. Federal Farmer, no. 14.

111. Ibid., no. 13.

112. Cato, no. 4.

113. The amendment was introduced on July 5, 1788. See *Elliot's Debates*, 2:408.

114. George Mason, Virginia Ratifying Convention, June 28, 1788, in *Elliot's Debates*, 3:494. Guggenheimer suggests that Mason's proposal "met with little support." Guggenheimer, "Development of the Executive Departments," 175.

115. See Remarks of Samuel Spencer, North Carolina Ratifying Convention, July 28, 1788, in *Elliot's Debates*, 4:116–17.

116. James Iredell, July 28, 1788, in *Elliot's Debates*, 4:108.

117. Ibid., 110.

118. *Federalist 39*, 250.

119. *Federalist 10*, 62. Emphasis added.

120. *Federalist 9*, 51.

121. *Federalist 57*, 384.

122. *Federalist 39*, 251. Emphasis in original.

123. Ibid.

124. Ibid.

125. The following analysis of Madison's argument for direct election of legislative representatives suggests the possible reasons for Madison's preference for direct popular election of both houses of Congress at the Constitutional Convention.

126. *Federalist 84*, 578. Emphasis in original.

127. *Federalist 22*, 146. Capitalization in original. Emphasis added.

128. Rohr, *To Run a Constitution*, 80. Emphasis in original.

129. Ibid., 79. Emphasis in original.

130. Ibid., 80. Emphasis added.

131. *Federalist 52*, 355. Emphasis added.

132. *Federalist 57*, 384.

133. See *Federalist 72*, 488: "The best security for the fidelity of mankind is to make their interest coincide with their duty."

134. For example, David B. Spence and Frank Cross argue from a "public choice" position that "agency policymaking is often desirable—and often desired by voters—irrespective of the ability of elected politicians to control what agencies do." David B. Spence and Frank Cross, "A Public Choice Case for the Administrative State," *Georgetown Law Journal* 89 (2000): 102.

135. Ibid., 131.

136. Ibid. To illustrate, Spence and Cross point to the Senate. There, the Framers sought to limit the direct influence of the people on government policy by "insulating Senate decisionmakers from direct electoral pressure." This would "create an environment conducive to deliberation and the development of expertise." But now the Senate is unable to produce this environment because it is directly elected. Thus we need administrative agencies to serve these original countermajoritarian purposes: "Although the Senate is no longer insulated from direct electoral pressure . . . administrative agencies are." Therefore, they argue, "When voters express a preference for vesting decisionmaking authority in administrative agencies, they echo the arguments of the Founders." Ibid., 132–33.

137. *Federalist 63*, 425.

138. As the famous passage of *Federalist 10* indicates, representatives "refine and enlarge the public views," implying of course that they pronounce the public voice. *Federalist 10*, 62.

139. *Federalist 57*, 385.

140. *Federalist 70*, 472.

141. This likely accounts for the specific phrasing of Madison's argument in *Federalist 52* that the legislature must have an "immediate connection" with the people. He was subtly indicating his disagreement with the indirect election of U.S. senators, and maintaining his position that legislators should be popularly elected and not indirectly appointed.

142. James Madison, speech on representation, 31 May 1787, quoted in *The Anti-Federalist Papers and the Constitutional Convention Debates*, ed. Ralph Ketcham (New York: First Mentor Printing, 1986), 41.

143. Again, Madison probably thought republican principles required even more than this. He consistently favored of the direct election of U.S. senators at the Constitutional Convention and offered a half-hearted defense of indirect election of senators in *Federalist 62*.

144. *Federalist 37*, 233.

145. *Federalist 70*, 471.

146. Ibid., 472.

147. Ibid., 473.

148. Ibid., 472.

149. Ibid., 476.

150. Ibid., 477–78.

151. Ibid., 472–73.

152. *Federalist 21*, 132.

153. *Federalist 47*, 324.

154. As he wrote: "Will it be sufficient to mark, with precision, the boundaries of these departments, in the constitution of the government, and to trust to these parchment barriers against the encroaching spirit of power? . . . [E]xperience assures us, that the efficacy of the provision has been greatly overrated; and that some more adequate defense is indispensably necessary for the more feeble, against the more powerful members of the government." *Federalist 48*: 332–33.

155. *Federalist 47*, 323

156. *Federalist 51*, 348.

157. Ibid., 349.

158. George Carey, *The Federalist: Design for a Constitutional Republic* (Urbana: University of Illinois Press, 1989), 68.

159. *Federalist 51:* 350.

160. Ibid.

161. Rohr, *To Run a Constitution*, 18. Emphasis in original.

162. Ibid.

163. *Federalist 47*, 325. Emphasis in original. This is the passage Rohr cites to support the argument being summarized.

164. Rohr, *To Run a Constitution*, 27.

165. Ibid., 83.

166. Charles de Secondat Montesquieu, *The Spirit of the Laws*, Book 11, chapter 6, "Of the Constitution of England," in *The Spirit of the Laws*, trans. and ed. Anne M. Cohler, Basia Carolyn Miller, and Harold Samuel Stone (New York: Cambridge University Press, 1989), 156.

167. *Federalist 47*, 326. Emphasis added.

168. Ibid., 325.

Chapter Two
Well-Regulated and Free: Administration and
Constitutionalism in the Early Republic

1. Some of the material contained in this chapter is based upon earlier publications: Joseph Postell, "Regulation, Administration, and the Rule of Law in the Early Republic," in *Freedom and the Rule of Law*, ed. Anthony A. Peacock (Lanham, MD: Lexington Books, 2010): 41–70; Joseph Postell, "The Right Kind of Regulation: How the Founders Thought about Regulation," in *Rediscovering Political Economy*, ed. Joseph Postell and Bradley C. S. Watson (Lanham, MD: Lexington Books, 2011): 209–30; and Joseph Postell, "Regulation during the American Founding: Achieving Liberalism and Republicanism," *American Political Thought* 5 (2016): 80–108.

2. Quoted in John Duffy, "Hogs, Dogs, and Dirt: Public Health in Early Pittsburgh," *Pennsylvania Magazine of History and Biography* 87, no. 3 (1963): 295, 296.

3. One newspaper wrote in 1857 that "this smoke," which "pervades the atmosphere to a large extent," is "from the carbon, sulphur, and iodine, contained in it, highly favorable to lung and cutaneous diseases." Quoted in ibid., 296.

4. Jonathan Hughes, *The Government Habit Redux: Economic Controls from Colonial Times to the Present* (Princeton, NJ: Princeton University Press, 1991), 48.

5. Quoted in Lawrence M. Friedman, *A History of American Law*, 2d ed. (New York: Simon and Schuster, 1985), 213.

6. L. Ray Gunn, *The Decline of Authority: Public Economic Policy and Political Development in New York State, 1800–1860* (Ithaca, NY: Cornell University Press, 1988), 101, 114.

7. Louis Hartz, *Economic Policy and Democratic Thought: Pennsylvania, 1776–1860* (Cambridge, MA: Harvard University Press, 1948), 56.

8. James Neal Primm, *Economic Policy in the Development of a Western State: Missouri, 1820–1860* (Cambridge, MA: Harvard University Press, 1954), 115–20.

9. See William Nelson, *The Americanization of the Common Law: The Impact of Legal Change on Massachusetts Society, 1760–1830* (Cambridge, MA: Harvard University Press, 1975), 121–22.

10. Friedman, *History of American Law*, 184–85; William Novak, *The People's Welfare: Law and Regulation in Nineteenth-Century America* (Chapel Hill: University of North Carolina Press, 1996), 15.

11. See generally William Novak, *The People's Welfare*.

12. Erwin C. Surrency, "'Calculated to Promote the General Good': The Development of Local Government in Georgia Towns and Cities," *Georgia Historical Quarterly* 84, no. 3 (2000): 403. The ordinance is dated "around 1807" because it is unclear when it was actually enacted, though it was included in an 1807 publication of the ordinances of the city council.

13. Quoted in Duffy, "Public Health in Early Pittsburgh," 297.

14. Ibid., 300.

15. Mary Fulton Green, "A Profile of Columbia in 1850," *South Carolina Historical Magazine* 70, no. 2 (1969): 108–9, 110.

16. Friedman, *History of American Law*, 185.

17. Oscar and Mary Handlin, *Commonwealth: A Study of the Role of Government in the American Economy: Massachusetts, 1774–1861* (Cambridge, MA: Harvard University Press, 1947), 64–68; Louis Hartz, *Economic Policy and Democratic Thought*, 204–5.

18. Friedman, *History of American Law*, 183; Novak, *The People's Welfare*, 15.

19. Handlin and Handlin, *Commonwealth*, 69–74; Hartz, *Economic Policy and Democratic Thought*, 206–7; Friedman, *History of American Law*, 185; Nelson, *Americanization of the Common Law*, 123–24.

20. Nelson, *Americanization of the Common Law*, 130; Handlin and Handlin, *Commonwealth*, 252–54; Hartz, *Economic Policy and Democratic Thought*, 208; Novak, *The People's Welfare*, 155–56.

21. Friedman, *History of American Law*, 179–80. Pennsylvania's charter to the first state bank it incorporated required it to lend $500,000 to the state at no higher than 6 percent interest. See Hartz, *Economic Policy and Democratic Thought*, 55.

22. See Friedman, *History of American Law*, 187.

23. Harry N. Scheiber, "Private Rights and Public Power: American Law, Capitalism, and the Republican Polity in Nineteenth-Century America," *Yale Law Journal* 107 (1997): 845.

24. John A. Fairlie, *Local Government in Counties, Towns and Villages* (New York: Century Co., 1906), 33. I rely on Fairlie's account (33–38), for much of the discussion of selection of local administrative officers.

25. Ibid., 34–35.

26. Virginia stands alone as an exception. In its constitutional convention of 1829–1830, an extensive debate over local government occurred, in which John Marshall and James Madison participated. Through their influence the traditional system of county courts and justices of the peace selected through appointment was retained. See ibid., 40.

27. Sunbury was a thriving port city during the 1780s in Georgia, but today is essentially uninhabited.

28. Surrency, "Calculated to Promote the General Good," 390.

29. Augusta, incorporated in 1789, was also empowered to select aldermen and a mayor in the same manner as Savannah. However, Savannah's 1798 charter switched it to the commissioner system, and an intendant could be appointed by the town commissioners. See ibid., 393–94.

30. Ibid., 391. It is clear that this phrase imposed a limitation on the kinds of bylaws that the local authorities could enact. See ibid., 399.

31. James H. Stone, "Economic Conditions in Macon, Georgia in the 1830s," *Georgia Historical Quarterly* 54 (1970): 210. Like other towns in Georgia, Macon moved by 1834 to a new form, consisting of a mayor, seven aldermen, and some minor officials. See ibid., 211.

32. Mary Fulton Green, "A Profile of Columbia in 1850," 108.

33. Gunn, *The Decline of Authority*, 84–85, 200–202.

34. Surrency, "Calculated to Promote the General Good," 392.

35. While the evidence is murky, Surrency suspects that "culprits were fined at the regular council meetings, and special sessions were probably called for the purpose of hearing cases." Ibid., 405.

36. Ibid., 404.

37. Stone, "Economic Conditions in Macon," 211.

38. Mary Fulton Green, "A Profile of Columbia in 1850," 116.

39. Duffy, "Public Health in Early Pittsburgh," 297–98.

40. Ibid., 303.

41. Hamburger, *Is Administrative Law Unlawful?* 101–2. See also 390–91.

42. Tocqueville, *Democracy in America*, trans. Delba Winthrop and Harvey C. Mansfield (Chicago: University of Chicago Press, 2000), 69.

43. Leonard White, *The Federalists: A Study in Administrative History*, paperback ed. (New York: The Free Press, 1965), 448.

44. Hartz, *Economic Policy and Democratic Thought*, 150–51.

45. Ibid., 152.

46. Quoted in ibid., 153.

47. Ibid., 159.

48. Ibid., 159–60.

49. Gunn, *The Decline of Authority*, 81.

50. Ibid., 85, 89.

51. Ibid., 199–200.

52. Ibid., 82.

53. Ibid., 90–91.

54. Quoted in ibid., 92.

55. Cass R. Sunstein, "Nondelegation Canons," *University of Chicago Law Review* 67 (2000): 322.

56. Paul D. Moreno, *The Bureaucrat Kings* (New York: ABC-Clio, 2016), 32. Italics original.

57. Tocqueville, *Democracy in America*, 70.

58. Ibid., 73.

59. See Novak, *The People's Welfare*, 173, 181. As Novak explains, in Massachusetts informers received half of the fine levied on those who sold liquor without a license: "six pounds for selling without a license, forty shillings for allowing gambling."

60. Handlin and Handlin, *Commonwealth*, 74, 95.

61. Ibid., 96.

62. *Austin v. Murray*, 127.

63. Ibid., 125.

64. As Thomas Cooley later summarized in his famous *Constitutional Limitations*: "Municipal by-laws must also be reasonable. Whenever they appear not to be so, the court must, as a matter of law, declare them void." Thomas M. Cooley, *A Treatise on the Constitutional Limitations Which Rest upon the Legislative Power of the States of the American Union* (Boston: Little, Brown & Co., 1868), 200.

65. W. F. Willoughby, *Principles of Judicial Administration* (Washington, DC: The Brookings Institution, 1929), 18.

66. Hartz, *Economic Policy and Democratic Thought*, 33.

67. Ibid., 310.

68. Gunn, *The Decline of Authority*, 83.

69. Ibid., 90.

70. Ellis W. Hawley, "The New Deal State and Anti-Bureaucratic Tradition," in *The New Deal and Its Legacy: Critique and Reappraisal*, ed. Robert Eden (Westport, CT:

Greenwood Press, 1989), 78. This is a central thesis of Stephen Skowronek's important book *Building a New American State: The Expansion of National Administrative Capacities, 1877–1920* (New York: Cambridge University Press, 1979), 3–35.

71. Tocqueville, *Democracy in America*, 67.

72. Mashaw, *Creating the Administrative Constitution*, 5.

73. Ibid., 45.

74. Kenneth Culp Davis, "A New Approach to Delegation," *University of Chicago Law Review* 36 (1969): 719–20.

75. Ibid., 719–20.

76. Hamburger, *Is Administrative Law Unlawful?* 84.

77. Ibid., 87.

78. Gary Lawson, "Delegation and Original Meaning," *Virginia Law Review* 88 (2002): 398.

79. Ibid., 400.

80. White, *The Federalists*, 53.

81. See F. W. Taussig, *The Tariff History of the United States*, 6th ed. (New York: G.P. Putnam's Sons, 1914), 1–108; in particular, for the 1789 Act see 14–15, and for later acts see 15–20.

82. *Annals of Congress*, 3:239–40 (December 7, 1791).

83. Ibid., 698–99 (November 19, 1792).

84. Ibid., 700 (November 19, 1792). Emphasis added.

85. Leonard D. White, *The Federalists: A Study in Administrative History, 1789–1801*, paperback ed. (New York: Free Press, 1965), 78.

86. Act of Feb. 20, 1792, ch. 7, § 1, 1 Stat. 232, cited in Lawson, "Delegation and Original Meaning," 403.

87. White, *The Federalists*, 68.

88. Cited in ibid., 69.

89. *Annals of Congress*, 3:351 (January 27, 1792). Italics added.

90. Ibid., 703 (November 20, 1792).

91. Ibid., 696 (November 19, 1792).

92. Ibid., 722 (November 21, 1792).

93. Ibid., 697 (November 19, 1792). See also Representative Livingston's repeated invocation of the nondelegation doctrine in a 1796 debate over the propriety of giving the Secretary of the Treasury power to remit fines. It is noteworthy that Fisher Ames, the primary respondent to Livingston's argument, countered by denying that this was legislative in nature, not by discrediting the nondelegation doctrine as such. See *Annals*, VI, 2284ff (February 24, 1796).

94. White, *The Federalists*, 77.

95. Mashaw, *Creating the Administrative Constitution*, 44.

96. White, *The Federalists*, 200.

97. Mashaw, *Creating the Administrative Constitution*, 90.

98. Mashaw concedes that "There is little doubt that the embargo, as established by statute and carried out in practice, violated virtually every constitutional principle that

the Jeffersonian Republicans held dear." Ibid., 96. The only sense in which the embargo is instructive was in its use of judicial review to *limit* administrative power, a practice that *was* in keeping with other more measured administrative arrangements during the early republic.

99. Paul D. Moreno, *The Bureaucrat Kings* (New York: ABC-Clio, 2016), 99.

100. Washington to de Moustier, May 25, 1789, in *Writings of George Washington*, ed. W.C. Ford, 11:397–98.

101. White, *The Federalists*, 448.

102. *Annals of Congress*, 3:937–38.

103. Ibid., 941.

104. Ibid.

105. Ibid., 942.

106. Ibid.

107. Ibid.

108. After a thorough examination of Washington's actions, Steven Calabresi and Christopher Yoo conclude that "Washington's statements and administrative practice strongly support the view that the President is responsible for execution of all federal law and thus may superintend all those authorized to execute it." Steven Calabresi and Christopher Yoo, "The Unitary Executive during the First Half-Century," *Case Western Reserve Law Review* 47 (1997): 1489.

109. White, *The Federalists*, 27.

110. As James Hart explains, these letters clearly demonstrated Washington's "clear conception . . . of the presidential function of over-all administrative management." James Hart, *The American Presidency in Action* (New York: Macmillan, 1948), 135.

111. See White, *The Federalists*, 32–36 (quote to Secretary Knox, 33).

112. Calabresi and Yoo, "First Half-Century," 1483. In the pages that follow I rely on several examples invoked by Calabresi and Yoo in this article.

113. See White, *The Federalists*, 448.

114. Ibid., 31.

115. Adams to Pickering, October 31, 1797, quoted in ibid., 29.

116. Quoted in ibid., 30.

117. Ibid., 17–18.

118. Ibid., 19.

119. Quoted in ibid., 35.

120. Calabresi and Yoo, "First Half-Century," 1498.

121. *Ex Parte Gilchrist*, 10 F. Cas. 355 (1808).

122. Mashaw, *Creating the Administrative Constitution*, 108.

123. Calabresi and Yoo, "First Half-Century," 1511.

124. Monroe to Rep. Adam Seybert, June 10, 1812, quoted in Leonard White, *The Jeffersonians: A Study in Administrative History, 1801–1829* (New York: Macmillan, 1956), 74.

125. 1 Op. Att'y Gen. (1823), 625.

126. See Calabresi and Yoo, "First Half-Century," 1519–20.

127. White, *The Jeffersonians*, vii.

128. Thomas Jefferson to Adamantios Koraes, October 31, 1823, in *The Writings of Thomas Jefferson*, ed. H. A. Washington (Washington, DC: Taylor and Maury, 1854), 7: 321.

129. Calabresi and Yoo, "First Half-Century," 1472–73.

130. *Annals of Congress*, 1:492.

131. Ibid., 542.

132. Ibid., 516.

133. Ibid., 531.

134. Ibid., 532.

135. Ibid., 548–49.

136. Cited in White, *The Federalists*, 21 (n.20).

137. James Kent, *Commentaries on American Law* (1826), 310.

138. Joseph Story, *Commentaries on the Constitution of the United States* (Boston: Hilliard, Gray, and Company, 1833), 3:395

139. Madison to Edward Coles, October 15, 1834, in *Letters and Other Writings of James Madison* (Philadelphia: J.B. Lippincott & Co., 1865), 4:368.

140. Jefferson to Madison, November 29, 1820.

141. Madison to Jefferson, December 10, 1820.

142. Mashaw, *Creating the Administrative Constitution*, 18.

143. Mashaw himself refers to "the significant power of common law remedies and local juries to stop administration in its tracks" in the context of the embargo, one page after implying that such remedies were unimportant. Ibid., 19. He also explains that common law "damage actions against officers . . . involved a court's de novo determination of whether an officer had acted legally and reasonably under the circumstances." Ibid., 24.

144. This happened with the Embargo Act and many other laws. See ibid., 104–12.

145. White, *The Federalists*, 425–26.

146. Ibid., 428.

147. Ibid., 415.

148. Ibid., 203.

149. Ibid., 253.

150. Ibid., 441, 443.

151. Ibid., 442–43.

152. Ibid., 446.

153. Ibid., 455.

154. Ibid., 439.

155. Ibid., 413.

156. *Otis v. Watkins*, 13 U.S. (9 Cranch) 339 (1815).

157. Ibid., 358.

158. Marshall explicitly stated that this standard of reasonableness did not require that the collector's judgment be *correct*. If it were erroneous, but arrived at in a reasonable manner, it would still be lawful.

159. Ann Woolhandler, "Judicial Deference to Administrative Action—A Revisionist History," *Administrative Law Journal* 43 (1991): 206.

160. *Little v. Barreme*, 6 U.S. 170 (1804).

Chapter Three
Executive-Centered Administration: Administrative Law and Constitutionalism during the Jacksonian Era

1. See Brian Balogh, *A Government Out of Sight: The Mystery of National Authority in Nineteenth-Century America* (New York: Cambridge University Press, 2009); Laura Jensen, *Patriots, Settlers, and the Origins of American Social Policy* (New York: Cambridge University Press, 2003); Jerry L. Mashaw, *Creating the Administrative Constitution: The Lost One Hundred Years of American Administrative Law* (New Haven: Yale University Press, 2012).

2. Ann Woolhandler, "Judicial Deference to Administrative Action—A Revisionist History," *Administrative Law Review* 43 (1991): 216.

3. Leonard D. White, *The Jacksonians: A Study in Administrative History, 1829–1861* (New York: Macmillan, 1954), 438.

4. White, *The Jacksonians*, 488–94.

5. Ibid., 502–3.

6. Ibid., 437.

7. Andrew Jackson, 1833 Annual Message to Congress.

8. See Mashaw, *Creating the Administrative Constitution*, 190. "Beyond these rudimentary inspection requirements, the 1838 statute relied on enhanced civil and criminal liability to promote steamboat safety. . . . [T]he statute relied heavily on traditional nonadministrative deterrence strategies—enhanced common law civil liability and criminal penalties for specified misconduct."

9. Sections 3–5, 12–14.

10. Sections 18 and 29.

11. White, *The Jacksonians*, 445.

12. Mashaw, *Creating the Administrative Constitution*, 187.

13. Ibid., 193, 194.

14. *Statutes at Large*, 32nd Congress, 1st Session (1852), 70.

15. *Congressional Globe*, Senate, 32nd Congress, 1st Session, July 9, 1852, 1710.

16. Ibid., 72.

17. Ibid., 1669.

18. Ibid., 1709.

19. Ibid.

20. Ibid., 1710.

21. Ibid., 2344–45.

22. Ibid., 2428.

23. Ibid.

24. *Statutes at Large*, 32nd Congress, 1st Session (1852), 61.

25. Philip Hamburger also rejects Mashaw's contention that the Steamboat Act is a significant first step towards an administrative state, but he does so on different grounds. Hamburger rests his case on the fact that the inspectors bound subjects on waters that were not within the jurisdiction of the United States, rather than focusing on the minimal and limited nature of the powers granted to the inspectors in the statute. See Hamburger, *Is Administrative Law Unlawful?* 106–7, 259, 526.

26. *Congressional Globe*, 32nd Congress, 1st Session (1852), 1710–11.

27. Decisions of the local inspectors could be appealed to the supervising inspectors, thus providing internal administrative appeals for initial decisions.

28. Mashaw, *Creating the Administrative Constitution*, 199.

29. Jefferson Davis, *Letters, Papers and Speeches*, 2:5 (Dec. 19, 1850), quoted in White, *The Jacksonians*, 145.

30. White, *The Jacksonians*, 147.

31. Henry Clay, *Works*, vol. 4, March 12, 1829, cited in White, *The Jacksonians*, 330.

32. White, *The Jacksonians,* 307. White relied on newspaper reports suggesting "a total of 919 removals out of 10,093 officeholders or somewhat less than 10 per cent." Ibid., 308. Thus, during the Jacksonian period, he concludes, "Two personnel systems were thus in operation in the public service. The patronage system held the public attention, but it was primarily the career system that enabled the government to maintain its armed forces, to collect its revenue, to operate its land system, to keep its accounts and audit its expenditures." White, *The Jacksonians*, 362. "Amidst the clamor for removals and partisan appointments to resulting vacancies," White concludes, "a hard core of experienced men consequently remained steadily at work." Ibid., 349.

33. President Polk lamented: "Will the pressure for office never cease! It is one year to-day since I entered on the duties of my office, and still the pressure for office has not abated. I most sincerely wish that I had no offices to bestow." Polk, March 4, 1846, in *The Diary of James K. Polk During his Presidency, 1845 to 1849*, vol. 1, ed. Milo Milton Quaife (Chicago, 1910), 261.

34. See White, *The Jacksonians*, 97.

35. Ibid., 115–18.

36. Ibid., 97.

37. Ibid., 395–96. Emphasis in original.

38. Ibid., 121.

39. Ibid., 534ff.

40. Ibid., 123.

41. Polk, *Diary*, 4:114 (September 1, 1848), quoted in White, *The Jacksonians*, 348.

42. White, *The Jacksonians*, 363–75 (quote, 365).

43. 10 *Statutes at Large* 189, Section 3.

44. See White, *The Jacksonians*, 371.

45. Ibid.

46. See Steven G. Calabresi and Christopher S. Yoo, "The Unitary Executive during the Second Half-Century," *Harvard Journal of Law & Public Policy* 26 (2003): 672.

47. Ibid., 678–79.

48. Ibid., 680.

49. The removal practices of Presidents Tyler, Polk, Taylor, Fillmore, Pierce, and Buchanan are described in Calabresi and Yoo, 686, 691–92, 696–97, 710–11.

50. Calabresi and Yoo, "Second Half-Century," 673.

51. 4 Op. Att'y Gen. (1842), 1–2, quoted in ibid., 679.

52. Remarks of Senator Calhoun in the U.S. Senate, Feb. 9, 1835, quoted in Morehead Committee Report of 1844, p. 59.

53. As Daniel Webster explained, "The law itself vacates the office, and gives the means of rewarding a friend without the exercise of the power of removal at all. Here

is increased power, with diminished responsibility." Remarks of Daniel Webster, Feb. 16, 1835, quoted in Morehead Committee on Retrenchment, 1844, p. 115.

54. See Forrest McDonald, *The American Presidency* (Lawrence: University Press of Kansas, 1994), 255–56.

55. Remarks of Senator Calhoun, Feb. 9, 1835, quoted in Morehead Committee on Retrenchment, 1844, 78.

56. Ibid., 64.

57. Ibid., 65–77.

58. Ibid., 77–78.

59. Remarks of Senator Ewing, Feb. 14, 1835, quoted in Morehead Committee on Retrenchment, 1844, 102–3.

60. Ibid., 106.

61. Ewing's analysis, along with other Whigs', perhaps points to the reasons Hamilton declares that the Senate would be required to concur in removals in *Federalist* no. 77.

62. Remarks of Senator Ewing, Feb. 14, 1835, quoted in Morehead Committee on Retrenchment, 1844, p. 109.

63. Remarks of Daniel Webster, Feb. 16, 1835, quoted in Morehead Report, 117.

64. Ibid.

65. Ibid., 119.

66. Cf. James Madison, *The Federalist*, no. 41: "If the different parts of the same instrument ought to be so expounded, as to give meaning to every part which shall bear it; shall one part of the same sentence be excluded altogether from a share in the meaning . . . ? For what purpose could the enumeration of particular powers be inserted, if these and all others were meant to be included in the preceding general power?"

67. Remarks of Senator Webster, Feb. 16, 1835, in Morehead Committee Report, 120–21.

68. Charles Francis Adams, "An Appeal from the New to the Old Whigs" (Boston: Russel, Odiorne & Co., 1835), p. 1.

69. Adams cites many statements of the Founders in favor of the President's removal power on pp. 27ff.

70. Adams, "Appeal from the New to the Old Whigs," 5. Emphasis in original.

71. Adams, "Appeal from the New to the Old Whigs," 9–11.

72. Morehead Committee Report of 1844, 28.

73. Ibid., 27. Italics added.

74. Ibid.

75. Ibid., 55.

76. Ibid.

77. President Lincoln, for example, removed 1,457 of the 1,639 offices that were under his control. See McDonald, *The American Presidency*, 320.

78. Ibid., 319; White, *The Jacksonians*, 86.

79. See Calabresi and Yoo, "Second Half-Century," 679.

80. Quoted in White, *The Jacksonians*, 86. In spite of his reputation and public pronouncements, Harrison also asserted his authority when he thought it necessary. At a cabinet meeting, reportedly, Webster informed Harrison that the Cabinet had decided

James Wilson to be the governor of Iowa. In response, Harrison wrote out the words "William Henry Harrison" on a piece of paper and asked Webster to read it aloud. After Webster did so, Harrison stood and allegedly said "And William Henry Harrison, President of the United States, tells you, gentlemen, that, by ———, John Chambers shall be Governor of Iowa." White, *The Jacksonians*, 47–48.

81. Ibid., 93.

82. Quoted in ibid., 43.

83. See Calabresi and Yoo, "Second Half-Century," 683.

84. Calabresi and Yoo, "First Half-Century," 1537.

85. Ibid., 1536 n. 298.

86. Quoted in ibid.

87. 3 Stat. 266, sec. 16 (April 10, 1816).

88. See White, *The Jacksonians*, 35. White quotes Jackson's letter to Duane, which states "it is not my intention to interfere with the independent exercise of the discretion committed to you by law over this subject."

89. Jackson, "Protest," quoted in ibid., 37–38.

90. Richard J. Ellis, *The Development of the American Presidency* (New York: Routledge, 2012), 314.

91. Clay's resolution declared that "the President has assumed the exercise of a power over the treasury of the United States, not granted to him by the constitution and laws, and dangerous to the liberties of the people." Quoted in Calabresi and Yoo, "First Half-Century," 1544.

92. Ellis, *Development of the American Presidency*, 315.

93. Quoted in Calabresi and Yoo, "First Half-Century," 1548.

94. Quoted in ibid., 1549.

95. Quoted in ibd., 1550.

96. Quoted in ibid., 1553.

97. See ibid., 1554–57.

98. As Calabresi and Yoo state, "even critics of unitary executive theory have been forced to concede that Jackson's removal of Duane represents a monument to the development of the unitary executive." Ibid., 1558–59.

99. Quoted in Calabresi and Yoo, "Second Half-Century," 693.

100. See ibid., 702–3. Calabresi and Yoo maintain that Crittenden's position is indefensible and therefore should not be weighed heavily in considering the historical evidence in favor of, or against, the unitary executive.

101. Including Reverdy Johnson, who served under President Zachary Taylor, and Caleb Cushing, who served under President Franklin Pierce. See ibid., 698, 706–8, for a fuller explication of their arguments.

102. White, *The Jacksonians*, 85.

103. *Kendall v. Stokes*, 44 U.S. (3 How) 87 (1845). *Kendall v. U.S.* is discussed in the context of mandamus later in this chapter.

104. Mashaw, *Creating the Administrative Constitution*, 214.

105. *Cary v. Curtis*, 44 U.S. (3 How.) 236 (1845).

106. Ibid., 252–53.

107. Ibid., 256.

108. Ibid., 253.

109. Ibid.

110. Ibid., 261.

111. Ibid., 263.

112. Ibid., 264.

113. Ibid., 265.

114. Ibid., 266.

115. See Ann Woolhandler, "Revisionist History," 222.

116. *Bartlett v. Kane*, 57 U.S. (16 How.) 263 (1853).

117. Ibid., 272.

118. *Decatur v. Paulding* 39 U.S. (14 Pet.) 497 (1840), 515.

119. I am grateful to Aditya Bamzai for this insight.

120. See Aditya Bamzai, "The Origins of Judicial Deference to Executive Interpretation," *Yale Law Journal* 126 (2016–17), 952–56.

121. *Converse v. Burgess*, 59 U.S. (18 How.) 413 (1855). See Ann Woolhandler, "Revisionist History," 223.

122. See *Greely v. Thompson*, 51 U.S. (10 How.) 225 (1850). In this case the Department presented an interpretation of the statute regarding the timing of the valuation, and a collector's refusal to require actual examination by appraisers. See Woolhandler, "Revisionist History," 223.

123. Woolhandler, "Revisionist History," 224.

124. *Kendall v. Stokes*, 37 U.S. (12 Pet.) 524 (1838).

125. Ibid., 610.

126. *Decatur*, 497.

127. Ibid., 515.

128. Mashaw, *Creating the Administrative Constitution*, 212.

129. Aditya Bamzai, "Origins of Judicial Deference," 953.

130. Mashaw, *Creating the Administrative Constitution*, 216.

131. Woolhandler, "Revisionist History," 199.

132. Ibid., 201. Woolhandler notes that "the judicially activist de novo method of review was at its height during the Marshall years, whereas the deferential res judicata model of review was at its height during the Taney years and then suffered a decline during and after Reconstruction." Ibid., 216.

133. Ibid., 230.

134. Mashaw, *Creating the Administrative Constitution*, 215.

135. *Bartlett v. Kane*, 272.

136. Woolhandler, "Revisionist History," 221.

137. Mashaw, *Creating the Administrative Constitution*, 216.

138. Kenneth M. Holland, "Roger Taney," in *American Political Thought: The Philosophic Dimension of American Statesmanship*, ed. Morton J. Frisch and Richard G. Stevens, 3d ed. (New Brunswick, NJ: Transaction Publishers, 2011), 226. James B. O'Hara has similarly argued that "Of the twenty-three Justices before Taney, only Samuel Chase had hinted that the constitutional decisions of the Court had to be founded

on the text of the Constitution, or on the text of laws, rather than on a 'higher' law believed to be from God. Taney set out on a new course. He was the first constitutional *positivist* to serve on the Court." "Out of the Shadows: Roger Brooke Taney as Chief Justice," *Journal of Supreme Court History* (1998): 29.

139. Ibid., 226.

140. 7 *Official Opinions of the Attorneys General of the United States*, 469–70 (August 31, 1855), quoted in White, *The Jacksonians*, 39.

Chapter Four
The Beginning of Bureaucracy?
Administrative Power after the Civil War

1. See, for instance, David Rosenbloom and Rosemary O'Leary, *Public Administration and Law*, 2d ed. (New York: Marcel Dekker, 1996), 2:22. "The American administrative state began to develop in earnest in the 1880s. . . . The Interstate Commerce Commission (ICC), generally viewed as the first federal independent regulatory agency, was created in 1887."

2. James Landis, *The Administrative Process* (New Haven: Yale University Press, 1938), 10.

3. Mashaw, *Creating the Administrative Constitution*, 233. Also, "Congressional abdication of regulatory policy making is the arena that tends most to exercise modern critics of the administrative state. And there is a tendency to imagine a pre-New Deal or pre-Progressive era world in which national regulatory policy, if adopted at all, was specified clearly by statute. As we have seen repeatedly . . . this image is false." Ibid., 244.

4. Ibid., 242.

5. Quoted in ibid., 244.

6. See Rosenbloom, *Public Administration and Law*, 265.

7. Stephen Skowronek, *Building a New American State: The Expansion of National Administrative Capacities, 1877–1920* (New York: Cambridge University Press, 1979), 30–31.

8. Four years earlier the National Currency Act also limited the president's removal power. See 12 *Stat.* 665 (1863).

9. *Congressional Globe*, 39th Congress, 2nd Session, 1340 (1867).

10. Andrew Johnson, "Veto of the Tenure of Office Act," March 2, 1867, in *The Papers of Andrew Johnson*, ed. Paul H. Bergeron (Knoxville: University of Tennessee Press, 1995), 12:95.

11. Andrew Johnson to the U.S. Senate, December 12, 1867, in *The Papers of Andrew Johnson*, 13:336

12. Mashaw, *Creating the Administrative Constitution*, 235.

13. Calabresi and Yoo, "The Unitary Executive during the Second Half-Century," 737.

14. Ibid., 746.

15. Typically the jurisdictional question arose when a claimant would allege that the government did not actually own the land when it issued the patent to a rival claimant. See Woolhandler, "Revisionist History," 218.

16. See Aditya Bamzai, "Origins of Judicial Deference to Executive Interpretation," *Yale Law Journal* 126 (2016–17), 962–65.

17. See Thomas W. Merrill, "Article III, Agency Adjudication, and the Origins of the Appellate Review Model of Administrative Law," *Columbia Law Review* 111 (2011): 940.

18. See Mashaw, *Creating the Administrative Constitution*, 136–37; Woolhandler, "Revisionist History," 218.

19. Woolhandler, "Revisionist History," 219.

20. Ibid.

21. Aditya Bamzai has recently drawn attention to the importance of the 1875 Judiciary Act in "Origins of Judicial Deference to Executive Interpretation," especially 962–65.

22. *Johnson v. Towsley*, 80 U.S. 72 (1871).

23. Ibid., 83.

24. Ibid., 86.

25. Ibid., 84.

26. Ibid., 86.

27. Ibid., 85.

28. Mashaw, *Creating the Administrative Constitution*, 248.

29. While the wording of these provisions varied slightly, they all tended to say the same thing. In 1819 Congress granted the circuit courts "original cognizance, as well in equity as the law, of all actions, suits, controversies, and cases, arising under" the patent and copyright laws. The "arising under" the laws phrase was the critical portion of each of these statutory provisions.

30. Bamzai, "Origins of Judicial Deference to Executive Interpretation," 955–58.

31. John Duffy, "Administrative Common Law in Judicial Review," *Texas Law Review* 77 (1998): 121–22.

32. Ann Woolhandler writes that "in the area of customs collection, the assumpsit action against customs and internal revenue officers who received payment under protest persisted, with congressional blessing, despite development of some administrative remedies." And "After Congress provided for general question jurisdiction in 1875, the trespass action against state officials for violation of federal norms became increasingly common." Woolhandler, "Revisionist History," 238n.209, 239.

33. Ari Hoogenboom, *Outlawing the Spoils: A History of the Civil Service Reform Movement, 1865–1883* (Urbana: University of Illinois Press, 1968), 10.

34. Soo-Young Park, *Who Is Our Master? Congressional Debates during Civil Service Reforms* (PhD Diss., Virginia Polytechnic Institute and State University, 2005), 116.

35. Charles Merriam, *American Political Ideas: Studies in the Development of American Political Thought, 1865–1917* (New York: Macmillan, 1920), 276.

36. Prominent among these scholarly treatments is Stephen Skowronek, *Building a New American State*, chapters 1–3.

37. Opinion of Attorney General Akerman on Questions Propounded by the Civil Service Commission, August 31, 1871, in *The Executive Documents for the Second Session of the Forty-Second Congress* (Washington, DC: Government Printing Office, 1872), 26.

38. Ibid., 27.

39. Ibid., 29.

40. Ibid.

41. Matthew Carpenter, January 10, 1872, in *The Congressional Globe: Containing the Debates and Proceedings of the Second Session Forty-Second Congress* (Washington, DC: Congressional Globe, 1872), 333.

42. Henry Snapp, January 17, 1872, in *Congressional Globe*, Second Session, Forty-Second Congress, 444.

43. Ibid.

44. Ibid.

45. Ibid.

46. Ibid., 445.

47. Matthew Carpenter, January 18, 1872, in *Congressional Globe*, Forty-Second Congress, Second Session, 453.

48. Ibid.

49. Ibid., 454.

50. Ibid.

51. Ibid.

52. Ibid.

53. *Congressional Globe*, 47th Congress, 2nd Session (December 27, 1882), 661.

54. Ibid. (December 15, 1882), 323.

55. Ibid., 355. Emphasis added.

56. Skowronek, *Building a New American State*, 78.

57. Ibid., 68.

58. Lyman Trumbull, December 11, 1871, in *The Congressional Globe: Containing The Debates and Proceedings of the Second Session Forty-Second Congress* (Washington, DC: Congressional Globe, 1872), 52. See also the speech of Reuben Fenton, Republican Senator from New York and supporter of civil service reform, on January 8, 1872: "I am aware that principles must be enforced in a large measure through party organization, and in no step toward civil service reform would I commit a wrong against the former or impair the latter. The very essence of popular government lies in associated political actions, and the cause which embarrasses the one strikes at the other." In *Congressional Globe*, Forty-Second Congress, Second Session, 300.

59. *Congressional Record*, 47th Congress, 2nd Session, 206. Emphasis added.

60. In further support of this interpretation, it is worth noting that Senator Pendleton himself introduced a bill proposing "the direct election of officers located outside of Washington," according to Ari Hoogenboom. See Hoogenboom, *Outlawing the Spoils*, 219.

61. Skowronek, *Building a New American State*, 69.

62. *Congressional Record*, 47th Congress, 2nd Session (December 15, 1882), 316

63. Donald P. Moynihan, "Protection versus Flexibility: The Civil Service Reform Act, Competing Administrative Doctrines, and the Roots of the Contemporary Public Management Debate," *Journal of Policy History* 16 (2004): 7.

64. See also the conclusion of Brian J. Cook, that the supporters of the Pendleton Act "pushed for a neutral, expert administration." Cook, *Bureaucracy and Self-Government: Reconsidering the Role of Public Administration* (Baltimore: Johns Hopkins University Press, 1996), 78.

65. Paul Van Riper, "Adapting a British Political Invention to American Needs," *Public Administration* 31 (1953): 317.

66. Paul Van Riper, *History of the United States Civil Service* (Evanston, IL: Row, Peterson, 1958), 105.

67. As Paul Moreno explains, "The Pendleton Act is often seen as a first step toward establishing the administrative state that progressives would soon call for. To some degree this is true. . . . Conversely, the civil service reformers were more backward-than forward-looking." Paul D. Moreno, *The Bureaucrat Kings* (New York: ABC-Clio, 2016), 40.

68. Cass Sunstein, *After the Rights Revolution: Reconceiving the Regulatory State* (Cambridge, MA: Harvard University Press, 1990), 19.

69. Robert Rabin, "Federal Regulation in Historical Perspective," *Stanford Law Review* 38 (1986): 1189.

70. Paul D. Moreno, "'The Legitimate Object of Government': Constitutional Problems of Civil War–Era Reconstruction Policy," in *Constitutionalism in the Approach and Aftermath of the Civil War*, ed. Paul D. Moreno and Johnathan O'Neill (New York: Fordham University Press, 2013), 174.

71. Paul D. Carrington, "Law and Economics in the Creation of Federal Administrative Law: Thomas Cooley, Elder to the Republic," *Iowa Law Review* 83 (1998): 373.

72. See Robert D. Cushman, *The Independent Regulatory Commissions* (1941; New York: Octagon Books, 1972), 19–36; John Rohr, *To Run a Constitution: The Legitimacy of the Administrative State* (Lawrence: University Press of Kansas, 1987), 92.

73. See Thomas K. McCraw, *Prophets of Regulation* (Cambridge: Harvard University Press, 1986), 57.

74. Cushman, *Independent Regulatory Commissions*, 40–41.

75. Ibid., 41.

76. Ibid., 45.

77. Ibid., 43.

78. Rohr, *To Run a Constitution*, 95.

79. Quoted in Cushman, *Independent Regulatory Commissions*, 51.

80. Quoted in ibid., 51.

81. Cushman downplays this feature of the legislative debates: "There was no imperative reason why the statesmen who were proposing an interstate commerce commission and discussing the problems associated with it should feel it necessary to apply a descriptive label to the job which the commission was to do. It was generally recognized that the commission must do several kinds of work, legislative, executive, and judicial; and that fact caused a few people some distress of mind." Ibid., 54. But

Cushman's assessment does not seem to fit the evidence that can be gleaned from the debates themselves. As Hiroshi Okayama has recently argued, "two related principles later used by lawyers to constrain administrative agencies, namely, separation of powers and the rule of law," were consistently invoked during the legislative debates over the ICC. These principles, Okayama notes, *were* heavily influential in the debates over the ICC, and the legislation that was eventually passed was a product of concerns about how to reconcile the Commission with constitutional principles. Okayama, "The Interstate Commerce Commission and the Political Origins of a Judicialized Administrative State" (paper Presented at the American Political Science Association Annual Meeting 2011), 10 and passim.

82. Quoted in Rohr, *To Run a Constitution*, 98.

83. See ibid., 97–98. Yale professor A. T. Hadley voiced similar views, emphasizing the purpose of ensuring publicity rather than that of exercising coercive legal power.

84. Skowronek, *Building a New American State*, 138.

85. *Congressional Record*, 48th Congress, 2nd Session, 1884, 16, 199. See also the statement of John Reagan himself, at the outset of the debate: "It will be well understood that I make a distinction between remedial provisions and those which relate to the action of a commission acting chiefly between the government and the companies, and not between aggrieved individuals and the wrongdoers." *Interstate Commerce Debate in Forty-Eighth Congress, Second Session* (Washington, DC: 1884), 14.

86. Okayama, "Political Origins of a Judicialized Administrative State," 21.

87. Quoted in ibid., 32.

88. *Interstate Commerce Debate*, 239. Reagan, the sponsor of the alternative legislation before the House, was even more explicit about the core difference between the two proposals: "I propose now, Mr. Speaker, to antagonize this idea of a commission by providing that certain things shall not be done, and that the doing of them shall be a violation of the law, and that certain things shall be done, and the non-doing of them shall be a violation of law." Ibid., 21.

89. Ibid., 231.

90. Ibid., 232.

91. See Joseph Postell, "Regulation, Administration and the Rule of Law in the Early Republic," in *Freedom and the Rule of Law*, ed. Anthony Peacock (Lanham, MD: Lexington Books, 2010), 41–70; Joseph Postell, "How the Founders Thought about Regulation," in *Rediscovering Political Economy*, ed. Joseph Postell and Bradley C. S. Watson (Lanham, MD: Lexington Books, 2011), 209–30.

92. *Interstate Commerce Debate*, 233. See generally ibid., 233–37. Dunn's analysis of the issue is highly sophisticated and faithful to the traditional approach that prevailed during the early republic.

93. Reagan noted, "It was felt then, as we all know to be the case now, that each road was a monopoly for the transportation of the freights and carrying of the travel on its particular line[,] . . . they felt and knew that they derived their life and being from the legislative authority of the country; and that the power which created them could regulate in a reasonable way their rates of charges as common carriers, as their charges and their actions have been regulated from time immemorial just as turnpikes are regulated and as hack-drivers in cities are regulated." Ibid., 19.

94. Ibid., 232.

95. Ibid.

96. Ibid., 238.

97. Ibid., 20.

98. Ibid. Reagan also predicted the "capture" of this new regulatory commission: "I doubt the expediency of providing for such a commission, and will state why. If we provide for the appointment of a railroad commission either by the president or any other authority (and if provided for it would seem most natural that the members should be appointed by the President), however honest and patriotic his intentions may be in making such appointments, we must remember that the railroad corporations . . . can easily combine their influence and bring to bear by indirection, if they dare not do it directly, influences which will be likely to control in the appointment of commissioners." Ibid., 20.

99. Ibid., 141.

100. Ibid., 68.

101. Ibid., 179. Benjamin Shively, of the Anti-Monopoly Party, had a different view: "I would lend special emphasis to the importance of the proposition embodied in the committee bill to create a railway commission. . . . I am not blind to the plain and palpable facts of the peculiar and overshadowing influence that must surround the board of commissioners. . . . I am opposed to such a mighty concentration of power in any appointed body of men." Ibid., 72–73.

102. As Benjamin Shively argued, "no legislation less radical than that contemplated by the bill offered by the gentleman from Texas [Mr. Reagan] will meet the exigencies of the occasion. The 'conservative' legislation of which gentlemen speak will only by its impotency retard rather than advance the settlement of existing difficulties." Ibid., 72.

103. Okayama, "Political Origins of a Judicialized Administrative State," 12.

104. As Okayama argues, "The 'quasi-judicial' nature of the ICC and other IRCs modeled after it . . . was not adopted accidentally; it was chosen intentionally within the institutional constraints that derived from the two principles, separation of powers and the rule of law." Ibid., 13.

105. ICA Section 9; Rohr, *To Run a Constitution*, 96; Okayama, "Political Origins of a Judicialized Administrative State," 31. This dual-enforcement mechanism was voided by the Supreme Court in 1907, on the grounds that it ran counter to the Act's purpose, which was to ensure a uniform standard of rates.

106. Quoted in Okayama, "Political Origins of a Judicialized Administrative State," 21–22.

107. Quoted in ibid., 31. Given these facts, while it is true that the Interstate Commerce Act "did not reflect a coherent ideological approach to railroad regulation . . . [but merely] addressed a discrete set of immediately pressing problems in an equivocal fashion that reflected the difficult process of hammering out legislative compromise," it goes too far to suggest that the final product was merely a hodgepodge of incompatible ideas. Robert L. Rabin, "Federal Regulation in Historical Perspective," *Stanford Law Review* 38 (1986): 1207–8. Rather, as the debates illustrate, the objections offered to the commission idea were carefully incorporated into the final product, not simply added in an incoherent manner.

108. Quoted in Okayama, "Political Origins of a Judicialized Administrative State," 24–25.

109. Marc Allen Eisner, *Regulatory Politics in Transition*, 2nd ed. (Baltimore: Johns Hopkins University Press, 2000), 48.

110. Eisner, *Regulatory Politics in Transition*, 48.

111. Merrill, "Origins of the Appellate Review Model," 950.

112. See Skowronek, *Building a New American State*, 157.

113. Alan Jones, "Thomas M. Cooley and the Interstate Commerce Commission: Continuity and Change in the Doctrine of Equal Rights," *Political Science Quarterly* 81 (1966): 602. Paul Carrington states that Cooley "regarded Jackson's bank veto message as a political text only slightly less sacred than the Declaration of Independence." Carrington, "Law and Economics," 363.

114. Howard Gillman, *The Constitution Besieged: The Rise and Demise of Lochner-Era Police Power Jurisprudence* (Durham, NC: Duke University Press, 1993).

115. Rohr, *To Run a Constitution*, 105. See also Alan Jones, "Thomas M. Cooley and Laissez-Faire Constitutionalism: A Reconsideration," *Journal of American History* 53 (1967): 763–64. Jones, importantly, cites Cooley agreeing to the proposition that "strictly speaking, there are no rights but those which are the creatures of law."

116. *People v. Salem*, 20 Mich. 487 (1870).

117. See Carrington, "Law and Economics," 363–71.

118. Ibid., 364–65.

119. Jones, "Cooley and the ICC," 605.

120. Carrington, "Law and Economics," 374–75. Cooley outlined this position in an essay titled "State Regulation of Corporate Profits," *North American Review* 137 (1883): 215.

121. Cooley, "Limits to State Control of Private Business," *Princeton Review* I (1878): 233–71.

122. Cooley, "State Regulation of Corporate Profits," *North American Review* 137 (1883): 207–17.

123. Jones, "Cooley and the ICC," 612.

124. *Bradstreet's*, Jan. 29, 1887, quoted in ibid., 612–13.

125. See ibid., 617.

126. Rohr, *To Run a Constitution*, 102.

127. Carrington, "Law and Economics," 384.

128. Jones, "Cooley and the Interstate Commerce Commission," 623.

129. See generally ibid., passim.

130. Carrington, "Law and Economics," 387.

131. Ibid.

132. See Rohr, *To Run a Constitution*, 109–10.

133. Quoted in Jones, "Cooley and the Interstate Commerce Commission," 615.

134. Ibid., 616. Jones is critical of Cooley's approach as ineffectual.

135. Carrington, "Law and Economics," 385.

136. Jones, "Cooley and the Interstate Commerce Commission," 627.

137. See ibid., 623.

138. *ICC v. Alabama Midland Railway Co.*, 168 U.S. 144 (1897). By 1890 Cooley noted (in the ICC's Annual Report) that reviewing courts were taking original testimony in appeals from the ICC. See Rohr, *To Run a Constitution*, 108.

139. Ibid., 174.

140. Ibid., 176.

141. *Texas and Pacific Railway Co. v. ICC*, 162 U.S. 197 (1896).

142. *ICC v. Cincinnati, New Orleans, and Texas Pacific Railway Co.*, 167 U.S. 479 (1897).

143. *ICC v. Alabama Midland*, 177.

144. Skowronek, *Building a New American State*, 154.

145. Ibid., 159.

146. Ibid., 160.

147. Ibid., 151.

148. Quoted in James Freedman, *Crisis and Legitimacy*, 59.

149. Marc Allen Eisner, *Regulatory Politics in Transition*, 2d ed. (Baltimore: Johns Hopkins University Press, 2000), 27.

150. McCraw, *Prophets of Regulation*, 54.

Chapter Five
A New Science of Administration:
Progressivism and the Administrative State

1. Marc Allen Eisner, *Regulatory Politics in Transition*, 2d ed. (Baltimore: Johns Hopkins University Press, 2000), 59. See also Thomas K. McCraw, *Prophets of Regulation* (Cambridge, MA: Harvard University Press, 1984), 78–79.

2. Daniel Ernst, *Tocqueville's Nightmare: The Administrative State Emerges in America, 1900–1940* (New York: Oxford University Press, 2014), 37.

3. See Aditya Bamzai, "The Origins of Judicial Deference to Executive Interpretation," *Yale Law Journal* 126 (2016–17), 955–58.

4. *American School of Magnetic Healing v. McAnnulty*, 187 U.S. 94 (1902)

5. Ibid., 110.

6. John F. Duffy, "Administrative Common Law in Judicial Review," *Texas Law Review* 77 (1998): 113–214.

7. Ronald Pestritto and William Atto, for instance, argue that, in spite of their important differences, "progressivism can be understood as a coherent set of principles with a common purpose." Pestritto and Atto, "Introduction," *American Progressivism: A Reader* (Lanham, MD: Lexington Books, 2008), 2. Richard Hofstadter, however, claims that progressivism was "a rather vague and not altogether cohesive or consistent movement," but "Its general theme was the effort to restore a type of economic individualism and political democracy that was widely believed . . . to have been destroyed by the great corporation and the corrupt political machine." Hofstadter, *The Age of Reform* (New York: Random House, 1955), 5.

8. Charles Merriam, *American Political Ideas: Studies in the Development of American Political Thought, 1865–1917*, with a new introduction by Sidney A. Pearson, Jr. (1920; reprint, New Brunswick, NJ: Transaction Publishers, 2008), 100.

9. Herbert Croly, *Progressive Democracy*, with a new introduction by Sidney A. Pearson, Jr. (New York: Macmillan Co., 1914; reprint, New Brunswick, NJ: Transaction Publishers, 1998), 256.

10. Ibid., 262.

11. Ibid., 273.

12. Ibid., 263–64.

13. See Merriam, *American Political Theories*, 103–5.

14. Croly, *Progressive Democracy*, 265.

15. Ibid., 266.

16. See Ronald J. Pestritto, *Woodrow Wilson and the Roots of Modern Liberalism* (Lanham, MD: Rowman and Littlefield, 2005), 33–98.

17. Woodrow Wilson, "The Modern Democratic State," December 1, 1885, in *The Papers of Woodrow Wilson* (hereafter cited as *PWW*), 69 vols., ed. Arthur S. Link (Princeton, N.J.: Princeton University Press, 1966–1993), 5:76, 80–81. Emphasis in original. I am indebted to Ronald Pestritto for this observation.

18. Croly, *Progressive Democracy*, 259.

19. Merriam, *American Political Theories*, 102.

20. Herbert Croly, *The Promise of American Life* (New York: Macmillan, 1909; reprint, Boston: Northeastern University Press, 1989), 208.

21. David W. Noble, *The Paradox of Progressivism* (St. Paul: University of Minnesota Press, 1958), 62–63.

22. Merriam, *American Political Theories*, 61.

23. John Dewey, "The Ethics of Democracy," in *John Dewey: The Early Works* (Carbondale: Southern Illinois University Press, 1969), 3:228.

24. Croly, *Promise of American Life*, 176. Italics added.

25. Croly, *Progressive Democracy*, 19.

26. Ibid., 17.

27. Croly, *Promise of American Life*, 17.

28. Ibid., 26.

29. Ibid., 25.

30. Ibid., 17.

31. Ibid., 6.

32. David K. Nichols, "The Promise of Progressivism: Herbert Croly and the Progressive Rejection of Individual Rights," *Publius: The Journal of Federalism* 17 (1987): 27, 35. Internal quotations omitted.

33. Croly, *Promise of American Life*, 271.

34. Ibid., 270.

35. Croly, *Progressive Democracy*, 270.

36. Ibid., 272.

37. Ibid.

38. Ibid., 279.

39. Woodrow Wilson, "The Study of Administration," *Political Science Quarterly* 2 (1887): 215.

40. Charles E. Merriam, *A History of American Political Theories* (New York: Macmillan, 1915), 322–23. Merriam cites Frank J. Goodnow, *Politics and Administration* (New York: Macmillan, 1914), 21.

41. Wilson, "The Study of Administration," 210. Emphasis in original.

42. Goodnow, *Politics and Administration*, 9.

43. Ibid., 13.

44. Ibid.

45. Woodrow Wilson, *Constitutional Government in the United States* (New York: Columbia University Press, 1911), 54.

46. Wilson, "The Study of Administration," 212.

47. Ronald Pestritto, *Woodrow Wilson and the Roots of Modern Liberalism*, 123–24.

48. See, in particular, Wilson's essay "Cabinet Government in the United States," August 1879, in *The Papers of Woodrow Wilson*, 69 vols., ed. Arthur S. Link (Princeton, NJ: Princeton University Press, 1966–1993) 1:497.

49. Wilson, *Constitutional Government*, 92.

50. Croly, *Progressive Democracy*, 364.

51. Wilson, "The Study of Administration," 207.

52. Ibid., 209.

53. Ibid., 214.

54. Ibid., 213.

55. Ibid., 214.

56. Hamburger, *Is Administrative Law Unlawful?* 472.

57. Ibid.

58. Friedrich Hayek, *The Constitution of Liberty*, paperback ed. (Chicago: University of Chicago Press, 1978), 198.

59. Ibid., 199.

60. See *Constitution of Liberty*, 200–201.

61. Ernst Freund, "The Law of the Administration in America," *Political Science Quarterly* 9 (1894): 405.

62. The best description of this relationship and the two competing views of administrative law held by Freund and Frankfurter is Daniel Ernst, "Ernst Freund, Felix Frankfurter, and the American *Rechtsstaat*: A Transatlantic Shipwreck," *Studies in American Political Development* 23 (2009): 171–88. This was reprinted as chapter 1 of Ernst, *Tocqueville's Nightmare*.

63. Frankfurter, "Some Observations on Supreme Court Litigation and Legal Education," Ernst Freund Lecture, The Law School, University of Chicago, February 11, 1953, 1.

64. Ernst, *Tocqueville's Nightmare*, 10.

65. Ernst Freund, "The Substitution of Rule for Discretion in Public Law," *American Political Science Review* 9 (1915): 666–76.

66. Ernst Freund, *Administrative Powers over Persons and Property: A Comparative Survey* (Chicago: University of Chicago Press, 1928). John Dickinson, one of the most

important Progressive administrative law theorists, criticized this book in the *American Political Science Review* in 1928.

67. Freund, *The Police Power: Public Policy and Constitutional Rights* (Chicago: Callaghan & Co., 1904); *Standards of American Legislation* (Chicago: University of Chicago Press, 1917).

68. Freund, "Law of the Administration in America," 405.

69. Ibid., 407.

70. Ibid., 409–10.

71. Ibid., 410.

72. Ibid., 414–15.

73. Ibid., 415–16.

74. Ibid., 418.

75. Ibid.

76. Ibid.

77. Ibid., 419.

78. Ibid., 424.

79. Ibid., 425.

80. See Ernst, *Tocqueville's Nightmare*, 13.

81. Quoted in ibid., 10.

82. Hamburger, *Is Administrative Law Unlawful?* 475.

83. Ernst, *Tocqueville's Nightmare*, 26.

84. Skowronek, *Building a New American State*, 179.

85. Ibid.

86. Alexander Hamilton, "The Federalist No. 73," in Alexander Hamilton et al., *The Federalist*, ed. Jacob Cooke (Hanover, NH: Wesleyan University Press, 1971), 493.

87. James Madison, "The Federalist, No. 51," in *The Federalist*, 348.

88. See Skowronek, *Building a New American State*, 181: "[Roosevelt] looked toward the creation of a stable career service directly attached to and exclusively managed by executive officers."

89. As Stephen Skowronek explains, when Elkins assumed the chair of the committee from Senator Shelby Cullom, he "immediately disposed of a comprehensive reform measure" that Cullom wanted to push through the Senate. Ibid., 250.

90. The question of judicial review was critical because of the fact that Commission orders went into effect in thirty days, even without judicial sanction. This meant that (as Thomas Merrill explains) preliminary injunctions would be the primary methods of seeking review of ICC orders. Consequently, "what mattered was determining the proper standard of review for preliminary injunctions, not the standard for deciding whether to penalize a railroad for defying a lawful order that had already gone into effect." Merrill, "Origins of the Appellate Review Model," 957.

91. Ibid., 958.

92. 40 *Congressional Record* 6685 (1906), quoted in ibid.

93. Merrill explains that "Shortly after the Hepburn Act was passed, the tenor of Supreme Court decisions in ICC matters changed dramatically." Ibid., 959.

94. *ICC v. Illinois Central Railroad Co.*, 215 U.S. 452 (1910). In explaining the reasons for the judicial retreat, Skowronek writes that it is "likely that the Court

understood the volatile nature of the question at hand and the growing precariousness of its own political position." *Building a New American State*, 260.

95. *ICC v. Illinois Central Railroad Co.*, 470.

96. *ICC v. Northern Pacific Railroad Co.*, 216 U.S. 538 (1910).

97. Ernst, *Tocqueville's Nightmare*, 39.

98. Merrill, "Origins of the Appellate Review Model," 953.

99. Skowronek, *Building a New American State*, 261.

100. Ibid., 262. He also writes that "Taft accepted the Progressives' zeal for expanding federal regulatory power and matched it with an acute sense of the need to control that power once it was created. Ibid., 262–63.

101. Ibid., 263.

102. Ibid., 265.

103. Ibid., 266.

104. Sidney M. Milkis, *Theodore Roosevelt, the Progressive Party, and the Transformation of American Democracy* (Lawrence: University Press of Kansas, 2009), 258.

105. Ibid., 209.

106. Ibid., 210.

107. Robert Wiebe, *The Search for Order: 1877–1920* (New York: Hill and Wang, 1967), 218.

108. Charles Forcey, *The Crossroads of Liberalism: Croly, Weyl, Lippmann and the Progressive Era, 1900–1925* (New York: Oxford University Press, 1967), xxiv.

109. "Suggestions for Letter to Governor Wilson on Trusts," Brandeis to Woodrow Wilson, September 30, 1912, in *Letters of Louis D. Brandeis*, ed. Melvin Urofsky and David Levy, vol. 2 (Albany: State University of New York Press, 1972), 688.

110. Theodore Roosevelt, *The Autobiography of Theodore Roosevelt* (New York: Scribner's & Sons, 1913), 423.

111. Ibid., 423.

112. Sidney Milkis notes that "Wilson's New Freedom campaign was thus gradually eclipsed by Roosevelt's bolder defense of the 'whole people.' . . . Wilson felt compelled, or saw the opportunity, to govern more as a New Nationalist than a New Freedom progressive." Milkis, *Theodore Roosevelt, the Progressive Party, and the Transformation of American Democracy*, 271. Milkis notes that Wilson supported the creation of the Federal Trade Commission, the Federal Reserve, and other administrative commissions that he denounced on the trail in 1912. This, Milkis observes, is what induced Herbert Croly to proclaim happily in 1913 that "the New Freedom had been discarded." Croly, "The Two Parties in 1916," *New Republic*, October 21, 1916, 286, cited in Milkis, *Theodore Roosevelt*, 272. Robert Wiebe similarly explains that by 1916 "every area of reform had been affected by the new values of bureaucratic management. The executive beyond a doubt was now the focus of national government. . . . Where the executive did not have jurisdiction, an independent commission usually did. This progressive favorite dominated the regulation of corporations and held promise of exercising a significant influence over finance and the tariff as well." Wiebe, *The Search for Order*, 221–22.

113. Roosevelt, *Autobiography*, 424.

114. Ibid.

115. Ibid.

116. Ibid., 425.
117. Charles A. Beard, "Jefferson and the New Freedom," *New Republic*, November 14, 1914, 18.
118. Ibid., 19.
119. See, for instance, Ronald J. Pestritto, *Woodrow Wilson and the Roots of Modern Liberalism* (Lanham, MD: Rowman & Littlefield Press, 2005); Will Morrisey, *The Dilemma of Progressivism: How Roosevelt, Taft, and Wilson Reshaped the American Regime of Self-Government* (Lanham, MD: Rowman & Littlefield, 2009); John Marini and Ken Masugi, eds., *The Progressive Revolution in Politics and Political Science* (Lanham, MD: Lexington Books, 2007). The notable exception is Eldon J. Eisenach, *The Lost Promise of Progressivism* (Lawrence: University Press of Kansas, 1994), which actually condemns Wilson for abandoning the true principles of progressivism due to his conservatism.
120. Pestritto notes that "The Study of Administration" is "arguably, responsible for launching the entire discipline of public administration, and public administrations journals to this day continue to publish articles on Wilson's essay." *Woodrow Wilson and the Roots of Modern Liberalism*, 225.
121. A leading historical account is Thomas K. McCraw, *Prophets of Regulation* (Cambridge, MA: Harvard University Press, 1984), 80–142. McCraw is especially interested in Brandeis's peculiar approach to the regulation of competition, but he concludes that Brandeis's judgment was clouded by a flawed understanding of economics. This led the Federal Trade Commission to be created in a problematic manner, which has plagued its effectiveness ever since. Thus McCraw blames Brandeis and Wilson for failing to embrace fully the need for centralized administration, rather than exploring the constitutional thought that might have undergirded their reluctance.
122. For a discussion of the effects of centralized administration on modern American civic life, see Sidney Milkis, *Theodore Roosevelt*, 290–98.
123. Harold Howland, *Chronicles of America: Theodore Roosevelt and His Times* (1921), 88.
124. Roosevelt, *Autobiography*, 425–26. Emphasis in original.
125. Ibid., 431.
126. Ibid.
127. Ibid., 433.
128. Ibid.
129. Charles McCarthy to Norman Hapgood, September 4, 1912, quoted in Sidney Milkis, *Theodore Roosevelt*, 210.
130. For Taft and the Republicans, see the remarks of Elihu Root in his Keynote Address as the chairman of the Republican National Convention of 1912. It is for this reason that Wilson characterized the difference between Roosevelt and Taft as a choice between "Tweedledum and Tweedledee." "They do not so much as propose to lay the knife at any one of the roots of the difficulties under which we now labor. . . . [T]hey intend to accept these evils and stagger along under the burden of excessive tariffs and intolerable monopolies as best they can through administrative commissions." *PWW* 25:324–25.

131. Wilson, "What Is Progress?" in *The New Freedom* (Garden City, NY: Doubleday, 1921), 42–43.

132. Wilson, "Freemen Need No Guardians," in ibid., 55.

133. Ibid., 56.

134. *PWW* 25:75, cited in Milkis, *Theodore Roosevelt*, 211.

135. Wilson, "Law or Personal Power," *PWW* 18:264.

136. Melvin Urofsky, *Louis D. Brandeis: A Life* (Random House, 2009), 347.

137. Wilson, "Benevolence, or Justice?" in *The New Freedom*, 196.

138. Wilson, "Monopoly, or Opportunity?" in *The New Freedom*, 172.

139. Brandeis, "Suggestions for Letter to Governor Wilson on Trusts," 688.

140. Charles Forcey, *The Crossroads of Liberalism*, 207–8.

141. Quoted in Arthur Schlesinger, Jr., *The Politics of Upheaval* (Boston: Houghton Mifflin, 1960), 280.

142. Arthur Link, cited in Strum, *Brandeis: Beyond Progressivism*, 83.

143. Milkis, *Theodore Roosevelt*, 206.

144. As Thomas McCraw writes, "Wilson never shared Brandeis's total aversion to industrial bigness." McCraw, *Prophets of Regulation*, 112. On the campaign trail in 1912, Wilson declared, "Big business is no doubt to a large extent necessary and natural . . . and, let me say, is probably desirable. But that is a very different matter from the development of trusts." Wilson, "Monopoly or Opportunity?" *The New Freedom*, 164–65.

145. McCraw, *Prophets of Regulation*, 111.

146. Wilson, "Monopoly, or Opportunity?" in *The New Freedom*, 172.

147. Wilson, "Draft of a Platform for the Democratic Party of Pennsylvania, April 4, 1910," *PWW* 20:316.

148. Wilson, "Interview," *New York Times*, December 24, 1911, *PWW* 23:613.

149. Wilson, "Law or Personal Power," *PWW* 18:264.

150. Skowronek, *Building a New American State*, 195.

151. Ibid., 196.

152. Thomas Merrill, "Origins of the Appellate Review Model," 969.

153. G. Edward White, *The Constitution and the New Deal* (Cambridge, MA: Harvard University Press, 2000), 108.

154. See Bamzai, "Origins of Judicial Deference to Executive Interpretation," 966–76.

155. *Bates v. Payne*, 194 U.S. 106, at 108 (1904).

156. Ibid., 109.

157. See ibid., 111.

158. Thomas Merrill explicitly links deference to the ICC and the Hepburn Act: "Shortly after the Hepburn Act was passed, the tenor of Supreme Court decisions in ICC matters changed dramatically." Merrill, "Origins of the Appellate Review Model," 959.

159. *Manufacturers' Railway Company v. United States*, 246 U.S. 457, at 481 (1918).

160. Reuel E. Schiller, "The Era of Deference: Courts, Expertise, and the Emergence of New Deal Administrative Law," *Michigan Law Review* 106 (2007): 408–9.

161. *Federal Trade Commission v. Gratz*, 253 U.S. 421 (1920); Thomas Merrill, "Origins of the Appellate Review Model, 970. Dan Ernst argues that the difference between the judiciary's treatment of the FTC and other agencies was a product of the "lifeless, formulaic opinions" the FTC offered in favor of its decisions. Thus the FTC was the outlier during this period because of "its failure to buttress its orders with findings of fact that conscientiously resolved conflicting evidence." Ernst, *Tocqueville's Nightmare*, 21.

Chapter Six
The Crisis of Legitimacy:
The New Deal Challenge to American Constitutionalism

1. David Lewis, *Presidents and the Politics of Agency Design: Political Insulation in the United States Government Bureaucracy, 1946–1997* (Stanford, CA: Stanford University Press, 2003), 7.

2. Quoted in Daniel Ernst, *Tocqueville's Nightmare: The Administrative State Emerges in America, 1900–1940* (New York: Oxford University Press, 2014), 57.

3. Joanna Grisinger, *The Unwieldy American State: Administrative Politics since the New Deal* (New York: Cambridge University Press, 2012), 1.

4. Ibid., 2–3.

5. *Panama Refining Co. v. Ryan*, 293 U.S. 418 (1935).

6. *Schecter Poultry Corp. v. United States*, 295 U.S. 495 (1935).

7. Ibid., 553.

8. The letter is quoted in the Court's opinion in *Humphrey's Executor v. United States*, 295 U.S. 602, 619 (1935).

9. *Myers v. U.S.*, 272 U.S. 52, at 114.

10. Ibid., 133–34.

11. Ibid., 135. Emphasis in original. Even in this case, however, Taft argued that the president "may consider the decision after its rendition as a reason for removing the officer, on the ground that the discretion regularly entrusted to that officer by statute has not been, on the whole, intelligently or wisely exercised." Ibid.

12. *Humphrey's Executor*, 624.

13. Ibid., 625.

14. Ibid., 628.

15. *Federal Trade Commission v. Ruberoid Co.*, 343 U.S. 487–88 (1952).

16. "Conference with Justice Brandeis at his request in the ante-room of the Clerk's office, at 2 P.M., May 27, 1935," box 20, Cohen MSS.

17. See Daniel Ernst, *Tocqueville's Nightmare*, 56–69; G. Edward White, *The Constitution and the New Deal* (Cambridge, MA: Harvard University Press, 2000), 109–14. Both authors argue that the Supreme Court's decisions in 1935 were not intended to undermine the New Deal but to send a message that regulatory programs and statutes would have to follow basic requirements of the rule of law, such as fact-finding requirements, procedural requirements, and structural components to ensure legality. In this reading, the cases were a confirmation of the legitimacy of agencies, so long

as they followed the blueprint that the Supreme Court could impose in future cases. Thus in their view the "switch in time" was not the result of the Court's caving to significant political pressure Roosevelt brought to bear on the institution but, rather, the acknowledgment that the New Deal had been adjusted to accommodate the Court's commandments. Of course, these two explanations of the Court's reversal in 1937 are not mutually exclusive.

18. Thomas W. Merrill, "Origins of the Appellate Review Model," 972–73.

19. John Dickinson, *Administrative Justice and the Supremacy of Law in the United States* (Cambridge, MA: Harvard University Press, 1927), 55.

20. Aditya Bamzai, "The Origins of Judicial Deference to Executive Interpretation," *Yale Law Journal* 126 (2016–17), 974–75.

21. Aditya Bamzai draws the connection between Dickinson's work, *Bates v. Payne*, and the 1940s administrative law cases in "Origins of Judicial Deference to Executive Interpretation," 976–85.

22. Reuel Schiller, "The Era of Deference," 415.

23. Ibid., 414.

24. Landis, *The Administrative Process*, 9.

25. Ibid., 46.

26. Mark Tushnet, "Administrative Law in the 1930s: The Supreme Court's Accommodation of Progressive Legal Theory," *Duke Law Journal* 60 (2011): 1576.

27. Sidney M. Milkis, *The President and the Parties: The Transformation of the American Party System since the New Deal* (New York: Oxford University Press, 1993), 117.

28. Ibid., 118.

29. Ibid., 105.

30. Ibid., 106.

31. As Milkis notes, FDR "viewed the Committee" and its work "as a surrogate constitutional convention." Ibid., 109.

32. "Report of the President's Committee on Administrative Management" (January 1937), 36.

33. Ibid., 29.

34. Milkis, *The President and the Parties*, 121.

35. See, for example, Cass R. Sunstein, "What's Standing after *Lujan*? Of Citizen Suits, 'Injuries,' and Article III," *Michigan Law Review* 91 (1992): 166; John A. Ferejohn and Larry D. Kramer, "Independent Judges, Dependent Judiciary: Institutionalizing Judicial Restraint," *New York University Law Review* 77 (2002): 1009.

36. Ann Woolhandler and Caleb Nelson, "Does History Defeat Standing?" *Michigan Law Review* 102 (2004): 691. Emphasis added.

37. Ibid., 692.

38. Ibid., 695–96. Internal citations omitted.

39. Maxwell L. Stearns, "Standing at the Crossroads: The Roberts Court in Historical Perspective," *Notre Dame Law Review* 83 (2008): 889.

40. Ibid., 882.

41. 297 U.S. 288 (1936).

42. Id., at 343 (Brandeis, J., concurring).

43. Id., at 345–46 (Brandeis, J., concurring).

44. 273 U.S. 299 (1927).

45. Id., at 309–310. Emphasis in original. Internal citations omitted.

46. 263 U.S. 143 (1923).

47. Id., at 148.

48. Id.

49. *Gray v. Powell*, 314 U.S. 402 (1941); *National Labor Relations Board v. Hearst Publications*, 322 U.S. 111 (1944).

50. Prior to determining that Seaboard was not a "producer" of coal, the Court also addressed whether there was a sale or disposal of coal if there was no transfer of title. On that question of law, the Court also sided with the agency, but without any deference to the agency. Thus *Powell* signaled that pure questions of law would not receive judicial deference, even while other questions would.

51. In spite of these general trends, which clearly pointed towards greater judicial deference to agencies, courts would still periodically assert the authority to review questions of law de novo. Ironically, the most prominent assertion of this power came from a concurring opinion from Justice Brandeis in a 1936 case involving an order of the Secretary of Agriculture fixing maximum stockyard rates. In that case, Brandeis declared that "[t]he supremacy of law demands that there shall be opportunity to have some court decide whether an erroneous rule of law was applied; and whether the proceeding in which facts were adjudicated was conducted regularly." *St. Joseph Stockyards v. United States*, 298 U.S. 38, at 84 (1936). Thus while Brandeis was willing to construct robust standing requirements to keep parties from bringing these disputes to the courts, he also asserted a wide scope of judicial review when they came. The Brandeis of *St. Joseph Stockyards* closely resembled the Brandeis of 1912 and the Brandeis that lectured FDR's advisors on "Black Monday."

52. *Crowell v. Benson*, 285 U.S. 22 (1932).

53. Ibid., 48.

54. *Murray's Lessee v. Hoboken Land & Improvement Co.*, 59 U.S. (18 How.) 272, 284 (1856).

55. *Crowell*, 50.

56. See also ibid., 45–46: "Rulings of the deputy commissioner upon questions of law are without finality. . . . [F]ull opportunity is afforded for their determination by the federal courts through proceedings to suspend or to set aside a compensation order."

57. Ibid., 50. The quote from *Murray's Lessee* followed: "there are matters, involving public rights, which may be presented in such form that the judicial power is capable of acting on them, and which are susceptible of judicial determination, but which Congress may or may not bring within the cognizance of the courts of the United States, as it may deem proper." *Murray's Lessee*, 284.

58. See Roscoe Pound, "The Need of a Sociological Jurisprudence," *Green Bag* 19 (1907): 607–15; Pound, "Mechanical Jurisprudence," *Columbia Law Review* 8 (1908): 605–23; Pound, "Liberty of Contract," *Yale Law Journal* 18 (1909): 454–87; Pound, "The Scope and Purpose of Sociological Jurisprudence," *Harvard Law Review* 24

(1911): 591–619; Pound, "The Scope and Purpose of Sociological Jurisprudence," *Harvard Law Review* 25 (1911): 140–68; Pound, "The Scope and Purpose of Sociological Jurisprudence, *Harvard Law Review* 25 (1912): 489–516.

59. Walter Gellhorn, "The Administrative Procedure Act: The Beginnings," *Virginia Law Review* 72 (1986): 219.

60. Ibid., 219–20.

61. Ibid., 220–21.

62. Franklin Delano Roosevelt, "Veto of a Bill Regulating Administrative Agencies," December 8, 1940, available online via "The American Presidency Project," at http://www.presidency.ucsb.edu/ws/index.php?pid=15914.

63. For a full discussion of Pound's political and legal thought, and a defense of his consistency, see Joseph Postell, "The Anti–New Deal Progressive: Roscoe Pound's Alternative Administrative State," *Review of Politics* 73 (2012): 53–85. The discussion that follows is expanded upon in that article.

64. Pound, *Interpretations of Legal History* (New York: Macmillan, 1923), 1. See also "Report of the Special Committee on Administrative Law," 63 *Annual Report of the American Bar Association* (1938), 331, 357.

65. Pound, "Executive Justice," *American Law Register* 55 (1907): 139.

66. "Report of the Special Committee on Administrative Law," 331, 352.

67. Pound, "The Organization of Courts" (Law Association of Philadelphia, 1913), 2.

68. Pound, "Executive Justice," 139.

69. Pound, "The Organization of Courts," 3.

70. Pound, "Executive Justice," 139.

71. Ibid., 145.

72. Pound, "The Growth of Administrative Justice," *Wisconsin Law Review* 2 (1924): 325.

73. Two prominent legal scholars responded in print to Pound's report, both expressing shock at its tone. See Kenneth Culp Davis, "Dean Pound and Administrative Law," *Columbia Law Review* 42 (1942): 89–103. Davis wrote that Pound's "sweeping strictures on administrative agencies have been widely influential" (89). See also Louis Jaffe, review of Roscoe Pound, *Administrative Law: Its Growth, Procedure, and Significance* (Pittsburgh: University of Pittsburgh Press, 1942), in *Columbia Law Review* 42 (1942): 1382–1385. Jaffe opened his review of Pound's book by noting, "The depth of controversy is attested by the violence and the distortion which it generates. . . . Not the least offender, both by reason of intellectual eminence and the extent of his transgression, is Dean Pound" (1382).

74. "Report of the Special Committee on Administrative Law," 338–39.

75. Ibid., 339.

76. Ibid.

77. Ibid., 346.

78. Ibid., 343.

79. Ibid., 352.

80. Ibid., 353.

81. Ibid.

82. Ibid., 344.

83. Ibid., 345.

84. Ibid., 359.

85. Ibid.

86. Ibid., 334.

87. As many legal scholars have noted, the typical agency practice up to the 1960s was to treat every case as unique, and use specific adjudication to deal with each particular case. During the 1960s, a "flight to rulemaking" took place where agencies began to use rules to achieve policy goals. See, for instance, Antonin Scalia, "*Vermont Yankee*, the APA, the D.C. Circuit, and the Supreme Court," *Supreme Court Review* (1978): 376.

88. "Report of the Special Committee on Administrative Law," 336.

89. "Judicial review in England and in the United States has had a marked effect in compelling the development of a technique of determination consonant with due process of law . . . commissions can be held to this balance only by legal checks judicially enforced." Ibid., 351.

90. Pound, "The Rule of Law and the Modern Social Welfare State," *Vanderbilt Law Review* 7 (1953): 30.

91. The distinction is given clear expression by Robert S. Lorch, *Democratic Process and Administrative Law* (Detroit: Wayne State University Press, 1980), 26–34. Lorch argues that administrative agencies decide cases with a forward-looking approach rather than one based on precedent; can initiate action and seek out cases unlike a court; and are designed to decide cases with a view to the public interest rather than the justice of the particular parties in any given case.

92. Pound, "The Rule of Law and the Modern Social Welfare State," 18.

93. Bernard Schwartz, "The Administrative Agency in Historical Perspective," *Indiana Law Journal* (1961): 279.

94. Ibid.

95. Quoted in Pound, "Organization of Courts," 15.

96. Ibid.

97. Ibid., 20.

98. Ibid., 21–22.

99. See Peter Woll, *Administrative Law, the Informal Process* (Berkeley: University of California Press, 1963), 18–19. As Joanna Grisinger explains, the Walter-Logan Act "sought to saddle agencies with more procedures and surround their actions with more judicial review." *The Unwieldy American State: Administrative Politics since the New Deal* (New York: Cambridge University Press, 2012), 60.

100. House Proceedings (statement of Rep. John Jennings Jr., May 24, 1946), reprinted in *Administrative Procedure Act: Legislative History, 79th Congress, 1944–1946* (Washington, DC: Government Printing Office, 1946), 392.

101. Ibid., 393.

102. Ibid., 382 (statement of Rep. Samuel Hobbs, May 24, 1946).

103. Senate Proceedings (statement of Sen. Alexander Wiley, March 12, 1946), in *Administrative Procedure Act: Legislative History*, 337–38.

104. House Proceedings (statement of Rep. Francis Walter, May 24, 1946), in *Administrative Procedure Act: Legislative History*, 349.

105. Senate Proceedings (statement of Sen. Pat McCarran, March 12, 1946), in *Administrative Procedure Act: Legislative History*, 297. The "bill of rights" phrase is found on 298.

106. *Hearings on S.674, S.675, and S.918*, Subcommittee of the Senate Committee on the Judiciary, quoted in Bernard Schwartz, "Adjudication and the Administrative Procedure Act," *Tulsa Law Journal 32* (1996): 207.

107. Senate Proceedings (statement of Sen. Pat McCarran, March 12, 1946), in *Administrative Procedure Act: Legislative History*, 307.

108. Ibid., 300.

109. See House Proceedings (statement of Rep. Francis Walter, May 24, 1946), in *Administrative Procedure Act: Legislative History*, 347, 351.

110. Reading the legislative debates suggests, in contrast to "McNollgast," that the Congress agreed with the basic reforms promised by the APA. It was not, in other words, an attempt by New Dealers to lock in their preferred policies in case the political tide turned against them in the late 1940s. See Mathew D. McCubbins, Roger G. Noll, and Barry R. Weingast, "The Political Origins of the Administrative Procedure Act," *Journal of Law, Economics, and Organization* 15 (1999): 180–217. The consensus was more likely the result of the widespread agreement that the APA would improve the working of the administrative state, even if there was disagreement about whether more needed to be done.

111. Senate Proceedings (statement of Sen. Pat McCarran, March 12, 1946), in *Administrative Procedure Act: Legislative History*, 299.

112. House Proceedings (statement of Rep. Howard W. Smith, May 24, 1946), in *Administrative Procedure Act: Legislative History*, 348.

113. Ibid., 362 (statement of Rep. Francis Walter, May 24, 1946).

114. Ibid., 374 (statement of Rep. John W. Gwynne, May 24, 1946).

115. Senate Proceedings (statement of Sen. Pat McCarran, March 12, 1946), in *Administrative Procedure Act: Legislative History*, 320.

116. House Proceedings (statement of Rep. Francis Walter, May 24, 1946), in *Administrative Procedure Act: Legislative History*, 365.

117. Senate Proceedings (exchange between Sen. Pat McCarran and Sen. Kenneth McKellar, March 12, 1946), in *Administrative Procedure Act: Legislative History*, 318–19.

118. House Proceedings (statement of Rep. Francis Walter, May 24, 1946), in *Administrative Procedure Act: Legislative History*, 368.

119. Ibid., 368–69 (statement of Rep. Francis Walter, May 24, 1946).

120. Ibid., 359 (statement of Rep. Francis Walter, May 24, 1946).

121. 5 U.S.C. § 706.

122. House Proceedings (statement of Rep. Raymond Springer, May 24, 1946), in *Administrative Procedure Act: Legislative History*, 378.

123. Ibid., 347 (statement of Rep. Earl Michener, May 24, 1946).

124. Ibid., 383 (statement of Rep. John Robsion, May 24, 1946).

125. Ibid., 372 (statement of Rep. Clarence Hancock, May 24, 1946).

126. Ibid., 373 (statement of Rep. John W. Gwynne, May 24, 1945).

127. Pat McCarran, "The Unwritten and Irrational Constitution of Regulatory Government in the United States," *Notre Dame Law Review* 24 (1948): 62.

128. One might raise objections to the use of the legislative history as a guide for interpreting the APA. Indeed, several scholars have noted the problems with such a project. See George Shepherd, "Fierce Compromise: The Administrative Procedure Act Emerges from New Deal Politics," *Northwestern Law Review* 90 (1996): 1662–63. Of course, many of the representatives may have sought to load the legislative history with statements favorable to their view of the law. Therefore, as a guide to legal interpretation, the legislative history may be problematic. Yet as a basis for explaining the political forces and principles at play in the debates, the legislative history is useful. And it reveals, at the very least, a substantial bloc in Congress that saw the APA as only the first step in a larger project of constraining administrative power.

129. Patrick McCarran, "Improving 'Administrative Justice': Hearings and Evidence; Scope of Judicial Review," *American Bar Association Journal* 32 (1946): 831, 893.

130. See John Dickinson, "Administrative Procedure Act: Scope and Grounds of Broadened Judicial Review," *American Bar Association Journal* 33 (1947): 434–37, 513–19. I am grateful to Aditya Bamzai for introducing me to this and the McCarran article cited above.

131. Ibid., 516.

132. Bamzai, "Origins of Judicial Deference," 995.

133. *Federal Trade Commission v. Cement Institute*, 333 U.S. 683 (1948).

134. *FTC v. Cement Institute*, 333 U.S. 720 (1948).

135. *O'Leary v. Brown-Pacific-Maxon*, 340 U.S. 504 (1951).

136. Kenneth Culp Davis, *Administrative Law* (St. Paul: West Publishing, 1951), 885.

Chapter Seven
"A Surrogate Political Process":
The 1970s Administrative Law Revolution

1. Quoted in Robert H. Ferrell, *Harry S. Truman: A Life* (Columbia: University of Missouri Press, 1996), 379.

2. Quoted in Michael Nelson, *The Presidency and the Political System*, 10th ed. (Washington, DC: CQ Press, 2013), 53.

3. David E. Lewis, *Presidents and the Politics of Agency Design: Political Insulation in the United States Government Bureaucracy, 1946–1997* (Stanford, CA: Stanford University Press, 2003).

4. Ibid., 19.

5. Ibid., 4.

6. Marc Allen Eisner, *Regulatory Politics in Transition*, 2d ed. (Baltimore: Johns Hopkins University Press, 2000), 119.

7. As Richard Harris and Sidney Milkis explain, "the term new social regulation refers to the numerous federal initiatives in environmental policy, occupational safety,

public health, consumer affairs, and equal opportunity that were enacted and implemented during the 1970s." *The Politics of Regulatory Change*, 2d ed. (New York: Oxford University Press, 1996), 6.

8. Of course, there was no perfect correlation between the New Deal and economic regulation, or the 1960s–1970s and social regulation. Some regulatory programs and agencies during the New Deal were social in nature, and some economic regulation was inaugurated in the 1960s and 1970s. But the correlation was strong. See Eisner, *Regulatory Politics*, 119–20.

9. The names of these agencies suggested a new emphasis on accountability: instead of multi-member *commissions* these new agencies were typically referred to as *agencies* or *administration*. While the names of these agencies were not always indicative of their composition (some "agencies" were independent and some "commissions" were housed in executive departments), they clearly signified a new division of the administrative state into "Independent Regulatory Commissions" and "Executive Agencies," an important distinction that carries considerable weight in administrative law.

10. Richard Nathan, *The Plot That Failed: Nixon and the Administrative Presidency* (New York: Wiley & Sons, 1975), 7.

11. Ibid., 5.

12. Ibid., 37.

13. Ibid., 39.

14. Ibid.

15. Ibid., 41.

16. Quoted in ibid., 40.

17. Ibid., 43.

18. Ibid., 45. For these developments, see ibid., 45–50.

19. See ibid., 49–53. In summary, Nathan writes, "Even with significantly enlarged White House and Executive office staffs," Nixon's counter-bureaucracy "was limited in relation to the far greater numbers of agency personnel. They simply could not get a handle on the multitudinous field of domestic affairs." Ibid., 61.

20. Richard B. Stewart, "The Reformation of American Administrative Law," *Harvard Law Review* 88 (1975): 1683.

21. Ibid., 1684.

22. Ibid., 1712.

23. Ibid., 1670. Also, "Courts have changed the focus of judicial review (in the process expanding and transforming traditional procedural devices) so that its dominant purpose is . . . the assurance of fair representation for all affected interests in the exercise of the legislative power delegated to agencies." Ibid., 1712.

24. Harris and Milkis, *The Politics of Regulatory Change*, 83.

25. Marver H. Bernstein, *Regulating Business by Independent Commission* (Princeton, NJ: Princeton University Press, 1955), 87.

26. Roger G. Noll, *Reforming Regulation* (Washington, DC: The Brookings Institution, 1971).

27. Landis, "Report to the President Elect," December 21, 1960, Senate Judiciary Committee, 86th Congress, 2nd Session.

28. Ibid.

29. Joanna Grisinger, *The Unwieldy American State*, 247.

30. Cass Sunstein, *After the Rights Revolution: Reconceiving the Regulatory State* (Cambridge, MA: Harvard University Press, 1990), 29.

31. 210 U.S. 373 (1908).

32. 239 U.S. 441 (1915).

33. 397 U.S. 254 (1970).

34. 408 U.S. 564 (1972).

35. *Vermont Yankee Nuclear Power Corporation v. Natural Resources Defense Council*, 435 U.S. 519 (1978).

36. 5 U.S.C. §553(b)(3); 5 U.S.C. §553(c).

37. Antonin Scalia, "*Vermont Yankee*, the APA, the D.C. Circuit, and the Supreme Court," *Supreme Court Review* (1978): 347.

38. Ibid., 376. As we will see, the *Vermont Yankee* decision involved this very thing, namely, the use of rulemaking to guide adjudication.

39. 410 U.S. 224 (1973).

40. Gary Lawson, *Federal Administrative Law*, 6th ed. (St. Paul, MN: West Publishing, 2013), 311.

41. The Supreme Court simply did not decide many cases involving administrative law during the 1960s and 1970s and still today decides a very small number of administrative law cases relative to the federal circuit courts. Given the institutional limitations of the Supreme Court (namely, that it can decide only a small number of cases each term), it can exercise only limited oversight of the circuit courts' supervision of the administrative state.

42. *O'Donnell v. Shaffer*, 491 F. 2d. 59, at 62 (DC Cir., 1974).

43. *American Airlines, Inc. v. Civil Aeronautics Board*, 359 F. 2d. 624, at 632 (D.C. Cir., 1966).

44. *Portland Cement Association v. Ruckleshaus*, 486 F. 2d 375 (D.C. Cir., 1973).

45. Ibid., 393, 402.

46. See Lawson, *Federal Administrative Law*, 319.

47. *Automotive Parts & Accessories Association v. Boyd*, 407 F. 2d. 330, at 338 (D.C. Cir., 1968).

48. See, for example, J. Skelly Wright, "New Judicial Requisites for Informal Rulemaking: Implications for the Environmental Impact Statement Process," *Administrative Law Review* 29 (1977): 59–64; Harold Leventhal, "Environmental Decisionmaking and the Role of the Courts," *University of Pennsylvania Law Review* 122 (1974): 536–41.

49. Jim Rossi, "Participation Run Amok," *Northwestern University Law Review* 92 (1997): 191.

50. Robert A. Kagan, *Adversarial Legalism: The American Way of Law* (Cambridge, MA: Harvard University Press, 2003), 173.

51. Landis, *The Administrative Process*, 69.

52. Alexander Hamilton et al., *The Federalist*, no. 78, in *The Federalist*, ed. Jacob E. Cooke (Hanover, NH: Wesleyan University Press, 1961), 523: the judiciary "may truly be said to have neither force nor will but merely judgment."

53. R. Shep Melnick, *Between the Lines: Interpreting Welfare Rights* (Washington, DC: The Brookings Institution, 1994), 266.

54. 5 U.S.C. § 702.

55. See Stewart, "Reformation of American Administrative Law," 1725–26.

56. In this discussion of the development of standing law in the 1960s and 1970s, I admittedly collapse the analytically distinct categories of constitutional and statutory standing. This is because I explain these cases as building on each other in a theoretical and a political sense, although these developments occurred along legally distinct lines. Although, for example, *Camp* involves statutory standing and *Sierra Club v. Morton* and *SCRAP* involve the question of injury that is central to constitutional standing, both cases occur in the same period of time and both expand access to the courts for reviewing administrative action.

57. For much of this historical overview, I draw upon Lawson, *Federal Administrative Law*, 1021–29.

58. 354 F. 2d 608 (2d Cir. 1965).

59. 359 F. 2d 994 (DC Cir. 1966).

60. *Scenic Hudson v. FPC*, 354 F. 2d 608, 615.

61. 397 U.S. 150, at 153 (1970). Here I depart slightly from Gary Lawson's presentation, which emphasizes the break between *Data Processing v. Camp* and the two cases just mentioned. It is true that in a legal sense there is a break between the expanded standing under the APA characteristic of *Scenic Hudson* and *United Church of Christ* and the "zone of interests" approach in *Camp*. However, on a deeper level *Camp*, in expanding access to the courts for interest groups, builds on these two cases rather than breaking with them.

62. See Lawson, *Federal Administrative Law*, 813–14: *Camp* and its progeny "construed section 702's reference to a 'relevant statute' to mean the *substantive* terms of the agency's organic statute rather than the terms of any *special review* provisions targeted specifically at standing." Emphasis in original.

63. 405 U.S. 727 (1972).

64. Id., at 733.

65. As the Court explained, "The trend of cases arising under the APA and other statutes authorizing judicial review of federal agency action has been toward recognizing that injuries other than economic harm are sufficient to bring a person within the meaning of the statutory language, and toward discarding the notion that an injury that is widely shared is *ipso facto* not an injury sufficient to provide the basis for judicial review. We noted this development with approval in *Data Processing*, in saying that the interest alleged to have been injured 'may reflect *aesthetic, conservational, and recreational*,' as well as economic, values." Id., at 738. Emphasis in original.

66. "A mere 'interest in a problem,' no matter how long-standing the interest and no matter how qualified the organization is in evaluating the problem, is not sufficient, by itself, to render the organization 'adversely affected' or 'aggrieved' within the meaning of the APA." Id., at 739.

67. 412 U.S. 669 (1973).

68. Id., at 687.

69. Id., at 690.

70. Stewart, "Reformation of American Administrative Law," 1735.

71. R. Shep Melnick chronicles these developments in *Regulation and the Courts: The Case of the Clean Air Act* (Washington, DC: Brookings Institution, 1983).

72. Eisner, *Regulatory Politics*, 129.

73. Stewart, "Reformation of American Administrative Law," 1761.

74. E. Donald Elliot, "*Chevron* Matters: How the Chevron Doctrine Redefined the Roles of Congress, Courts and Agencies in Environmental Law," *Villanova Environmental Law Journal* 16 (2005): 6.

75. Ibid., 11.

76. The cases were *Kaelin v. Grubbs,* and *Stuart v. Nappi*. See Shep Melnick, *Between the Lines: Interpreting Welfare Rights* (Washington, DC: The Brookings Institution Press, 1994), 165–66. It is also worth noting that these cases were decided by different federal circuit courts, namely, the Fourth and Fifth Circuit Courts. Melnick does note that an Eleventh Circuit Court decision differed from this trend by permitting the expulsion of an emotionally disturbed student who brought weapons to school and threatened to kill another student. Ibid.

77. *Honig v. Doe*, 484 U.S. 305 (1988).

78. Note, "Enforcing the Right to an 'Appropriate' Education: The Education for All Handicapped Children Act of 1975," *Harvard Law Review* 92 (1979): 1127, cited in Melnick, *Between the Lines*, 168.

79. *Hendrick Hudson District Board of Education v. Rowley*, 458 U.S. 176 (1982), 188–89.

80. See Jeremy Rabkin, *Judicial Compulsions* (New York: Basic Books, 1989), 149.

81. Ibid., 151.

82. In a few areas, however, the courts refrained from intervening to reinterpret statutes when pressed to do so by advocacy groups. Robert Katzmann explains that, "In the early 1970s, the federal judiciary had a number of opportunities to impose its vision on legislative and administrative processes in the area of transportation for the disabled, but it acted with considerable restraint." Katzmann, *Institutional Disability: The Saga of Transportation Policy for the Disabled* (Washington DC: Brookings Institution Press, 1986), 154, and 154–87.

83. 5 U.S.C. § 706(2)(A).

84. Lawson, *Federal Administrative Law*, 700.

85. *Greater Boston Television Corp. v. Federal Communication Commission*, 444 F. 2d (1970), 851.

86. 499 F. 2d. 467 at 475 (DC Cir, 1974). For another famous and illustrative case, see *Ethyl Corp v. EPA*, 541 F2d 1 (DC Cir 1976).

87. Stewart, "Reformation of American Administrative Law," 1757.

88. Melnick, *Regulation and the Courts*, 11.

89. Eisner, *Regulatory Politics*, 118.

90. Anne M. Kornhauser, *Debating the American State: Liberal Anxieties and the New Leviathan, 1930–1970* (Philadelphia: University of Pennsylvania Press, 2015), 9.

91. R. Shep Melnick, "Executive Power and Administrative Law," *The Public Interest* 97 (1989): 134–35.

92. See Eisner, *Regulatory Politics*, 124.

93. Harris and Milkis, *Politics of Regulatory Change*, 10

94. 57 F. 3d 1129 (DC Cir. 1995).

95. Id., at 1132.

96. Robert A. Kagan, *Adversarial Legalism: The American Way of Law* (Cambridge, MA: Harvard University Press, 2003), 216–17. Emphasis in original.

97. Mark Seidenfeld, "Demystifying Deossification: Rethinking Recent Proposals to Modify Judicial Review of Notice and Comment Rulemaking," *Texas Law Review* 75 (1997): 502.

98. Ibid., 506.

99. Ibid., 521.

100. Richard A. Harris and Sidney M. Milkis, *The Politics of Regulatory Change: A Tale of Two Agencies*, 2d ed. (New York and London: Oxford University Press, 1996), 61.

101. See ibid., 66–92.

102. Rossi, "Participation Run Amok," 182.

103. Ibid., 193.

104. Hudson P. Henry, "A Shift in Citizen Suit Standing: *Friends of the Earth, Inc. v. Laidlaw Environmental Services*," *Ecology Law Quarterly* 28 (2001): 241.

105. Harris and Milkis, *Politics of Regulatory Change*, 241–42.

106. Ibid., 243.

107. Richard Stewart, "The Reformation of American Administrative Law," 1761. Internal citations omitted.

108. Kagan, *Adversarial Legalism*, 214.

109. Ibid.

110. Seidenfeld, "Demystifying Deossification," 512. Although Seidenfeld's comment here is in relation to "hard look" review, procedural requirements, and ossification, his argument equally applies to standing questions, namely, without judicial review agencies will serve private as opposed to public interests.

111. Ibid., 513.

112. Lisa Schultz Bressman, "Beyond Accountability: Arbitrariness and Legitimacy in the Administrative State," *New York University Law Review* 78 (2003): 496.

113. Ibid., 504.

114. See Professor Rabkin's excellent summary of scholars such as Richard Stewart and Cass Sunstein in *Judicial Compulsions*, 137–38.

115. Ibid., 139.

116. As Robert Kagan explains, one "distinctive feature of America regulatory law" is "the unique extent to which it encourages *private* enforcement of *public* law." *Adversarial Legalism*, 193. Emphasis in original.

117. Ibid., 225. Emphasis in original.

118. Rabkin, *Judicial Compulsions*, 142–43.

119. Cass R. Sunstein, "Beyond the Republican Revival," *Yale Law Journal* 97 (1988): 1556.

120. See Kornhauser, *Debating the American State*, 53: "The modern state had opened up a yawning gap between traditional democratic institutions and the actual practice

of democracy. . . . Critics of the 1960s would revisit [concerns about democracy] with more success, at least in terms of legal avenues of participation and redress."

121. Harris and Milkis, *The Politics of Regulatory Change*, 5, also ibid., chapter 3.

122. Ibid., 74.

123. See R. Shep Melnick, "The Politics of Partnership," *Public Administration Review* 45 (1985): 654–56.

124. Ibid., 658.

125. Ibid.

Chapter Eight
The Conservative Counterrevolution?
The Rise of a Jurisprudence of Deference

1. R. Shep Melnick, *Between the Lines: Interpreting Welfare Rights* (Washington, DC: Brookings Institution Press, 1994), 17.

2. Cass R. Sunstein, "Law and Administration after *Chevron*," *Columbia Law Review* 90 (1990): 2082.

3. 435 U.S. 519 (1978).

4. The vote was 7–0, as Justices Blackmun and Powell did not take part in the consideration or decision of the case.

5. Id., 557.

6. Id., 557.

7. Id., 558.

8. Id., 557.

9. 295 U.S. 495, at 553 (Cardozo, J., concurring). The *Schecter* case was discussed in Chapter Six.

10. 673 F.2d 525 (DC Cir. 1982).

11. Jack M. Beermann and Gary S. Lawson, "Reprocessing *Vermont Yankee*," *George Washington Law Review* 75 (2007): 860.

12. See *Portland Cement Ass'n v. Ruckelshaus*, 486 F.2d 375 (DC Cir. 1973), discussed in Chapter Seven. Today, consequently, almost every NPR includes significant data and findings alongside the proposed rule.

13. See *MCI Telecommunications Corp.* v. *Federal Communications Commission*, 57 F. 3d 1136 (DC Cir. 1995).

14. In *Chocolate Manufacturers Association of U.S. v. Block*, 755 F. 2d 1098 (4th Cir. 1985), for instance, the Fourth Circuit ruled that the NPR issued by the Department of Agriculture, determining which foods could be purchased with WIC [Women with Infant Children] coupons, was deficient because flavored milk was removed from the list of foods during the comment process. The court determined that this required additional notice and opportunity for comment since the rule had been changed through the rulemaking process. The court argued that the removal of flavored milk was not a "logical outgrowth" of the notice, but this seemed to ignore that, given the comments received and the notice given, the final rule delisting flavored milk was quite logical.

15. See *Reythlatt v. United States Nuclear Regulatory Commission*, 105 F.3d 715 (DC Cir. 1997).

16. Not the least of which is the fact that the Supreme Court can only review a limited number of cases per year. See Peter L. Strauss, "One Hundred and Fifty Cases per Year: Some Implications of the Supreme Court's Limited Resources for Judicial Review of Agency Action," *Columbia Law Review* 87 (1987): 1093–136. For this reason then-Professor Scalia described the Supreme Court as an "absentee landlord" in administrative law, while the DC Circuit is "a resident manager." Scalia, "*Vermont Yankee*," 371.

17. This term was first used in scholarship by Thomas McGarity, in "Some Thoughts on 'Deossifying' the Rulemaking Process," *Duke Law Journal* 41 (1992): 1385–462, although he attributes first usage of the term to E. Donald Elliot. See ibid., 1386 n.4.

18. McGarity, "Some Thoughts," 1385.

19. 5 U.S.C. § 553(b)(3)(A).

20. For two recent examples involving the Department of Education and the Food and Drug Administration, see R. Shep Melnick, "The Odd Evolution of the Civil Rights State," *Harvard Journal of Law and Public Policy* 37 (2014): 113–34, and Joseph Postell, "The Cheese(makers) Stand Alone," June 18, 2014, at http://www.libertylawsite.org/2014/06/18/the-cheesemakers-stand-alone/ (accessed 4/24/2016). In the legislative debates on the APA, supporters consistently explained that these exceptions were not to be abused, that courts would be able to review the agencies' rationale for invoking the exceptions, and that amendments to the APA would be needed if the exceptions were abused. As Senator McCarran explained, the "good cause" exemption for informal rulemaking would be allowed only if a reviewing court determined, independently of the agency, that it was justified: "it will be the duty of reviewing courts to prevent avoidance of the requirements of the bill by any manner or form of indirection, and to determine the meaning of the words and phrases used, insofar as they have not been defined in the bill itself." Senate Proceedings (statement of Sen. Pat McCarran, March 12, 1946) in *Administrative Procedure Act: Legislative History*, 326.

21. *Paralyzed Veterans of America v. D.C. Arena L.P.*, 117 F. 3d 579 (D.C. Cir., 1997).

22. *Perez v. Mortgage Bankers Association*, 575 U.S. ____ (2015).

23. 504 U.S. 555 (1992).

24. Id., at 560.

25. *Federal Election Commission v. Akins*, 524 U.S. 11 (1998). The kind of informational injury at issue in *FEC v. Atkins* closely resembled the *U.S. v. Salt Lake and Los Angeles Railroad* (discussed in Chapter Six), in which Brandeis argued that the ICC's valuation of a railroad was not subject to judicial review because it was not an order which affected the rights of the railroad. Those on the left who supported the loosening of standing requirements in *Akins* were opposed to Brandeis's view of standing in the *Salt Lake and Los Angeles Railroad* decision—another illustration of the shift in institutional allegiances.

26. 528 U.S. 167 (2000).

27. Id., at 185–86.

28. Major agency rules are those costing $100 million or more.

29. By Reagan's second term, roughly 30 percent of proposed rules were modified or abandoned altogether after undergoing OIRA review. During the presidency of George W. Bush, 150 regulations were withdrawn after OIRA review. Thus OIRA

review has clearly given the president some influence, but that influence has been limited.

30. As Christopher DeMuth explains, "Closer cases are typically the subject of vigorous internal disagreement; sometimes OMB prevails, sometimes the agencies prevail, sometimes OMB and the agencies compromise." DeMuth, "The Regulatory State," *National Affairs* (Summer 2012): 80.

31. As Lisa Heinzerling summarizes, "The process is utterly opaque . . . [and] diffuses power to such an extent . . . that at the end of the day no one is accountable for the results it demands." Heinzerling, "Inside EPA: A Former Insider's Reflections on the Relationship between the Obama EPA and the Obama White House," *Pace Environmental Law Review* 31 (2014): 326. Christopher DeMuth similarly explains that while "White House review has, with little ado, culled many clearly bad agency proposals and fortified many clearly good ones . . . these improvements, while real, have been marginal." DeMuth, "The Regulatory State," 80.

32. *Chevron U.S.A. Inc., v. Natural Resources Defense Council, Inc.*, 467 U.S. 837 (1984).

33. Ibid., 842–43.

34. Justice Stevens, generally considered to be a liberal, was the author of the Court's opinion in *Chevron*; however, conservative jurists and legal scholars quickly seized on the ruling in *Chevron* and sought to make it an across-the-board presumption in favor of agency legal interpretations. Thus it was conservatives who made *Chevron* into an important precedent, by invoking it in subsequent opinions, rather than the author of the opinion itself.

35. Linda Jellum, "*Chevron*'s Demise: A Survey of *Chevron* from Infancy to Senescence," *Administrative Law Review* 59 (2007): 730. See also Ann Graham, "Searching for *Chevron* in Muddy Waters: The Roberts Court and Judicial Review of Agency Decisions," *Administrative Law Review* 60 (2008): 271: "Analysis of the Roberts Court cases shows that classic *Chevron* analysis is dead—or at least critically wounded." See also Michael Herz, "The Rehnquist Court and Administrative Law," *Northwestern Law Review* 99 (2004): 321: "The Court is not actually as deferential to agencies as all the fuss about *Chevron* would make it seem. It is generally accepted that the Supreme Court has not been more deferential to agency interpretations since *Chevron* was decided than it was before."

36. Thomas W. Merrill and Kristin E. Hickman, "*Chevron*'s Domain," *Georgetown Law Journal* 89 (2001): 833–921.

37. Sunstein, "*Chevron* Step Zero," 191.

38. For instance, in *Young v. Community Nutrition Institute*, 476 U.S. 974 (1986), the Court reviewed an agency's interpretation of the Federal Food, Drug and Cosmetic Act. The language of the statute said that the Secretary of Health and Human Services "shall promulgate regulations limiting the quantity [of any poisonous or deleterious substance added to food] to such extent as he finds necessary for the protection of public health." (21 U.S.C. § 346) The question was whether the term "shall" limited the secretary's discretion, in essence depriving the secretary of the discretion *not* to issue regulations, or whether "to the extent necessary" granted the discretion not to regulate,

rather than merely allowing the administrator to regulate less or more as needed to protect public health. The FDA had adopted the former interpretation through informal procedures rather than a formal rulemaking. Without asking whether *Chevron* should apply at all to an interpretation adopted by informal procedures, the Court invoked *Chevron* and deferred to the FDA's interpretation, overturning a Court of Appeals decision that had rejected that same interpretation. It made no distinction between agency interpretation adopted through formal procedures and those adopted through informal procedures.

39. 529 U.S. 576 (2000).

40. Id., at 587.

41. Id., at 589.

42. 533 U.S. 218 (2001).

43. Id., at 226–27.

44. This formulation is taken from the case of *Skidmore v. Swift & Co.*, 323 U.S. 134 (1944), which declared that agency interpretations of law, "while not controlling upon the courts by reason of their authority, do constitute a body of expertise and informed judgment to which courts and litigants may properly resort for guidance. The weight of such a judgment . . . will depend upon the thoroughness evident in its consideration, the vitality of its reasoning, its consistency with earlier and later pronouncements, and all those factors which give it power to persuade, if lacking power to control." Ibid., 140.

45. *U.S. v. Mead*, 235–36.

46. Ibid., 241 (Scalia, J., dissenting).

47. 512 U.S. 218 (1994).

48. 529 U.S. 120 (2000).

49. Ibid., 159–60.

50. 547 U.S. 715 (2006).

51. Ibid., 734.

52. Note, "How Clear Is Clear in *Chevron* Step One?" *Harvard Law Review* 118 (2005): 1693.

53. Ibid. Emphasis added.

54. Ibid., 1699, citing Thomas W. Merrill, "Textualism and the Future of the *Chevron* Doctrine," *Washington University Law Quarterly* 72 (1994): 362.

55. William N. Eskridge Jr. and Lauren E. Baer, "The Continuum of Deference: Supreme Court Treatment of Agency Statutory Interpretations from *Chevron* to *Hamdan*," *Georgetown Law Journal* 96 (2008): 1083–226, is an empirical analysis of how Supreme Court judges vote on cases of agency statutory interpretation that draws this conclusion.

56. "How Clear Is Clear?" 1699.

57. Elena Kagan, "Presidential Administration," *Harvard Law Review* 114 (2001): 2376–77.

58. Elliot, "*Chevron* Matters," 5.

59. Juliet Eilperin, "EPA Presses Obama to Regulate Warming under Clean Air Act," *Washington Post*, March 24, 2009.

60. See Andrew Grossman, "TARP: Now a Slush Fund for Detroit?" *The Foundry*, December 12, 2008.

61. Sunstein, "Law and Administration after *Chevron*," 2086–89.

62. 569 U.S. _____ (2013).

63. Cass R. Sunstein, "The Catch in the Obamacare Opinion," *Bloomberg View*, June 25, 2015.

64. *Michigan v. Environmental Protection Agency*, 576 U.S. ___ (2015).

65. Ibid. (Thomas, J., concurring).

66. 463 U.S. 29 (1983).

67. 463 U.S. at 43.

68. Mark Seidenfeld, "Demystifying Deossification: Rethinking Recent Proposals to Modify Judicial Review of Notice and Comment Rulemaking," *Texas Law Review* 75 (1997): 491.

69. Ibid., 491–92.

70. *State Farm*, 463 U.S. at 59 (footnote omitted).

71. Thomas J. Miles and Cass R. Sunstein, "The Real World of Arbitrariness Review," *University of Chicago Law Review* 75 (2008): 761.

72. Robert A. Schapiro, "Judicial Deference and Interpretive Coordinacy in State and Federal Constitutional Law," *Cornell Law Review* 85 (2000): 682.

73. Richard J. Pierce, "Democratizing the Administrative State," *William and Mary Law Review* 48 (2006): 562. The case to which Pierce is referring is the "Benzene" case, *Industrial Union Department, AFL-CIO v. American Petroleum Institute*, 448 U.S. 607 (1980).

74. For Thomas's most explicit indication that he would entertain reviving judicial enforcement of the nondelegation doctrine, see his concurring opinion in *Whitman v. American Trucking Association*, 531 U.S. 486–87 (2001).

75. 488 U.S. 361 (1989).

76. 487 U.S. 654 (1988).

77. 561 U.S. 477 (2010).

78. 435 U.S. at 548.

79. Scalia, "*Vermont Yankee*," 387–88.

80. 435 U.S. at 524.

81. Id., at 543, quoting *FCC v. Schreiber*, 381 U.S. 279, 290 (1965), which quoted *FCC v. Pottsville Broadcasting Co.*, 309 U.S. 134, 143 (1940).

82. *FCC v. Pottsville Broadcasting Co.*, 309 U.S. 134, 141–43. Internal citations omitted.

83. Scalia, "*Vermont Yankee*," 403.

84. Ibid.

85. Ibid., 403–4.

86. Antonin Scalia, "The Doctrine of Standing as an Essential Element of the Separation of Powers," *Suffolk University Law Review* 17 (1983): 881–99.

87. 524 U.S. 36–37 (1998).

88. 528 U.S. 215 (2000).

89. Scalia, "Doctrine of Standing as an Essential Element," 896.

90. Ibid., 894.

91. 528 U.S. 210 (2000).

92. Elliot, "*Chevron* Matters," 14.

93. Antonin Scalia, "The Role of the Judiciary in Deregulation," *Antitrust Law Journal* 55 (1986): 193.

94. Antonin Scalia, "Judicial Deference to Administrative Interpretations of Law," *Duke Law Journal* (1989): 516.

95. Ibid.

96. Ibid., 516–17.

97. Herz, "The Rehnquist Court and Administrative Law," 303.

98. Bernard Schwartz, "Federalism, Administrative Law, and the Rehnquist Court in Action," *Tulsa Law Journal* 32 (1997): 480.

Conclusion
The Ongoing Crisis of Legitimacy

1. See Daniel Ernst, *Tocqueville's Nightmare: The Administrative State Arrives in America, 1900–1940* (New York: Oxford University Press, 2014), 7–8, 142–46.

2. Herman Belz, *A Living Constitution or Fundamental Law? American Constitutionalism in Historical Perspective* (Lanham, MD: Rowman & Littlefield, 1988), 159, 154.

3. See *City of Arlington v. FCC*, 569 U.S. ___ (2013) (Roberts, C.J., dissenting); *Perez v. Mortgage Bankers Ass'n*, 575 U.S. ___ (2015) (Thomas, J., concurring).

4. David Rosenbloom, *Public Administration and Law*, 9. See also "constitutional values and administrative values are often incompatible." Ibid., 263.

5. Ibid., v.

6. Ibid., 259, 265.

7. G. Edward White, *The Constitution and the New Deal* (Cambridge, MA: Harvard University Press, 2000), 95.

BIBLIOGRAPHY

Adams, Charles Francis. *An Appeal from the New to the Old Whigs*. Boston: Russel, Odiorne & Co., 1835.

American Airlines, Inc. v. Civil Aeronautics Board, 359 F. 2d. 624 (DC Cir., 1966).

American Medical Association v. Reno, 57 F. 3d. 1129 (DC Cir., 1995).

American School of Magnetic Healing v. McAnnulty, 187 U.S. 94 (1902).

Ashwander v. Tennessee Valley Authority, 297 U.S. 288 (1936).

Association of Data Processing Service Organizations v. Camp, 397 U.S. 150 (1970).

Automotive Parts & Accessories Association v. Boyd, 407 F. 2d. 330 (DC Cir., 1968).

Balogh, Brian. *A Government Out of Sight: The Mystery of National Authority in Nineteenth-Century America*. New York: Cambridge University Press, 2009.

Bamzai, Aditya. "The Origins of Judicial Deference to Executive Interpretation." *Yale Law Journal* 126 (2016–17): 908–1001.

Barck, Oscar Theodore Jr., and Hugh Talmage Lefler. *Colonial America*, 2d ed. New York: Macmillan, 1968.

Bartlett v. Kane, 57 U.S. (16 How.) 263 (1853).

Bates v. Payne, 194 U.S. 106 (1904).

Beard, Charles A. "Jefferson and the New Freedom." *The New Republic*, November 14, 1914.

Beermann, Jack M., and Gary S. Lawson. "Reprocessing *Vermont Yankee*." *George Washington Law Review* 75 (2007): 856–901.

Belz, Herman. *A Living Constitution or Fundamental Law? American Constitutionalism in Historical Perspective*. Lanham, MD: Rowman & Littlefield, 1988.

Bernstein, Marver H. *Regulating Business by Independent Commission*. Princeton, NJ: Princeton University Press, 1955.

Best, Judith. "The Presidency and the Executive Power." In *The Framing and Ratification of the Constitution*, edited by Leonard W. Levy and Dennis J. Mahoney, 209–21. New York: Macmillan, 1987.

Bestor, Arthur. "The American Civil War as a Constitutional Crisis." *American Historical Review* 69 (1964): 327–52.

Bi-Metallic Investment Co. v. State Board of Equalization of Colorado, 239 U.S. 441 (1915).

Board of Regents of State Colleges v. Roth, 408 U.S. 564 (1972).

Bressman, Lisa Schultz. "Beyond Accountability: Arbitrariness and Legitimacy in the Administrative State." *New York University Law Review* 78 (2003): 461–556.

Calabresi, Steven G., and Christopher S. Yoo. "The Unitary Executive during the First Half-Century." *Case Western Reserve Law Review* 47 (1997): 1451–561.

———. "The Unitary Executive during the Second Half-Century." *Harvard Journal of Law & Public Policy* 26 (2003): 667–801.

Carey, George. *The Federalist: Design for a Constitutional Republic*. Urbana: University of Illinois Press, 1989.

Carrington, Paul D. "Law and Economics in the Creation of Federal Administrative Law: Thomas Cooley, Elder to the Republic." *Iowa Law Review* 83 (1998): 363–90.

Cary v. Curtis, 44 U.S. (3 How.) 236 (1845).

City of Arlington v. FCC. 569 U.S. _____ (2013).

Chocolate Manufacturers Association of U.S. v. Block, 755 F. 2d. 1098 (4th Cir., 1985).

Christensen v. Harris County, 529 U.S. 576 (2000).

Converse v. Burgess, 59 U.S. (18 How.) 413 (1855).

Cook, Brian J. *Bureaucracy and Self-Government: Reconsidering the Role of Public Administration*. Baltimore: Johns Hopkins University Press, 1996.

Cooley, Thomas M. "Limits to State Control of Private Business." *Princeton Review* 1 (1878): 233–71.

———. "State Regulation of Corporate Profits." *North American Review* 137 (1883): 207–17.

———. *A Treatise on the Constitutional Limitations Which Rest upon the Legislative Power of the States of the American Union*. Boston: Little, Brown & Co., 1868.

Connecticut Light and Power Company v. Nuclear Regulatory Commission, 673 F. 2d. 525 (DC Cir., 1982).

Cooper, Charles J. "Confronting the Administrative State." *National Affairs* 25 (2015): 96–108.

Croly, Herbert D. *Progressive Democracy*. New York: Macmillan Co., 1914; reprint, New Brunswick, NJ: Transaction Publishers, 1998.

———. *The Promise of American Life*. New York: Macmillan, 1909; reprint, Boston: Northeastern University Press, 1989.

Crowell v. Benson, 285 U.S. 22 (1932).

Cushing, Harry Alonzo. *History of the Transition from Provincial to Commonwealth Government in Massachusetts*. New York, 1896.

Cushman, Robert D. *The Independent Regulatory Commissions*. 1941; reprint New York: Octagon Books, 1972.

Davis, Kenneth Culp. *Administrative Law*. St. Paul: West Publishing Co., 1951.

———. "Dean Pound and Administrative Law." *Columbia Law Review* 42 (1942): 89–103.

———. "A New Approach to Delegation." *University of Chicago Law Review* 36 (1969): 713–33.

Decatur v. Paulding, 57 U.S. (14 Pet.) 497 (1840).

DeMuth, Christopher. "The Regulatory State." *National Affairs* 12 (2012): 70–91.

Dewey, John. "The Ethics of Democracy." In *John Dewey: the Early Works*, vol. 3. Carbondale: Southern Illinois University Press, 1969.

Dickerson, Oliver Morton. *American Colonial Government 1696–1765*. Cleveland: Arthur Clark Co., 1912.

Dickinson, John. *Administrative Justice and the Supremacy of Law in the United States.* Cambridge, MA: Harvard University Press, 1927.

———. "Administrative Procedure Act: Scope and Grounds of Broadened Judicial Review." *American Bar Association Journal* 33 (1947): 434–37, 513–19.

Dry, Murray. "The Case against Ratification: Anti-Federalist Constitutional Thought." In *The Framing and Ratification of the Constitution*, edited by Leonard W. Levy and Dennis J. Mahoney, 271–91. New York: Macmillan, 1987.

Duffy, John. "Hogs, Dogs, and Dirt: Public Health in Early Pittsburgh." *Pennsylvania Magazine of History and Biography* 87 (1963): 204–305.

Duffy, John F. "Administrative Common Law in Judicial Review." *Texas Law Review* 77 (1998): 113–214.

Edward Hines Yellow Pines Trustees v. United States, 263 U.S. 143 (1923).

Eisenach, Eldon J. *The Lost Promise of Progressivism*. Lawrence: University Press of Kansas, 1994.

Eisner, Marc Allen. *Regulatory Politics in Transition*, 2d ed. Baltimore: Johns Hopkins University Press, 2000.

Elliot, E. Donald. "*Chevron* Matters: How the Chevron Doctrine Redefined the Roles of Congress, Courts and Agencies in Environmental Law." *Villanova Environmental Law Journal* 16 (2005): 1–18.

Ellis, Richard J. *The Development of the American Presidency*. New York: Routledge, 2012.

Elson, Henry William. *History of the United States of America*. New York: Macmillan, 1904.

Ernst, Daniel R. "Ernst Freund, Felix Frankfurter, and the American *Rechtstaat*: A Transatlantic Shipwreck." *Studies in American Political Development* 23 (2009): 171–88.

———. *Tocqueville's Nightmare: The Administrative State Emerges in America, 1900–1940*. New York: Oxford University Press, 2014.

Eskridge, William N. Jr., and Lauren E. Baer. "The Continuum of Deference: Supreme Court Treatment of Agency Statutory Interpretations from *Chevron* to *Hamdan*." *Georgetown Law Journal* 96 (2008): 1083–226.

Ethyl Corp. v. EPA, 541 F. 2d. 1 (DC Cir., 1976).

Ex Parte Gilchrist, 10 F. Cas. 355 (1808).

Fairlie, John A. *Local Government in Counties, Towns and Villages*. New York: Century Co., 1906.

Farrand, Max. *The Records of the Federal Convention of 1787*. New Haven: Yale University Press, 1911.

Federal Communications Commission v. Pottsville Broadcasting Co., 309 U.S. 134 (1940).

Federal Election Commission v. Akins, 524 U.S. 11 (1998).

Federal Trade Commission v. Cement Institute, 333 U.S. 683 (1948).

Federal Trade Commission v. Gratz, 253 U.S. 421 (1920).

Federal Trade Commission v. Ruberoid Co., 343 U.S. 470 (1952).

Ferejohn, John A., and Larry D. Kramer. "Independent Judges, Dependent Judiciary: Institutionalizing Judicial Restraint." *New York University Law Review* 77 (2002): 962–1039.

Ferrell, Robert H. *Harry S. Truman: A Life*. Columbia, MO: University of Missouri Press, 1996.

Food and Drug Administration v. Brown & Williamson, 529 U.S. 120 (2000).

Forcey, Charles. *The Crossroads of Liberalism: Croly, Weyl, Lippmann and the Progressive Era, 1900–1925*. New York: Oxford University Press, 1967.

Free Enterprise Fund v. Public Company Accounting Oversight Board (PCAOB), 561 U.S. 477 (2010).

Freedman, James. *Crisis and Legitimacy: The Administrative Process and American Government*. New York: Cambridge University Press, 1980.

Freund, Ernst. *Administrative Powers over Persons and Property: A Comparative Survey*. Chicago: University of Chicago Press, 1928.

———. "The Law of the Administration in America." *Political Science Quarterly* 9 (1894): 403–25.

———. *The Police Power: Public Policy and Constitutional Rights*. Chicago: Callaghan & Co., 1904.

———. *Standards of American Legislation*. Chicago: University of Chicago Press, 1917.

———. "The Substitution of Rule for Discretion in Public Law." *American Political Science Review* 9 (1915): 666–76.

Friedman, Lawrence M. *A History of American Law*. 2d ed. New York: Simon and Schuster, 1985.

Friends of the Earth vs. Laidlaw Environmental Services, 528 U.S. 167 (2000).

Gellhorn, Walter. "The Administrative Procedure Act: The Beginnings." *Virginia Law Review* 72 (1986): 219–33.

Gillman, Howard. *The Constitution Besieged: The Rise and Demise of Lochner-Era Police Power Jurisprudence*. Durham, NC: Duke University Press, 1993.

Goldberg v. Kelly, 397 U.S. 254 (1970).

Goodnow, Frank J. *Politics and Administration*. New York: Macmillan Co., 1914.

Graham, Ann. "Searching for *Chevron* in Muddy Waters: The Roberts Court and Judicial Review of Agency Decisions." *Administrative Law Review* 60 (2008): 229–72.

Gray v. Powell, 314 U.S. 402 (1941).

Greater Boston Television Corp. v. Federal Communication Commission, 444 F. 2d. 841 (1970).

Greely v. Thompson, 51 U.S. (10 How.) 225 (1850).

Green, Fletcher M. *Constitutional Development in the South Atlantic States: A Study in the Evolution of Democracy*. Chapel Hill: University of North Carolina Press, 1930.

Green, Mary Fulton. "A Profile of Columbia in 1850." *South Carolina Historical Magazine* 70 (1969): 104–21.

Grisinger, Joanna L. *The Unwieldy American State: Administrative Politics since the New Deal*. New York: Cambridge University Press, 2012.

Guggenheimer, Jay Caesar. "The Development of the Executive Departments, 1775–1789. In *Essays on the Constitutional History of the United States during the Formative Period, 1775–1789*, edited by J. Franklin Jameson, 116–85. Boston: Houghton, Mifflin & Co., 1889.

Gunn, L. Ray. *The Decline of Authority: Public Economic Policy and Political Development in New York State, 1800–1860*. Ithaca, NY: Cornell University Press, 1988.

Hamburger, Philip. *Is Administrative Law Unlawful?* Chicago: University of Chicago Press, 2014.

Hamilton, Alexander, James Madison, and John Jay. *The Federalist*. Edited by Jacob E. Cooke. Middletown, CT: Wesleyan University Press, 1961.

Handlin, Oscar, and Mary Handlin. *Commonwealth: A Study of the Role of Government in the American Economy: Massachusetts, 1774–1861*. Revised ed. Cambridge, MA: Harvard University Press, 1969.

Harris, Richard A., and Sidney M. Milkis. *The Politics of Regulatory Change: A Tale of Two Agencies*. 2d ed. New York: Oxford University Press, 1996.

Hart, James. *The American Presidency in Action*. New York: Macmillan Co., 1948.

Hartz, Louis. *Economic Policy and Democratic Thought: Pennsylvania 1776–1860*. Cambridge, MA: Harvard University Press, 1948.

Hawley, Ellis W. "The New Deal State and Anti-Bureaucratic Tradition." In *The New Deal and Its Legacy: Critique and Reappraisal*, edited by Robert Eden, 77–92. Westport, CT: Greenwood Press, 1989.

Hayek, Friedrich. *The Constitution of Liberty*. Paperback ed. Chicago: University of Chicago Press, 1978.

Heinzerling, Lisa. "Inside EPA: A Former Insider's Reflection on the Relationship between the Obama EPA and the Obama White House." *Pace Environmental Law Review* 31 (2014): 325–69.

Hendrick Hudson District Board of Education v. Rowley, 458 U.S. 176 (1982).

Henry, Hudson P. "A Shift in Citizen Suit Standing: *Friends of the Earth, Inc. v. Laidlaw Environmental Services*." *Ecology Law Quarterly* 28 (2001): 233–52.

Herz, Michael. "The Rehnquist Court and Administrative Law." *Northwestern University Law Review* 99 (2004): 368–81.

Hofstadter, Richard. *The Age of Reform: From Bryan to FDR*. New York: Random House, 1955.

Holland, Kenneth M. "Roger Taney." In *American Political Thought: The Philosophic Dimension of American Statesmanship*, edited by Morton J. Frisch and Richard G. Stevens, 3d ed., 225–50. New Bruswick, NJ: Transaction Publishers, 2011.

Honig v. Doe, 484 U.S. 305 (1988).

Hoogenboom, Ari. *Outlawing the Spoils: A History of the Civil Service Reform Movement, 1865–1883*. Urbana: University of Illinois Press, 1968.

Howland, Harold. *Theodore Roosevelt and His Times: A Chronicle of the Progressive Movement*. New Haven: Yale University Press, 1921.

Hughes, Jonathan. *The Government Habit Redux: Economic Controls from Colonial Times to the Present*. Princeton, NJ: Princeton University Press, 1991.

Humphrey's Executor v. United States, 295 U.S. 602 (1935).

Industrial Union Department, AFL-CIO v. American Petroleum Institute, 448 U.S. 607 (1980).

Industrial Union Department, AFL-CIO v. Hodgson, 499 F. 2d. 476 (DC Cir., 1974).

Interstate Commerce Commission v. Alabama Midland Railway Co., 168 U.S. 144 (1897).

Interstate Commerce Commission v. Cincinnati, New Orleans, and Texas Pacific Railway Co., 167 U.S. 479 (1897).

Interstate Commerce Commission v. Illinois Central Railroad Co., 215 U.S. 470 (1910).

Interstate Commerce Commission v. Northern Pacific Railroad Co., 216 U.S. 538 (1910).

Jaffe, Louis. Review of Roscoe Pound, *Administrative Law: Its Growth, Procedure, and Significance*. In *Columbia Law Review* 42 (1942): 1382–85.

Jellum, Linda. "*Chevron's* Demise: A Survey of *Chevron* from Infancy to Senescence." *Administrative Law Review* 59 (2007): 725–82.

Jensen, Laura. *Patriots, Settlers, and the Origins of American Social Policy*. New York: Cambridge University Press, 2003.

Johnson v. Towsley, 80 U.S. 72 (1871).

Jones, Alan. "Thomas M. Cooley and Laissez-Faire Constitutionalism: A Reconsideration." *Journal of American History* 53 (1967): 751–71.

———. "Thomas M. Cooley and the Interstate Commerce Commission: Continuity and Change in the Doctrine of Equal Rights." *Political Science Quarterly* 81 (1966): 602–27.

Kagan, Elena. "Presidential Administration." *Harvard Law Review* 114 (2001): 2246–385.

Kagan, Robert A. *Adversarial Legalism: The American Way of Law*. Cambridge, MA: Harvard University Press, 2003.

Katzmann, Robert. *Institutional Disability: The Saga of Transportation Policy for the Disabled*. Washington DC: The Brookings Institution Press, 1986.

Keller, Morton. *America's Three Regimes*. New York: Oxford University Press, 2007.

Kendall v. Stokes, 44. U.S. (3 How) 87 (1845).

Landis, James. *The Administrative Process*. New Haven, CT: Yale University Press, 1938.

———. "Report to the President-Elect." December 21, 1960, Senate Judiciary Committee, 86th Congress, 2nd Session.

Lawson, Gary S. "Delegation and Original Meaning." *Virginia Law Review* 88 (2002): 327–404.

———. *Federal Administrative Law*, 6th ed. St. Paul: West Publishing, 2013.

———. "The Rise and Rise of the Administrative State." *Harvard Law Review* 107 (1994): 1231–54.

Lewis, David. *Presidents and the Politics of Agency Design: Political Insulation in the United States Government Bureaucracy, 1946–1997*. Stanford, CA: Stanford University Press, 2003.

Leventhal, Harold. "Environmental Decisionmaking and the Role of the Courts." *University of Pennsylvania Law Review* 122 (1974): 536–41.

Little v. Barreme, 6. U.S. 170 (1804).

Lockridge, Kenneth A., and Alan Kreider. "The Evolution of Massachusetts Town Government, 1640 to 1740." *William and Mary Quarterly* 23 (1966): 549–74.

Londoner v. City and County of Denver, 210 U.S. 373 (1908).

Lorch, Robert S. *Democratic Process and Administrative Law*. Detroit: Wayne State University Press, 1980.

Lowi, Theodore. *The End of Liberalism: The Second Republic of the United States*. 2d ed. New York: W.W. Norton, 1979.

Lujan v. Defenders of Wildlife, 504 U.S. 555 (1992).

Kornhauser, Anne M. *Debating the American State: Liberal Anxieties and the New Leviathan, 1930–1970*. Philadelphia: University of Pennsylvania Press, 2015.

Manufacturers' Railway Company v. United States, 246 U.S. 457 (1918).

Marini, John, and Ken Masugi, eds. *The Progressive Revolution in Politics and Political Science*. Lanham, MD: Lexington Books, 2007.

Mashaw, Jerry L. *Creating the Administrative Constitution: The Lost Hundred Years of Administrative Law*. New Haven: Yale University Press, 2012.

McCarran, Pat. "Improving 'Administrative Justice': Hearings and Evidence; Scope of Judicial Review." *American Bar Association Journal* 32 (1946): 827–31, 893–94.

———. "The Unwritten and Irrational Constitution of Regulatory Government in the United States." *Notre Dame Law Review* 24 (1948): 62–69.

McCraw, Thomas K. *Prophets of Regulation*. Cambridge, MA: Harvard University Press, 1986.

McCubbins, Mathew D., Roger G. Noll, and Barry R. Weingast. "Administrative Procedures as Instruments of Political Control." *Journal of Law, Economics, and Organization* 3 (1987): 243–77.

———. "The Political Origins of the Administrative Procedure Act." *Journal of Law, Economics, and Organization* 15 (1999): 180–217.

McDonald, Forrest. *The American Presidency: An Intellectual History*. Lawrence: University Press of Kansas, 1994.

McGarity, Thomas O. "Some Thoughts on 'Deossifying' the Rulemaking Process." *Duke Law Journal* 41 (1992): 1385–1462.

MCI Telecommunications Corp. v. Federal Communications Commission, 57 F. 3d. 1136 (DC Cir., 1995).

Melnick, R. Shep. *Between the Lines: Interpreting Welfare Rights*. Washington, DC: The Brookings Institution Press, 1994.

———. *Clearing the Air: The Case of the Clean Air Act*. Washington, DC.: The Brookings Institution Press, 1983.

———. "Executive Power and Administrative Law." *The Public Interest* 97 (1989): 134–39.

———. "The Odd Evolution of the Civil Rights State." *Harvard Journal of Law and Public Policy* 37 (2014): 113–34.

———. "The Politics of Partnership." *Public Administration Review* 45 (1985): 653–60.

Merriam, Charles E. *American Political Ideas: Studies in the Development of American Political Thought, 1865–1917.* New York: Macmillan Co., 1920.

———. *A History of American Political Theories.* New York: Macmillan Co., 1915.

Merrill, Thomas W. "Article III, Agency Adjudication, and the Origins of the Appellate Review Model of Administrative Law." *Columbia Law Review* 111 (2011): 939–1003.

———, and Kristin E. Hickman. "*Chevron*'s Domain." *Georgetown Law Journal* 89 (2001): 833–921.

Miles, Thomas J., and Cass R. Sunstein. "The Real World of Arbitrariness Review." *University of Chicago Law Review* 75 (2008): 761–814.

Milkis, Sidney M. *The President and the Parties: The Transformation of the American Party System since the New Deal.* New York: Oxford University Press, 1993.

———. *Theodore Roosevelt, the Progressive Party, and the Transformation of American Democracy.* Lawrence: University Press of Kansas, 2009.

Mistretta v. United States, 488 U.S. 361 (1989).

Moreno, Paul D. *The Bureaucrat Kings: The Origins and Underpinnings of America's Bureaucratic State.* New York: ABC-Clio, 2016.

———. "'The Legitimate Object of Government': Constitutional Problems of Civil War-Era Reconstruction Policy." In *Constitutionalism in the Approach and Aftermath of the Civil War*, edited by Paul D. Moreno and Johnathan O'Neill, 161–82. New York: Fordham University Press, 2013.

Morgan, Edmund S. *The Birth of the Republic.* 3d ed. Chicago: University of Chicago Press, 1992.

Morrisey, Will. *The Dilemma of Progressivism: How Roosevelt, Taft, and Wilson Reshaped the American Regime of Self-Government.* Lanham, MD: Rowman & Littlefield, 2009.

Morrison v. Olson, 487 U.S. 654 (1988).

Motor Vehicle Manufacturers Association v. State Farm, 463 U.S. 29 (1983).

Moynihan, Donald P. "Protection versus Flexibility: The Civil Service Reform Act, Competing Administrative Doctrines, and the Roots of the Contemporary Public Management Debate. *Journal of Policy History* 16 (2004): 1–33.

Murray's Lessee v. Hoboken Land & Improvement Co., 59 U.S. (18 How.) 272 (1856).

Myers v. United States, 272 U.S. 52 (1926).

Nathan, Richard. *The Plot that Failed: Nixon and the Administrative Presidency.* New York: Wiley & Sons, Inc., 1975.

National Labor Relations Board v. Hearst Publications, 322 U.S. 111 (1944).

Nelson, Michael. *The Presidency and the Political System.* 10th ed. Washington, DC: CQ Press, 2013.

Nelson, William E. *The Americanization of the Common Law: The Impact of Legal Change on Massachusetts Society, 1760–1830.* Cambridge, MA: Harvard University Press, 1975.

Newman, Bruce. *Against that 'Powerful Engine of Despotism': The Fourth Amendment and General Warrants at the Founding and Today.* Lanham, MD: University Press of America, 2007.

Nichols, David K. "The Promise of Progressivism: Herbert Croly and the Progressive Rejection of Individual Rights." *Publius: The Journal of Federalism* 17 (1987): 27–39.

Noble, David W. *The Paradox of Progressivism.* St. Paul: University of Minnesota Press, 1958.

Noll, Roger G. *Reforming Regulation.* Washington, DC: The Brookings Institution, 1971.

Novak, William J. *The People's Welfare: Law and Regulation in Nineteenth-Century America.* Chapel Hill: North Carolina University Press, 1996.

O'Donnell v. Shaffer, 491 F. 2d. 59 (DC Cir., 1974).

Office of Communication of United Church of Christ v. Federal Communications Commission, 359 F. 2d. 994 (DC Cir., 1966).

O'Hara, James B. "Out of the Shadows: Roger Brooke Taney as Chief Justice." *Journal of Supreme Court History* 23 (1998): 21–38.

O'Leary v. Brown-Pacific-Maxon, 340 U.S. 504 (1951).

Okayama, Hiroshi. "The Interstate Commerce Commission and the Political Origins of a Judicialized Administrative State." Paper presented at the Annual Meeting for the American Political Science Association, 2011.

Otis v. Watkins, 13 U.S. (9 Cranch) 339 (1815).

Panama Refining Co. v. Ryan, 293 U.S. 418 (1935).

Paralyzed Veterans of America v. D.C. Arena L.P., 117 F. 3d. 579 (DC Cir., 1997).

Park, Soo-Young. "Who Is Our Master? Congressional Debates during Civil Service Reforms." PhD diss., Virginia Polytechnic Institute and State University, 2005.

People v. Salem, 20 Mich. 487 (1870).

Perez v. Mortgage Bankers Association, 575 U.S. ___ (2015).

Pestritto, Ronald J., and William Atto. Introduction to *American Progressivism: A Reader,* 1–32. Lanham, MD: Lexington Books, 2008.

Pestritto, Ronald J. *Woodrow Wilson and the Roots of Modern Liberalism.* Lanham, MD: Rowman & Littlefield, 2005.

Pierce, Richard J. "Democratizing the Administrative State." *William and Mary Law Review* 48 (2006): 559–611.

Portland Cement Association v. Ruckleshaus, 486 F. 2d. 375 (DC Cir., 1973).

Postell, Joseph. "The Anti-New Deal Progressive: Roscoe Pound's Alternative Administrative State." *Review of Politics* 73 (2012): 53–85.

———. "Regulation, Administration, and the Rule of Law in the Early Republic." In *Freedom and the Rule of Law,* edited by Anthony A. Peacock, 41–70. Lanham, MD: Lexington Books, 2010.

———. "Regulation during the American Founding: Achieving Liberalism and Republicanism." *American Political Thought* 5 (2016): 80–108.

———. "The Right Kind of Regulation: How the Founders Thought about Regulation." In *Rediscovering Political Economy,* edited by Joseph Postell and Bradley C.S. Watson, 209–30. Lanham, MD: Lexington Books, 2011.

Pound, Roscoe. "Executive Justice." *American Law Register* 55 (1907): 137–46.
———. "The Growth of Administrative Justice." *Wisconsin Law Review* 2 (1924): 321–29.
———. *Interpretations of Legal History*. New York: Macmillan Co., 1923.
———. "Liberty of Contract." *Yale Law Journal* 18 (1909): 454–87.
———. "Mechanical Jurisprudence." *Columbia Law Review* 8 (1908): 605–23.
———. "The Need of a Sociological Jurisprudence." *Green Bag* 19 (1907): 607–15.
———. *The Organization of Courts*. Law Association of Philadelphia, 1913.
———. "The Rule of Law and the Modern Social Welfare State." *Vanderbilt Law Review* 7 (1953): 1–33.
———. "The Scope and Purpose of Sociological Jurisprudence." *Harvard Law Review* 24 (1911): 591–619.
———. "The Scope and Purpose of Sociological Jurisprudence." *Harvard Law Review* 25 (1911): 489–516.
Prakash, Saikrishna. "Hail to the Chief Administrator: The Framers and the President's Administrative Powers." *Yale Law Journal* 102 (1993): 991–1017.
Primm, James Neal. *Economic Policy in the Development of a Western State: Missouri, 1820–1860*. Cambridge, MA: Harvard University Press, 1954.
Rabin, Robert L. "Federal Regulation in Historical Perspective." *Stanford Law Review* 38 (1986): 1189–326.
Rabkin, Jeremy. *Judicial Compulsions*. New York: Basic Books, 1989.
Rapanos v. U.S., 547 U.S. 715 (2006).
Reytblatt v. United States Nuclear Regulatory Commission, 105 F. 3d. 715 (DC Cir., 1997).
Rohr, John A. *To Run a Constitution: The Legitimacy of the Administrative State*. Lawrence: University Press of Kansas, 1986.
Roosevelt, Franklin. "Veto of a Bill Regulating Administrative Agencies." December 8, 1940. Available online at http://www.presidency.ucsb.edu/ws/index.php?pid=15914.
Roosevelt, Theodore. *The Autobiography of Theodore Roosevelt*. New York: Scribner's & Sons, 1913.
Rosenbloom, David H., and Rosemary O'Leary. *Public Administration and Law*. 2d ed. New York: Marcel Dekker, 1996.
Rossi, Jim. "Participation Run Amok: The Costs of Mass Participation for Deliberative Agency Decisionmaking." *Northwestern University Law Review* 92 (1997): 173–250.
Scalia, Antonin. "The Doctrine of Standing as an Essential Element of the Separation of Powers." *Suffolk University Law Review* 17 (1983): 881–99.
———. "Judicial Deference to Administrative Interpretations of Law." *Duke Law Journal* 1989 (1989): 511–21.
———. "The Role of the Judiciary in Deregulation." *Antitrust Law Journal* 55 (1986): 191–98.
———. "Vermont Yankee: The APA, the D.C. Circuit, and the Supreme Court." *Supreme Court Review* (1978): 856–901.

Scenic Hudson Preservation Conference v. Federal Power Commission, 354 F. 2d. 608 (2nd Cir., 1965).

Schapiro, Robert A. "Judicial Deference and Interpretive Coordinacy in State and Federal Constitutional Law." *Cornell Law Review* 85 (2000): 656–716.

Schecter Poultry Corp. v. United States, 295 U.S. 495 (1935).

Scheiber, Harry N. "Private Rights and Public Power: American Law, Capitalism, and the Republican Polity in Nineteenth-Century America. *Yale Law Journal* 107 (1997): 823–61.

Schiller, Reuel L. "The Era of Deference: Courts, Expertise, and the Emergence of New Deal Administrative Law." *Michigan Law Review* 106 (2007): 399–441.

Schlesinger, Arthur Jr. *The Politics of Upheaval*. Boston: Houghton Mifflin, 1960.

Schwartz, Bernard. "Adjudication and the Administrative Procedure Act." *Tulsa Law Journal* 32 (1996): 203–19.

———. "The Administrative Agency in Historical Perspective." *Indiana Law Journal* 36 (1961): 263–81.

———. "Federalism, Administrative Law, and the Rehnquist Court in Action." *Tulsa Law Journal* 32 (1997): 477–91.

Seidenfeld, Mark. "Demystifying Deossification: Rethinking Recent Proposals to Modify Judicial Review of Notice and Comment Rulemaking." *Texas Law Review* 75 (1997): 483–524.

Shepherd, George. "Fierce Compromise: The Administrative Procedure Act Emerges from New Deal Politics." *Northwestern Law Review* 90 (1996): 1557–683.

Sierra Club v. Morton, 405 U.S. 727 (1972).

Skidmore v. Swift & Co., 323 U.S. 134 (1944).

Skowronek, Stephen. *Building a New American State: The Expansion of National Administrative Capacities, 1877–1920*. New York: Cambridge University Press, 1979.

Spence, David B., and Frank Cross. "A Public Choice Case for the Administrative State." *Georgetown Law Journal* 89 (2000): 97–142.

St. Joseph Stockyards v. United States, 298 U.S. 38 (1936).

Stearns, Maxwell L. "Standing at the Crossroads: The Roberts Court in Historical Perspective." *Notre Dame Law Review* 83 (2008): 875–964.

Stewart, Richard B. "The Reformation of American Administrative Law." *Harvard Law Review* 88 (1975): 1667–813.

Stone, James H. "Economic Conditions in Macon, Georgia in the 1830s." *Georgia Historical Quarterly* 54 (1970): 209–25.

Storing, Herbert. "What the Anti-Federalists Were For." In *The Complete Anti-Federalist*, edited by Herbert Storing, I: 1–76. Chicago: University of Chicago Press, 1981.

Strauss, Peter L. "One Hundred and Fifty Cases per Year: Some Implications of the Supreme Court's Limited Resources for Judicial Review of Agency Action." *Columbia Law Review* 87 (1987): 1093–136.

Street, Alfred Billings. *The Council of Revision of the State of New York*. Albany: William Gould, 1859.

Sunstein, Cass R. *After the Rights Revolution: Reconceiving the Regulatory State*. Cambridge, MA: Harvard University Press, 1990.

———. "Beyond the Republican Revival." *Yale Law Journal* 97 (1988): 1539–90.

———. "Chevron Step Zero." *Virginia Law Review* 92 (2006): 187–249.

———. "Law and Administration after *Chevron*." *Columbia Law Review* 90 (1990): 2071–120.

———. "Nondelegation Canons." *University of Chicago Law Review* 67 (2000): 315–43.

———. "What's Standing after *Lujan*? Of Citizen Suits, 'Injuries,' and Article III." *Michigan Law Review* 91 (1992): 163–236.

Surrency, Erwin C. "'Calculated to Promote the General Good': The Development of Local Government in Georgia Towns and Cities." *Georgia Historical Quarterly* 84 (2000): 381–409.

Taussig, F. W. *The Tariff History of the United States*. 6th ed. New York: G.P. Putnam's Sons, 1914.

Texas and Pacific Railway Co. v. Interstate Commerce Commission, 162 U.S. 197 (1896).

Thach, Charles C. Jr. *The Creation of the Presidency, 1775–1789: A Study in Constitutional History*. Reprint. Indianapolis: Liberty Fund, 2010.

de Tocqueville, Alexis. *Democracy in America*. Translated by Delba Winthrop and Harvey C. Mansfield. Chicago: University of Chicago Press, 2000.

Turley, Jonathan. "The Rise of the Fourth Branch of Government." *Washington Post*, May 24, 2013.

Tushnet, Mark. "Administrative Law in the 1930s: The Supreme Court's Accommodation of Progressive Legal Theory. *Duke Law Journal* 60 (2011): 1565–637.

United States v. Florida East Coast Railway, 410 U.S. 224 (1973).

United States v. Los Angeles and Salt Lake Railroad Company, 273 U.S. 299 (1927).

United States v. Mead Corporation, 533 U.S. 218 (2001).

United States v. Students Challenging Regulatory Agency Procedures, 412 U.S. 669 (1973).

van Riper, Paul. "Adapting a British Political Invention to American Needs." *Public Administration* 31 (1953): 317–30.

———. *History of the United States Civil Service*. Evanston, IL: Row, Peterson, 1958.

Vermont Yankee Nuclear Power Corporation v. Natural Resources Defense Council, 435 U.S. 519 (1978).

White, Adam J. "Reining in the Agencies." *National Affairs* 11 (2012): 42–58.

White, G. Edward. *The Constitution and the New Deal*. Cambridge, MA: Harvard University Press, 2000.

White, Leonard D. *The Federalists: A Study in Administrative History, 1789–1801*. Paperback ed. New York: Basic Books, Inc., 1952.

———. *The Jacksonians: A Study in Administrative History, 1829–1861*. New York: Macmillan Co., 1954.

———. *The Jeffersonians: A Study in Administrative History, 1801–1829*. New York: Macmillan Co., 1956.

Whitman v. American Trucking Association, 531 U.S. 457 (2001).

Wiebe, Robert. *The Search for Order: 1877–1920.* New York: Hill and Wang, 1967.

Will, George. "Battling the Modern American Administrative State." *Washington Post,* November 27, 2015.

Willoughby, W. F. *Principles of Judicial Administration.* Washington, DC: The Brookings Institution, 1929.

Wilson, Woodrow. "Cabinet Government in the United States." In *The Papers of Woodrow Wilson,* 69 vols., edited by Arthur S. Link. Princeton, NJ: Princeton University Press, 1966–1993.

———. *Constitutional Government in the United States.* New York: Columbia University Press, 1911.

———. *The New Freedom.* Garden City, NY: Doubleday, 1921.

———. "The Study of Administration." *Political Science Quarterly* 2 (1887): 197–222.

Woll, Peter. *Administrative Law, the Informal Process* (Berkeley: University of California Press, 1963.

Woolhandler, Ann. "Judicial Deference to Administrative Action: A Revisionist History." *Administrative Law Review* 43 (1991): 197–245.

———, and Caleb Nelson. "Does History Defeat Standing Doctrine?" *Michigan Law Review* 102 (2004): 689–732.

Wright, J. Skelly. "New Judicial Requisites for Informal Rulemaking: Implications for the Environmental Impact Statement Process." *Administrative Law Review* 29 (1977): 59–64.

Wroth, L. Kinvin, and Hiller B. Zobel, eds. *Legal Papers of John Adams,* vol. 1. Cambridge, MA: Harvard University Press, 1965.

Young v. Community Nutrition Institute, 476 U.S. 974 (1986).

INDEX

Adams, John: and American Independence, 17; as chair of Board of War, 27; and department heads, 81; and election of officers, 29; and *Little v. Barreme*, 92; and president's powers, 82, 88; and removal of administrative officers, 88, 142; and subordinate officers, 81

Adams, John Quincy, 88, 111

administrative agencies: and accountability, 295; and administrative discretion, 208, 308; and administrative power, 188, 202, 208–209, 212, 231, 235; and Administrative Procedure Act, 298–299; and administrative process, 226, 236, 252, 272–275; and agencies' functions, 242, 252; and agencies of war, naval affairs, foreign relations and finance, 27, 29; and agency heads, 238; and appointment of administrative officers, 103, 144; and blending of powers, 54; Coast Survey, 96; and colonial courts, 15, 16; combination of functions in, 54–56; Commission on Economy and Efficiency, 217; and Congress, 248; and consolidation of powers, 177; and Constitution, 206; and courts, 8–9, 15–17, 168, 188, 204–205, 215, 228, 256, 267–268, 274; CPSC, 249; and creation of by Continental Congress, 27; and crisis of legitimacy, 319; and decentralization, 216; and delegation of power, 68–69, 95, 130, 208, 210, 215–216, 301; Dockery-Cockrell Commission, 216; and due process, 159; EEOC, 249; and Environmental Protection Agency, 249, 258–259, 265, 287, 289–290, 296;

executive agencies, 209, 289; and expansion of federal agencies, 128, 136, 208–209; and expertise, 177, 214, 232–233, 250, 251, 269, 273, 291, 295, 299, 302; Federal Communications Commission, 208; Federal Power Commission, 207; and Federal Power Commission, 261; Federal Reserve, 249; Federal Trade Commission, 207, 210, 211–212, 216, 217, 249, 257, 354n121, 356n161; and findings of facts, 8–9, 188, 205; General Land Office, 134–135; and "hard look" standard, 268–270, 299; and implementation of policy, 215, 217; independence of, 205–206, 217, 218, 252; and interest groups, 272, 273; and interpretation of statutes, 8, 295–297, 298; and Interstate Commerce Commission, 127, 128, 205, 216, 217, 221–222, 249; and judicial deference, 10, 204–205, 213–215, 219, 291–292, 300–301; judicial function of, 234–235; and judicial power, 235; and judicial review, 3, 8–9, 10, 204, 205, 213–214, 223, 227, 231, 234, 235–236, 259, 260, 265, 266, 272–273, 289; Keep Committee, 216; and legal interpretation, 214, 223, 224, 225–226, 241, 243, 244, 265, 288, 289, 290, 291; and legislative powers, 7, 102, 130; Naval Observatory, 96; and the New Deal, 10, 207–209, 232–236, 249; NHTSA, 98, 249, 299; NLRB, 225, 249; and Office of Information and Regulatory Affairs, 288–289, 289; OSHA, 98, 249; and PA's Canal Board, 67–68; and policies, 3, 8–9, 279, 283, 285, 286, 288; Post Office, 204, 205;